Sports Economics, Management and Policy

Volume 14

The aim of this series is to provide academics, students, sports business executives, and policy makers with information and analysis on the cutting edge of sports economics, sport management, and public policy on sporting issues.

Volumes in this series can focus on individual sports, issues that cut across sports, issues unique to professional sports, or topics in amateur sports. Each volume will provide rigorous analysis with the purpose of advancing understanding of the sport and the sport business, improving decision making within the sport business and regarding policy toward sports, or both. Volumes may include any or all of the following: theoretical modelling and analysis, empirical investigations, or description and interpretation of institutions, policies, regulations, and law.

More information about this series at http://www.springer.com/series/8343

Antti Laine • Hanna Vehmas
Editors

The Private Sport Sector in Europe

A Cross-National Comparative Perspective

Springer

Editors
Antti Laine
Faculty of Sport and Health Sciences
University of Jyväskylä
Jyväskylä, Finland

Hanna Vehmas
Faculty of Sport and Health Sciences
University of Jyväskylä
Jyväskyla, Finland

ISSN 2191-298X ISSN 2191-2998 (electronic)
Sports Economics, Management and Policy
ISBN 978-3-319-61309-3 ISBN 978-3-319-61310-9 (eBook)
https://doi.org/10.1007/978-3-319-61310-9

Library of Congress Control Number: 2017958868

Printed on acid-free paper

This Springer imprint is published by Springer Nature
The registered company is Springer International Publishing AG
The registered company address is: Gewerbestrasse 11, 6330 Cham, Switzerland

Preface

The first initiative of this *Private Sport Sector in Europe* project took place in May 2015 when we as editors started the planning. The idea was introduced in the MEASURE group meeting during the 12th EASS (European Association for the Sociology of Sport) conference in Dublin in June 2015. In August, selected scholars within sport sociology and related sport disciplines from 32 European countries were contacted and invited to contribute to this book.

We contacted scholars from all the European Union (EU) member states (28 countries) and from all countries that are members of the European Free Trade Association (EFTA), but not members of the EU (four countries). Eventually, authors from altogether 19 countries agreed to participate in the project, out of which 18 countries, all of them EU member states, submitted their country chapters. Around two years after the first initiative, it is time to express gratitude.

We would like to thank Dennis Coates, the editor of this book series *Sport Economics, Management and Policy*, for the instant positive response and guiding comments to our project. We are grateful to Lorraine Klimowich and Kelly Daugherty of Springer (Economics & Political Science) for being adaptable and professional throughout the publication process. We are also thankful to Ville Korkiakangas, who helped us finalize the manuscript.

Most of all, we would like to truly thank all the authors who contributed to this book. Starting to study a subject with fragmental statistics and limited amount of other source material available was most certainly a challenging and time-consuming task. We are grateful that you managed to keep up with us in this project. On the other hand, we are also sure that this project is a very important opening, which hopefully encourages and eases future endeavors in the field.

Jyväskylä, Finland

Antti Laine
Hanna Vehmas

Contents

Getting a Grip on the Private Sport Sector in Europe

Antti Laine and Hanna Vehmas

Introduction

Sport and physical activity are enormous areas of contemporary human action. At various levels and in different parts of the world they are seen to have significant health, social and economic impacts in the lives of the individual human beings and societies more broadly. Sport participation is widely recognized as one of the key preventives of several illnesses and promoters of social cohesion and community

A. Laine (✉) • H. Vehmas
Faculty of Sport and Health Sciences, University of Jyväskylä, Jyväskylä, Finland
e-mail: antti.laine@jyu.fi; hanna.m.vehmas@jyu.fi

A. Laine, H. Vehmas (eds.), *The Private Sport Sector in Europe*, Sports Economics, Management and Policy 14, https://doi.org/10.1007/978-3-319-61310-9_1

spirit in many ways. In increasing variety sport also offers business and employment opportunities and this way contributes to the national and global economies.

In order to make sense how contemporary sport is organized and developed around its above mentioned impacts, it is useful to see sport comprising three distinct sectors: (1) state/public sector, (2) civic/voluntary sector and (3) private/professional sector. Especially public and voluntary sport sectors have been approached in several recent publications (e.g., Breuer, Hoekman, Nagel, & Van der Werff, 2015; Hallmann & Petry, 2013; Nicholson, Hoye, & Houlihan 2010; Scheerder, Willem, & Claes, 2017). This seems only natural because in many parts of the world, and particularly in Europe, sport and physical culture have traditionally been formed around these sectors.

The **public sector** comprises governmental organisations at different levels. In most countries this usually means national and federal governments and their ministries and other top-level political institutions at the state level; regional, county, and territorial departments at the regional level; and municipalities (i.e., cities, towns and other urban and rural districts) at the local level. The public sport sector has received a great deal of attention in the academic studies over the years. This is because its role has been significant in providing financial and political support for the sport infrastructure, especially in the forms of sport facility construction, physical education at schools and state subsidies for non-governmental sport organisations, such as sport clubs and other sport associations.

Especially in Europe, sport has been traditionally perceived as a form of public good and basic right of the citizens that should be supported by the state. This applies to both competition and recreational sports. Success in the international sporting competitions on one hand and promotion of recreational mass sport on the other hand have been among the publicly financed societal goals in many societies. In some countries more than in others, promotion of sport and physical activity of the citizens has been an obvious part of the political agenda. This has been the case for example in Finland, where the state has since 1970s through its sport policies and subsidies directed and guided citizens' sport participation in the spirit of the Nordic welfare state model, which emphasizes the equal access and participation possibilities of all citizens in sport and physical activity (Suomi et al., 2012; Vasara, 2004; Vehmas & Ilmanen, 2013). In some other countries, for example in Belgium the subsidization policy of the state has led to the situation in which the non-profit sport sector has become dependent on the government funding (Theeboom, Haudenhuyse, & De Knop, 2010).

The role of the public sector may be realized in the form of Sports Act in which sport has been given a special legislative position. The range and contents of these acts vary across the countries, and they are often so called skeleton laws, which mean that they are merely guidelines rather than juridical bindings or sanctioning forms of legislation (Vehmas & Ilmanen, 2017). Despite this, the sphere of sport is directed, guided and sanctioned by many other legal bindings and acts, such as association, business and employment laws.

The **voluntary sector** refers to the non-governmental organisations, which are in many countries the core actors in providing sport services to the citizens. At the national level, voluntary sector usually refers to the national sport federations, for example National Olympic committees (NOCs) and domain organisations of different sport disciplines. In many countries, there are also regional, county, provincial or territorial level sport organisations (e.g., Hallman & Petry, 2013). Local level civic sector services are usually provided by the sport clubs and in some countries educational institutions. These organisations often function on voluntary and non-profit basis, although there are differences between the countries. Voluntary sport organisations have been approached in a great number of studies especially in Europe where sport and physical culture have historically been formed around the amateur voluntary organisations.

The third major sport sector comprises profit making private companies that produce and sell sport products and services. This sector also includes professional athletes and consumers who spend money on participating in and watching sports. Companies and organizations produce goods and services to facilitate this, thereby generating money, and 'value added' to the economy. In this book all flows of profit-making companies supplying sport goods and services are referred to as the **private sport sector**.

There is a trajectory that in the current global market economy situation and within the crisis of the public sector in many countries, in Europe particularly, the states cannot anymore fulfil all of their sport-related responsibilities. Also the voluntary sector as a sport provider is in the state of flux as the motives and reasons for volunteering are becoming more diverse. In addition to the traditional, altruistic and social motives, today's volunteers are seen to expect more than before, also monetary and tangible forms of compensation in return of their voluntary commitments (e.g., Emrich, Pitsch, Flatau, & Pierdzioch, 2014; Monga, 2006). This has led to a situation in which the private sport sector is expected to provide new solutions to these challenges. This refers not only to the professional elite sport sector, but also to the recreational physical culture more broadly. The significance of the private sport sector as the employer in sport is also increasing. For these reasons it is extremely important to update the current knowledge of the sport-related enterprises in the private sector in Europe.

Neglected Field of Private Sport Sector

In some discussions, particularly in the United States, private sport sector often refers to sport businesses that are mainly related to the top-level individual athletes or major professional team sports that generate vast income through sponsorship, payments for broadcasting rights, and income from paying spectators. In the European context however, sport industry is perceived more broadly encompassing also businesses that are involved in supplying goods and services across the whole sport and physical culture. These include also those organizations and businesses that operate mainly in the area of mass participation sport. (See e.g., Gratton & Taylor, 2000; Standeven & De Knop, 1999.)

Although it is widely recognized that sport is nowadays a significant sector of the economic activity, and thus there is no question about the importance of the sport industry and sport business and any other profit making sport actors, this sector has received less attention in the sport-related research especially in Europe (see e.g., Laine, 2015). Several reasons can be pointed out for that.

By the **first** token and dating back to its origins, European sport, unlike North American has traditionally been formed around sport clubs and state support, which have taken the academic attention away from the private sport sector. To a certain degree, private sport sector is an ambivalent field that includes aspects, which might have refrained scholars for example in sociology from fully concentrating in this area of sport.

When approaching private sport sector in Europe, the amateur versus professional dichotomy that is rooted in its origins, needs to be taken into consideration. It is widely recognised that modern sport was first established in Britain in the nineteenth century where it referred to the pastime folk games and activities that eventually became transformed into instruments of education. The core origins of the modern European sport are thus linked with the idea of amateur, not professional mentality. This was also the ideal of the Olympic movement until the very recent decades of the twentieth century. The civic sector thinking of sport spread across Europe and was further connected to the interpretations of the civilization of the societies in which sport was seen as a socially accepted form of violence and aggression release. (See e.g., Elias & Dunning, 2008; Giulianotti & Robertson, 2007; Maguire, 1999.) This then implies that sport and physical culture stem from the activities that can be seen to belong to the grassroots spheres of the human life. Or as expressed in the Habermasian (1989) terms, spheres of the *life world*, in which they were not targets of monetary profit-making or other professional activities where there is a risk of the communicative spirit to become colonialized and exploited as a source of value added.

However, within the modernisation and globalisation developments of the societies in general, also sport in Europe eventually started to professionalize. This happened later in Europe than for example in North America where sport was much earlier perceived as a professional activity. There are interesting stories for example about the successful athletes during the first decades of the twentieth century, among them Finnish well-known long distance runners Hannes Kolehmainen, Paavo Nurmi and Ville Ritola, who all moved to the United States at some points of their running careers in order to receive financial compensation for their running performances and achievements. This was highly forbidden in their home country at that time. (See e.g., Vehmas & Lahti, 2015; Viita, 2003.)

European sport, too, is nowadays to a great deal organised, financed and developed around the private profit-making sector. However, this field has, to some extent been disregarded by sociology or passed over to the observations of sport economics or sport marketing, which "ex officio" deal with the economic indicators and business enhancement of sport. It might be that there is a tendency of the scholars in sociology to perceive research interests in this field somewhat superficial, or as enhancing neo-liberal consumer behaviour and thus, assumingly inequalities in society. It was after all already Max Weber (see e.g., Lewis, 1975; Weber, 1922/1978), one of the most referred classic thinkers in sociology and economics, who introduced the idea of value free sociology. This means that the function of the scientific research is merely to offer tools, not finalised solutions for the societal problems. Despite this according to Weber, the values of sociologists come out in what he or she chooses to examine. This then releases sociologists from the expectations that if and when they study private sport sector, they are expected to find 'business solutions' that would support neo-liberal world capitalist ideology, but on the other hand, in the same Weberian spirit, they might be categorized as business promoters.

The **second** reason why private sport sector might have been neglected in the academic studies is the fact that the field is very multidimensional, fragmental and in a constant state of flux. It is difficult to get a grip on it. New companies and actors come and go, and trends in the sport consumer behaviour are difficult to predict. Information technology shapes and changes the products and services in the industry in such a speed that it is difficult or almost impossible to keep up with the field in in-depth and more thorough academic investigations. This can be expressed in line with the consumer logic that 'today's results are easily yesterdays' news'. Therefore, more stable structures, organisations and behaviour patterns, such as traditional sport clubs or sport supporting political institutions are more "research-friendly" objects, because they remain unchangeable at least a bit longer for the scholars to grasp an interpretation about their whereabouts and existence.

Thirdly, and closely linked with the previous justifications, private sport sector has been neglected in the academic studies at least partially because the companies in the field do not constitute a single and clearly defined business field. Therefore it is difficult to exactly define what the private sport sector field actually comprises. (See e.g., Laine, 2015.) Most of the scholars in sport sciences have an idea what type of companies and organisations are included in the sector. Yet, at the same time it is extremely difficult, if possible at all, with the current state of statistics and other business records to precisely know what for example the economic or employment impact of the private sport sector is.

The diverse field of sport-related companies is illustrated in Fig. 1. This figure was originally outlined for the Development strategy of the sport entrepreneurship 2020 in Finland. The aim of the strategy was to make visible the different sport-related business possibilities, instances, roles and interactions between the fields. (See Koivisto, 2010; Kosonen, 2014.)

The center of the figure illustrates companies to whom sport and physical activity are core activities. Typical examples in this field are professional leagues, corporate sport clubs, private sport facilities, and athletes and coaches who have started their own businesses. The further away the businesses are situated from the center of the figure the more loosely they are connected to the sport business. In these fields sport sector becomes more mixed with several other industries, such as tourism, media, construction, technology and wellbeing. In addition, the actors along the ring of the figure do not necessarily identify themselves as 'sport actors'. Instead sport for them is seen as a means of business, a part of the larger business operations or merely a context where the business is located. (Koivisto, 2010.)

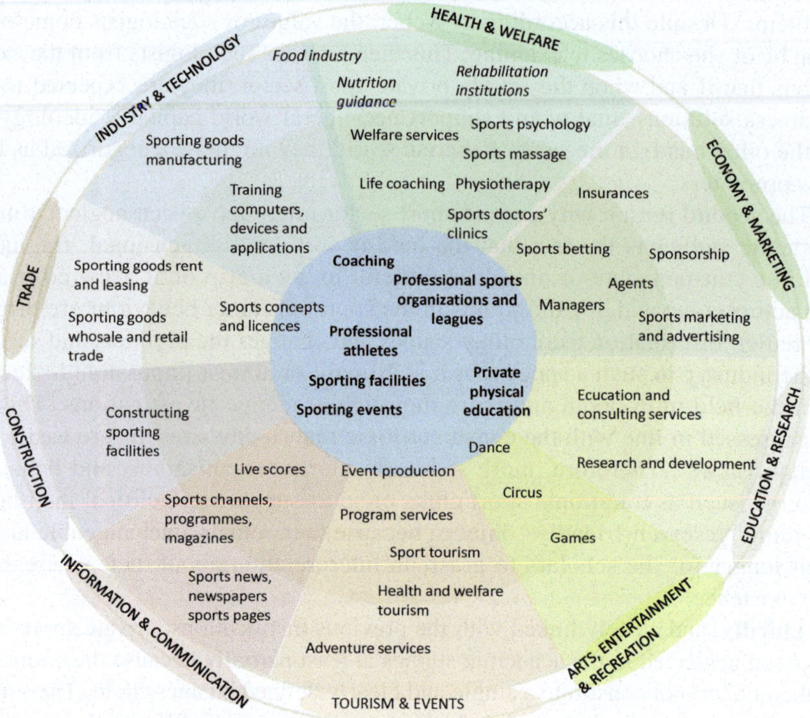

Fig. 1 Sport business field. Source: Koivisto (2010).

Need for a Social Study Approach on the Private Sport Sector

With the above mentioned arguments in mind, we as sport sociologists chose to launch this book project. Whether we like it or not, private sport sector is a growing field in sport that needs to be examined also with the background statements from social sciences. This is to provide our students and graduates, as well as decision makers and the entrepreneurs with the current knowledge and potential of the business and employment opportunities in the field.

Private sport sector has been evolving at a fast speed during this millennium. Despite the economic downturns there have been for many years a strong upward trend and expectations in this sector. Sport, physical activity, health and wellbeing are growing areas of consumption, entertainment, education, lifestyles and thus, business and employment opportunities for the citizens of the postmodern contemporary societies. Media, technology and even science have been harnessed to influence the growth and popularity of the business of sport. Sport, health and wellness technology with heart rate and other activity monitoring devices and technical clothing product development alone encompasses vast areas of business potential for companies and expert individuals in this field. People spend more than before money on sport participation, sport equipment and other sport-related goods and services, such as travelling and sport media consumption. Postmodern societies are going through uncertain economic and social times at the moment, and sometimes we can perceive leisure commitments and control over one's own body as sources of meaning and sustainability in life (see e.g., Stebbins, 2008; Vehmas, 2010).

Fitness and health clubs are one of the most obvious forms of industries in this field. As it will be presented in the number of articles of this book, the fitness boom that is evidenced in many of the European countries is enhancing the consumption and product development in sport. Ageing of the western societies, problems related to the sedentary lifestyle and non-communicable diseases together with the increasing health and body awareness all have influenced the demand and supply of the services and products in this field. In addition, sport-related tourism and sport events are nowadays significant niche markets that move millions of people worldwide. Skiing, golf and for example the popularity of running and other endurance sports events offer a huge amount of business opportunities for companies, facilities, manufacturers and other organisations. Top-level sport clubs, in Europe especially in football, as referred to soccer here, have become more professional in their activities as they attract millions of people across the globe and bear tremendous amount of business operations in various directions.

What also makes private sport sector worth investigating is the fact that the public sector is in many European countries at least partially withdrawing from the sport service supply. Traditionally research has regarded the welfare state being based on two main ideas. First, sport practices have contributed to building the welfare state through integration, social networks and the promotion of equality of opportunities. Second, it is assumed that the opportunities to participate in sport activities are linked with the way welfare state subsidies and develops sport facilities and sport participation.

However, the power of the state in the Keynesian economic spirit to influence the sport sector has been diminishing due to economic recessions and replaced by the neo-liberal monetary systems that offer more space for privately run sport service production. The overall consequence of this has been that the state is pulling back from these sectors where it traditionally had a monopoly position. The funding resources of the state for sport associations and social projects have become stretched, and the role of the state in developing a sport-for-all provision is weakened in many countries simply by the position it is forced to take. This implies that the state may not be able to take up this task alone. There are some who would argue for the state to leave providers to compete for participants. This would allow the open market to provide for a range of public needs, without subsidizing public facilities and services, and take the burden away from the public sector. (Ilmanen, 2015; Theeboom et al., 2010.)

The private sector then either on its own or more likely in collaboration with the public and voluntary sectors, is expected to supply sport and health-related services to the citizens in the future. There is a constant revision of the relationship between the public, private and voluntary sectors. The challenge for these sectors is the polarisation of physical activity and how the population as whole can be motivated to be active enough for their well-being and health. With the current global 'inactivity crisis' and the scarcity of resources, public organizations in sport and physical activity are expected to form successful and responsible partnerships with private organizations. In the sport and physical activity contexts, public-private partnerships across multiple sectors have pooled financial, product, and human resources to create sporting facilities, events, products, and programs. (Heikkala, 2009; Itkonen & Salmikangas, 2015; O'Reilly & Brunette, 2014.)

Last but by all means not least, private sport sector should receive academic attention because of its potential to employ people now and in the future. According the *broad definition of sport* (of which definition is presented later), number of employees in sport in the European Union (EU) in 2012 (27 countries) was 4.46 million and the share of employment in sport from total employment was 2.12% (SportsEconAustria, 2012). Croatia joined the EU in 2013 and is not included in those figures.

It is also estimated that more than before graduates with sport studies will find work in the private sport sector in the future. Therefore, it is seen important to update the current industry situation so that there will be updated information and knowledge about the future job qualifications in the field. This is seen vitally important also for the curricula development in higher education in sport. (Laine & Ilmola, 2016; Vehmas & Salmikangas, 2016.)

Aim of the Book

For the reasons mentioned above about private sport sector having received less attention in sport research, and particularly within sociological approaches, this book intends to fill in the gaps of knowledge that have been prevailing in the field. This is done by contributors from 18 selected European countries answering to the following questions:

1. How sport in the *basic level* is organised in the public, private and voluntary sectors and *more precisely*, what is the private sport sector's position among the three sport sectors?
2. What is the structure and characteristics of the private sport sector?
3. What are the most significant sport business fields and the largest companies of those fields?

4. In which way has the private sport sector changed during the 2000s?
5. What are the special cases that illustrate the development and future scenarios of the private sport sector?

Statistical Data About the Private Sport Sector in Europe

In order to evaluate the significance and future trajectories of the private sport sector, adequate and comparable statistics need to be available. Due to its growing economic and social impact, sport has gained an important place in the European strategies and programmes. It is seen that harmonised and comparable statistics are needed to strengthen the evidence-based policies in this field. Under the EU Work Plan for Sport 2014–2017 (Council resolution 2014/C 183/03), Eurostat with the European Commission's Directorate General for Education and Culture (DG EAC), initiated the regular dissemination of harmonized statistics on sport. (Eurostat, 2016b.)

As it is presented in more detail in some of the articles of this book, the European sport market development in the early 1970s requested properly arranged economic data, which would allow an easier overview of the market. The first attempts were to find the initial indicators of the economic value of sport in nine European countries. This was followed by introductions of more standardized methodology, and studies about the macroeconomic relationship between sport and the economy, particularly focusing on the sources of sport on a larger sample of European countries. (Andreff, 2006; 2011.)

Despite the strong need to collect such data due to the rapid development of all types of sports across Europe and even though there have been improvements in the availability of cross-national compiling of statistics (e.g., Satellite Account System and Sports Observatory) researchers still to some extent have to rely on the results acquired in individual countries. As no Eurostat data collection is devoted specifically to sport, sport statistics are derived from already existing EU surveys. The sport-related statistics currently cover: employment in sport (data from the EU Labour Force Survey); international trade in sporting goods (data from COMEXT); attendance at live sports events (data from the Adult Education Survey); and private expenditure on sporting goods and services (data from the Household Budget Survey). (Eurostat, 2016b.)

Statistics on international trade in sporting goods enable the measurement of the value of sporting goods traded between EU Member States and between EU and non-EU countries. The data are extracted from Eurostat's COMEXT database, which contains statistics for the Member States and also for the EFTA and candidate countries. (Eurostat, 2016b.)

Following the EU Commission's 2007 White Paper on Sport, the former Working Group on 'Sport & Economics' has developed the 'Vilnius Definition of Sport'. The purpose of the definition was to define sport statistically and in an economically meaningful way. The 'Vilnius Definition of Sport' distinguishes (1) *statistical definition of sport*, (2) *narrow definition of sport* and (3) *broad definition of sport*.

Statistical definition of sport corresponds with the NACE Rev. 2 division (93) *sports activities and amusement and recreation activities*, the only part of the sport sector having its own NACE division (see Appendix: NACE Rev. 2 Directly Sport-Related Classes). *Narrow definition of sport* consists of all activities which are inputs to sport (i.e., all goods and services which are necessary for doing sport) plus the *statistical definition of sport*. *Broad definition of sport* consists of all activities which require sport as an input (i.e., all goods and services which are related to a sport activity, but without being necessary for doing sport) plus the *statistical definition of sport* and *the narrow definition of sport*. (See e.g., Eurostat, 2017c; SportsEconAustria, 2012; Sport Satellite Accounts, 2013.)

The basis for Eurostat's sport employment data are laid down in the 'Vilnius definition of sport'. Thus the Eurostat definition of employment in sport refers to the core statistical definition (economic sector of sport activities according to the NACE classification) and introduces additionally the dimension of occupation according to the ISCO classification (sport and fitness workers employed also outside of the sport sector). (Eurostat, 2016b.)

The employment and international trade data are updated every year. The dissemination of data on participation in live sport events and household expenditure on sporting goods and services coincides with the publication of the results of the respective surveys. Other indicators, such as levels of physical activity or time spent in sport participation, are likely to be added to the database once relevant survey results become available. Data on physical activity was about to be gathered in 2016 from the new round of the European Health Interview Survey and the Time Use Survey. (Eurostat, 2016b.)

Statistical Framework of the Book

As it was mentioned earlier, the private sport sector is very multidimensional and fragmented. Defining the sector is difficult, because the companies in the field do not constitute a single and clearly defined field of business. Some of the fields can be illustrated by taking advantage of the *Statistical classification of economic activities in the European Community* (NACE Rev. 2, 2008). (See e.g., Laine, 2015.) NACE is in use in all European countries, although the national name of the classification varies.

The term NACE is derived from the French *Nomenclature statistique des activités économiques dans la Communauté européenne*. Various NACE versions have been developed since 1970. NACE is a four-digit classification providing the framework for collecting and presenting a large range of statistical data according to economic activity in the fields of economic statistics and in other statistical domains developed within the European statistical system (ESS). NACE Rev. 2 is a revised classification that was adopted at the end of 2006 and, in 2007, its implementation began. The first reference year for NACE Rev. 2 compatible statistics is 2008. (Eurostat, 2016a.) NACE Rev. 2 is used as the basic statistical framework of this book.

NACE uses four hierarchical levels and national implementations may also introduce additional levels. In level 1 there is 21 *sections* identified by alphabetical letters from A to U. In levels 2–4 classes are identified with numbers. In level 2 classes are called *divisions*, in level 3 *groups* and in level 4 *classes*. Four-digit level 4 includes sport-related classes. In this book we call those directly sport-related classes, economic activities or business fields. The amount of the directly sport-related classes varies somewhat between countries as some countries have additional sport-related classes (e.g., skiing centre activities) with more detailed coding system, usually five-digit. Table 1 introduces those directly sport-related NACE Rev. 2 classes that can be found from the Eurostat (2016a) Metadata. Grouping and definition of each class is presented in Appendix: NACE Rev. 2 Directly Sport-Related Classes. Building of pleasure and sporting boats (NACE code 30.12) is not defined here as a directly sport-related class.

Table 1 Directly sport-related NACE Rev. 2 classes.

Business field	NACE code
Manufacture of sport goods	32.30
Retail sale of sporting equipment in specialised stores	47.64
Renting and leasing of recreational and sport goods	77.21
Sport and recreation education	85.51
Operation of sport facilities	93.11
Activities of sport clubs	93.12
Fitness facilities	93.13
Other sport activities	93.19

Source: Eurostat (2016a).

There are also a lot of other classes that include sport-related economic activities, but those are not statistically classified. For example section J (Information and communication) does not include separate class for sport media or under section K (Financial and insurance activities) it is not possible to find a class for sport insurances. However, presenting the key figures of the statistically classified sport-related classes enable to outline and compare different sport business fields within one country and also to some extent between different European countries.

As editors of this book we requested the authors to gather information from all statistically classified directly sport-related classes that are in use in their countries NACE equivalent classifications. This information was advised to be gathered from the countries' national statistical offices, not from Eurostat, because Eurostat does not cover all available data (Eurostat coverage is limited to sections B-N and to four digit level). The authors were instructed to use data from the year 2013. However, if that was not possible, another proximate year was taken into account.

According the basic framework of this book sport statistically consists of all directly sport-related NACE classes (not only those classes that are included in the *statistical definition of sport*, i.e., to NACE division 93). Our definition is thus broader than the *statistical definition of sport*, but not so comprehensive as the *narrow definition of sport* or the *broad definition of sport*. On the other hand, also both the narrow and broad definitions are utilized in this book.

Except Austria and the United Kingdom, authors of this book used the proposed NACE classification. Austria and United Kingdom instead presented their private sport sector statistics based on the Sport Satellite Account (SSA) system. Also the Netherlands utilized SSA. SSA is more comprehensive statistical system to measure sport-related economic activity, but only a limited number of European countries have produced a national SSA. With the help of Satellite Accounts such sectors that are an amalgam of industries can be measured.

Following the statistical framework, each country contributor was asked to present the following economic key figures from all directly sport-related classes: (1) number of companies, (2) number of employees, (3) total revenue, (4) revenue per company and (5) employees average salary. According to our up-front enquiries to European national statistical institutes such data was informed to be available most parts, although some differences and limitations were expected.

In addition to the sport business field comparisons, authors were encouraged to gather information about the largest companies from the most significant sport business fields. The objective was to present 1–3 of the most significant sport business fields in detail and to discuss other sport business fields briefly. Company information was requested to be gathered by utilising such national sources that provide key facts and financial figures (e.g., amount of offices and employees, revenue, EBITDA-%[1]) of private companies, and if possible Amadeus database that provide comparable financial information for public and private companies across Europe (see Bureau van Dijk, 2016).

Although, authors were requested to use above mentioned statistics, it was emphasized that the aim of the book was not to become merely a statistical presentation. In this book statistics are used to support the outlining of the private sport sector.

Structure of the Book

This book covers detailed information about altogether 18 European countries' private sport sectors. All the countries are EU member states. West-Central European countries are represented by Austria, France, Germany, Portugal and United Kingdom (UK is scheduled to leave EU in 2019); Mediterranean countries by Cyprus, Greece, Italy and Spain; Benelux countries by Belgium and the Netherlands, East-Central countries by the Czech Republic, Hungary and Romania, Baltic states by Estonia, Latvia and Lithuania; and Nordic countries by

[1] EBITDA (Earnings before interest, taxes, depreciation and amortization) shows how much of the company's revenue remains uncovered after the reduction of the company's operating costs. EBITDA-% = 100 × EBITDA/revenue. EBITDA-% = EBITDA margin.

Finland. These countries are presented in Fig. 2 along with other EU member states[2] and countries that are members of The European Free Trade Association (EFTA), but not members of the EU[3].

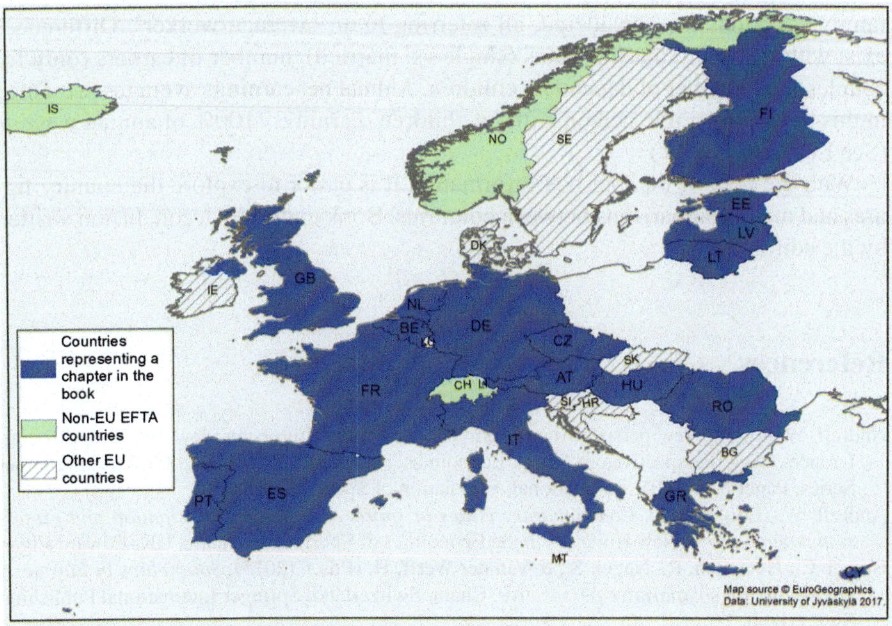

Fig. 2 Countries representing a chapter in the book.

The country chapters are presented in alphabetical order by the country names. The chapters have been produced either individually or as joint projects between the scholars from respective countries. A fact box has been placed in the beginning of each country chapter. Fact boxes include countries' capital name; geographical size in square kilometres; population in million; gross domestic products (GDP) both per capita and in Purchasing Power Standards (PPS); as well as annual net earnings average. Fact boxes have been compiled by the editors from Eurostat database using statistics from the year 2013[4]. In total in 2013 EU (28 countries) population was 505.2 million, GDP per capita 26,700 euros and annual net earnings average 22,663 euros (Eurostat, 2017a).

GDP is a measure for the economic activity. It is defined as the value of all goods and services produced less the value of any goods or services used in their creation.

---

[2] Bulgaria, Croatia, Denmark, Ireland, Luxembourg, Malta, Poland, Slovakia, Slovenia and Sweden.

[3] Iceland, Liechtenstein, Norway and Switzerland.

[4] Annual net earnings figure in Cyprus is from 2007.

The volume index of GDP per capita in Purchasing Power Standards (PPS) is expressed in relation to the European Union (EU28) average set to equal 100. If the index of a country is higher than 100, this country's level of GDP per head is higher than the EU average and vice versa. (Eurostat, 2017d.)

Annual net earnings depend on the personal situation of the worker. Different family situations are considered, all referring to an 'average worker'. Differences exist with respect to marital status (single vs. married), number of earners (only for couples) and number of dependent children. Annual net earnings averages presented in this book are 'single person without children' earnings (100% of annual wages). (See Eurostat, 2017b.)

With the help of the fact box information it is easier to explore the country figures and make comparisons between countries. Book ends with a conclusion written by the editors.

References

Andreff, W. (2006). New perspectives in sports economics: A European view. In: 8th IASE conference: "New Perspectives in Sports Economics", Bochum, May 4–6, 2006. Working Paper Series, Paper No. 06-05. International Association of Sports Economics.

Andreff, W. (Ed.). (2011). *Contemporary issues in sports economics. Participation and professional team sports*. New Horizons in the Economics of Sport. Cheltenham, UK: Edward Elgar.

Breuer, C., Hoekman, R., Nagel, S., & Van der Werff, H. (Eds.). (2015). *Sport clubs in Europe. A cross-national comparative perspective*. Cham, Switzerland: Springer International Publishing Switzerland.

Bureau van Dijk. (2016). Amadeus database. Retrieved October 22, 2016 from http://www.bvdinfo.com/en-gb/our-products/company-information/international-products/amadeus

Elias, N., & Dunning, E. (2008). *Quest for excitement. Sport and leisure in the civilizing process*. Dublin, Ireland: University College Dublin Press.

Emrich, E., Pitsch, W., Flatau, J., & Pierdzioch, C. (2014). Voluntary engagement in sports clubs: A behavioral model and some empirical evidence. *International Review for the Sociology of Sport, 49*(2), 227–240.

Eurostat. (2016a). Glossary: Statistical classification of economic activities in the European Community (NACE). Retrieved October 8, 2016 from http://ec.europa.eu/eurostat/statistics-explained/index.php/Glossary:Statistical_classification_of_economic_activities_in_the_European_Community_(NACE)

Eurostat. (2016b). *Sport statistics*. 2016 edition. Retrieved November 12, 2016 from http://ec.europa.eu/eurostat/documents/4031688/7203321/KS-04-15-823-EN-N.pdf

Eurostat. (2017a). Database. Retrieved February 24, 2017 from http://ec.europa.eu/eurostat/data/database

Eurostat. (2017b). Earnings. Retrieved February 24, 2017 from http://ec.europa.eu/eurostat/web/labour-market/earnings

Eurostat. (2017c). Employment in sport. Retrieved February 24, 2017 from http://ec.europa.eu/eurostat/web/sport/employment-in-sport

Eurostat. (2017d). GDP per capita in PPS. Retrieved February 24, 2017 from http://ec.europa.eu/eurostat/web/products-datasets/-/tec00114

Giulianotti, R., & Robertson, R. (Eds.). (2007). *Globalization and sport*. Malden, MA: Blackwell.

Gratton, C., & Taylor, P. (2000). *Economics of sport and recreation*. London, UK: E & FN Spon.

Habermas, J. (1989). *The theory of communicative action. Volume two. Lifeworld and system: A critique of functionalist reason*. Boston, MA: Beacon Press.
Hallmann, K., & Petry, K. (Eds.). (2013). *Comparative sport development. Systems, participation and public policy*. New York, NY: Springer.
Heikkala, J. (2009). *Sport governance in Finland*. Reports. Helsinki, Finland: Suomen Liikunta ja Urheilu.
Ilmanen, K. (2015). Liikuntapalvelujen muutos 1800-luvun lopulta 2000-luvulle [The change of sport services from the end of 19th century to 21st century]. In: H. Itkonen, & A. Laine (Eds.), *Liikunta yhteiskunnallisena ilmiönä* (pp. 19–37). University of Jyväskylä. Department of Sport Sciences. Studies 1/2015.
Itkonen, H., & Salmikangas, A.-K. (2015). The changing roles of public, civic and private sectors in Finnish Sports Culture. *Viesoji politika ir administravimas, 14*(4), 545–556.
Koivisto, N. (2010). *Liikunta-alan yrittäjyyden kehittämisstrategia 2020* [The Development Strategy 2020 for sports industry entrepreneurship]. Helsinki, Finland: Diges ry.
Kosonen, H. (2014). *Liikuntaliiketoiminnan ekosysteemin muutokset* [Changes in the sports business ecosystem]. Tem raportteja 20/2014.
Laine, A. (2015). Liikunta- ja urheilualan yrityskenttä [Sport business field]. In: H. Itkonen, & A. Laine (Eds.), *Liikunta yhteiskunnallisena ilmiönä* (pp. 77–98). University of Jyväskylä. Department of Sport Sciences. Studies 1/2015.
Laine, A., & Ilmola, R. (2016). Liikunnan yhteiskuntatieteilijät työmarkkinoilla – vuosina 2000–2014 valmistuneiden maistereiden sijoittuminen työelämään [Social scientists of sport on the employment market – How the MSSc graduates from 2000–2014 are positioning themselves in working life]. *Liikunta & Tiede, 53*(1), 60–67.
Lewis, J. (1975). *Max Weber and value-free sociology: A marxist critique*. London, UK: Lawrence and Wishart.
Maguire, J. (1999). *Global sport. Identities, societies, civilizations*. Cambridge, UK: Polity Press.
Monga, M. (2006). Measuring motivation to volunteer for special events. *Event Management, 10*(1), 47–61.
Nicholson, M., Hoye, R., & Houlihan, B. (Eds.). (2010). *Participation in sport. International policy perspectives*. London, UK: Routledge.
O'Reilly, N., & Brunette, M. K. (2014). *Public-private partnerships in physical activity and sport*. Physical activity intervention series. Champaign, IL: Human Kinetics.
Scheerder, J., Willem, A., & Claes, E. (Eds.). (2017). *Sport policy systems and sport federations. A cross-national perspective*. London, UK: Palgrave Macmillan.
Sport Satellite Accounts. (2013). *Sport satellite accounts – A European Project: New results*. European Commission.
SportsEconAustria. (2012). *Study on the contribution of sport to economic growth and employment in the EU*. European Commission, D-G Education and Culture.
Stebbins, R. A. (2008). *Serious leisure. A perspective for our time*. New Brunswick, NJ: Transaction Publishers.
Standeven, J., & De Knop, P. (1999). *Sport tourism*. Champaign, IL: Human Kinetics.
Suomi, K., Sjöholm, K., Matilainen, P., Glan, V., Nuutinen, L., Myllylä, S. … Lee, A. (2012). *Liikuntapaikkapalvelut ja väestön tasa-arvo. Seurantatutkimus liikuntapaikkapalveluiden muutoksista 1998–2009*. [Sport facility services and equality. Follow up study about the changes in sport facilities in 1998–2009]. Helsinki, Finland: Opetus- ja kulttuuriministeriö.
Theeboom, M., Haudenhuyse, R., & De Knop, P. (2010). Community sports development for socially deprived groups: A wider role for the commercial sports sector? A look at the Flemish situation. *Sport in Society, 13*(9), 1392–1410.
Vasara, E. (2004). *Valtion liikuntahallinnon historia* [History of State sports governance]. Helsinki, Finland: Liikuntatieteellinen Seura.
Vehmas, H. (2010). *Liikuntamatkalla Suomessa – vapaa-ajan valintoja jälkimodernissa yhteiskunnassa* [Sport tourism in Finland. Leisure choices in postmodern society]. Studies in sport, physical education and health 143 (PhD dissertation). University of Jyväskylä.

Vehmas, H., & Ilmanen, K. (2013). Finland. In K. Hallman & K. Petry (Eds.), *Comparative sport development. Systems, participation and public policy* (pp. 47–59). New York, NY: Springer.
Vehmas, H., & Ilmanen, K. (2017). Finland: From steering to the evaluation of the effectiveness. In J. Scheerder, A. Willem, & E. Claes (Eds.), *Sport policy systems and sport federations. A cross-national perspective* (pp. 113–134). London, UK: Palgrave Macmillan.
Vehmas, H., & Lahti, J. (2015). Finland: From elite running to mass running events. In J. Scheerder & K. Breedveld (Eds.), *Running across Europe the rise and size of one of the largest sport markets* (pp. 105–118). London, UK: Palgrave Macmillan.
Vehmas, H., & Salmikangas, A.-K. (2016). Higher education and employment in Sport management. Oral presentation in the 13th European Association for Sociology of Sport conference in Copenhagen, May 7, 2016.
Viita, O. (2003). *Hymyilevä Hannes. Työläisurheilija Hannes Kolehmaisen sankaruus porvarillisessa Suomessa* [Smiling Hannes. The heroism of working-class Athlete Hannes Kolehmainen in Bourgeois Finland] (PhD dissertation). Helsinki, Finland: Otava.
Weber, M. (1922/1978). *Economy and society. An outline of interpretive sociology* (Vol. 2). Berkeley, CA: University of Califormia Press.

AUSTRIA: Winter Tourism and Sport Retail Most Significant Sport Business Fields

Philipp Vejchoda

Selected country facts (in 2013)	
Capital	Vienna
Geographical size (km^2)	83,879
Population (million)	8.45
GDP (euro per capita)	38,000
GDP (per capita in PPS)	131
Annual net earnings average (€)	27,521

Getting to Know the Austrian Sport Profile

Sport in Austria has a rich history which began around 150 years ago. The first signs of organized sport associations in Austria can be found as early as between 1880 and 1890 when activities such as alpine sports and mountain climbing began to establish themselves in an organized way. (Marschik, 2011.) Due to the long history of the Austrian sport, various key stakeholders have emerged and innumerable changes have shaped the Austrian sport scene and its organizations. In present times three sectors have emerged as the main providers of sport. Two of these sectors, namely public and voluntary, can be seen as the key stakeholders even though the private sector is gaining importance. (Pratscher, 2000.)

Sport was predominantly described by values such as performance, discipline, success and records during the 1950s in Austria. Nowadays sport is more likely to be associated with attributes such as happiness, wellbeing and individualism.

P. Vejchoda (✉)
Faculty of Sport and Health Sciences, University of Jyväskylä, Jyväskylä, Finland
e-mail: philipp.vejchoda@gmail.com

A. Laine, H. Vehmas (eds.), *The Private Sport Sector in Europe*, Sports Economics, Management and Policy 14, https://doi.org/10.1007/978-3-319-61310-9_2

(Wagner, 2010.) This change was mainly led by the differentiation in sport which shifted from competition-based thinking towards non-competitive physical activity programs. These programs were developed for more health-oriented people in the society. (Nagel, 2006.) Norden (2007) also describes this change in the understanding of sport. Nowadays it is seen that people tend to exercise and move more on their own, which shows why the private sector is becoming stronger (Norden, 2007). For this article sport is used to describe both of the above mentioned definitions. It includes both competitive sport and non-competitive physical activity.

In the public sector, sport is mainly governed by the Austrian Federal Ministry of Defence and Sports. Other parties that govern sport at the state level are the Ministry for Education, Arts and Culture, and the Ministry for Science and Research. These ministries oversee the allocation of the budget and funding of projects in order to strengthen sport in Austria. (Spindler-Oswald, 2016.) Even though these organizations oversee the federal agenda of the sport, every single federal state in Austria has its own regulations regarding sport as stated in the Austrian constitutional law (Bundesverfassungsgesetz, 2015).

In the non-governmental side of the organized sport in Austria the "Österreichische Bundes-Sportorganisation" (BSO) is responsible for overseeing the sport agenda. The overall target of the BSO is to act as a lobbyist for organized sport and subsequently for its member associations. The main tasks are to foster and to develop sport and physical activity within Austria and to represent the interests of sport to the society, and to public and other institutions. Furthermore three roof organisations for grassroots level sport have a great stake in the organization of sport in Austria, having membership numbers which exceed three million individuals. ASKÖ ("Arbeitsgemeinschaft für Sport und Körperkultur in Österreich"), ASVÖ ("Allgemeiner Sportverband Österreichs") and SPORTUNION provide Austrian citizens with a nation-wide network of sport clubs and thus opportunities to be physically active (Spindler-Oswald, 2016). This network of sport clubs consists of around 14,000 clubs spread all over Austria. Within this network football (2284 clubs), Bavarian curling (1675), tennis (1612), equestrian sport (1359) and skiing (1171) represent the five biggest sports in Austria according to the amount of clubs. (Braunstingl, 2015.) This well established network of sport clubs enables Austrian citizens to participate in sport club activities; per capita one sport club is available for approximately 610 people (Statistik Austria, 2016a). These numbers highlight also the importance of the voluntary sector in Austria as within the clubs approximately 576,000 people spend their time to work voluntarily. In terms of time, people working voluntarily within sport give almost 2.2 million hours per week of their free time to the sport clubs with either zero or marginal costs for those clubs. Both the number of voluntary workers and the hours spent for voluntary work put the sport sector in the first place compared to all other categories and possibilities in which voluntary work can be done. (Bundesministerium für Arbeit, Soziales und Konsumentenschutz, 2015.)

The private sport sector in Austria on the other hand has developed considerably over the last years as professionalization and globalization have shaped all three sectors within sport. This increase in importance can be also seen in higher and more frequent media coverage and increased general recognition of sport as an important part of the Austrian economy. The economy is supported by sport in various ways as sport and all its connected in- and outputs have an impact in terms of direct and indirect gross value added. In 2013 this impact on the economy amounted to a total of approximately 17.1 billion euros in direct and indirect gross value added. (Klafl, 2015.) Subsequently it can be stated that the share of sport within the whole economy lies at around 6% as the total gross value added in Austria for the year 2013 showed a total of approximately 288 billion euros (Statistik Austria, 2016b). Another way to observe the relationship between sport and economy in Austria is to state that approximately every 17th euro that is generated within the economy can be traced back to sport activities (Klafl, 2015).

The importance of sport and physical activity more broadly for the Austrian economy can be further seen when it is compared to other European countries. The Austrian institute SportsEconAustria (SpEA) has examined the direct economic impact of sport within countries of the European Union. This study shows that Austria – as a relatively small country in size – leads this comparison. For this comparison, the direct gross value added was used, which in Austria amounts to around 11.6 billion euros. (SportsEconAustria, 2012a.) The European Union average for the relationship between sport and economy in this matter lies at 1.8%. For Austria an average of 4% can be calculated. The proportion leaves traditionally strong sport countries such as Germany and the United Kingdom behind. (Gaulhofer, 2015.)

Thus it can be concluded that the sport sector is a highly vital part of the Austrian economy. This article draws upon the importance of sport and will further describe the historical evolution of the private sport sector in Austria. The role of Austria in building a common framework to measure the economic impact of sport within the countries of the European Union will also be explained. This is followed by the description of the biggest stakeholders within the Austrian sport economy and their specific impact. Third part of the article reviews the statistical representation of the sport sector and, as concluding remarks, discusses the possible future developments of the Austrian sport economy.

Private Sport Sector Starts to Count

As many other countries, Austria has also witnessed significant changes in the private sport sector from the beginning of this millennium onwards. With the emergence of higher levels of disposable income and higher prevalence of leisure options more money flows into the experiential driven consumption, such as cinema and theatre visits. Whereas cinema and theatre visits can be seen as more traditional ways of spending leisure, sport has emerged as an important part of this sector as well. (Soltész, 2002.) As sport has various peculiarities the measurement of its economic impact has been and to some extent still is difficult. Peculiarities for example in the skiing industry range from building sufficient infrastructure to educating skiing instructors, all the way to accident insurances for skiing injuries.

(SportsEconAustria, 2012a.) Under the circumstance that sport is overall important for the society and its values, a higher focus on quantifying this sector is justifiable. Thus, even though it is rather hard to measure an exact impact, more resources should be put into this matter to resolve this issue. (Schmidl, 2004.)

Even though Austria is a relatively sport dependent country, analyses of the impact of sport on the economy only started to gain importance by the verge of this millennium. The first comprehensive study on this topic was conducted by the Institute for Industrial Sciences (Industriewissenschaftliches Institut [IWI]) in 1999. This report combined everything that was known about the private sport sector at that time and showed extensively how important tourism was. Half of the economic value added of around 4.7 billion euros – which amounted to 2.5% of the gross domestic product (GDP) in 1998 – derived from sport tourism. (Dachs, Macek, Preissl, Steindl, & Zwickl, 2001.) It is clear to see that this sector has developed considerably over the last decade as the value added figure in 2013 stood for 11.6 billion euros. Nowadays, sport tourism still has an extensive impact in the sport economy. (Gaulhofer, 2015.) Moreover the comparison of the GDP shows that the sport economy has grown as the percentage of sport-related GDP rose to 4% in 2013 (Klafl, 2015). This increase in the private sector of sport can be explained by the emergence of commercialization in sport. Due to the increased popularity of sport as a mean to mass entertainment, commercialization was able to penetrate this sector. (Heinilä 1989.) Houlihan (2007) furthermore states that even though business has always had a stake in sport, the intensity of the process of commercialization within sport, has been a phenomenon of the late twentieth century. Thus it does not come surprising that the private sport sector in Austria has also grown over the last years.

Another important part of the study of Dachs et al. (2001) was that it showed how the private sport sector nurtures employment in Austria. Camy (2006) also states that sport is a growth area in terms of development and creation of jobs in Europe. Again here it can be stated that commercialization of sport is one of the main reasons for this development. Due to the interconnectivity of sport with many other sectors a wide network can be identified. (Camy, 2006.) Additionally, the European Union has identified sport as a means to create jobs and thus sport has been playing a significant role in various strategies and programmes (Eurostat, 2016). The potential of sport as a creator of workplaces can be verified at least in Austria as nowadays over 330,000 workplaces are directly or indirectly connected to the sport sector (Klafl, 2015; SportsEconAustria, 2016). In terms of employment, the sport tourism sector leads again in importance in regard to this matter, as it amounted to over half of the 99,400 workplaces in Austria in 1998 and around 130,000 workplaces for the winter sports season of 2010/2011 (Dachs et al. 2001; SportsEconAustria, 2012a).

The last interesting part of the IWI report was the outlook of the possible developments in the future. Dachs et al. (2001) state that the importance of sport in the future is likely to increase and more importantly the sector will remain stable as it is more crisis-resilient than other sectors in an economy. Szabó Földesi (2014) verifies that sport is partly more resilient to economic crises than other sectors. Whereas mega sport events do not suffer as much from the latest economic crisis as other sectors, grassroots level sport suffered the most in the realm of sport. Furthermore, Dachs et al. (2001) point out that sport participation is likely to grow as women and older generations will engage more in sport. This acts as a catalyst for a higher demand in sporting goods and sufficient infrastructure. In terms of regular participation in sport and physical activity, Austria witnessed an increase of 7% points during the span from 2009 to 2013, showing that an increase in sport participation has occurred (European Commission, 2014).

As aforementioned, this analysis of the Austrian sport sector marked the beginning of the quantification of this specific sector and thus paved way to control the importance and development over the future. Another step forward in this quest of quantification was the Austrian EU presidency in 2006. During its presidency, Austria launched various projects related to sport and economy in Europe. Main focus points of the presidency period were to find out the macroeconomic effects of sport, employment effects of sport, economic effects of large-scale sporting events, sport and tourism, sport and health, and sport and the aging society. (Austria working on sport and the EU economy study, 2006.) All of those focus points were targeted towards the Lisbon strategy of the European Union which aims to strengthen employment and growth to transform Europe into the most dynamic and most competitive economic area worldwide. Experts in this topic saw sport as an opportunity to achieve those goals both on a national and European level. (Sportministerium, 2012.)

One important partner in the quest of achieving these EU goals – at least in Austria – is the institute SportsEconAustria. This institute was founded in 2004 and since then it has been acting as the key stakeholder for the economic measurements of sport in Austria by regularly producing data about the economic of sport sector and further delivering researches about various topics within the sphere of sport. (SportsEconAustria, n.d.) The data that is produced within SpEA provides valuable insights and thus is used to further describe the development of the sport economy in Austria. To gain this data, the so called sport satellite accounts are being used. In short, these accounts can be seen as a system in which all economic effects of sport are being taken into consideration. Those effects are the gross domestic production, economic value added and, employment. Another important part of the satellite account system is that with its help it is possible to show consistent figures from different countries despite the fact that some national accounts would not show this data properly. (SportsEconAustria, 2012b.) Furthermore, SpEA has been given the task to introduce the sport satellite accounts in all countries within the European Union. This decision was made in December 2014 and was issued by the before inaugurated working group for "Sport and Economics". (Lampl, 2015.) Due to this decision, and the importance of the topic of sport and economy, it can be stated that Austria and especially SpEA play a crucial role in developing reporting standards and processes further, in order to better quantify and compare statistical representation of sport all over the European Union.

Tourism and Retail Dominate the Private Sport Sector

The previous chapter about the history of the sport economy and furthermore the private sport sector shortly introduced the institute SpEA and its valuable impact on sport. This impact justifies itself as SpEA delivers annual figures about the Austrian sport sector and thus these figures can and will be used to show the various sport business fields within Austria. Even though the data does not show figures such as revenues and EBITDA – of which a definition is given later – it identifies the most important fields within the Austrian sport sphere. Figure 1 shows the development of the sport sector clearly.

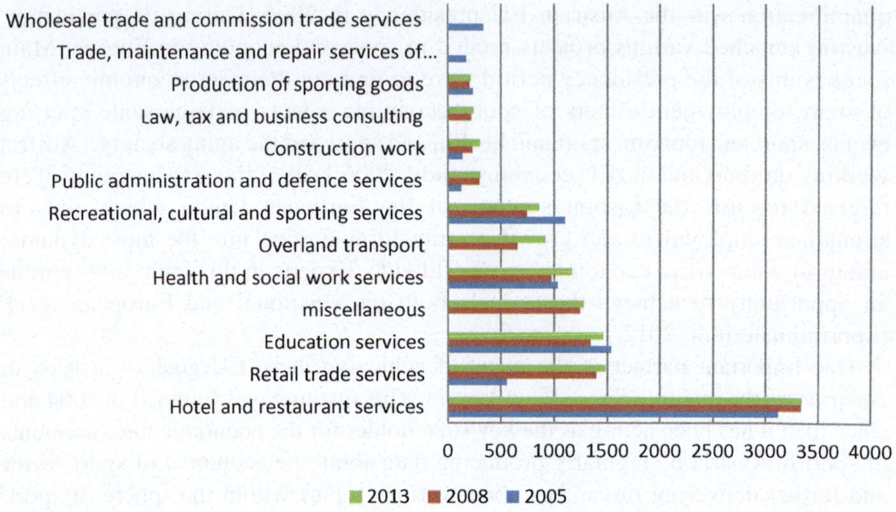

Fig. 1 Direct inland gross value added in Austria in 2005–2013 (in MEUR; broad sport definition). Sources: SportsEconAustria (2009; 2014; 2016).

The numbers in Fig. 1 are calculated through the earlier described sport satellite accounts which extract the impact of sport from other services. These figures deal with the direct inland gross added value that sport has on Austria, which means that only those business transactions are being used which derive directly from sport. The definition that is used for sport stems from the Vilnius Definition of Sport – Version 2.0. (EC EG Sport & Economics/Team SportsEconAustria, 2015.) Within this agreement a broad, a narrow and a statistical definition of sport were drawn to unify and simplify the process of calculating numbers for national sport satellite accounts within the European Union. The leading party of this unification was SpEA which proves their importance in this field. (Bundes-Sportorganisation, n.d.) According to the broad Vilnius definition of sport all transactions are being taken into account which draws upon sport as an input and an output plus all core sport services (EC EG Sport & Economics/Team SportsEconAustria, 2015). This definition acts as the broadest of the three formulated definitions and in fact shows how many different aspects about sport need to be taken into account (Felderer et al., 2006).

According to the broad definition of sport, hotel and restaurant services have the highest shares of economic value added in Austria. The first place for this sector does not come as a surprise, as Austria is a traditionally strong country in tourism – both in summer and winter. The tourism sector in Austria has remained stable over the last 10 years with amounts of approximately 3.3 billion euros total of value added to the economy. (SportsEconAustria, 2009; 2014; 2016.) Especially winter tourism has remained as one of the sport sectors that are vital for the Austrian economy. The importance of this sector can be seen in the statement that Austria would lose its first place among the European countries in terms of economic value added, if winter sport tourism would be taken out of the equation. Thus, without winter sport tourism and all its positive side effects Austria would only have half of the value added per year (Dachs et al., 2001), and subsequently rank only among the average countries within the European Union (Gaulhofer, 2015).

Winter sport tourism is the most important source of revenue in private sport business in Austria. Not only take the skiing centres advantage of the high numbers of visitors every year but also other actors, for example sport retailers and restaurants benefit from it.

For the winter season from November 2015 until April 2016 new records in arrivals and overnight stays were achieved in Austria, which further confirms the previously mentioned trend that winter tourism is very important for Austria and that this field will grow further in the future. For this mentioned period of time, statistical institutes have measured that the winter sport tourism in Austria has attracted over 18.4 million people from all over the world with all together over 68.5 million overnight stays. In addition, this sector has generated revenues of approximately 13.2 billion euros over this period of time. The highest numbers of arrivals and overnight stays were recorded in the federal states of Tyrol and Salzburg. With their location in the heart of the Alps and their long history in winter sports, those two federal states can be seen as the key players within the winter sport tourism sector in Austria. Especially the outstanding quality of the infrastructure (e.g., ski lifts, slopes and accommodation) and a very good price-performance ratio secure their places on the top within Austria. (Kuprian, 2016.)

Another big stakeholder in the private sport sector in Austria is the sport retail trade services. According to the latest data from SpEA this sector generated around 1.5 billion euros in value added during 2013. (SportsEconAustria, 2016.) This lifts the retail trade services to place number two in terms of sport contribution for the whole economy in Austria. One interesting factor within those services is that due to the latest fitness trends a big change within this sector has occurred. With only 87 million euros generated in 2005, sport retail services were ranked only fifth among the biggest contributors of sport in the Austrian economy. As mentioned in the analysis of the changes in the private sport sector in Austria, the fitness boom and subsequently a higher demand for clothing, sporting equipment and other necessities to exercise, can be seen as the drivers behind this outstanding development within this sphere of sport business. (Dachs et al., 2001.)

Furthermore, the advent of online shopping and the continuation of fitness trends make this sector grow more in importance. This development can be seen through the increasing shares of sporting goods retail transactions that are done by means of e-commerce. Even though online sporting goods retail achieved 7% of its revenues through online transactions and thus ranked in the first place among online shopping in Austria in 2010, there was still room for improvement and development in the future. (Austrian Press Agency, 2011.) This room for improvement was fulfilled and thus the online sport retail market more than doubled to take a share of 15% of all transactions in 2015. Despite this already ongoing development, experts within the field of sport retail still expect higher growth rates in this specific sector. (Richter, 2016.)

In 2015, 2.5 billion euros were spent in total for sporting goods and sport clothing in Austria. Only 1.5 billion euros of those sales stem from the traditional stationary sales in the sporting goods shops. The remaining amount of one billion euros flowed through either other stationary sales, such as conventional shoe and clothing shops, and supermarkets, or the above mentioned online sales. Among the non-traditional sellers, mono label stores such as North Face or Salewa, and other specialized sport stores such as running shops, fitness shops, outdoor shops and bike shops have emerged especially due to the problems among the traditional sellers. (Pressberger, 2015; Richter, 2016.) One of the reasons for that is that brands and other assortments have not felt valued anymore within the big sport retail stores (Richter, 2016). Specialized stores can also give customers better expertise in their areas and other services such as maintenance and repair (Gutbrunner, 2015). On the other hand, in online sales, the biggest profiteers among this sector are for example Amazon and Zalando (Richter, 2016). Due to their easy accessibility and around the clock services the online services have been successful in entering also the sport retail market. To counteract the strong development of the online retailers, Austrian sport retail shops have started to expand their existing online distribution channels and put more emphasis on online sales. (Pressberger, 2014; Richter, 2016.)

Sport retail sector has been in constant flux over the last years due to these changes and there is no sign of long lasting stability within this sector. Thus it will remain subject of possibly significant changes over the next years. One of those changes that might shake the Austrian sporting goods landscape is that other sporting goods retailers aim to enter the market within the next years. One of those retailers is Norwegian XXL Sports & Outdoor Group which has successfully handled operations in Scandinavian countries. XXL has signed its first two lease contracts in Austria with an intention to open at least one store late 2017 (XXL ASA – Third quarter 2016 results, 2016). This new competitor might take away market shares of the existing retailers and thus shape the sporting goods retail landscape even further. Especially with a sophisticated presence in the online market XXL might be able to fulfil changes the analysts expect about higher online sales.

Key Stakeholders Within Sport Tourism and Sport Retail

As it was established before, the two biggest sectors within the Austrian sport sphere are winter tourism and sporting goods retailers. Due to the various contributors in the winter sport tourism ski lift operators will be presented as an example in this article as they closely and directly contribute to this sector. The ski lift operators fall under the ÖNACE2008[1] code of 49.39-1 – "Transport by cable railways, funiculars and ski lifts". Besides ski lift operators, sport retailers will be further introduced with the help of the ÖNACE2008 codes 46.49-3 – "Wholesale of sport goods" – and 47.64-0 – "Retail sale of sporting equipment in specialised stores". (Statistik Austria, 2016c.) The following data was gathered through the Amadeus database due to the reason that in reports of Statistik Austria some of the codes were summarized with other irrelevant sectors and thus could not show a precise picture about these particular fields. Within this database the codes shown above were used to extract the biggest companies within the particular fields.

[1] ÖNACE2008 is the Austrian equivalent of the *Statistical classification of economic activities in the European Community* (NACE Rev. 2, 2008).

Table 1 **Biggest ski lift operators by revenue in Austria in 2013.**

Name	Revenue (MEUR)	EBITDA-%	Staff (n)	Slope kilometres
Silvrettaseilbahn AG	72.9	45.6	326	172
Zillertal arena	49.9	38.7	403	143
4-Berge-Skischaukel	48.8	30.5	160	123
Bergbahn AG Kitzbühel	46.1	34.4	274	173
Arlberger Bergbahnen AG	39.3	35.3	246	350
Mayrhofner Bergbahnen AG	31.2	34.2	165	136
SkiWelt Wilder Kaiser – Brixental marketing GmbH	25.2	27.2	250	284
Skicircus Saalbach Hinterglemm Leogang Fieberbrunn	12.3	n/a	252	270
Ötztaler Gletscherbahn GmbH & co KG	6.9	n/a	377	144
Serfaus-Fiss-Ladis information	1.6	n/a	594	160

Sources: Bureau van Dijk (2016); TirolWerbung GmbH (2016); Österreich: größte Skigebiete – Größtes Skigebiet in Österreich (2016).

Table 1 shows the ten biggest ski resort areas and their ski lift operators according to slope kilometres (Tirol Werbung GmbH, 2016; Österreich: größte Skigebiete – Größtes Skigebiet in Österreich, 2016). It can be seen that the top four operators all have revenues above 45 million euros with the number five coming close to them with approximately 40 million euros revenue. Those revenue figures show that the operators have a significant contribution towards the Austrian economy.

Furthermore, the EBITDA-% shows that the ski lift operators can be seen as profitable businesses. The EBITDA margin (i.e., EBITDA-%) is used to measure a company's operating profitability as the EBITDA ("Earnings before interest, tax, depreciation and amortization") is divided by the total revenue. (Investopedia, 2010.) What is interesting about this sector is that many ski operators have joined forces during the last years to further increase their revenues and the quality for their customers. For example "Skicircus Saalbach Hinterglemm Leogang" just recently started its cooperation with the ski operator in Fieberbrunn which makes it one of the biggest ski resorts in the world. (Tourismusverband Saalbach, 2016.) Another interesting factor is that only the first eight operators can report revenues over ten million euros. Following those operators, a clear gap can be seen. This hints at a further necessity to form cooperation between geographically close skiing resorts. It might ensure that with a stronger portfolio of slopes more customers could be attracted and revenues could be increased. In terms of people employed, the top ten of this sector combined have over 3000 workplaces as seen in Table 1. Thus those operators employ around 300 people per average which puts them in the sector of large-scale enterprises. This shows again that winter sport tourism is highly contributing to the employment situation in Austria. (Kleissner, 2012.)

Table 2 Biggest sport retailers by revenue in Austria in 2013.

Name	Revenue (MEUR)	EBITDA-%	Staff (n)
Intersport Österreich Einkaufsgenossenschaft	262.5	0.6	3600
Hervis sport- und Modegesellschaft m.b.H.	228.0	7.1	1176
SportsDirect.Com Austria GmbH	199.5	−15.7	2000
Zentrasport Österreich Einkaufsgenossenschaft	129.9	1.0	93
Blue tomato GmbH	58.0	1.1	144
Titus GmbH	26.2	4.3	n/a
Pryde group GmbH branch Austria	20.8	3.5	n/a
Nike retail B.V. Branch Austria	17.9	4.5	34
Foot locker Austria GmbH	14.3	7.5	n/a

Source: Bureau van Dijk (2016).

Table 2 shows the biggest sporting goods retailers in Austria. The top four companies in this sector can all report revenues of at least around 130 million euros per year. The leader in this sector is Intersport Österreich with a value of more than 262 million euros. Intersport Österreich acts as the group for all connected Intersport branches in Austria which amounts to around 150 locations (Intersport Österreich, 2016). The first competitor of Intersport is the Hervis Sport- und Modegesellschaft GmbH which accumulates revenues of 228 million euros. SportsDirect.com Austria GmbH follows behind the top two. This group is the first which cannot break the 200 million euros' line. Another interesting fact for SportsDirect.com Austria is that it is the only company with a negative EBITDA-%. The reason lies behind the fact that SportsDirect.com with its headquarters in Great Britain only acquired Eybl Sports & Sports Experts (EAG) in 2013 and started to remodel its previous assortment, and rebrand its stores according to SportDirect.com (Austrian Press Agency, 2014). This remodelling into a sporting equipment discount shop was not well received by the Austrian population and thus the group lost market shares and revenues (Richter, 2016). After the big four, specialized stores such as Blue Tomato GmbH, Titus GmbH and the Austrian branch of Pryde Group GmbH placed themselves in this sector. They provide subculture sports like snowboarding, skateboarding, surfing and wakeboarding with products and expertise in the field. In terms of employment this sector provides even more jobs than the ski lift operators as combined they accumulate over 7000 workplaces.

Conclusions

In general the Austrian sport sector has witnessed and undergone many changes over the last decades. Various factors such as the emergence of new trends in the fitness industry and higher disposable income and leisure have shaped the sport sector especially since the beginning of this century. Furthermore, professionalization and scarceness of public funding has led to a strong private sport sector in Austria. Another factor for the development of this sector is that online sales for sporting goods have skyrocketed in revenues over the last years. Despite these changes however, it can be still stated that the public and the voluntary sport sectors play a significant role in Austria.

Nevertheless, the private sport sector with its contribution to the Austrian economy has gained more importance and is likely to be further developed over the next years and decades. This is evident especially because the private side of sport is more as resilient to crises as the rest of the economy (Szabó Földesi, 2014) as people do not tend to change their habits so quickly and frequently (Klafl, 2015). Another reason is that sport not only has effects on the value added and employment but also fosters technological advancements. This can be transferred into other fields as well – for example synthetics in sporting goods which were adapted for the aircraft industry. (Dachs et al., 2001.) The Austrian ski manufacturer Fischer for example invested heavily in research and development for their ski production. Due to the harsh economic climate in the sport industry in the 1970s, Fischer used their acquired knowledge in the field of synthetics to open the subsidiary FACC (Fischer Advanced Composite Components). The daughter company develops and produces light constructional components for the aircraft and helicopter industry all over the world. (Koprax, Garaus, & Güttel, 2015.) Thus private sport sector investments and evermore stronger developments are expected also in the future.

As it was mentioned earlier, the private sport sector is expected to gain importance and furthermore help to employ people in Austria. Unemployment numbers in general have increased during the last years with a total of over 333,000 inhabitants, which puts Austria in a challenging situation (AMS Österreich, 2016). The sport sector in general and the private sport sector in particular are however expected to be able to provide job opportunities for Austrians despite the overall hard economic recession situation. According to the Vilnius definition, the sport sector was able to produce directly and indirectly approximately 333,000 jobs in Austria for the last year. (SportsEconAustria, 2016.) This shows that the Austrian private sport sector has an impact in the job market and thus can be seen as a significantly positive contributor to the employment rates.

In terms of the biggest contributors to the Austrian private sport sector, data shows that winter tourism and sport retail have the biggest offerings to the Austrian economy and thus can be seen as the strongest actors in the sector. Especially winter sport is vital for Austria as it does not only consist of operating ski slopes, ski lifts, skiing equipment and accommodation but also has various other contributions. Examples for other contributions are instruction of skiing and snowboarding, production of sporting goods, and betting on the outcomes of alpine skiing, cross country skiing, biathlon and other winter sports. Furthermore, the technology used nowadays in the ski lifts in Austria is highly appreciated all over the world and for that reason heavily exported to other countries. (SportsEconAustria, 2012a.)

Regarding the statistical reporting some limitations in Austria still exist. Even though SpEA delivers qualitative work in the field of reporting it is not possible to find data according to ÖNACE 2008 codes from the website of the statistical office in Austria. Especially the codes for sport remain missing because either data is not collected for those codes or the collected data contradicts each other. Thus not even rough estimates can be made and separate research needs to be conducted to find numbers and figures according to senior researcher at SpEA, Günther Grohall. (Grohall, personal communication, November 11, 2015.)

As a conclusion it can be stated that Austrian private sport sector has a vital part for the Austrian economy. It provides not only monetary profits and jobs but also fosters technological advancement and spreads out far among the Austrian economy and other sectors. Sport and its services have a big network of upstream and downstream contributors which make the private sport sector strong. It can be assumed that this sector due to above mentioned reasons will remain strong and even grow bigger during the upcoming years.

References

AMS Österreich. (2016). *Übersicht über den Arbeitsmarkt Mai 2016* [Overview of the labour market May 2016]. Retrieved June 16, 2016 from http://www.ams.at/_docs/001_uebersicht_aktuell.pdf

Austria working on sport and the EU economy study. (2006). *EurActiv.com*. Retrieved September 21, 2016 from http://www.euractiv.com/section/sports/news/austria-working-on-sport-and-the-eu-economy-study/

Austrian Press Agency. (2011). Online-Handel in Österreich wächst rasant [Online-retail in Austria grows rapidly]. *Futurezone.at*. Retrieved June 5, 2016 from http://futurezone.at/b2b/online-handel-in-oesterreich-waechst-rasant/24.570.346

Austrian Press Agency. (2014). Aus für Traditionsmarke Sport Eybl [Tradiotional brand Eybl folds]. *derStandard.at*. Retrieved June 14, 2016 from http://derstandard.at/1399507037060/Marken-Sport-Eybl-und-Sports-Experts-verschwinden

Braunstingl, A. (2015). *BSO_Mitgliederstatistik 2015* [BSO member statistic 2015]. Retrieved May 15, 2016 from http://www.bso.or.at/de/ueber-uns/mitglieder/mitgliederstatistik/

Bundesministerium für Arbeit, Soziales und Konsumentenschutz. (2015). *Bericht zur Lage und zu den Perspektiven des Freiwilligen Engagements in Österreich – 2.Freiwilligenbericht* [Report on the current state and the perspectives of voluntary engagement in Austria – 2nd volunteer report]. Retrieved May 15, 2016 from http://bmsk2.cms.apa.at/cms/freiwilligenweb/attachments/2/4/2/CH3095/CMS1401440787892/2._freiwilligenbericht.pdf

Bundes-Sportorganisation. (n.d.). *Sport und Wirtschaft* [Sport and economy]. Retrieved May 16, 2016 from http://www.bso.or.at/de/sport-in-oesterreich/sport-und-gesellschaft/sport-und-wirtschaft/

Bundesverfassungsgesetz, B-VG §15. (2015).

Bureau van Dijk. (2016). *Company reports*. Retrieved May 26, 2016 from Amadeus database.

Camy, J. (2006). Employment opportunities in the sports sector: A review of the European situation. In G. Di Cola (Ed.), *Beyond the scoreboard: Youth employment opportunities and skills development in the sports sector* (pp. 85–112). Geneva, Switzerland: International Labour Office.

Dachs, B., Macek, S., Preissl, M., Steindl, G., & Zwickl, G. (2001). *Die wirtschaftliche Bedeutung des Sports in Österreich* [The economic significance of sport in Austria]. Vienna, Austria: Industriewissenschaftliches Institut.

EC EG Sport & Economics/Team SportsEconAustria. (2015). *The Vilnius Definition of Sport – Version 2.0*. Retrieved June 2, 2016 from http://ec.europa.eu/eurostat/documents/6921402/0/Vilnius+Definition+Sport+CPA2008+official+2013_09_19.pdf

European Commission. (2014). *Sport and physical activity*. Special Eurobarometer 412/wave 80.2. Brussels, Belgium: D-G Education and Culture.

Eurostat. (2016). *Employment in sport*. Retrieved September 19, 2016 from http://ec.europa.eu/eurostat/statisticsexplained/index.php/Employment_in_sport

Felderer, B., Helmenstein, C., Kleissner, A., Moser, B., Schindler, J., & Treitler, R. (2006). *Sport und Ökonomie in Europa – Ein Tour d' Horizon* [Sport and economics in Europe – A tour d' Horizon]. Vienna, Austria: Bundeskanzleramt Österreich – Sektion Sport.

Gaulhofer, K. (2015). Sport und Wirtschaft: Österreichs "Goldene beim" Geld [Sport and economy: Austrias Gold medal]. *Die Presse*. Retrieved May 19, 2016 from http://diepresse.com/home/wirtschaft/economist/4739941/Sport-und-Wirtschaft_Osterreichs-Goldene-beim-Geld

Gutbrunner, S. (2015). Sports Direct floppt, andere Händler profitieren [Sport Direct flops, other sellers benefits]. *Wirtschaftsblatt*. Retrieved August 17, 2016 from http://wirtschaftsblatt.at/home/nachrichten/oesterreich/4655863/Sports-Direct-floppt-andere-Haendler-profitieren

Heinilä, K. (1989). The sports club as a social organization in Finland. *International Review for the Sociology of Sport, 24*(3), 225–248.

Houlihan, B. (2007). *Sport and society: A student introduction*. London, UK: Sage.

Intersport Österreich. (2016). Unternehmen [company]. *Intersport.at*. Retrieved June 13, 2016 from http://www.intersport.at/unternehmen/organisation/index.html?lang=de&ixn=-6afd180c:1554eb9bf59:-1b8f&jsessionid=3448D22DFF94F338733240DEF22B91E4

Investopedia. (2010). EBITDA margin definition. *Investopedia.com*. Retrieved June 12, 2016 from http://www.investopedia.com/terms/e/ebitda-margin.asp

Klafl, C. (2015). Sport bringt Österreich Milliarden [Sport brings billions to Austria]. *Kurier*. Retrieved May 16, 2016 from http://kurier.at/wirtschaft/sport-bringt-oesterreich-milliarden/132.765.010

Kleissner, A. (2012). *Die gesamtwirtschaftliche Bedeutung des Wintersports in Österreich* [The macroeconomic significance of winter sport in Austria]. Retrieved August 17, 2016 from http://www.allianz-zukunft-winter.at/assets/content/Meinungsbildung/2012_Anna_Kleissner_Gesamtwirtschaftliche_Bedeutung_Wintersport.pdf?PHPSESSID=068c09d7ec5db822886ae0680e77f246

Koprax, I., Garaus, C., & Güttel, W. (2015). Dieser Weg wird kein leichter sein. Wie durch Pfadkreation dem eingeschlagenen Pfade der Unternehmensentwicklung eine neue Richtung gegeben werden kann [This path won't be easy. How through path creation a new path for business development can be realized]. In W. Güttel (Ed.), *Austrian management review* (pp. 60–68). München, Germany: Rainer Hampp Verlag.

Kuprian, B. (2016). *Winter 2015/16: Österreich ist "Darling" des Wintersporturlaubs, Ankünfte +5%, Nächtigungen +4%* [Austria winter sport holiday "darling", arrivals +5%, overnight stays +4%]. Retrieved June 2, 2016 from https://www.austriatourism.com/wp-content/uploads/2016/05/2016g_wintersaison_hochrechnung-zusfass.pdf

Lampl, S. (2015). Sportminister Klug: Sport ist bedeutender Wirtschaftsfaktor [Sport minister Klug: Sport is a significant economical factor]. *ots.at*. Retrieved May 16, 2016 from http://www.ots.at/presseaussendung/OTS_20150420_OTS0043/sportminister-klug-sport-ist-bedeutender-wirtschaftsfaktor

Marschik, M. (2011). Austrian sport and the challenges of its recent historiography. *Journal of Sport History, 38*(2), 189–198.

Nagel, S. (2006). *Sportverein im Wandel. Akteurtheoretische Analyse zur Entwicklung von Sportvereinen* [Sport clubs in transition. Actor-theoretical analysis on the development of sport clubs]. Schorndorf, Germany: Hofmann Verlag.

Norden, G. (2007). Sportaktivität in der Freizeitgesellschaft: Entwicklung, Tendenzen und Szenarien [Sport activity of the leisure-loving society: Development, tendencies and scenarios]. In P. Hilscher, G. Norden, M. Russo, & O. Weiß (Eds.), *Entwicklungstendenzen im Sport* (2nd ed., pp. 13–59). Wien, Austria: Lit-Verlag.

Österreich: größte Skigebiete – Größtes Skigebiet in Österreich. (2016). *Skiresort.de*. Retrieved June 12, 2016 from http://www.skiresort.de/skigebiete/europa/oesterreich/sortiert-nach/laenge-pisten/

Pratscher, H. (2000). Sportverhalten in Österreich [Sport behaviour in Austria]. *Journal für Ernährungsmedizin, 2*(5), 18–23.

Pressberger, T. (2014). Chancen für KMU im Sporthandel [Chances for SME's in sport retail]. *Wirtschaftsblatt*. Retrieved September 21, 2016 from http://wirtschaftsblatt.at/home/nachrichten/newsletter/3850977/Chancen-fur-KMU-im-Sporthandel?from=suche.intern.portal

Pressberger, T. (2015). Wer sich spezialisiert, macht das Rennen [The ones who specialize will win the race]. *Wirtschaftsblatt*. Retrieved August 17, 2016 from http://www.vsso.at/dokumente/File/vsso_medienecho-w-blatt_fcgi.pdf

Richter, W. (2016). *Großbaustelle Sportartikelhandel* [Construction site: Sport retail]. Retrieved June 4, 2016 from http://www.regiodata.eu/images/attachments/article/987/PRA_Sportartikelhandel_in_Oesterreich_03.05.2016.pdf

Schmidl, B. S. (2004). Die ökonomische Bedeutung des Sports in Österreich [The economic significance of sport in Austria]. *Kurswechsel, 2*, 56–66.

Soltész, S. (2002). *Trendsportarten* [Trend sports]. Hamburg, Germany: Diplomica.

Spindler-Oswald, B. (2016). *Die Organisation des Sports in Österreich, in Europa und International* [The organisation of sport in Austria, Europe and internationally]. Retrieved May 15, 2016 from http://www.bso.or.at/fileadmin/Inhalte/Dokumente/BSO-Skriptum_Organisation_des_Sports.pdf

Sportministerium. (2012). *Österreichische EU-Ratspräsidentschaft 2006* [Austrian EU-presidency 2006]. Retrieved May 30, 2016 from https://www.sportministerium.at/de/themen/europaeische-sportpolitik/eu-ratspraesidentschaften/oesterreichische-eu-ratspraesidentschaft

SportsEconAustria. (2009). *Das Sport-Datenvademecum Ausgabe 4* [The sport-datavademecum edition 4]. Retrieved May 15, 2016 from http://www.esce.at/spea/speafile/0909%20BMLVS%20IV%20SportAustria%20Datenvademecum%20SpEA%20DE.pdf

SportsEconAustria. (2012a). *Das Sport-Datenvademecum Ausgabe 6* [The sport-datavademecum edition 6]. Retrieved May 15, 2016 from http://www.esce.at/spea/speafile/1206%20BMLVS%20IV%20Sportaustria%20Datenvademecum%20Nr.6.pdf

SportsEconAustria. (2012b). *Study on the contribution of sport to economic growth and employment in the EU*. European Commission, D-G Education and Culture.

SportsEconAustria. (2014). *Das Sport-Datenvademecum Ausgabe 7* [The sport-datavademecum edition 7]. Retrieved May 15, 2016 from http://www.esce.at/spea/uploads/Sportaustria%20NR7%202014-low%20FINAL.pdf

SportsEconAustria. (2016). *Das Sport-Datenvademecum Ausgabe 8* [The sport-datavademecum edition 8]. Retrieved May 15, 2016 from http://www.esce.at/spea/uploads/Sportaustria%20NR8%20012016-lr.pdf

SportsEconAustria. (n.d.). *INSTITUT* [Institute]. Retrieved May 30, 2016 from http://www.esce.at/spea/index.php?page=institut

Statistik Austria. (2016a). *Bevölkerungsstand* [Population]. Retrieved May 15, 2016 from http://statistik.at/web_de/statistiken/menschen_und_gesellschaft/bevoelkerung/volkszaehlungen_registerzaehlungen_abgestimmte_erwerbsstatistik/bevoelkerungsstand/078392.html

Statistik Austria. (2016b). *Jahresdaten* [Yearly statistics]. Retrieved May 24, 2016 from http://statistik.at/web_de/statistiken/wirtschaft/volkswirtschaftliche_gesamtrechnungen/bruttoinlandsprodukt_und_hauptaggregate/jahresdaten/019715.html

Statistik Austria. (2016c). *ÖNACE2008 – Struktur* [ÖNACE2008 – structure]. Retrieved May 16, 2016, from http://www.statistik.at/KDBWeb/kdb_VersionAuswahl.do?KDBtoken=null&versID=10438&sprache=EN

Szabó Földesi, G. (2014). The impact of the global economic crisis on sport. *Physical Culture & Sport. Studies & Research, 63*(1), 22–30.

Tirol Werbung GmbH. (2016). Die 10 größten Skigebiete [The 10 biggest skiing areas]. *Tirol.at*. Retrieved June 3, 2016 from http://www.tirol.at/reisefuehrer/sport/skifahren/die-10-groessten-skigebiete

Tourismusverband Saalbach. (2016). TirolS – Zwei Länder. Eine Bahn [TirolS – Two federal states. One ski lift]. *saalbach.com*. Retrieved June 14, 2016 from http://www.saalbach.com/de/winter/service/pressebereich/presse-detail/article//TirolS-Zwei-Laender-Eine-Bahn.html

Wagner, T. (2010). *Entwicklungstendenzen des Sports am Beispiel der ASKÖ Steg Dornach* [Development tendencies of sport on the example of ASKÖ Steg Dornach]. Vienna, Austria: University of Vienna.

XXL ASA – Third quarter 2016 results. (2016). Retrieved November 7, 2016 from http://schjarven-2014-elb-1ozfug6ewdf39-1589988198.eu-west-1.elb.amazonaws.com/investor/download-center/announcements/announcement/?release_id=0D98274F60FE81BC

BELGIUM: The Rise and Size of the Sport Industry in the Flemish Region and the Brussels-Capital Region

Julie Borgers and Jeroen Scheerder

Selected country facts, whole Belgium (in 2013)	
Capital	Brussels
Geographical size (km^2)	30,528
Population (million)	11.16
GDP (euro per capita)	35,300
GDP (per capita in PPS)	120
Annual net earnings average (€)	26,609

Introduction

As in different other European countries, sport in Belgium is organised in three main sectors, representing a variety of sport organisations with different rationales, goals and values (Scheerder, Zintz, & Delheye, 2011b; Scheerder & Vos, 2013; 2014). A triangle of mass sport providers can be distinguished in the governmental, the commercial and the civil society sector. Furthermore, a number of professional companies is involved with the production and distribution of sporting goods and equipment. These activities are needed to support the provision of sport-related services, thus account for an important part of the total sport industry in Belgium (see

J. Borgers
Policy in Sports & Physical Activity Research Group, University of Leuven,
Leuven 3000, Belgium
e-mail: julie.borgers@kuleuven.be

J. Scheerder (✉)
University of Leuven, Faculty of Kinesiology & Rehabilitation Sciences, Gymnasium,
Tervuursevest 101, B-3001 Leuven, Belgium
e-mail: jeroen.scheerder@kuleuven.be

A. Laine, H. Vehmas (eds.), *The Private Sport Sector in Europe*, Sports Economics, Management and Policy 14, https://doi.org/10.1007/978-3-319-61310-9_3

also Scheerder, Vos, Pabian, & Pauwels, 2010c). As the sport policy in Belgium is organised on a community level,[1] this chapter addresses the emergence and the current size of the sport industry in Flanders, which entails the Flemish Region and part of the Brussels-Capital Region (BCR). The Flemish Region is the northern and Dutch-speaking part of Belgium and counts for 6,444,127 inhabitants, which is about 58% of the Belgian population (Statistics Belgium, 2015). The Brussels-Capital Region is also included in the analysis because the headquarters of some companies operating in the Flemish Region are located here.

In the first part of this chapter, findings of research on sport organisations, sport participation and sport-related employment are presented to further clarify the position of different sectors in the landscape of sport organisations (Scheerder et al., 2011a; Scheerder, Borgers, & Willem, 2015a; 2015b). Secondly, the size of the total sport industry is estimated based on structural, professional and financial characteristics. More specifically, the growth of the sport industry and its subsectors is illustrated and an estimation of its current size in terms of the number of companies, employment rates and revenue is made. The third part provides a more detailed picture of the characteristics of the largest sport-related companies and the fitness industry as a particular example of a profit making business. The chapter ends with a summary and discussion of the main findings.

The Organisation of Sport

In different studies on sport organisations and sport participation, the three main sport sectors are illustrated by archetype examples of organisations such as fitness centres in the commercial sector, local sport authorities in the governmental sector, and non-profit sport clubs in the civil society sector (Scheerder et al., 2010a; Scheerder, Vos, Breesch, Lagae, & Van Hoecke, 2010b; Scheerder, Vos, Vandermeerschen, & van Poppel, 2014; Scheerder, Seghers, Meganck, Vandermeerschen, & Vos 2015c). The civil society sector can be considered as the oldest, most traditional and still the most prominent sector for the organisation of sport. About 24,000 sport clubs are functioning on a voluntary and a non-profit basis. Approximately half of these clubs were established before the 1980's (Scheerder et al., 2010a; Scheerder & Vos, 2014). With Flanders being one of the pioneering regions in the European Sport for All charter, early initiatives in the promotion of sport and the construction of sport facilities were also taken by state administrators and municipalities. The first decree on the organisation of sport at a local level in 1976 resulted in the establishment of municipal sport administrations, which have been held responsible for the facilitation and promotion of sport ever since (Scheerder & Vos, 2014; Scheerder et al., 2014). Whilst

[1] Cultural autonomy of language communities was gained in 1969 (Scheerder et al., 2011b).

approximately 30% of these administrations was introduced before 1980, more than half (55.1%) were established in the 1980's-1990's. The remaining 15% of the municipalities completed the picture by establishing a local sport administration in the period between 2000 and 2010. Thirdly, the commercial sector has been engaged in the production of sport goods and the delivery of sport-related services mainly from the 1980's onwards (Van Bottenburg, 2006). Besides its relevance in the scenery of professional sport events and elite sport, this growing sector has influenced the organisation of leisure sport and sport-related employment due to the establishment of fitness and health centres and other private sport facilities, such as bowling and karting centres.

A study by Scheerder and colleagues (2010c) estimated the share of sport-related (salaried) employment in the total economy in the Flemish Region for less than 1%. These authors found that the private, profit making sector constitutes for approximately 56% of the employment in the sport industry, whereas the public and private non-profit sectors represented respectively 28% and 16%. Furthermore, the non-profit sector is an important source of volunteer work in Flanders: more than 400,000 volunteers deliver services in sport clubs, which equals to about 8% of the Flemish population aged 15 years and older (Scheerder et al., 2010a; Scheerder & Vos, 2014).

Participation Rates in Different Organisational Settings for Sport Participation

The Participation Survey on Culture, Youth, Sports and Media was carried out in 2009 and again in 2014 by the Flemish government (Scheerder et al., 2011a; 2015a; 2015b). This is a large scale and repeated cross-sectional survey that contains data, among others, on sport participation behaviour of a representative sample of 15 to 85-years old Flemish citizens ($\bar{X}_{2009}=47.05 \pm 18.62$ years; $\bar{X}_{2014}=48.29 \pm 19.01$ years). General participation rates are similar at both times, with about 63% of the total population practicing sport at least once a year (Scheerder et al., 2015a).

Figure 1 shows that non-organised forms of sport participation, either individually or in informal groups, are the most popular: more than 40% of the total sample in both surveys practiced at least one sport activity in a non-organised way. However, over the past 5 years a slight decrease in the share of non-organised sport is compensated by an increase in participation in the private sport sector, that is in civil society organisations (+1.0%) and commercial organisations (+2.8%). Other research also showed that commercial organisations such as fitness centres have the ability to attract other participants as compared to traditional sport providers, such as more women, young adults and people with financial constraints (Borgers, Pilgaard, Vanreusel, & Scheerder, 2016).

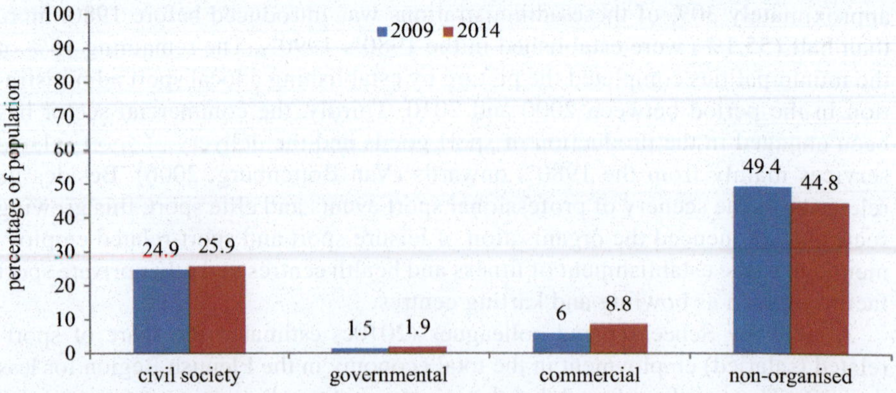

Fig. 1 Participation rates in civil society, governmental and commercial sport organisations and non-organised sport in Flanders, in 2009 (n = 3090) and 2014 (n = 3949), percentages of 15 to 85-years old population. Sources: Based on Scheerder et al. (2011a; 2015a; 2015b).

Data and Methods

The size of the sport industry is estimated based on structural, professional and financial characteristics of sport-related economic activities. Structural characteristics refer to the number of companies in the sport industry, professional characteristics concern the number of employees, and financial characteristics refer to the revenue of sport-related companies. In the second part of the analysis, a more detailed picture is provided with professional and financial parameters of individual companies (i.e., staff members, revenue and EBITDA-%[2]).

The Belgian equivalent (NACE-BEL 2008) of the *Statistical classification of economic activities in the European Community* (NACE Rev. 2, 2008) is used as an outset for the collection of sport industry data. For the present study, two databases are accessed, namely ADS and Bel-First. General information on sport-related companies comes from ADS (Algemene Directie Statistiek) (Statistics Belgium, 2016a). The in-depth analysis of the largest sport-related companies is based on the Bel-First database (Bureau Van Dijk, 2016). In total 15,696 sport-related companies are located in Belgium. Further analyses in this chapter, however, are again restricted to the Flemish Region and the BCR. About 71% of all sport-related companies are located in this region (Table 1).

[2] EBITDA stands for Earnings Before Interests, Taxes, Depreciation and Amortisation. EBITDA-% = 100 x EBITDA/revenue. EBITDA-% = EBITDA margin.

Table 1 Number of sport-related companies according to ADS and Bel-First data, in 2015.

	ADS	Bel-First
Flemish region	10,168 (64.8%)	4720 (62.2%)
Brussels-Capital region	932 (5.9%)	574 (7.6%)
Walloon region[a]	4596 (29.3%)	2291 (30.2%)
Total	**15,696 (100%)**	**7585 (100%)**

Sources: Bureau Van Dijk (2016); Statistics Belgium (2016a).
[a]Walloon Region is the southern, French-speaking part of Belgium. 32% of the Belgian population (3,589,744 people) lives in the region (Statistics Belgium, 2015).

The number of companies in the ADS database is higher than in the Bel-First database because Bel-First only includes companies that need to deliver annual invoices. These account for about 48% of all companies in the ADS database. Another limitation of the Bel-First data is that the high amount of missing data hinders a reliable estimation of the total size of the sport industry or of average parameters like revenue and staff members.[3] Also, whereas ADS contains NACE codes up to five digits, Bel-First is limited to information based on four digits. This implies that some specific sport-related classes could not be identified with Bel-First data. Nevertheless, because ADS did not provide company specific information, the in-depth analysis of the largest sport companies is based on Bel-First data. Hence, this analysis does not include companies involved with the wholesale of sport and camping goods (46946) and those with the exploitation of snooker and billiards facilities (93291).

Selection of Economic Activities

Relevant sport-related economic activities were selected based on the NACE Rev. 2 classification (Eurostat, 2008; Statistics Belgium, 2013). Companies' primary codes were screened, thus only companies that focus on sport as their main activity are included. This resulted in ten categories of economic activities (see Table 2). The selected economic activities were categorised as activities related to (i) the distribution of sporting goods, (ii) the production of sporting goods, or (iii) the delivery of services in the sport industry.

[3] Information on the business size in Bel-First is available for 54% of all companies. The majority of these companies is classified as 'small' (87.8%), whereas a minority is labelled 'medium-sized' (11.0%), 'large' (1.2%) or 'very large' (0.04%). No information on the operationalisation of the size is provided by Bureau Van Dijk (2016). Information on staff members and company revenue is mainly available for large companies.

Table 2 Overview of selected sport-related economic activities in the Flemish Region and the BCR, based on NACE Rev. 2 Classification (2008).

Type of activity	Category of economic activities	NACE codes
Service delivery	*Exploitation of sport facilities*	93110
	Activities of sport clubs and federations	93121, 93122, 93123, 93124, 93125, 93126, 93127, 93128, 93129, 93191
	Exploitation of fitness facilities	93130
	Sport and recreation education	85510
	Renting and leasing of sport and camping goods	77210
	Exploitation of snooker and billiards facilities	93291
	Other sport activities	93199
Distribution	*Retail sale of sport and camping goods in specialised shops*	47640
	Wholesale of sport and camping goods, except bicycles	46496
Production	*Manufacturing of sport goods*	32300

The selection of relevant codes is limited to the economic activities that only represent sport and recreation. This means that, for example, the manufacture of sport clothes and the construction of sport and recreation crafts is not included in the current analyses, as they make part of wider categories of activities in the NACE Rev. 2 Classification – respectively 14,199 ('manufacturing of clothes and other accessories') and 33,150 ('construction and maintenance of crafts'). Furthermore, time-trend analyses are limited to the period between 2008 and 2015 because of a different classification of activities and different company registration procedures before 2008.

Calculation of Average Yearly Growth Rates

The relative growth of the number of companies, the number of employees or the companies' revenue is expressed by the Average Yearly Growth Rate (AYGR). The AYGR between 2008 and 2015 is measured by the following formula (see also Scheerder et al., 2010c):

$$\text{AYGR} = \left(\left(X_{2015} / X_{2008}\right) \wedge \left(1/\left(2015-2008\right)\right) - 1\right)^{*} 100$$

- X_{2015} is the value of the parameter in 2015
- X_{2008} is the value of the parameter in 2008

The Sport Industry in 2015

In 2015, a total number of 11,100 sport-related companies located in the Flemish Region and the BCR employed a total number of 11,554 staff members. Table 3 shows that the biggest share of sport-related companies is involved with the delivery of services (87.9%). Also the majority of employees work in companies that deliver sport-related services (68.7%), whereas almost one third (31.2%) works in the sector of distribution. Hence, the findings of this study align with Scheerder et al.'s (2010c) statement that the majority of jobs in the sport industry concerns the delivery of services rather than distributing and manufacturing products. In contrast, companies involved with the distribution of sport goods deliver a big share to the total revenue in the sport sector: almost half of the revenue (48.6%) is generated by distributing activities. Companies involved with service delivery generate about 51% of the revenue.

Table 3 **Share of economic activities related to service delivery, distribution and production in the number of sport-related companies, the number of employees and the total revenue in the sport industry, in the Flemish Region and the BCR, in 2015.**

Type of activity	Number of companies (%)	Number of employees (%)	Revenue (%)
Service delivery	87.9	68.7	51.1
Distribution	11.7	31.2	48.6
Production	0.4	0.1	0.2
Total	**11,100 (n)**	**11,554 (n)**	**3579 (MEUR)**

Source: Based on ADS (Statistics Belgium, 2016a).

As shown in Table 4 and Fig. 2, the majority of companies operates in the business of activities of sport clubs and sport federations (24.1%), sport and recreation education (22.9%), and the exploitation of sport facilities (17.7%). Companies providing activities as sport clubs or federations and those involved with the exploitation of sport facilities also constitute for the majority of sport-related jobs (respectively 27.5% and 25.1%). Sport and recreation education companies, however, deliver less than 1% of all jobs in the sport industry. This implies that many of these companies are one-person businesses (i.e., independent teachers, coaches and trainers). In contrast, the retail sale of sport and camping goods in specialised shops (7.4% of all sport-related companies) and the exploitation of fitness facilities (4.5% of all sport-related companies) represent bigger companies that employ more people, representing respectively 24 and 11% of all sport-related jobs.

Table 4 Number of companies, staff members and revenue in different categories of sport-related economic activities in the Flemish Region and the BCR, in 2015.

Type of activity	Category of economic activities	Number of companies	Number of staff members[a]	Revenue (x 1000 €)
Service delivery	*Activities of sport clubs and federations*	2674	3171	775,805
	Sport and recreation education	2539	70	36,977
	Exploitation of sport facilities	1962	2894	574,654
	Other sport activities, not specified	1638	381	194,002
	Exploitation of fitness facilities	499	1240	210,840
	Renting and leasing of sport and recreation goods	383	140	29,867
	Exploitation of snooker and billiards facilities	59	44	7705
Distribution	*Retail sale of sport and camping goods in specialised shops*	826	2809	761,129
	Wholesale of sport and camping goods, except bicycles	475	794	979,161
Production	*Manufacturing of sport goods*	45	11	8799
	Total	**11,100**	**11,554**	**3,578,938**

Source: Based on ADS (Statistics Belgium, 2016a).

[a]Note: The reported number of employees concerns the number of salaried employees, not independent managers of (one-person) companies. For this reason the reported number of staff members may be lower than the number of companies. Not all staff members are working full-time (no full-time equivalents/FTEs).

The sport industry in 2015 had a total revenue of about three-and-a-half billion euros. It is shown, however, that the revenue is not necessarily linked to the number of companies and/or employees in a particular business field. That is, the large share of companies in sport and recreation education generates only 1% of the revenue in the sport sector. In contrast, the largest share of revenue is generated by companies involved with the distribution of sporting goods, namely in the wholesale (27.4%) or the retail sale (21.3%). In the next paragraphs these variables are approached from a time-trend perspective between 2008 and 2015.

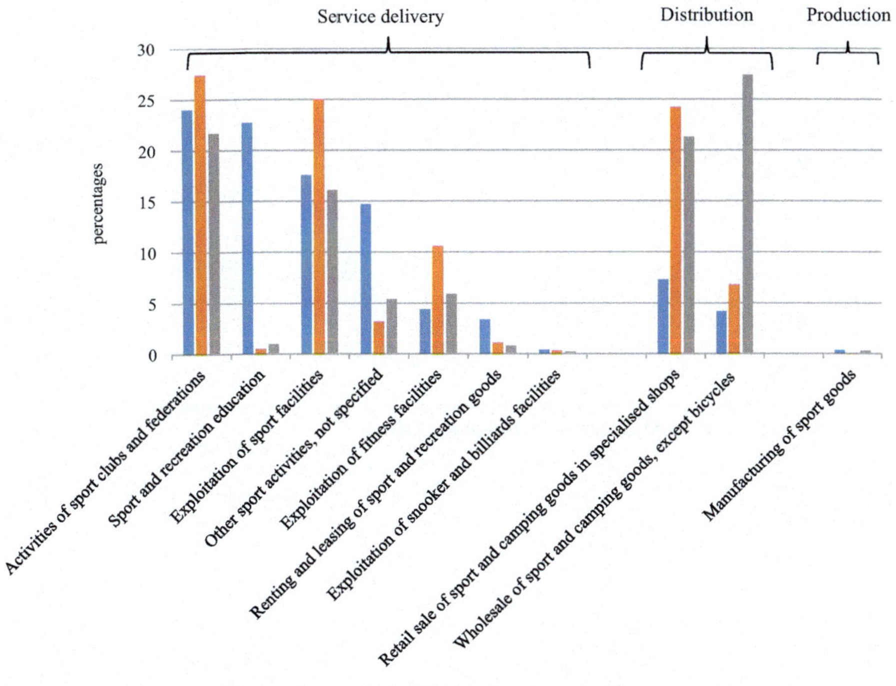

Fig. 2 Relative share of companies, staff members and revenues in different categories of sport-related economic activities in the Flemish Region and the BCR, in 2015, percentages of total number of sport-related companies (n = 11,100), total number of staff members (n = 11,554) and total revenue in the sport industry (3579 MEUR). Source: Based on ADS (Statistics Belgium, 2016a).

Number of Sport-Related Companies

Figure 3 shows the evolution in the number of sport-related companies between 2008 and 2015. A continuous rise is observed with an increase in the number of companies from 7799 in 2008 to 11,100 in 2015, which equals an AYGR of about 5%. Furthermore, the share of sport-related companies in the total economy rose from 1.5% in 2008 to 1.8% in 2015 (Fig. 4). The AYGR shows that the sport-related business has grown relatively stronger than the total industry.

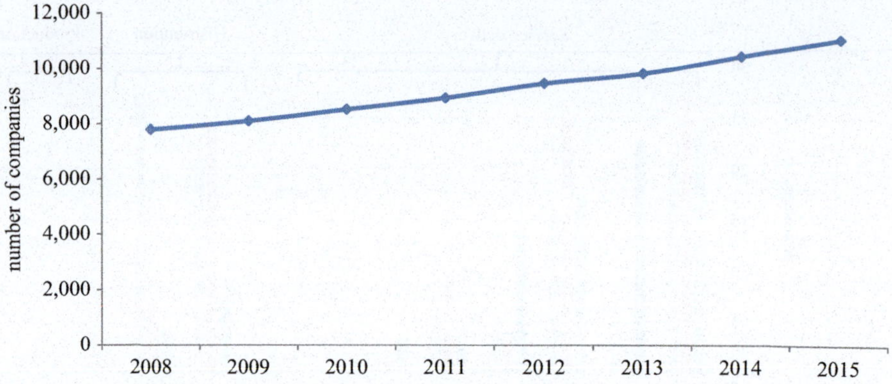

Fig. 3 Total number of sport-related companies in the Flemish Region and the BCR, in 2008–2015. Source: Based on ADS (Statistics Belgium, 2016a).

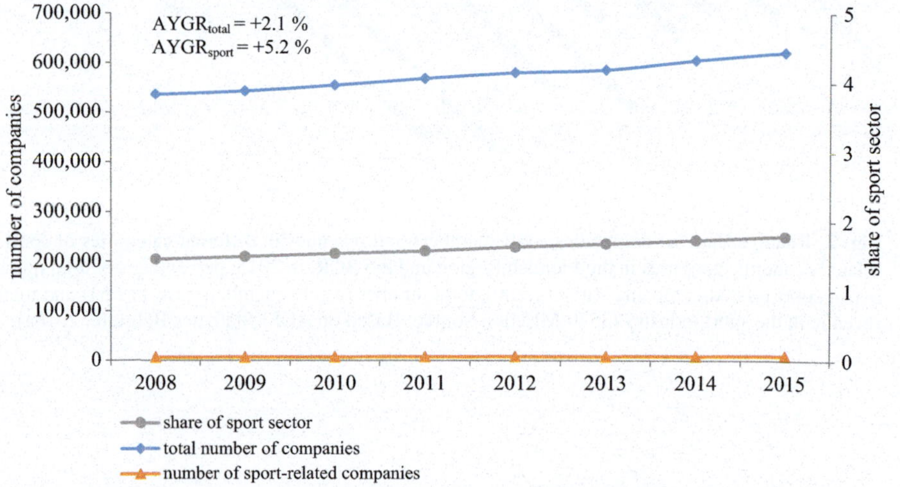

Fig. 4 Share and evolution of sport-related companies in relation to total economy in the Flemish Region and the BCR, in 2008–2015. Source: Based on ADS (Statistics Belgium, 2016a).

A more detailed picture on the number of sport-related companies in specific business fields shows the importance to distinguish between different economic activities (Fig. 5). The strongest increase can be ascribed to a rise in the number of companies involved with sport and recreation education (AYGR = +13.4%), the exploitation of fitness facilities (AYGR = +9.3%), activities of sport clubs and federations (AYGR = +8.0%), and other sport activities (AYGR = +8.9%). Also the number of sport-related renting and leasing companies (AYGR = +6.4%) and the manufacturing of sport goods (AYGR = +1.3%) has risen. In contrast, a decrease is observed in the number of companies exploiting sport facilities (AYGR = −1.2%) and snooker and billiards facilities (AYGR = −3.4%). Also the number of companies involved with the wholesale (AYGR = −3.8%) and retail sale (AYGR = −1.2%) of sport and camping goods has lost share.

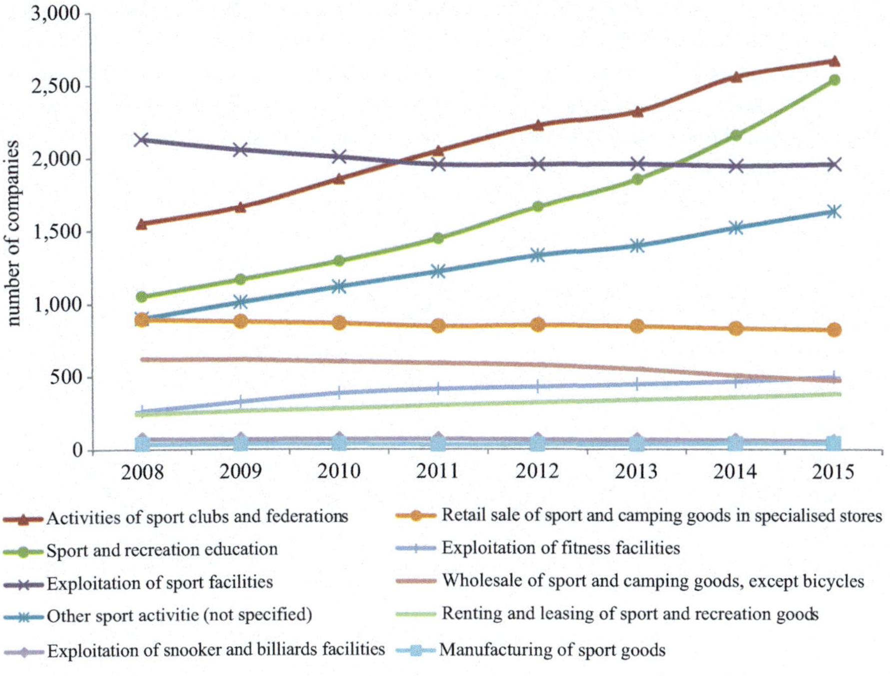

Fig. 5 Number of sport-related companies in specific categories of economic activities in the Flemish Region and the BCR, in 2008–2015. Source: Based on ADS (Statistics Belgium, 2016a).

In addition to the graphics developed with ADS data, Fig. 6 provides a broader perspective on developments in the sport industry since the end of the nineteenth century. This picture was drawn based on Bel-First data because this dataset provided company-specific information on the year of foundation. The number of companies per category here is lower than in analyses using ADS data because the Bel-First only contains companies that have to deliver annual invoices (see Table 1). We therefore focus on trends, not on absolute numbers, in this graphic.

Three waves can be distinguished in the establishment of sport-related companies particularly since the mid-twentieth century. Sport clubs and federations, as well as companies concerned with the exploitation of sport facilities, have the longest tradition. The number of this kind of companies gradually expanded in the aftermath of the Second World War and particularly since the 1970's (see also Scheerder et al., 2011b; Scheerder & Vos, 2014). This phase can be referred to as the *emergence of the non-profit sport industry*. Secondly, companies involved with the retail sale of sport and camping goods and other sport activities have been established since the end of the 1960's but mainly rose during eighties and nineties. This second phase is called the *emergence of the sport goods trading industry*. A third wave is witnessed since the end of the 1980's with the exploitation of fitness facilities, sport and recreation education and the renting and leasing of sport and recreation goods. This phase can be called the *emergence of the commercial sport services industry.*

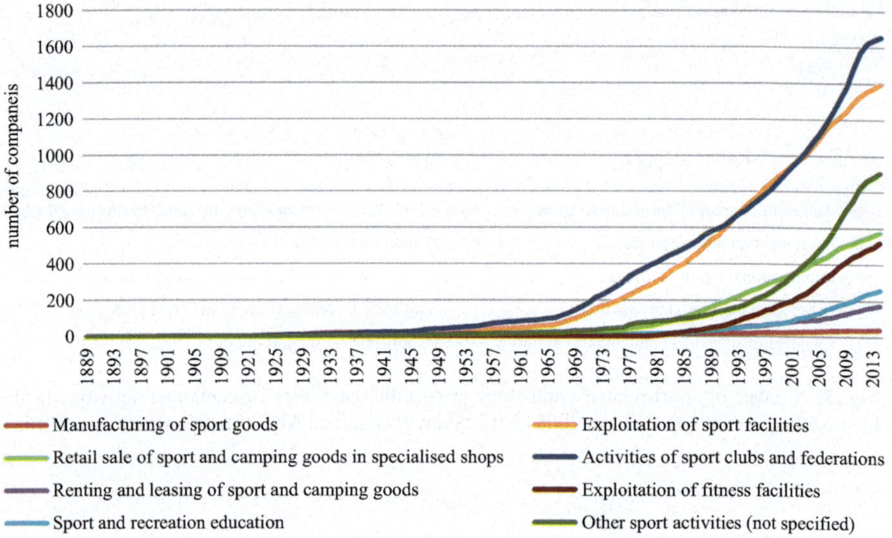

Fig. 6 Year of the foundation of companies in different categories of sport-related economic activities in the Flemish Region and the BCR, cumulative numbers. Source: Based on Bel-First (Bureau Van Dijk, 2016).

Employment in the Sport Industry

Generally, a rise from about 9422 employees in 2008 up to 11,554 employees in 2015 is observed (see Fig. 7). Sport-related employment rose with, on average, 3% per year over the observed period. After a stagnation in sport-related employment in the aftermath of the economic recession (2008–2011), a substantial rise is observed after 2011.

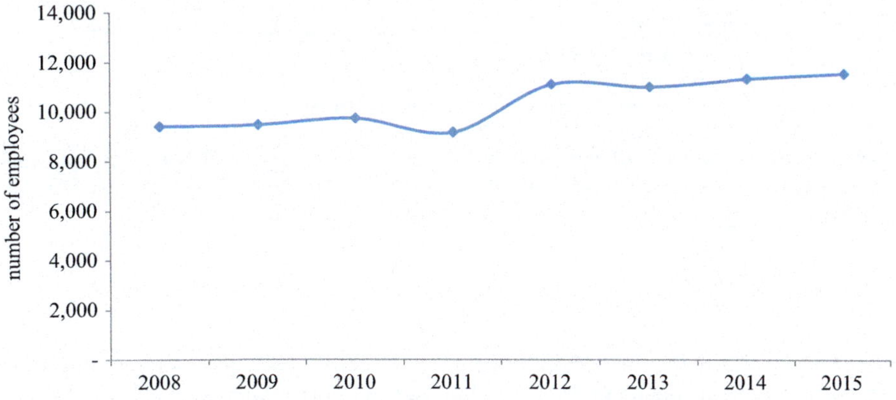

Fig. 7 Evolution of total employment rates in sport-related companies in the Flemish Region and the BCR, in 2008–2015. Source: Based on ADS (Statistics Belgium, 2016a).

Sport-related employment accounts for less than 1% of the total employment in the Flemish Region and the BCR (Fig. 8). It can be noted, however, that the AYGR of employment in the sport-sector is higher than in the total economy. Overall, this trend is in line with findings of Scheerder and colleagues (2010c) who studied developments in employment in the sport sector prior to the economic recession (1993–2007).

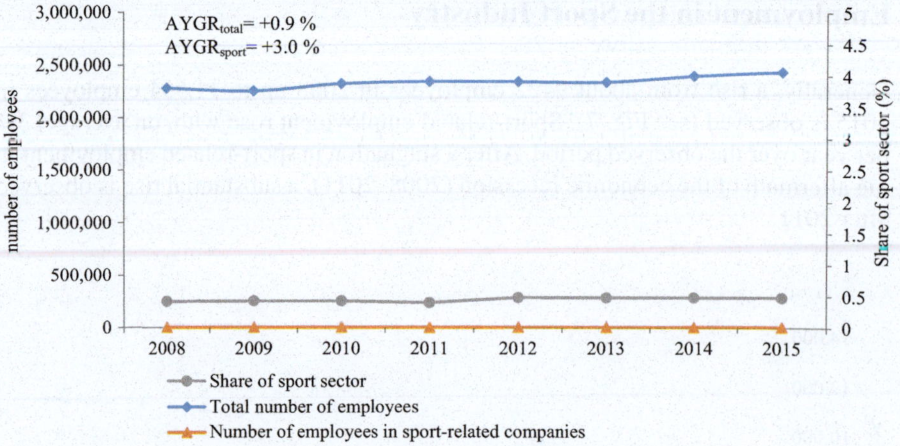

Fig. 8 Share and evolution of employees in sport-related companies in relation to total economy in the Flemish Region and the BCR, in 2008–2015. Source: Based on ADS (Statistics Belgium, 2016a).

Figure 9 shows that both employment in the sector of services delivered by sport clubs and federations (AYGR = +3.4%) and in sport-related renting and leasing companies (AYGR = +3.6%) has grown slightly but continuously over the observed period. Also the number of jobs in the sector of the retail sale of sporting goods shows a general increase (+10.1%). The strongest increase in the number of sport-related jobs, however, is observed in the sector of the exploitation of fitness facilities (AYGR = +24.5%) and sport and recreation education (AYGR = +22.4%). The number of jobs in the fitness sector particularly increased between 2009 and 2010 and stabilised afterwards.

Employment in the exploitation of sport facilities has decreased in the period of economic recession between 2008 and 2010 but remained stable thereafter (AYGR = −3.7). The number of jobs in the wholesale of sport and camping goods (AYGR = −2.9%), the exploitation of snooker and billiards facilities (AYGR = −8.5%) and the manufacturing of sport goods (AYGR = −23.8%), however, decreased continuously over the observed period.

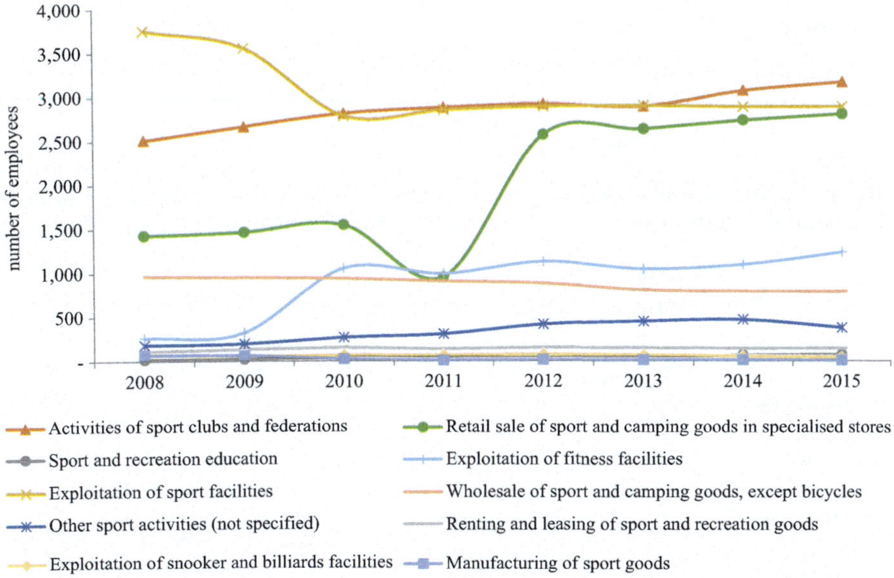

Fig. 9 Evolution of employment rates in sport-related companies in different categories of economic activities in the Flemish Region and the BCR, in 2008–2015. Source: Based on ADS (Statistics Belgium, 2016a).

Revenues of the Sport-Related Companies

The revenue of sport-related companies has risen substantially over the past 7 years (Fig. 10). The sport industry represents less than 1% of the revenue in the total economy (Fig. 11). It is noted, though, that the AYGR of the sport sector over the past years (+6.0%) has been bigger than that of the total economy ($AYGR_{total}$ = +2.3%). Revenues have been recalculated for inflation effects based on the Consumer Price Index in 2016 (Statistics Belgium, 2016b).

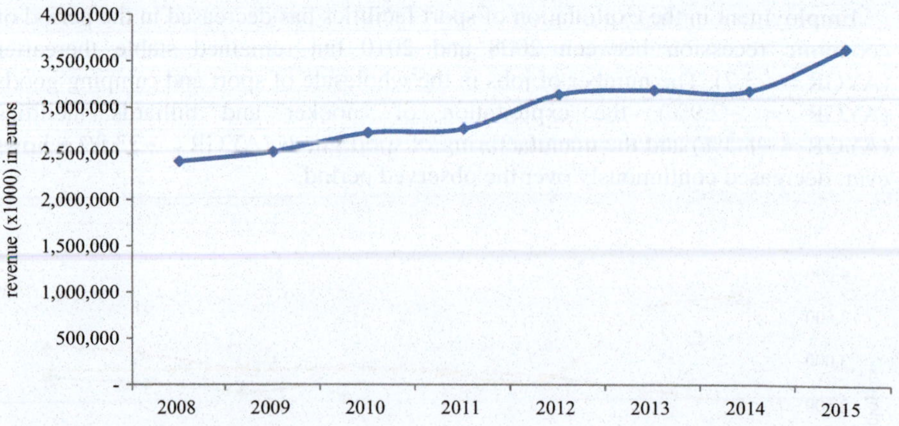

Fig. 10 Evolution of total revenue of sport-related companies in the Flemish Region and the BCR, revenue in euros (x1000), in 2008–2015. Source: Based on ADS (Statistics Belgium, 2016a).

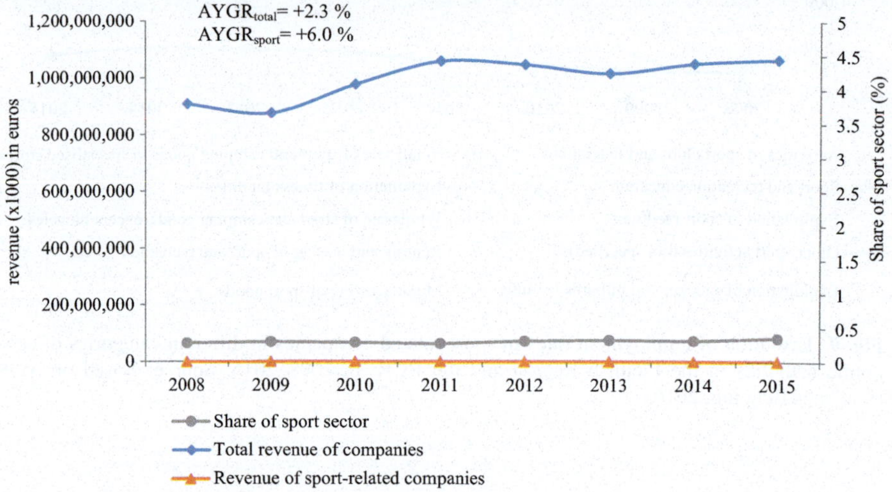

Fig. 11 Share and evolution of revenue in sport-related companies in relation to total economy in the Flemish Region and the BCR, in 2008–2015. Source: Based on ADS (Statistics Belgium, 2016a).

The evolution of revenues differs according to the particular business field (Fig. 12). The wholesale of sport and camping goods has always delivered the largest share of sport-related revenue to the economy, even though its share in the number of companies has been relatively low. The revenue of this business field has grown continuously (AYGR = +2.4%). Also the revenue of companies involved with the retail sale of sport and camping goods in specialised stores has risen over the observed period (AYGR = +8.4%), albeit with a more fluctuating pattern. The largest relative increase in revenue is observed in the exploitation of fitness facilities (AYGR = +31.1%). Also the revenue of companies involved with activities of sport clubs and federations (AYGR = +8.8%), sport and recreation education (AYGR = +6.8%) and other sport activities (AYGR = +8.9%), as well as companies involved in the exploitation of sport facilities (AYGR = +3.2%), increased. Furthermore, whereas the revenue of renting and leasing companies remained more or less stable (AYGR = −0.5%), a negative trend is observed for companies involved with the exploitation of snooker and billiards facilities (AYGR = −5.8%) and the manufacturing of sport goods (AYGR = −8.7%).

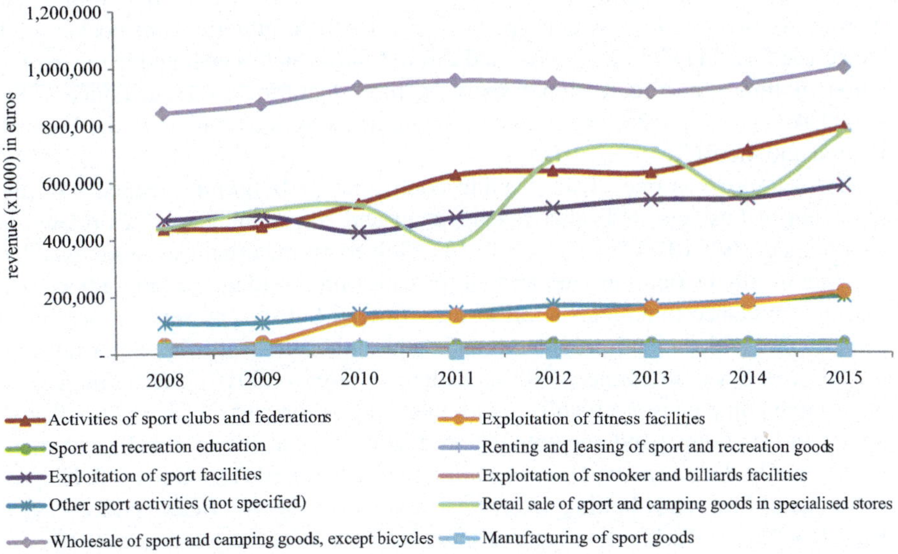

Fig. 12 Evolution in revenue of sport-related companies in different categories of economic activities in the Flemish Region and the BCR, revenue in euros (x1000), in 2008–2015. Source: Based on ADS (Statistics Belgium, 2016a).

Largest Sport Companies

According to Bel-First data, 33 large to very large sport companies are located in the Flemish Region and the BCR. This section introduces the largest companies, their main activities, year of foundation and EBITDA-%. After that, a focus is put on characteristics of the largest fitness companies.

Overall, the largest company in the sample is *Decathlon Belgium*, with 151 chain stores located in the Benelux (since 1993, EBITDA-$\%_{2013} = 6.73$). Decathlon's primary business line is the retail trade of sport and camping goods. Other large companies in this sector are *Scouts & Gidsen Vlaanderen* (since 1934, EBITDA-$\%_{2013} = -0.95$), *S.S.A. Sporting Goods* (since 1965, EBITDA-$\%_{2013} = 5.75$), *Thule* (since 1977, EBITDA-$\%_{2013}$ = 18.13), *PM United Brands* (since 1981, EBITDA-$\%_{2013} = 0.34$), *America Today Belgium* (since 1990, EBITDA-$\%_{2013} = 2.28$),

D.D.C. (since 1994, EBITDA-$\%_{2013}$ = −0.77) and *Snow & Surf* (since 1999, EBITDA-$\%_{2014}$ = 5.18). Furthermore, the subsample of large companies entails a number of professional sport clubs for soccer,[4] hockey[5] and other sports,[6] as well as chains of health and fitness clubs (see also Table 5).

Remarkably, also some non-profit sport organisations appear in the list of large sport companies. Examples of national level organisations are the *Belgian Olympic and Interfederal Committee (BOIC)* (since 1962, EBITDA-$\%_{2013}$ = 4.22) and the *Union Royale Belge des Sociétés de Football-Association,* which represents the football clubs in the country (since 1923, EBITDA-$\%_{2013}$ = 5.22). Also *Koninklijke Atletiek Associatie Gent*, which operates as a football, athletics and hockey club (since 1964, EBITDA-$\%_{2014}$ = 5.64) and *2 Sportstad*, which is engaged in the exploitation of fitness and recreational sport facilities featuring exercise (since 1986, EBITDA-$\%_{2014}$ = 210.25) stand among the largest sport companies in the Flemish Region and the BCR.

Golazo Sports is one of the leading companies in Belgium engaged with the provision of business and other management and consultancy services related to sport (since 1990, EBITDA-$\%_{2013}$ = 18.01). Golazo Sports organises more than 250 sporting events in Belgium and abroad, provides professional training advice and nutrition guidance to athletes at all levels ('Energy Lab'), represents a number of professional athletes and provides brands and authorities with the opportunity to use sport as a way to connect with its audience (Golazo, 2016). Furthermore, two other large companies are involved with the exploitation and management of sport arenas and stadiums,[7] and one with the production of seats for sport halls and stadiums.[8] Finally, *Lotto Sports Organisation* (since 2002, EBITDA-$\%_{2013}$ = 0.48) provides gambling and betting activities related to sport. *Elaut* (since 1977, EBITDA-$\%_{2014}$ = 12.1) manufactures sport apparel. A few large companies are not further considered because, to the authors' knowledge, their link with sport is limited.[9]

---

[4] Cf. *Club Brugge* (since 1997, EBITDA-$\%_{2014}$ = −28.92), *Koninklijke Racing Club Genk* (since 1998, EBITDA-$\%_{2014}$ = −25.79), *Koninklijke Beerschot 2 Club* (since 1999, EBITDA-$\%_{2012}$ = −40.66), *Stayen* (since 1999, EBITDA-% not available), *Royal Sporting Club Anderlecht* (since 2010, EBITDA-$\%_{2014}$ = 6.93) and Kortrijk Voetbalt (since 2010, EBITDA-$\%_{2014}$ = −4.46).

[5] Cf. *La Rasante* (since 2000, EBITDA-$\%_{2013}$ = 8.39)

[6] Cf. *Pipa Trading* (since 2006, EBITDA-$\%_{2014}$ = −1.26), *David Lloyd Leisure Operations* (since 2009, EBITDA-$\%_{2013}$ = 26.04), *S&R Gent* (since 2010, EBITDA-$\%_{2013}$ = −74.82), *S&R Beveren* (since 2010, EBITDA-$\%_{2013}$ = −73.85).

[7] Cf. *Compagnie Le Zoute* (since 1931, EBITDA-$\%_{2013}$ = 6.51), *Koninklijke Renvereniging Oostende* (since 1989, EBITDA-$\%_{2013}$ = −262.34).

[8] *Jezet Seating* (since 1989, EBITDA-$\%_{2013}$ = −0.71)

[9] Cf. *Kodak* (printing plates, professional digital cameras, printing software, etc.) and *Evedec* (facilities support management services).

The number of fitness centres in the Flemish Region and the Brussels-Capital Region has risen substantially since the mid-1980's. However, the growth in the number of employees and its revenue over the past decade is relatively higher than the increase in the number of companies in this sector. This shows that the fitness sector in Belgium is a profitable business. The trends may be explained by the attractiveness of fitness activities by consumer groups that have previously been found to be at risk of inactivity, such as women and lower income groups.

Overview of Largest Health and Fitness Companies

In accordance with previous and ongoing research on the fitness sector in the Flemish Region and the BCR (Scheerder et al., 2010b; Breesch, Vos, & Scheerder, 2015), the remaining part of this chapter focuses on financial and economic measures of individual companies that are primarily involved in fitness activities. Table 5 provides company specific data on the year of foundation, number of offices, the company's total revenue, staff number and EBITDA-% of the last available year among the largest fitness companies in the Flemish Region and the BCR. Within the subsample of fitness companies with information available on the company size (NACE Rev. 2 primary code = 9313; $n = 473$), three companies were classified as large (0.6%), 18 companies as middle-sized (3.8%) and 452 companies as small (95.6%). Two middle-sized fitness companies were excluded from the analysis due to bankruptcy. Additionally, all other large and middle-sized companies in the Flemish Region and the BCR (n = 346) were screened on links with the fitness industry. It appeared that some prominent fitness companies were coded with 9311 (exploitation of sport facilities), whereas they are known to manage fitness facilities (*Groep Sportoase*, *Just Fit*, *Sports Club de Wezembeek-Oppem*).

EBITDA-% numbers of large sport companies (see earlier) have shown that the operating profitability of a company is often related to the subsector wherein one operates. Whereas large companies engaged in the retail trade of sport and camping goods, as well as non-profit sport associations such as the *BOIC*, usually have a positive EBITDA-%, the management and exploitation of professional soccer clubs, multisport centres (e.g., *S&R Group*) or a chain of fitness facilities often show a negative cash flow. A detailed look at the management and exploitation of fitness facilities in Table 5, however, suggests that the profitability of managing fitness facilities may relate to the size and the age of a company. Fitness companies with negative EBITDA-% are among the younger and large companies of the selected sample. This can be explained by recent investments needed to start up a company, which may rebalance in neutral or positive cash flow over the years.

Table 5 Large and middle-sized fitness companies in the Flemish Region (FR) and the Brussels-Capital Region (BCR), data of last available year per company.

Name	Location	Size	Year of foundation	Offices (n)	Staff (n)	Revenue (1000 €)	EBITDA-%
Aspria City	BCR	MS	2004	1	17	3153	1.98
Aspria Club	BCR	MS	2000	3	23	6163	8.33
Basic-fit Belgium	BCR	L	2009	4	122	22,271	−14.98
Bugo invest	FR	MS	1999	1	n/a	424	25.81
DLL (David Lloyd leisure)	BCR	L	1997	2	n/a	3021	69.11
Do invest	FR	MS	2009	1	32	4637	2.29
Fanatics	FR	MS	1993	1	4	n/a	n/a
Fitness and health Schaffen	FR	MS	1995	6	9	n/a	n/a
Fitopia	FR	MS	1994	1	28	n/a	n/a
Groep Sportoase	BCR	MS	2005	10	4	658	12,45
Healthcity Belgium	BCR	L	2006	1	300	38,433	−10.03
IFitness peer	FR	MS	2012	1	2	n/a	n/a
Just fit	BCR	MS	2009	4	30	5763	−13.47
Karteria Diest	FR	MS	1991	2	6	n/a	n/a
Lovani	FR	MS	1995	1	n/a	n/a	n/a
O2Xygen	FR	MS	2002	2	12	n/a	n/a
Oxygen clubs	FR	MS	2004	2	21	n/a	n/a
Sports Club de Wezembeek-Oppem	FR	MS	1974	1	11	1407	n/a
Thermae sports	FR	MS	2001	3	24	1139	n/a
Thermen Dilbeek	FR	MS	1989	2	23	n/a	n/a
Wellness systems	FR	MS	1994	2	n/a	n/a	n/a

Notes: *L* large, *MS* middle-sized, *n/a* not available.
Source: Based on Bel-First data (Bureau Van Dijk, 2016).

Conclusions

This article has outlined how the sport industry in the Flemish Region and the BCR has been developing by focusing on particular sport-related subsectors that were selected by the Belgian equivalent (NACE-BEL, 2008) of the *Statistical classification of economic activities in the European Community* (NACE Rev. 2) (Eurostat, 2008; Statistics Belgium, 2013). Generally, three waves can be distinguished in the development of the sport industry since the mid-twentieth century: (i) the emergence of the non-profit sport industry since the 1950's, (ii) the emergence of the sport goods trading industry since the 1970's, and (iii) the emergence of the commercial sport services industry since the 1990's. More specifically, the current size of the sport industry and evolutions between 2008 and 2015 were estimated by focusing on structural, professional and financial characteristics of this sector as a whole and of particular subsectors. Overall, it can be concluded that the sport industry has grown over the past 7 years and, despite it represents only a small share of the total economy, its AYGR is stronger as compared to the total industry. The majority of companies is involved with the delivery of sport-related services. However, almost half of the sport sector's revenue is generated by companies that are involved with the distribution of sport and camping goods. The sector of manufacturing products represents a relatively small share of the sport industry.

In line with other research the current analysis has shown that private, profit-making companies have gained a prominent position in the sport industry (see also Scheerder et al., 2010b; 2010c; Van Bottenburg, 2006; Woolf, 2008). Over the last decade, the number of sport-related companies has grown substantially and continuously, particularly due to the business of sport and recreation education and the exploitation of fitness facilities. The rise in these particular business fields can be explained by an interaction between trends of commercialisation and consumerism (e.g., Sassatelli, 2010; Van Bottenburg, 2006; Van der Roest, Vermeulen, & Van Bottenburg, 2015). The fitness sector is an example of a flexible service industry that targets new markets by focusing on changing demands of potential consumers (Sassatelli, 2010; Woolf, 2008). As an example, the services offered by fitness clubs have developed over the past decades from traditional power and cardio facilities to full-service arrangements including access to fitness, group sessions, wellness and personal coaching. It is also noted that companies involved in sport and recreation education are mostly one-person companies (no paid staff), which suggests that part of the observed increase in this sector can be attributed to personal coaches. Nevertheless, also the so-called *traditional* sport business, with sport activities provided by sport clubs and federations, is still on the rise. As different population groups are reached by different settings for participation, this supports the idea that new, *lighter* forms of sport participation are not necessarily replacing old sport cultures, but are an addition to the increasingly diversified landscape of sport providers (see also Borgers et al., 2015; Borgers, Pilgaard, Vanreusel, & Scheerder, 2016).

The growth of the fitness industry is also noted by an obvious increase in the revenue generated by this sector. The AYGR in revenue over the past seven years shows that the fitness industry is an important profit-making business. This is also confirmed by the mainly positive EBITDA-%, which indicates a positive cash flow of fitness companies. Obviously, two large chains of fitness facilities in Belgium (Health City and Basic Fit) have a negative operating profitability. This can be clarified by the fact that these chains have been expanding their number of branches rapidly, which requires big investments in terms of accommodation and staff (Breesch et al., 2015). Also, *Basic Fit* is an example of a low budget fitness club that offers only basic fitness services at reduced prices.

In contrast to the rise of the fitness industry, other business fields such as the retail sale of sport and camping goods appear to be more vulnerable to economic fluctuations, both in the number of employees and in the revenue generated by this sector. The exploitation of sport facilities has lost share in terms of the number of companies and employees, however, it remains an important source of revenue in the sport industry. Even though the data does not allow for drawing conclusions on causality and mechanisms underpinning the observed trends, a possible explanation for the decrease in this subsector could be financial savings on sport facilities by companies and government actors during economic recession. A general downward trend was also observed in the share of the manufacturing of sport goods in the economy. The decreasing trend of the snooker and billiards industry may be linked to a decreasing popularity of the related activities in Flanders (Scheerder, Vandermeerschen, Borgers, Thibaut, & Vos, 2013).

To finish this chapter and to enhance understanding of its potential for comparability with other countries, some limitations need to be highlighted. First, the international coding of primary business fields is unclear at some points. On the one hand, some economic activities are classified under different codes. For example, fitness companies were mostly classified as 9313, but in some cases also as 9311 whereas their business activities were similar to that of the exploitation of fitness facilities. On the other hand, some non-sport oriented companies (e.g., Kodak) seem to use sport-related NACE codes to describe their main activities. As it was impossible to check and correct the reliability of codes over the entire sample, it is suggested that some bias may occur in the classification of economic activities. Secondly, the NACE Rev. 2 classification does not allow for making a total calculation of the sport industry. That is, the manufacturing of sport clothes and the construction of sport crafts, for example, are included in bigger categories in which no classes can be filtered. In this view, the numbers presented in this chapter may be an underrepresentation of the total sport industry. The inclusion of camping and recreation goods in certain categories, in contrast, may result in an overestimation of parameters in specific business fields. Obviously, many of the so-called 'large' companies are involved with the trading of camping goods, which might be considered a bias in the estimation of the total sport industry. A third point of attention concerns the differences between the available databases. The authors have aimed to provide a detailed picture of the size of the sport industry based on the strengths of each data source.

Acknowledgements The authors are grateful to Michael Goethals and Guy Pauwels of the Research Administration of the Flemish Government for their support in providing the data for this chapter. We also thank Erik Thibaut (KU Leuven) for his support in the analysis and the interpretation of economic measures.

References

Borgers, J., Pilgaard, M., Vanreusel, B., & Scheerder, J. (2016). Can we consider changes in sports participation as institutional change? A conceptual framework. *International Review for the Sociology of Sport*. https://doi.org/10.1177/1012690216639598.

Borgers, J., Thibaut, E., Vandermeerschen, H., Vanreusel, B., Vos, S., & Scheerder, J. (2015). Sports participation styles revisited. A time-trend study in Belgium from the 1970s to the 2000s. *International Review for the Sociology of Sport, 50*(1), 45–63.

Breesch, D., Vos, S., & Scheerder, J. (2015). The financial viability of the fitness industry in Belgium. *Sport, Business and Management: An International Journal, 5*(4), 365–385.

Bureau Van Dijk. (2016). *Bel-First. Financiële en economische informatie over bedrijven in België en Luxemburg* [Bel-First. Financial and economic information on companies in Belgium and Luxembourg]. Retrieved June 28, 2016 from http://www.bvdinfo.com/nl-be/our-products/company-information/national-products/Bel-First

Eurostat. (2008). *NACE Rev. 2. Statistical classification of economic activities in the European Community*. Retrieved June 20, 2016 from http://ec.europa.eu/eurostat/documents/3859598/5902521/KS-RA-07-015-EN.PDF

Golazo. (2016). *About Golazo*. Retrieved July 6, 2016 from http://www.golazo.com/about-golazo/

Sassatelli, R. (2010). *Fitness culture. Gyms and the commercialisation of discipline and fun*. New York, NY: Palgrave MacMillan.

Scheerder, J., Borgers, J., & Willem, A. (2015a). Sportdeelname in Vlaanderen. Trends en profielen [Sport participation in Flanders. Trends and profiles]. In J. Lievens, J. Siongers, & H. Waege (Eds.), *Participatie in Vlaanderen 2. Eerste analyses van de Participatiesurvey 2014* (pp. 209–249). Leuven/Den Haag, Belgium: Acco.

Scheerder, J., Borgers, J., & Willem, A. (2015b). Sportdeelname in Vlaanderen. De organisatorische context van sportbeoefening [Sport participation in Flanders. The organisational settings of sport participation]. In J. Lievens, J. Siongers, & H. Waege (Eds.), *Participatie in Vlaanderen 2. Eerste analyses van de Participatiesurvey 2014* (pp. 251–281). Leuven/Den Haag, Belgium: Acco.

Scheerder, J., Seghers, J., Meganck, J., Vandermeerschen, H., & Vos, S. (2015c). *Sportclubs in beeld. Resultaten van het Vlaamse Sportclub Panel 2.0 (VSP2.0)* [Sport clubs in the picture. Results of the Flemish Sport Club Panel 2.0]. Leuven, Belgium: KU Leuven/Onderzoeksgroep Sport- & Bewegingsbeleid.

Scheerder, J., Vandermeerschen, H., Borgers, J., Thibaut, E., & Vos, S. (2013). *Vlaanderen sport! Vier decennia sportbeleid en sportparticipatie* [Sports in Flanders! Four decades of sport policy and sports participation]. Ghent, Belgium: Academia Press.

Scheerder, J., & Vos, S. (2013). Belgium: Flanders. In K. Hallmann & K. Petry (Eds.), *Sports comparative sport development. Systems, participation and public policy* (pp. 7–21). New York, NY: Springer.

Scheerder, J., & Vos, S. (2014). *De krijtlijnen van het speelveld. Organisatie en planning van sport en sportbeleid in Vlaanderen* [The lines of the playground. Organisation and planning of sport and sport policy in Flanders] (2nd ed.). Ghent, Belgium: Academia Press.

Scheerder, J., Vos, S., Breesch, D., Késenne, S., Van Hoecke, J., & Vanreusel, B. (2010a). *Sportclubs in beeld. Basisrapportering over het Vlaamse Sportclub Panel 2009 (VSP09)* [Sport clubs in the picture. Report on the Flemish Sport Club Panel 2009]. Leuven, Belgium: KU Leuven/Department of Human Kinesiology.

Scheerder, J., Vos, S., Breesch, D., Lagae, W., & Van Hoecke, J. (2010b). *De fitnesssector in beeld. Basisrapportering over het Vlaamse Fitness Panel 2009 (VFP09)* [A picture of the fitness sector. Report on the Flemish Fitness Panel 2009]. Leuven, Belgium: KU Leuven/Afdeling Sociale Kinesiologie & Sportmanagement.

Scheerder, J., Vos, S., Pabian, S., De Martelaer, K., Lefevre, J., & Philippaerts, R. (2011a). Actieve vrijetijdssport in Vlaanderen. Trends, profielen en settings [Leisure-time sports in Flanders. Trends, profiles and settings]. In J. Lievens & H. Waege (Eds.), *Participatie in Vlaanderen 2. Eerste analyses van de Participatiesurvey 2009* (pp. 43–82). Leuven/Den Haag, Belgium: Acco Academic.

Scheerder, J., Vos, S., Pabian, S., & Pauwels, G. (2010c). De Vlaamse sportarbeidsmarkt in kaart gebracht. Enkele ontwikkelingen en kenmerken van de tewerkstelling in de sportsector [An analysis of employment in the sport sector in Flanders. Developments and characteristics of employment in the sport sector]. *Vlaams Tijdschrift voor Sportbeheer, 215*, 21–33.

Scheerder, J., Vos, S., Vandermeerschen, H., & van Poppel, M. (2014). *Sportdiensten in beeld. Basisrapportering over het Vlaamse Sportdienst Panel 1.0 (VSDP1.0)* [Local sport services in the picture. Report on the Panel of Flemish Local Sport Services]. Leuven, Belgium: KU Leuven/Onderzoeksgroep Sport- & Bewegingsbeleid.

Scheerder, J., Zintz, T., & Delheye, P. (2011b). The organisation of sports in Belgium. Between public, economic and social profit. In C. Sobry (Ed.), *Sports governance in the world: A socio-historic approach. The organization of sport in Europe: A patch-work of institutions, with few shared points* (pp. 84–113). Paris, France: Le Manuscrit.

Statistics Belgium. (2013). *NACE-BEL 2008*. Retrieved June 20, 2016 from http://statbel.fgov.be/nl/statistieken/gegevensinzameling/nomenclaturen/nacebel/

Statistics Belgium. (2015). *Kerncijfers: statistisch overzicht van België* [Core numbers: statistical overview of Belgium]. Retrieved October 10, 2016 from http://statbel.fgov.be/nl/binaries/NL_kerncijfers_2015_WEB_COMPLET_tcm325-275721.pdf

Statistics Belgium. (2016a). *Evolutie van het aantal BTW-plichtige ondernemingen volgens activiteit* [Evolution of the number of VAT-obliged companies by economic activity]. Retrieved October 10, 2016 from http://statbel.fgov.be/nl/statistieken/cijfers/economie/ondernemingen/levensloop/histo/evolutie/#.WBbgMfNTGpo

Statistics Belgium. (2016b). *Consumer Price Index according to the COICOP nomenclature base year, per year and month.* Retrieved October 10, 2016 from https://bestat.economie.fgov.be/bestat/crosstable.xhtml?view=208b69bd-05c5-4947-b7f9-2d2300f517b8

Van Bottenburg, M. (2006). Commercialisering van de sport. Potentieel of bedreiging? [The commercialisation of sport. Opportunities or threats?]. In M. Van Bottenburg, B. Vanreusel, P. Verweel, & M. Teeuwen (Eds.), *Inzichten vanaf de zijlijn. Wetenschappelijke coaching van het sportbeleid?* (pp. 19–35). The Hague, The Netherlands: WRR.

Van der Roest, J. W., Vermeulen, J., & Van Bottenburg, M. (2015). Creating sport consumers in Dutch sport policy. *International Journal of Sport Policy and Politics, 7*(1), 105–121.

Woolf, J. (2008). Competitive advantage in the health and fitness industry. Developing service bundles. *Sport Management Review, 11*(1), 51–75.

CYPRUS: A Small Island Country, Full of History and Passion for Sport

Nicos Kartakoullis, Theofilos Pouliopoulos, and Christina Loizou

Selected country facts (in 2013)	
Capital	Nicosia
Geographical size (km^2)	9251
Population (million)	0.87
GDP (euro per capita)	21,000
GDP (per capita in PPS)	84
Annual net earnings average (€)	20,434

Cyprus – A Brief Overview

Cyprus is the largest island in the Mediterranean Sea, located at the crossroads of the cultures and civilizations from the ancient years until today. The strategic position of the island, bridging Europe, Middle East and north southern Africa has been a blessing and a curse at the same time throughout the centuries. The colonization of Cyprus by the Greeks started at about the middle of the second millennium BC and was completed during the twelfth to eleventh century BC (Hadjistefanou, 2004). The island was occupied by several empires across the centuries, such as the

N. Kartakoullis (✉)
University of Nicosia, Engomi, Cyprus
e-mail: kartakoullis.n@unic.ac.cy

T. Pouliopoulos
University of Peloponnese, Sparti, Greece
e-mail: thpouliop@uop.gr

C. Loizou
University of Nicosia, Engomi, Cyprus
e-mail: loizou.c@unic.ac.cy

A. Laine, H. Vehmas (eds.), *The Private Sport Sector in Europe*, Sports Economics, Management and Policy 14, https://doi.org/10.1007/978-3-319-61310-9_4

Persians, Romans, Ottomans and others, but the dominant culture from ancient times until today has been the Greek.

The island was liberated from British Colonization in 1960, but it was divided in 1974 after a coop d'état by the Greek Junta and the Turkish invasion. Since then, the negotiations between Greek-Cypriots and Turkish-Cypriots for the reunification of the country have been unsuccessful. Despite this difficult situation, the Cypriot economy (the Republic of Cyprus government-controlled area) achieved enviable progress in the 50-year period after the country's independence.[1] Indeed, the traditional agricultural economy of the early 1960s was gradually transformed into an economy characterized by the high standard of living and a robust financial sector, based especially on tourism and services (Central Bank of Cyprus, 2012). Cyprus became an EU member in 2004 and joined the Euro zone in January 2008. Although the recent economic crisis in 2013 was a setback for the Cypriots, the economy is recovering and the future seems to be bright again.

As for the demographics, the population reached 838,897 persons on the 1st of October 2011 compared to 689,565 in the previous census which was held in 2001, (recording an increase of 21.7% in the last 10 years) (Statistical Service of the Republic of Cyprus, 2011). These data refers only to the government-controlled part of the island, or else the Republic of Cyprus. In the entire island, there are estimations of a 1,133,803 population, from which the 80% are Greek-Cypriots, 18% Turkish Cypriots and Turkish settlers and 2%, other minorities (Maronites, Armenians, Latins and others). The total area of the island is 9251 sq km (of which 3355 sq km are in north Cyprus) and the climate is Mediterranean with hot, dry summers and cool winters. The dominant religion is the Eastern Orthodox Christianity, as the majority of the population is Greek Orthodox while in the northern part of the island the majority of the population is Muslim.

Cyprus and Sport

The roots of sport in the island date back to the ancient Greek civilization years. There is archeological evidence from the early arrival of the Greeks (1500 BC) in the island that sports like boxing, wrestling, bull riding and others were practiced in Cyprus, either as ritual or as a festival based competition (Hadjistefanou, 2004). In the classic era of the Greek civilization (fifth and fourth centuries BC) there was a gymnasium/palaistra (a place for physical training and gymnastics) in the ancient towns of Salamis and Curium, as in Greece's mainland city-states and the other Greek colonies. In addition, Cypriot athletes participated regularly in the ancient Olympic Games. Dimitrios Salaminios was the most successful

[1] Since the division of the island the northern part of Cyprus is inhabited by Turkish-Cypriots while the southern part of the island is inhabited by Greek-Cypriots and it is referred to as the government-controlled area (or Republic of Cyprus).

Cypriot athlete in the third century BC. He won five times in the Olympic Games (race and pentathlon), but he was also victorious in other crown Games in mainland Greece (Pythian Games, Isthmian Games) and Asia Minor. (Cyprus Sport Organisation, 2012b.)

Nowadays sport in Cyprus has special importance. It has become part of the Cypriot society over the years, and is considered to be one of the most important social institutions and phenomena that permeates all levels of the Cypriot society (Kartakoullis, 2006). Although Cyprus is a "football crazy nation" (Kartakoullis, Kriemadis, & Pouloukas, 2009), around 40% of the Cypriots aged 15 and above engage in all kinds of sports and exercise leisure activities (Cyprus Sport Organisation, 2012a).

Regarding the physical activity, data from the World Health Organization (WHO) - Global Health Observatory (GHO) in 2010, show that 64.7% of the Cypriot adult population meets WHO's Global Recommendations on Physical Activity for Health (2010), with males being more active (70.7%) than females (58.5%) (World Health Organization, 2010). More specifically, the results of a study conducted by the University of Nicosia for the Cyprus Sport Organisation, show that regarding team sports, the majority of people were involved in football (13.2%). Other participated team sports were dancing (5.0%), basketball (3.8%), volleyball (2.7%) and futsal (1.7%). Walking for exercise purposes was the most popular individual sport (47.6%). Many people exercise at a gym (26.4%).Swimming is practiced by 9.2%, tennis by 3.4% and cycling by 1.7% of the population in Cyprus. Various other individual sport activities were participated by less than 1% of the population, 10.4% of the population in total. (Cyprus Sport Organisation, 2012a.) These facts are rather encouraging about the physical and sport activities in Cyprus. Despite the high temperatures during the summer, the car-oriented culture and the lack of national schemes promoting active travel to schools and workplaces, Cyprus shows decent levels of sport and physical activity participation.

In addition, "sport in Cyprus has developed over the last two decades in terms of competitive results as well as in terms of the money available in the sport industry of the country" (Kartakoullis, Karlis, Walker, & Locke, 2015). In the London Olympic Games in 2012, the sailor Pavlos Kontidis won the very first and so far the only Olympic medal (silver) for Cyprus. In addition, Cyprus was the most successful country in Europe's games of small states until last year (Games of the Small States of Europe History, 2015). These achievements are significant when the population of the country is taken into consideration. Additionally, it is worth mentioning that until recently very few sport facilities in the country were in accordance to the international standards of the sport federations, a disadvantage for the Cypriot athletes who aimed to compete in the elite international level.

The structure of sport in Cyprus is rather similar to other European countries (pyramid form), but due to the small size of the country the central administration model is followed (see Fig. 1). Consequently, Cyprus Sport Organisation, the state funded sport organisation is the highest sports authority in Cyprus. More specifically, the stakeholders of sport in Cyprus are:

- The Cyprus Sport Organisation
- The Cyprus Olympic Committee
- National sport federations
- Athletic clubs and associations
- The Ministry of Education of the Republic of Cyprus
- Universities and colleges
- The National Association of Physical Education Teachers
- The Association of Employers of Cyprus
- The Association of the owners of Fitness centers and facilities
- Coaches' associations
- The Cyprus Association of Sport management
- Parents' associations (Kartakoullis, 2014).

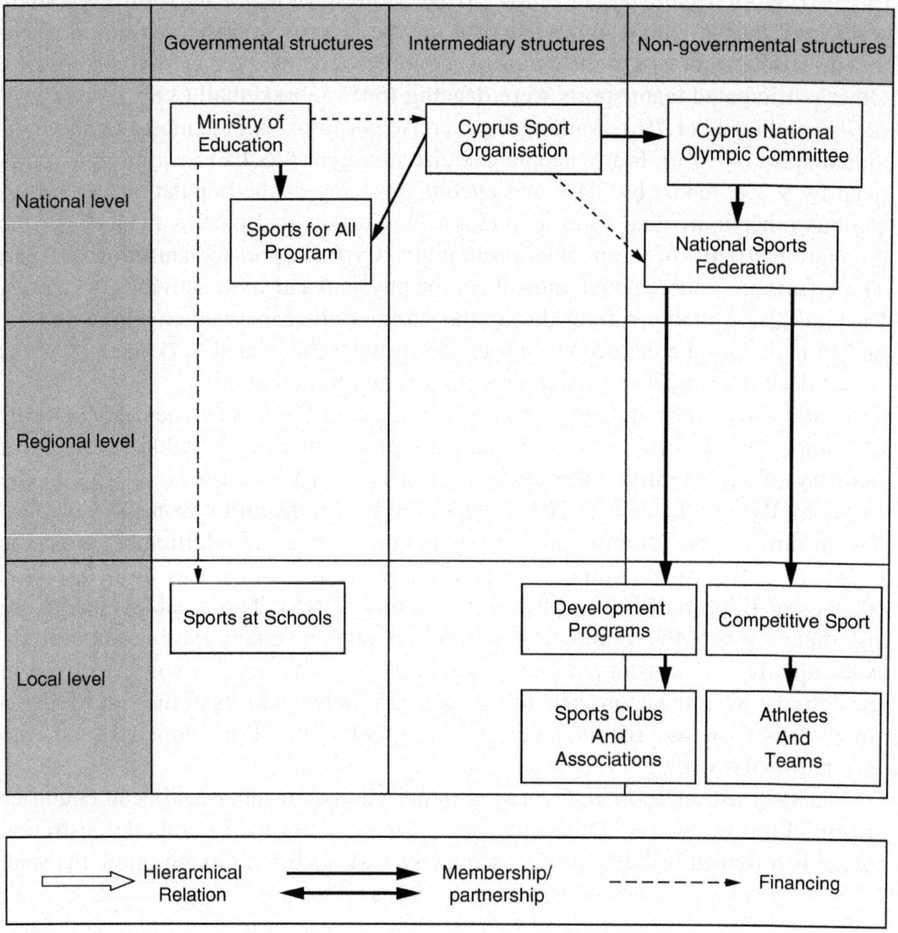

Fig. 1 The organisation of sport in Cyprus. Source: Kartakoullis (2014).

Cyprus Sport Organisation

Cyprus Sport Organisation (CSO) is the highest sport authority in the country with the responsibilities of planning and policy making in the field of sport. The CSO is a legal entity and it is considered as a semi-governmental organisation. It is funded by the government budget each year and it is in charge of allocating financial resources to the national sport federations. The CSO is governed by the Board of Directors which consists of nine members: a President and eight members, who are appointed by the President of the Republic and the Council of Ministers. The CSO provides financial support, develops infrastructure and monitors the work of national sport federations and sport clubs at all levels; from competitive to mass sport, including grassroots sport. (Cyprus Sport Organisation, 2012a.)

The main platform for promoting mass sport is the ‘Sport for all Programme’ (SFA). The CSO began to operate the SFA movement in 1985 aiming at wellbeing, improvement of the physical condition and health and the recreation of all citizens engaging in sport and physical activities. Adopting the philosophy of the Sports for All Movement for offering equal opportunity to all population, the SFA addresses all citizens regardless of gender, age, ethnicity and race, social and economic status, physical or mental condition.

According to the 2011 data, 700 sport centers operated all around the free part of Cyprus, where more than 17,000 members of all ages participated in sport programmes. At the same time 103 qualified physical education graduates were employed in the programmes, of whom 89 manned the sport centers all around Cyprus and 14 had coordination and managerial duties. (Cyprus Sport Organisation, 2012a.)

Another sport scheme provided by the CSO is the National Scheme of Developmental Sport Support (NSDSS). The NSDSS basically supports the team sport club academies, but during its course, it has also included a small number of individual sports with potential of development and need for support. The NSDSS covers athletes aged 12–16, while quite a similar planning covers ages 16–18 in three team sports (basketball, volleyball and handball) for which the relevant federations organize teenage championships. The other three national programmes of CSO (five in total) are talent planning, elite-category and planning high performance. (Cyprus Sport Organisation, 2008.)

A research report carried out by the University of Nicosia for the Cyprus Sport Organisation (2012a), under the title “Leisure Sports Participation in Cyprus” showed that 70,000 people are involved in the practice of sport in Cyprus. The main aim of the CSO’s strategy is to involve more citizens in sport and recreational physical activity, and on the competitive sport improve results in national and international competitions in both individual and team sports. As far as the non-competitive side of sport, an increase by 0.5% in active sport participation would reach the expectations of the 2020 National Sports Policy. (Kartakoullis et al., 2015.)

Table 1 Cyprus Sport Organisation budget in 2013.

Source of income	EUR
State subsidy	28,000,000
Income from renting of facilities	862,470
Income from other sources	1,4856,070
Security services of sports events	90,000
Total income	**30,437,540**

Source: Cyprus Sport Organisation (2013).

For the year 2013 CSO had a budget of roughly 30 million euros, of which 28 million was received from the state funding. Roughly 11 million euros was the total amount that CSO gave to all the national federations in 2013. As we can see in Table 1, the state is by far the main supporter of the CSO, national federations and Cypriot sport in general.

Cyprus Olympic Committee

The Cyprus Olympic Committee (COC) was founded in 1974 and was officially recognized by the IOC in 1978. The main purpose of COC is to encourage interest in the Olympic Games and to foster the aims and ideals of the Olympic movement in the Republic of Cyprus. Since 1980 the COC has ensured that Cyprus is represented with athletes at the summer and winter Olympic Games, as well as at Regional and Continental Games which have the patronage of the IOC. In addition to participating in the Games, the Cyprus Olympic Committee actively participates in the activities organized by the IOC, the Association of the European Olympic Committees (EOC) and other NOC's. Overall, COC is responsible for developing the Olympic Movement and the Olympic ideals in Cyprus in collaboration with the national sport federations. (Kartakoullis et al., 2015.)

National Sport Federations and Cooperating Organisations

National sport federations in Cyprus are autonomous bodies that operate independently as they conduct their operations based on the principles of the international sport federations and the International Olympic Committee. Apart from football and its governing body, the Cyprus Football Association, the rest of the national sport federations fully depend on the funding that they receive from the state through the CSO. These associations are small sized organisations, based mainly on volunteers, and they employ only a small number of full time staff (Kartakoullis, 2014). Table 2 below shows the organisations with whom the federations who filled the template cooperate in running their programmes.

Table 2 Federations and cooperating organisations.

Federation	Nature of programme	Cooperating organisation
Billiards	Billiards	CSO
Ski	Alpine ski	CSO, Cyprus Olympic Committee, Cyprus tourism organisation
Amateur Athletics	Track development	CSO
Shooting	Hunting gun and air gun	CSO
Football	n/a	
Cycling	Cycling academy	CSO
Basketball	Basketball academies	CSO
Waterski	Slalom	CSO
Special Olympics	Basket	Engomi school management board
	Football	Gymnastic Association Pangypria
	Track	Cyprus police
	Swimming	CSO
	Rhythmic gymnastics	CSO
Tennis	Tennis	CSO, COC, tennis Europe, ITF
Swimming	Swimming	CSO
Bowling	Bowling	CSO, COC, ETBF, WTBA
Hockey	Hockey	CSO, COC, EHF, FIH
Bridge	Training courses	CSO, Ministry of Education
Table tennis	Table tennis	SFA
Taekwondo	Taekwondo	CSO, COC, SFA
Judo	Judo	CSO, COC, SFA
Handball	Handball	CSO

Source: Cyprus Sport Organisation (2012a).

Data, as provided by the federations, show that most of the programmes provided, run in cooperation with the Cyprus Sport Organisation and the Cyprus Olympic Committee. Some federations run programmes in cooperation with their respective European or international federations. (Cyprus Sport Organisation, 2012a.)

Voluntary Sport Sector

According to a survey undertaken by the CSO in 2006, there were approximately 12,500 volunteers in sport in Cyprus, which amounts to 1.5% of the population. It is estimated that the number and share of volunteers remained stable in the period of 2000–2009. The sport sector includes 48 sport federations (umbrella organisations for a particular sport) and 600 sport clubs representing Olympic and non-Olympic sports. All federations and clubs rely on volunteers, including 50 clubs which also employ professional staff. Along these lines, volunteers are involved to some extent in proffessionalised sport clubs, which in Cyprus consist mostly of large football clubs, for example through participating in the board of management or coaching at youth level. Around 80% of the volunteers are involved through clubs while the remaining 20% participate through federations. (GHK, 2010.)

In addition to the federations and clubs, individuals may volunteer in sport through the Cyprus Olympic Committee, the Cyprus Commonwealth Games Committee, the Cyprus University Sport Federation, the Cyprus Federation of Sport Medicine and the Cyprus Sportswriters' Union. The economic value of volunteering in sport in Cyprus is estimated to be 80 million euros. This calculation is based on four million hours of volunteering per year at a rate of 20 euros per hour. In full-time equivalent (FTE) volunteers represent 90% of the employment in the sports sector. It is widely accepted that without volunteers a large section of the sports movement would not exist. (GHK, 2010.)

The Private Sport Sector

According to the Central Bank of Cyprus (2012), the economy of Cyprus has been dominated by the service sector during the recent years. Trade, financial and business services, together with shipping, have been the key drivers of the economic growth. Despite these facts, Cypriot economy, compared to other European countries, is a very small market and thus, the sport market is equally small. In addition, the powerful role of CSO and the state funding leaves only a small niche for the private sport sector. Therefore, the private sport sector is largely based on professional football and as we see in Table 3 in the sporting goods sector and in the private sport services sector (e.g., sporting goods, sport services and fitness facilities). Table 3 presents the directly sport-related business fields, according the *Statistical classification of economic activities in the European Community* (NACE Rev. 2, 2008), in Cyprus in 2013.

Table 3 Directly sport-related business fields in Cyprus in 2013.

Business field	NACE code	Enterprises (n)	Revenue (1000 €)	Persons engaged	Total wages & salaries (1000 €)
Wholesale of sport goods	46492	20	5424	42	693
Wholesale of bicycles and their parts and accessories	46493	7	1392	11	116
Retail sale of sporting equipment in specialised stores (incl. Bicycles, fishing goods, camping and hunting equipment, boats and yachts)	4764	163	18,299	240	3426
Renting and leasing of recreational and sport goods	7721	29	348	12	119
Sport and recreation education	8551	123	3868	155	1876
Operation of sport facilities	9311	43	8677	180	2690
Activities of sport clubs	9312	85	49,171	671	29,173
Fitness facilities	9313	228	12,239	358	3568
Other sport activities	9319	141	39,920	551	9427
Total		**839**	**139,338**	**2220**	**51,088**

Source: Statistical Service of the Republic of Cyprus (2016).

Football, the True Passion of Cypriots

The football sector comprises the main pillar of the sport industry in Cyprus. In 2004–2005 the football industry represented 1.84% of the GDP of Cypriot economy. Cyprus can be considered as a football-loving nation, as football competitions draw significant attention in large number of audiences, and are extensively covered by the media. In this regard, it is worth noting that when the two major men's football teams of the country (APOEL Nicosia and Omonoia Nicosia) play against each other, they attract more than 25,000 people to the stadium. This is indeed a large number, compared to the size of the country and the population. (Kartakoullis et al., 2009.)

Nevertheless, in the elite sport level Cyprus recently enjoyed some exceptional sporting successes, mainly in men's professional football. Over the last years three Cypriot football teams (APOEL, Anorthosis, AEL) have performed exceptionally well in the European top-level competitions (UEFA Champions League and Europa League). APOEL qualified to the quarterfinals of the UEFA Champions League during the season 2011/2012, which was a great achievement that introduced Cyprus to the "world football map". Additionally, the performance of the men's national football team in the group B of the qualification stage for Euro 2016 was more than decent (4 wins, 6 defeats).

Concerning the major expenses of the football clubs, these include salaries which are paid to football players, coaches, and administrative staff, accommodation and board when the club is traveling for away games, transfer fees, and expenses for the organisation of matches (Theophanous & Kartakoullis, 2008). As an illustration, the magazine "In Business" published data for two major football clubs in Cyprus for the year 2013. The first one was APOEL which for that year declared 5.5 million euros annual budget and a staff of 55 persons while the second one was Apollon Limassol which declared 3.5 million euros and a staff of 54 persons (The 700+ biggest companies in Cyprus, 2014).

Another significant part of the football industry in Cyprus is the private football academy sector, where thousands of children pay a monthly or annual fee to learn and practice football. In addition, the private football academies organize their own annual championships, in parallel with the official "grassroots" tournaments of the Cyprus Football Federation. However, no official data exist about the exact number of private football academies and their contribution in Cypriot economy.

Private Expenditure of Sporting Goods and Services

The fact that Cypriot economy was flourishing for decades, allowed Cypriots to spend great amounts of money buying products and services. More specifically in the field of sport, the most recent sport statistics edition of Eurostat (2016) shows that Cyprus is in the first place in Europe in the expenditure of recreational and sporting services (see Fig. 2). This means that Cypriots spend a large amount of money to take care of their physical condition and appearance by enjoying sport, recreation or fitness services. The last available data on the consumption of sporting goods was extracted from the 2010 Household Budget Surveys (HBS). The HBS is a sample survey of private households carried out regularly under the responsibility of the national statistical offices in each of the 28 EU Member States. This survey provides information about household consumption expenditure on goods and services with detailed categories and breakdowns and income and possession of consumer durables and cars.

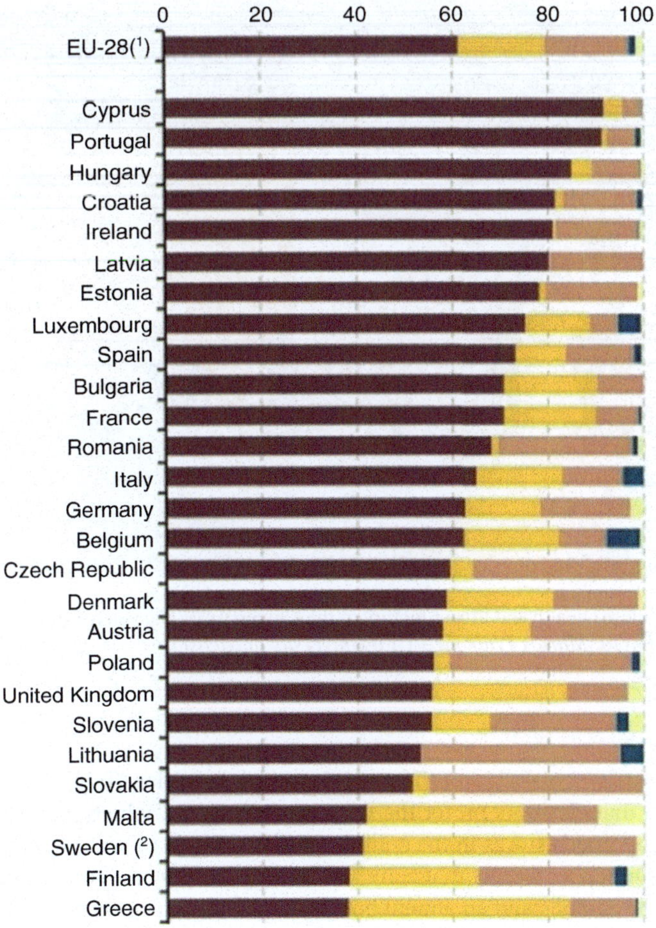

Fig. 2 Private household expenditure on recreational and sporting services (purple), major durables for outdoor recreation (*orange*), equipment for sport, camping and open-air recreation (*light purple*), major durables for indoor recreation (*blue*) and maintenance and repair of other major durables for recreation and culture (*yellow*). Source: Eurostat (2016).

Figure 2 shows that Cypriots are frequent consumers of sport services. This is also confirmed by the data shown in Table 4 where it is evident that in 2013 there were 228 fitness facilities that provided fitness and sport services all over Cyprus. In Table 4 it is seen that there are 163 retail sale enterprises of sporting equipment in specialized stores (including bicycles, fishing goods, camping and hunting equipment, boats and yachts). Cyprus, being an island, gives the opportunity for fishing, yachting and other sea water activities. (The 700+ biggest companies in Cyprus, 2014.)

UFit State of the art health and fitness facility of the University of Nicosia for students and the local community. *Photo: Marios Tziakouris/UFit University of Nicosia.*

In the sporting goods sector there are five big companies (Table 4). As a result, it can be seen that Cypriots prefer the well-known brands, which they are offered in most sporting goods stores in the country. It is important to highlight the success of the "Sport Direct" company that is by far the biggest sporting goods enterprise with a staff of 140 persons and an annual budget of 19 million euros in 2013. (The 700+ biggest companies in Cyprus, 2014.)

Table 4 The biggest sporting goods companies in Cyprus in 2013.

Company	Brands	Staff (n)	Revenue (MEUR)
A.M PAPAKYRIAKOU	Reebok, body talk, Asics, speedo, champion, quicksilver	90	9
Adidas CYPRUS	Adidas	55	n/a
Intersport athletics (CYPRUS)	Adidas, Nike, reebok, Asics, firefly	30	3.5
Sport DIRECTCOM CYPRUS	Dunlop, Slazenger, Everlast, firetrap, Karrimor, Lonsdale	140	19
VASSOS CHRISTOFOROU	Nike, Adidas, puma, Converse, Freddy, Varis	68	7.5

Source: The 700+ biggest companies in Cyprus (2014).

Sport Tourism Sector

Tourism is the core industry of Cyprus. The island of Cyprus is one of the most popular tourism destinations in Europe, if not internationally. In 2013 the direct contribution of travel and tourism to GDP was 1136.8 million euros (6.8% of total GDP), with a forecast of 2070.9 million euros (10.5% of total GDP) in 2024. Also, in 2013 Travel & Tourism directly supported 27,000 jobs, which represents the 7.8% of total employment. (World Travel and Tourism Council, 2014.)

As a result, sport tourism also, has been a growing field in Cypriot economy recently. A research conducted on behalf of the Cyprus Tourism Organization showed that the total number of international sport-related visitors to Cyprus in 2013 was estimated to be 20,803 visitors, which is an estimated 5% increase from the previous year (2012). The revenues of the sport tourism sector to the Cyprus economy for 2013, was estimated at about 30.5 million euros. (Cyprus Tourism Organization, 2014.)

The largest share of sport visitors in Cyprus came for the sake of football (34% of visitors), for diving (21%) for cycling (17% of visitors) and for swimming (15%). The majority of sport visitors preferred to visit the country during the months of February, March and April, which accounted for 45% of the annual visits. These months are popular probably because of the lower temperatures in Cyprus, while in summer the practice of sport activities is difficult due to hot temperatures and humidity. The main countries of origin were Russia, Great Britain and Germany, from where the majority of sport visitors (44%) came in Cyprus. (Cyprus Tourism Organization, 2014.)

Private Sport Sector in the 2000s

The 2000s was a transformative and growing decade for Cyprus. The country became a member of the European Union and the Eurozone, and the economy witnessed an unprecedented growth. Also, the sport sector developed towards more professional and closer to the European quality standards. The building of new stadia and the first successes of Cyprus in international competitions showed that there was a positive trend for the future. However, for the private sport sector the change was not so significant. According to the European Foundation for the Improvement of Living and Working Conditions (2013), "in terms of employment, aggregate employment in the sport and active leisure sector in Cyprus accounted only for 0.65% of the total the employment in 2009".

Due to the small market size and the domination of the public and voluntary sectors in the Cypriot sport, there are no professional organisations or trade unions in the sport sector. However, the European Foundation for the Improvement of Living and Working Conditions, an organisation that provides data about the 2000s in Cyprus (see Table 5) shows that in a nine-year period and despite the growth of the wider economy, the sport and leisure sector showed no significant changes.

Moreover, there is a loss of 0.5% in the share of sectoral employment for the sport industry, meaning that especially the private sport sector could not follow the general growth of economy. (European Foundation for the Improvement of Living and Working Conditions, 2013.)

Table 5 Sport and leisure sector properties in 2000 and 2009.

	2000	2009
Number of companies in the sector	527	560
Aggregate employment	1867	2206
Male employment	1464	n/a
Female employment	403	n/a
Share of sectoral employment (%)	0.7	0.65
Source of company data and employment figures	Business register	

Source: European Foundation for the Improvement of Living and Working Conditions (2013).

Conclusions

Cyprus is a historic island with the paradox of being a divided country. Nevertheless, the Republic of Cyprus is a modern, developed state with some unique cultural characteristics that have arisen from the fact that Cyprus acts as a bridge between the West and the East. Sport is one of the most popular social phenomena in the Cypriot society and has recently become an important social institution for the economy as well. Sport in Cyprus has developed significantly over the last two decades in the elite international level. The recent exceptional performances in individual (sailing) and team sports (football), together with the traditional passion of the Cypriots for football, indicate that Cyprus can be considered a sport oriented nation.

Cypriot sport is mainly based on state funding and central administration. The Cyprus Sport Organisation is in charge of most of the sport activities in the country, providing financial support to clubs, federations and sport facilities' construction and function. The privatization process of the western countries has not yet reached Cypriot sport and only football and the football federation are financially independent from state funding. While football is the most valuable and important asset of the sport industry, recently also sport tourism, recreational activities and sporting good products have contributed to the national economy. Another great pillar of Cypriot sport is the voluntary sector. That is because the whole structure of Cypriot sport is based on volunteers. Their contribution as club and federation members, managers, officials, coaches and volunteers is the backbone of the national sport system.

As a result, the private sport sector has a secondary role in relation to the public and voluntary sport sectors, even though recently there has been a significant growth in private sport services and products. Cypriots are good consumers of sport products and also active members of fitness clubs and other sport services. The question is whether sport in Cyprus can become more professional and financially independent from the state funding. For example, although Cypriot economy and market grew in the period after the 2000s, no significant changes were observed in the private sport sector. Thus, professionalisation and good governance are the key words for the future of sport in Cyprus. As the sport industry is growing, the administration of sport organisations calls for better management practices and good governance (Kartakoullis et al., 2015).

In conclusion, despite the recent progress of the sport industry in Cyprus, there is a great challenge for the Cypriot sport to become more professional, financially independent, well-managed and market-oriented. Although Cyprus is a small country, the recent successes in the UEFA Champions League, the Olympic Games and in other international competitions show that Cyprus has the potential to become competitive in the elite level, but also inspire more Cypriots to get involved in sport. The voluntary sector, which is the main pillar of the Cypriot sport structure, must be enhanced with professionals who are aware of the international sport industry and sport management practices. The challenge for the private sport sector is to be advanced from the inferior sector that it is today, to an equally significant contributor in the Cypriot sport, national economy and society in general.

References

Central Bank of Cyprus. (2012). *The Cyprus economy – Historical review, prospects, challenges*. Retrieved July 15, 2016 from http://www.centralbank.gov.cy/media/pdf/CBC_book_EN.pdf

Cyprus Sport Organisation. (2008). *White bible for sport in Cyprus*. Nicosia, Cyprus: CSO Press-Promotion Office.

Cyprus Sport Organisation. (2012a). *Study on leisure sports participation in Cyprus*. Nicosia, Cyprus: University of Nicosia.

Cyprus Sport Organisation. (2012b). *Sports in Cyprus – A history of centuries*. Nicosia, Cyprus: Konos.

Cyprus Sport Organisation. (2013). Προϋπολογισμός έτους 2013 [Annual Budget for the year 2013]. Retrieved July 5, 2016 from http://cyprussports.org/koa/general-information/financial/financial-budget/file/142---2013.html

Cyprus Tourism Organization. (2014). *Sports Tourism Report for the Year 2013*. Retrieved February 10, 2015 from http://media.visitcyprus.com/media/b2b_en/Research_Projects/Statistica_Athlitikos_Tourismos_2013_en.pdf

European Foundation for the Improvement of Living and Working Conditions. (2013). *Cyprus: The representativeness of trade unions and employer associations in the sport and active leisure sector*. Retrieved July 12, 2016 from http://www.eurofound.europa.eu/observatories/eurwork/comparative-information/national-contributions/cyprus/cyprus-the-representativeness-of-trade-unions-and-employer-associations-in-the-sport-and-active

Eurostat. (2016). *Sport statistics*. Retrieved March 18, 2016 from http://ec.europa.eu/eurostat/documents/4031688/7203321/KS-04-15-823-EN-N.pdf/b911c74d-c336-421e-bdf7-cfcba4037f94

Games of the Small States of Europe History. (2015). Retrieved July 7, 2016 from http://www.iceland2015.is/english/the-games/history/

GHK. (2010). *Volunteering in the European Union*. Study on behalf of the European Commission. D-G education and culture. Retrieved July 9, 2016 from http://ec.europa.eu/citizenship/pdf/doc1018_en.pdf

Hadjistefanou, C. (2004). *Athletics in ancient Cyprus and the Greek tradition: 1500 BC 330 AD*. Nicosia, Cyprus: Kyproepeia Publishing House.

Kartakoullis, N. (2006). *Challenges facing sport: The way ahead*. Paper presented at the Physical Education Teachers' Conference – February 2006. Limassol, Cyprus.

Kartakoullis, N., Kriemadis, T., & Pouloukas, S. (2009). Cyprus: A football crazy nation? *Soccer & Society, 10*(2), 226–244.

Kartakoullis, N. (2014). *European observatoire of sport and employment V Sport+ Strategy for a competent workforce – National Dissemination Report – Cyprus*. Retrieved April 12, 2016 from http://www.vsportplus.eu/wp/wp-content/uploads/2014/05/D18.2_VSPORT_National_Report_-Cyprus.pdf

Kartakoullis, N., Karlis, G., Walker, T., & Locke, M. C. (2015). Good governance and management practices: The perspectives of Cyprus national sport federations administrators. *International Journal of Sport Management, Recreation and Tourism, 19*, 62–74.

Statistical Service of the Republic of Cyprus. (2011). *Preliminary Results of the Census of Population, 2011*. Retrieved July 12, 2016 from http://www.mof.gov.cy/mof/cystat/statistics.nsf/All/732265957BAC953AC225798300406903?OpenDocument&sub=2&sel=1&e=&print

Statistical Service of the Republic of Cyprus. (2016). Unpublished raw data for the private sport sector in Cyprus for the year 2013.

The 700+ biggest companies in Cyprus. (2014). *In Business magazine* (May, 2014). Retrieved July 8, 2016 from https://issuu.com/eventsteamimh/docs/pdf700

Theophanous, A., & Kartakoullis, N. (2008). The financial dimensions of the football industry in Cyprus. *Economics and Sports, 8*(1), 25–32.

World Health Organization. (2010). *Global recommendations on physical activity for health*. Retrieved May 10, 2015 from http://apps.who.int/iris/bitstream/10665/44399/1/9789241599979_eng.pdf

World Travel and Tourism Council. (2014). *Economic impact 2014 world, London, WTTC*. Retrieved March 25, 2016 from http://www.ontit.it/opencms/export/sites/default/ont/it/documenti/files/ONT_2014-03-31_03008.pdf

CZECH REPUBLIC: Growth of the Profit-Making Sport Sector After Economic and Political Transformations

Irena Slepičková, Petr Laník, and Jakub Popelka

Selected country facts (in 2013)	
Capital	Prague
Geographical size (km^2)	78,868
Population (million)	10.52
GDP (euro per capita)	15,000
GDP (per capita in PPS)	84
Annual net earnings average (€)	8880

The Changing Role and Position of Different Sectors in Sport Development

The Czech Republic has a long sporting tradition. The first sport clubs and physical exercise organizations were founded as early as in the second half of the nineteenth century. The Czech Jiří Stanislav Guth-Jarkovský, was an active figure in establishing the International Olympic Committee in 1894, and thus, become the Secretary-General of the IOC in 1919. Sport and physical activity spread similarly to the

I. Slepičková (✉)
Charles University, Prague, Czech Republic
e-mail: slepickova@ftvs.cuni.cz

P. Laník
University of Economics, Prague, Czech Republic
e-mail: lanikpetr1@gmail.com

J. Popelka
Lokal Sport, Beroun, Czech Republic
e-mail: popelka.jakub@gmail.com

A. Laine, H. Vehmas (eds.), *The Private Sport Sector in Europe*, Sports Economics, Management and Policy 14, https://doi.org/10.1007/978-3-319-61310-9_5

countries to the west of the Czech region. Especially after the independent Czechoslovakia was created in 1918, voluntary sport organizations, such as independent sport clubs and associations began to increase rapidly in number. (Kössl, Štumbauer, & Waic, 2008.)

Sport has always been part of life for the Czech people, which has reflected in social, economic and political events. To describe the main features of the Czech sport development since the beginning of this millennium and to analyse the position of the private sport sector during this period, recent history of the Czech Republic and its impact in the field of sport needs to be explored. The breaking point was evidenced at the end of 1989 with political changes throughout the former Eastern Bloc. Before these events, the guarantor of the sport development was a unified umbrella sport organization – the Czechoslovak Union of Physical Education (ČSTV) with a well-established structure, both vertically (state, two republics, 10 regions, 72 districts and about 8500 sport clubs) and horizontally – fulfilling the needs of the sport associations, and financing of the sport clubs and sport facilities at each territorial level.

Private sport services already began to appear during the 1980s, with the permission of the communist regime. Nevertheless, the private entities did not have the characteristics of the independent enterprises yet. For example, *ČSTV – Sportpropag* organized sport and recreation activities for the public or for sport instructors, especially those from sport clubs. *Pragosport* was a division of ČSTV that made money by exporting Czechoslovak athletes abroad. The rest of the sport services were represented by small businesses such as sport instructors who rented out school gyms and organized paid services for the visitors. This was typical, for example, in the globally developing women's jazz gymnastics and aerobics. (Slepičková, 2007.)

A turning point for the future of the private sector in sport took place in 1989. This process was evidenced in the Central and Eastern European countries and initiated radical changes with respect to political, economic and social foundations. New principles which undoubtedly affected the development of sport, contributed to the creation of the current institutions with all their strengths and weaknesses, and were inspired by the work of authors from fields of political sciences and public administration, and of the field of sport science. (E.g., Dvořáková & Kunc, 1994; Mlčoch, Machonin, & Sojka, 2000; Novotný, 2000; Slepičková, 2007; 2011.)

Thus, four principles of the new Czech society can be recognized: (1) society transitioned from the totalitarian regime to democracy; (2) establishment of the Rule of Law and Civil Liberty; (3) change from closed to diversified society and (4) stress on the national identity instead of internationalism. These principles have also influenced sport. Sport governance was decentralized; all sporting entities attained legal independence and became owners of their sport facilities. This transformation of the society also opened space for both increased professionalism and sport entrepreneurship. (Slepičková, 2011.) This process was also related to cheating and criminal behaviour from time to time. Football, for example, is known for a series of scandals with actors on the fringes or beyond the fringes of the law (Slepičková, 2010).

The consequences of the privatization strongly affected ice hockey, another popular sport in the Czech Republic. At present, issues connected with social justice are being discussed and the attitudes to youth training are being criticized. Professionalization and privatization even affect transfers of young pupils, some as young as 9 years old, between clubs as subjects of trades. (Český svaz ledního hokeje, 2016; Kalenda, 2011.)

Organization of Sport in the Czech Republic

The process of democratization, liberalization, and transition to the free market economy has affected also sport in the Czech Republic. It has caused fragmentation of the voluntary sport movement, mainly because each national sport federation and each sport club became an independent legal entity. Sport organizations incorporated into the unified sport organization ČSTV at the turn of the 1950s, restored their activities. New brand organizations were created. Sometimes, this fragmentation resulted in competitions on sharing sport infrastructure and club members. This situation weakened the voluntary sector with regards to their relations with the government. However, voluntary organizations gradually recognized that it is necessary to cooperate with the state when negotiating government subsidies.

In 1993, the Ministry of Education, Youth, and Sport as the coordinator of the sport affairs was established by the government. Moreover, municipalities began to engage in the sport development work. Nevertheless, the public support for sport at the municipal level often depended on local deputies, who decided to support sport or not.

Procedural preparations for the accession to the European Union and the left-wing government at the turn of the millennium brought in changes in the forms of the newly approved governmental documents and the final the Sport Act (Česká republika, 2001). As a result, the Ministry of Education, Youth and Sport is now the guarantor and coordinator responsible for sport development and funding of elite sport. Nevertheless, the act remains very general, without detailed specification of duties, control mechanisms or sport financing rules.

When it comes to the sport sector in the Czech Republic it can be noted that the voluntary sector could have kept its independence when it became an absolute stakeholder of SAZKA, a lottery corporation. Poorly run financial operations of this company by its president and oligarchs from nine sport umbrella organizations led to bankruptcies and enormous financial problems in the voluntary sector in 2011. The top-level sport received resources from the state budget and from sponsors. However, the lack of financial support for small and medium-sized sport clubs, which had no subsidies for the sporting milieu for 3–4 years, forced some of them into liquidation. Nevertheless, regions and municipalities gave them financial support. Without this support of local administrations, sport infrastructure and sporting activities in clubs would have needed to develop their activities in a very challenging environment.

Nonetheless, to date, umbrella voluntary sport organizations have remained relatively strong in the Czech Republic. These organizations are the principal bodies in negotiations with the government for sport funding. This can be seen in the current *National Sport Board*, a consultative body of the Minister of Education, Youth, and Sport. The board consists of 26 members with voting rights, who are mostly managers from sport umbrella organizations including the minister in charge. Three representatives of the regional and local administrations only have an advisory capacity. (Ministerstvo školství, mládeže a tělovýchovy ČR, 2016.)

At present, there are intense discussions about sport financing, increasing support through the state budget, and, which body would administer these funds. Intense discussions are also held about the new Sport Act. Soon, it will be clear as to whether a financially and socially effective model will be found.

Private Sport Sector – Current Position and Legislative Framework

The above mentioned political and social processes led to the development of the private sector in the Czech Republic, which opened possibilities for business activities in the sport as well. Elite sport turned fully professional and commercialized and began earn its financial resources through sponsorships and other alternatives, mostly state funding. National sport representation and several premier-league teams, most of them in football and ice hockey, are financed directly from the state budget and partly from municipal budgets (Kraus, 2016). Developments in the private profit-making sector has not only changed the elite sport, but also provided space for enhanced sporting possibilities amongst the "non-organized" public.

The private sector can be seen as a kind of competitor to the voluntary sector, for example from the point of view of providing sporting facilities and services. Many active recreational athletes have left sport clubs and taken advantage of the paid services, mainly in big towns and cities with higher purchasing power. Hence, a significant decrease in the number of members of the voluntary sport organizations has been seen. The approximately 30% decrease was detected even in the number of children and youth in organized sport between 1988 and 2014 (Slepičková, Slepička, & Mudrák, 2016).

Private actors providing sport business activities are registered in various legal forms in accordance with the current Czech legislation. Both formal and informal aspects of these entities significantly determine the nature of the business activities. As indicated by Kraft and Bednářová (2006), the number of employees, requirements for material equipment, level of administrative complexity, flexibility of decision-making, tax optimization issues, characteristics of the costs and the domain of the subject's activities are considered as important items regarding the choice of business form. Firms that are active in sport, both directly and indirectly, can be divided into two major categories – self-employed and private companies. (Kraft & Bednářová, 2006.)

Self-employment is a situation where anybody can on a short notice start his or her business in sport based on a trading license. One of the advantages of a self-employed business is a lower tax burden. The most important disadvantages are: full personal liability for the business extending to the totality of one's personal property; low hourly income; and/or providing other administrative activities virtually without remuneration. This business form is most often used in small or medium-sized businesses. However, it is also used by people considered to be employees rather than entrepreneurs. The main reason for this "exception" is more favourable obligations towards the state both on the part of the self-employed person and on the part of the employer. (Holman, 2001; Synek, 1996.)

In sport, professional trades and unqualified trades are prevailing in the Czech Republic. To obtain a professional trade licence, professional competence must be proven in the respective field of business. In sport, these are most often provisions of physical education and sport services, massage, reconditioning, and regeneration services. Professional competence is evidenced by higher education, further vocational education or by a retraining certificate issued to the respective party. (Holman, 2001; Synek, 1996.)

In order to conduct unqualified trade, professional competence does not have to be proven. These trades include the operation of sport facilities and organization of sport activities, or manufacture, repair, and maintenance of sport products, or other activities related to sport, for example in the promotion, marketing or research activities. Unqualified trades may also be conducted by professional athletes or trainers that need not be employees of the respective club.

Private Companies are the next dominant form used mainly for medium-sized and larger businesses. These companies are directly or indirectly active in all sport sectors. In the Czech Republic, there are several different types of companies classified into two main categories – personal enterprises and private limited companies. Personal enterprises can be unlimited or limited partnerships. In sport, most enterprises in this group are unlimited partnerships. Their advantage, compared to the private limited companies, is tax advantages under the same principles as is the case with self-employed persons. (Kraft & Bednářová, 2006.)

Private limited companies, particularly *limited liability companies* (Ltd.) and the *joint-stock companies* (JSC) are more popular than personal enterprises. Currently, limited liability companies are, together with the self-employed businesses, the most popular legal form of establishing new businesses. The difference between a limited liability company and a joint-stock company is that a Ltd. requires zero registered capital (CZK 1). A joint-stock company on the other hand usually has a broader business territory, and sometimes is active in other countries. (Kraft & Bednářová, 2006; Synek, 1996.)

Specifics of the Private Sport Sector Development

Before 1990, the private sector did not exist in the Czech Republic. At that time, not even small tradesmen were found in the country. This was the same in Poland and in the former German Democratic Republic. In 1948, all privately-owned businesses were nationalized and replaced by state-owned companies or cooperatives, some of which were active in sport. Many of these former or newly-founded businesses (e.g., *Sport and Artis* cross-country ski company) succeeded in developing competitive production of good quality sport equipment that did well in foreign markets. Trade targeted mainly Eastern Bloc countries. Aside from production, actual sport business was conducted by enterprises which were part of the umbrella sport organization ČSTV (*Sportprojekt, SAZKA, Sportpropag*) (MO ČÚV ČSTV, 1989). At that time, sport clubs in particular, were given permission to do business independently (Kábele, 2011).

The year 1990 brought general privatization of the companies, including those focused on sport. The government sold these companies (sometimes for very low prices) to domestic or foreign private owners, or they were given back to their original owners or their descendants. The new owners had to face up to the competitive environment, and they either aimed for further development of production, or closed and sold out the property. This involved some well-known and successful companies, such as sport shoe manufacturer *Botana*, terminated or significantly reduced their activities. A successful bike company, *Favorit*, is an illustrative case study about the significant changes in the Czech (Czechoslovak) economy, including production of sporting goods.

Favorit bikes had been produced in Rokycany since 1922. The popularity of cycling grew after World War II, and private bicycle production was turned over to a national company called *Eska-Cheb*. The bike brand *Favorit* was popular not just in Czechoslovakia, but also worldwide. These bikes were exported to 38 different countries including the US, Canada and the Federal Republic of Germany in 1980s. After 1990, the factory was privatized and was called the *Favorit Rokycany Company*. However, this company did not keep up with the global trends – above all the growing popularity of mountain bikes. Thus, the sales decreased and the company went bankrupt in 2001. In 2011 however, Richard Galovič bought the original trademark of the defunct *Favorit* and set up a company called *Favorit Czechoslovakia*. Between 2012 and 2014, he re-established the bicycle production under the *Favorit* brand, which has reinstated the tradition of high-quality handmade bikes that fulfil the current exacting standards. (Favorit Czechoslovakia s. r. o., 2016.)

Sport clubs have been also registered themselves as business enterprises, mainly those that are involved in popular sports and at elite performance levels (e.g., in football, ice hockey, basketball and volleyball). Sport clubs have been transformed from voluntary organizations into private companies, usually as joint stock companies. Private sport clubs have been also launched for sports at the lower performance level. In golf for example, there are today nearly 140 outdoor golf courses, 50 of them with 18 or more holes (Česká golfová federace, 2016).

Popularity of golf has risen in the Czech Republic. In the photo there is scenery from the Golf Course Karlštejn, which is around 15 kilometres from Prague. The course opened in 1993, and is located alongside one of the most famous Czech castles, Karlštejn Castle, founded in 1348 by the Czech King and Holy Roman Emperor Charles IV. *Photo: Andrej Halada.*

Self-employed businesses are popular in the Czech Republic and they have witnessed a rapid growth since the beginning of the private sport sector in 1990. This has been typical for businesses in fitness and wellness, and sales and service of sport equipment. Individuals opened body-conditioning gyms in various premises, for examples in warehouses of the liquidated companies. These services started to become progressively more professional with a number of complementary services (e.g., consulting, sale of sports equipment and catering). When they are successful in larger towns, they are transformed, one after another, either to joint stock or limited liability businesses.

At the same time, large foreign corporations, such as *BBC*, *FactoryPro*, and *Holmes Place* started penetrating the Czech market. With competition from big business corporations, fitness centers run as self-employed entities and have survived mostly in municipalities and smaller towns. A similar pattern has been observed in the case of sport equipment and bicycle retail shops.

Private sector development has been also connected with new trends of sport in general when the voluntary sector was not able to cover the wide spectrum of the needs amongst the population. To satisfy the increasingly varying and demanding requirements from both active and passive participants, availability of sporting goods and services, of both domestic and foreign origins, has grown substantially.

The private sport sector has had to cope with the problems caused by the recession, which began in the United States in the beginning of the 2000s. Dubská (2011) from the Czech Statistical Office has summarized the situation. She saw that the Czech Republic emerged relatively well from the crisis and was not clearly affected by it. However, the period following the global economic crisis seemed to have been more serious for the Czech economy. Compared to the EU, the slow down tempo of the economy, as well as the ensuing decrease in household consumption expenditures and investments in the Czech Republic was not as extreme as in some other European countries. (Dubská, 2011.)

It is then fair to assume that household expenditures on sport were not significantly reduced due to the crisis. Neverthless the global economic crisis hit the Czech Republic in a sensitive place – its openness to global goods and capital flows, to which the above mentioned import of sport goods is related. In 2009 the Czech crown declined in value against both the euro and the US dollar. Thus, the crisis lowered significantly the income of the premier-league teams from their sponsors, who could not afford to be so generous. This was evident for example in ice hockey. (Sport.cz, 2016.)

Sport Business Fields

Table 1 shows the directly sport-related business fields in the Czech Republic in 2013, according the Czech equivalent (CZ-NACE) of the *Statistical classification of economic activities in the European Community* (NACE Rev. 2, 2008). Profit-making organizations are not exclusively involved, as organizations from other sectors can also be active in the field. In addition to core activities, sport clubs are also permitted by the new Civil Code to have secondary economic activities, or other profit-making activities, if these support the main activity or economic utilization of the organization's property (Česká republika, 2012). Organizations are allowed to establish business entities (limited liability companies) to support sport, usually for operating their own sport facilities. Basic data about the companies can be found in the economic databases, but their accessibility is limited.

Several databases have been used to analyse the situation in the Czech Republic. Amadeus (Bureau van Dijk Electronic Publishing, 2016) served as the fundamental database. Access was granted through a subscriber, the University of Economics in Prague. Data was completed from the Albertina (Bisnode Česká republika, 2016) and Merk (IMPER CZ, s.r.o., 2016) databases that also use the NACE classification. Unfortunately Albertina does not provide a sufficiently detailed view on individual business fields.

Staff and revenue data was available only for limited number of companies. All this data is italicized in Table 1.

Table 1 Directly sport-related business fields in the Czech Republic in 2013[a].

Business field	NACE code	Companies (n)	*Companies with staff data available (n)*	*Staff (n)*	*Companies with revenue data available (n)*	*Revenue (1000 €)*	*Revenue/ Company (1000 €)*
Retail sale of sport equipment and bicycles	4764	893	*385*	*7635*	*578*	*345,871*	*598.4*
Operation of sport facilities	9311	17,788	*1785*	*13,217*	*1091*	*326,591*	*299.4*
Activities of sport clubs	9312	6926	*293*	*1949*	*1696*	*167,555*	*98.8*
Other sport activities	9319	6086	*277*	*1581*	*2069*	*103,931*	*50.2*
Manufacture of sport goods	3230	707	*106*	*3021*	*314*	*79,261*	*252.4*
Fitness facilities	9313	180	*101*	*678*	*112*	*26,440*	*236.1*
Sport and recreation education	8551	326	*73*	*397*	*185*	*9902*	*53.5*
Renting and leasing of recreational and sport goods	7721	78	*31*	*187*	*58*	*5579*	*96.2*
Total		**32,984**	***3051***	***28,665***	***6103***	***1,065,130***	***174,5***

Source: IMPER CZ, s.r.o (2016).

[a]The exchange rate of the Czech National Bank as of 31.12.2013 was used (1 EUR = 27.065 CZK). The utilized databases do not indicate the average salary in individual business fields according to NACE. According to the Czech Statistical Office, average monthly salary in 2013 was 25,035 CZK = 925 EUR. Thus, average annual salary was 11,100 EUR. Albertina provided a general view of the number of companies according to the NACE classification, shown in the Companies column. Albertina also provides information about the number of employees and annual revenue for companies only in specific intervals (e.g., 1–3 employees). For a simplified interpretation, the average value of the number of employees rounded to the nearest integer was used for each interval. Values received in this way were subsequently summarized and can be considered for an estimation of the average number of employees of companies in individual NACE classes. The annual estimates of revenues were calculated following the same method.

Table 1 shows that the largest number of companies operate in the field of sport facilities, as either owners, managers, or renters. These companies are mostly sport clubs, municipal and regional organizations or private firms with newly constructed facilities, such as golf courses and tennis courts. They also have the largest number of employees and highest revenues. For example, swimming pools and ice arenas spend more than 30% of their budget on energy costs and another 30% on salaries (including health and social taxes) (Novotný et al., 2011).

The second most important field is the activities of sport clubs. Regrettably, the database covers staff numbers in only 293 of the 6926 registered clubs (4%) and annual revenue in only 1696 registered clubs (25%). Table 1 also shows a relatively high number of educational companies. Privatization and commercialization of sport has impacted this field which was formerly covered by the public education system and the voluntary sector.

In retail, there are less than 900 companies. As big foreign chains belong to this category with total revenue of 345 million euros in 2013, this is one of the strongest business fields. The popular field of fitness and wellness offers fitness facilities. The databases cover about 56% of them, with an average of 6–7 employees. They provide services, for example, in sport, spa and restaurant operations, including personnel and maintenance.

Companies manufacturing sporting goods have relatively high revenues; there are about 700 of them in the Czech Republic with 30 employees on average. During the last 25 years, this field has witnessed a rather interesting development. After 1990, people found themselves in self-employed sport businesses, similar to other economic sectors. These commercial activities were mainly in the area of fitness, retail and service of sport equipment, mostly bikes. There was a growing demand for sporting goods and services, and small to large retail shops appeared practically in all Czech towns.

Due to the entry of multinational corporations into the Czech Republic after 2000, a portion of small businesses closed down. Large chain stores entered the market. Table 2 shows data on the most important players in 2010–2013. For example Intersport has operated in the Czech Republic since 2001 and has consistently increased the number of stores (from 21 to 32) (Intersport, 2016). SPORTISIMO launched Czech operations in Brno, the second largest city in the Czech Republic, in autumn 2001. In 2015 they opened their 90th store. (Sportisimo, 2016.) Recently, Sports Direct, the biggest sport equipment retailer in Great Britain entered the Czech market. Decathlon, another global firm, has been in the Czech market since 2010. These companies have their stores above all in larger cities and in metropolitan agglomerations.

Despite the above mentioned development in the retail sales, some large companies have not been able to successfully compete in the market. For example GIGA SPORT registered a huge loss in 2012 (EBITDA[1]-% -58.56), and left the Czech

---

[1] EBITDA (Earnings Before Interest, Taxes, Depreciation and Amortization) is one indicator of a company's financial performance (Investopedia 2016). EBITDA-% = 100 x EBITDA/revenue. EBITDA-% = EBITDA margin.

market. An interesting company, HUDI sport, founded by a Czech entrepreneur, producing and selling quality sport clothing for outdoor activities is very popular among Czech consumers. Internet shopping is also increasingly popular and has given new companies that produce clothing for sport and outdoor activities, an opportunity to sell they products directly to the consumers (e.g., the Czech firm SAM 73 Apparel). In spite of the negative EBITDA-% figures in Table 2 for some companies, they still open new stores and are active in the market.

Table 2 Biggest retail sale of sport equipment and bicycles (NACE code 4764) companies by revenue in the Czech Republic[a].

Company	Brand	Stores (n)	Revenue (1000 €)	EBITDA-%	Staff (n)	Report (year)
A3 sport, s.r.o.	A3	54	51,827	−4.31	750	2013
Hervis sport a móda, s.r.o.	Hervis	27	35,704	−5.93	375	2013
Intersport ČR, s.r.o.	Intersport	21	27,381	−0.34	375	2011
Decasport, s.r.o.	Decathlon	8	19,263	−14.77	375	2013
Rock point, a.s.	Rock point	40	15,809	−1.58	375	2010
SAM 73 apparel, s.r.o.	Sam 73	93	12,601	2.88	225	2013
Alpine pro stores, s.r.o.	Alpine pro	32	9148	n/a	375	2010
Kastner + Öhler, s.r.o.	GIGA sport	n/a	7481	−58.56	n/a	2012
Destiny distribution, s.r.o.	Snowbitch	6	3706	11.34	37	2012
Ing. Viktor Walzel	HUDI sport	7	n/a	n/a	75	2013

Sources: Firmy.cz (2016) and IMPER CZ, s.r.o. (2016).
[a]s.r.o. means Ltd., a.s. means JSC.

Football as a Business

Large sport clubs that organize professional sports have transformed into business entities in the Czech Republic as it has happened also in most other European countries and globally. Football, as an example is the most popular sport in the Czech Republic both from the audience perspective and in the number of registered members. In 2014, the Football Association of the Czech Republic had 427,000 members, out of which 326,000 were adults and 101,000 children and youth. As with participation in organized sport in general, football has seen a decline in memberships; the number of adolescent members declined by 30,000 since 1997 (Slepičková et al., 2016). Nevertheless, these facts have not affected the Czech elite football, when viewed as a business. In the Czech Republic (population ca 10.5 million), there are 16 football clubs competing in the premier league and 12 clubs in the penultimate league. Almost all clubs are business entities. Table 3 describes basic economic data for the most important Czech football clubs. Since Albertina (Bisnode Česká republika, 2016) does not contain full data, it is not possible to include 2013 data for all clubs. Instead data has been retrieved from 2010 to 2014.

Table 3 Biggest Czech football clubs (NACE code 9311 and/or 9312) by revenue.

Company	Brand	Revenue (1000 €)	EBITDA-%	Staff (n)	Report (year)
AC SPARTA PRAHA FOTBAL, a.s.	Sparta	9157	−92.7	75	2010
SK SLAVIA PRAHA – FOTBAL a.s.	Slavia	6701	n/a	37	2013
FK MLADÁ BOLESLAV a.s.	Škoda	4499	3.0	15	2012
SK SIGMA OLOMOUC, a.s.	Sigma	3515	2.7	37	2010
FK TEPLICE a.s.		2669	−22.3	22	2013
FC ZBROJOVKA BRNO, a.s.	Zbrojovka	2637	−16.7	15	2010
FC VIKTORIA PLZEŇ, a.s.	Viktoria	2617	−146.6	37	2010
FK DUKLA Praha a.s.	Dukla	2221	n/a	8	2013
FC BANÍK OSTRAVA, a.s.	Baník	2221	n/a	15	2013
FC VYSOČINA JIHLAVA, a.s.		2032	−5.9	22	2014
1.FC SLOVÁCKO, a.s.	Slovácko	1999	n/a	37	2014
FC FASTAV Zlín, a.s.	Fastav	1175	−2.1	8	2010
FC SLOVAN LIBEREC a.s.	Slovan	1119	−211.0	37	2011
BOHEMIANS PRAHA 1905, a.s.	Bohemians	1040	−20.1	8	2013
1. FK PŘÍBRAM, a.s.	–	111	n/a	0	2013
FK JABLONEC, z.s.[a]	–	7	n/a	3	2013

Source: IMPER CZ, s.r.o (2016).
[a]z.s. means voluntary sport club.

Clubs are listed in Table 3 by their total annual revenues. It is obvious that economic strength between individual clubs differs remarkably. The highest revenues can be found in clubs with the longest traditions (i.e., Sparta and Slavia). During 2010–2014, Sparta won the league once, and was in the second place three times. Currently, the most successful club is Viktoria Plzeň – four times Czech champion and once in the second place in 2010–2015. Bohemians Praha 1905 on the other hand was rescued from bankruptcy by their fans, a unique situation from the global perspective. This club‘s revenues are one ninth of the richest club Sparta Praha.

EBITDA-% is unfavourable for most of the clubs, which means that many clubs have witnessed financial losses. Only Škoda Mladá Boleslav seems to be in good financial health; they are linked with a thriving company Škoda Auto. This company is also a long-term sponsor of the World ice hockey championships and the Tour de France.

Clubs that are unsuccessful from the sport-competition point of view must fight against disfavour with their financial partners, who either desert them, or face financial losses. For example FC Liberec, although a Czech champion several years ago, has had long-term financial problems (EBITDA-% -211 in 2011). The club's commercial sponsor, Precioza, is also in financial difficulty.

Another interesting club is Viktoria Plzeň. It was not doing well in 2010 (EBITDA-% -146). Data for further years is not available in the databases used. However, it can be assumed that the situation of the club improved significantly after they won the Czech championship several times in the recent years. The follow-up participation in the UEFA Europa League and UEFA Champions League brought in 700 million CZK (26 million euros) over 3 years (IDnes, 2014). Data in Table 3 and of the team standings in premier league (Fotbal.cz – FAČR, 2016), imply an inverse relation between the club revenues and competitive success.

Regrettably, in the Czech legal environment, objective information about the financial status of clubs, dealings with partner businesses, and/or business activities of owners or stakeholders are internal and confidential matters of these clubs, even when they are subsidized by public municipal resources in cities where they are active. (Novotný et al., 2011.)

Conclusions

The analysis presented above illustrates the transformation and dynamics of the sport sector and especially the profit-making organizations in the Czech Republic. Nowadays, sport business holds an important position in producing goods and services in the similar way as in other economically developed countries. Even though the voluntary and public sport sectors are still seeking their optimal roles in sport promotion, the sport market has been stabilized.

The analysis also shows a lack of easily accessible and objective data on sport businesses and the private sport sector more broadly. There are two main reasons for this. First, sport is not classified as an economic sector in the Czech Republic and, therefore, methodology for data collection and data processing has not yet been developed. Moreover, the Czech Statistical Office only works with the NACE classification at the second-order resolution level, and, therefore, the business entities in the field of sport are not identified within this methodology. Second, the Czech government, which incorporated sport into the competencies of the Ministry of Education, Youth and Sport, has shown little interest in periodically obtaining sufficient objective information about sport, which could be used for support and development of the field. For example, until now, no structured sport infrastructure list has been compiled. Further, no summary of sport financing through district or municipal budgets exists. As a result, it is not possible to assess the real social and economic contribution of sport, including private sport sector.

However, a catalyst from the editors of this publication has initiated deeper insight into the private sport sector in the Czech Republic based on the economic databases applying NACE classification. Distinction of the individual sport business fields was possible through the four-digit coding system. Different databases use the NACE classification, but unfortunately they are not freely available, free of charge or easily accessible. The basis for the above presented analysis was not only data retrieved from Amadeus, but also from other sources, such as Albertina and Merk. Another database, namely Firmy.cz (2016), contains data that make the presented tables and analysis more precise and were counted "by hand". These companies, however, did not provide us information from their official databases. Therefore, NACE classes were complemented based on the needs of our study. Despite these limitations, we chose two interesting business fields for more detailed illustration: (1) retail sale of sport equipment and bicycles and (2) top-level football. It was evident that economic data corresponds to the findings regarding development of these fields. Future development will show how much sources of economic data improve and whether those databases will be more detailed and freely available.

References

Bisnode Česká republika. (2016). *Albertina CZ Silver Edition. Ver.5.2.8.8. Smart database for business and marketing* [DVD]. Prague, Czech Republic: Bisnode Česká republika, a.s.

Bureau van Dijk Electronic Publishing. (2016). *Amadeus. A database of comparable financial information for public and private companies across Essurope.* Retrieved March 5, 2016 from https://amadeus.bvdinfo.com/version-20161125/home.serv?product=amadeusneo

Česká golfová federace. (2016). Seznam hřišť [The list of golf courses]. Retrieved May 15, 2016 from http://www.cgf.cz/GolfPlaces.aspx?IDMenu=84052184

Česká republika. (2001). *Zákon o podpoře sportu č. 115 ze dne 28. února 2001* [The sports act No. 115 from February 28, 2001]. Retrieved October 25, 2016 from http://www.msmt.cz/sport/zakon-o-podpore-sportu

Česká republika. (2012). *Zákon občanský zákoník č. 89 ze dne 3. února 2012* [The Civic Code No. 89 from February 3, 2012]. Retrieved December 19, 2016 from http://www.aplikace.mvcr.cz/sbirka-zakonu/ViewFile.aspx?type=c&id=6144

Český svaz ledního hokeje. (2016). Stanovy a řády [Statutes and rules]. Retrieved September 6, 2016 from http://www.cslh.cz/text/121-stanovy-a-rady.html

Dubská, D. (2011). Dopady světové finanční a hospodářské krize na ekonomiku České republiky [Impact of world financial and economic crisis on the Economy of the Czech Republic]. Retrieved September 6, 2016 from http://www.apic-ak.cz/data_ak/11/k/Stat/DopadyKrizeCR.pdf

Dvořáková, V., & Kunc, J. (1994). *O přechodech k demokracii* [On transition to the democracy]. Prague, Czech Republic: SLON.

Favorit Czechoslovakia s. r. o. (2016). History of Favorit: 65 years of a sporting legend from Rokycany. Retrieved May 6, 2016 from http://www.favorit.cz/en/favorit/history

Firmy.cz. (2016). Retrieved March 8, 2016 from https://www.firmy.cz/

Fotbal.cz – FAČR. (2016). Historie ligy [History of premier-league]. Retrieved October 10, 2016 from http://www.epojisteniliga.cz/historie-landing

Holman, R. (2001). *Ekonomie* [Economics]. Prague, Czech Republic: C.H. Beck.

IDnes. (2014). Plzeň za tři roky v pohárech vydělala téměř 700 milionů korun [Plzeň earned nearly 700 million Crowns in cups during three years]. Retrieved May 15, 2016 from http://fotbal.idnes.cz/fotbaliste-plzne-prijmy-z-evropskych-poharu-fnk-/fot_pohary.aspx?c=A140321_113628_fot_pohary_tru

IMPER CZ, s.r.o. (2016). *Merk. Database of economics subjects in the Czech Republic*. Retrieved February 20, 2016 from http://www.merk.cz

Intersport. (2016). O společnosti [On the company]. Retrieved June 14, 2016 from http://www.intersport.cz/unternehmen/organisation/index.html?lang=cs&ixn=-6afd180c:155d3da58f5:6ee4

Investopedia. (2016). What is 'EBITDA'. Retrieved December 21, 2016 from http://www.investopedia.com/terms/e/ebitda.asp

Kábele, J. (2011). Sportpropag – nepravděpodobné místo pro studium společnosti: Osobní pohled [Sportpropag – Improbable place for studying society: personal view]. *Sociální studia, 8*(1), 17–32.

Kalenda, J. (2011). Hokejová šlechta? [Ice hockey nobility?]. In P. Slepička & I. Slepičková (Eds.), *Sport a sociální stratifikace* (pp. 44–57). Prague, Czech Republic: FTVS.

Kössl, J., Štumbauer, J., & Waic, M. (2008). *Vybrané kapitoly z dějin tělesné kultury* [Selected chapters from history of physical culture] (3rd ed.). Prague, Czech Republic: Karolinum.

Kraft, J., & Bednářová, P. (2006). *Ekonomie I* [Economics I]. Liberec, Czech Republic: Technická univerzita v Liberci.

Kraus, M. (2016). *Zdroje nezbytné pro realizaci vládní politiky a vládních koncepcí v oblasti podpory sportu do roku 2020* [Necessary sources for realization of government policy and government concepts of sport promotion till the year 2020]. Oral presentation in Národní sportovní konference.

Ministerstvo školství, mládeže a tělovýchovy ČR. (2016). Seznam členů Národní rady pro sport [The list of members of National Council for sport]. Retrieved May 20, 2015 from http://www.msmt.cz/file/36956/

Mlčoch, L., Machonin, P., & Sojka, M. (2000). *Ekonomické a společenské změny v české společnosti po roce 1989/alternativní pohled/* [Economical and societal changes in the Czech society after year 1989/alternative view]. Prague, Czech Republic: Karolinum.

MO ČÚV ČSTV. (1989). *K problematice placených tělovýchovných služeb* [Problems of paid sport services]. Prague, Czech Republic: Sportpropag.

Novotný, J. (2000). *Ekonomika sportu* [Sport economics]. Prague, Czech Republic: ISV.

Novotný, J., Eysseltová, S., Fukalová, N., Hobza, V., Kotáb, J., Marešová, K., ... Vltavská, K. (2011). *Sport v ekonomice* [Sport in economics]. Prague, Czech Republic: Wolters Kluwer.

Slepičková, I. (2007). *Sportovní organizace. Teoretická východiska a situace v ČR po roce 1990* [Sport organizations. Theoretical background and situation in the Czech Republic after the year 1990]. Prague, Czech Republic: Karolinum.

Slepičková, I. (2010). Football as a field of new professionalization in sport in the Czech Republic. In C. Sobry (Ed.), *Sport et travail* (pp. 321–226). Paris, France: L'Harmattan.

Slepičková, I. (2011). New space for a new face of sport in central and Eastern European countries. In S. G. Földesiné & T. Dóczi (Eds.), *The interaction of sport and society in the V4 countries* (pp. 35–48). Budapest, Hungary: Hungarian Society of Sport Science.

Slepičková, I., Slepička, P., & Mudrák, J. (2016). Změny sportu jako sociálního jevu ve vztahu k dopingu [Changes of sport as social phenomenon in relation to the doping]. In P. Slepička (Ed.), *Problematika dopingu ve sportu se zaměřením na děti a mládež* (pp. 62–71). Prague, Czech Republic: FTVS UK.

Sport. cz. (2016). Kluby hokejové extraligy snižují rozpočty, došlo i na propouštění [Extra league ice hockey clubs cut down their budgets; Including dismissals employees]. Retrieved September 29, 2016 from https://www.sport.cz/hokej/extraliga/clanek/151739-kluby-hokejove-extraligy-snizuji-rozpocty-doslo-i-na-propousteni.html

Sportisimo. (2016). Sportisimo – život v pohybu [Sportisimo – Life in movement]. Retrieved June 14, 2016 from http://www.sportisimo.cz/o-spolecnosti/

Synek, M. (1996). *Manažerská ekonomika* [Managerial economics]. Prague, Czech Republic: Grada.

ESTONIA: To Buy or Not to Buy Is a Question for Many Estonians in Sport and Leisure Participation

Kristjan Port and Karel Kulbin

Selected country facts (in 2013)	
Capital	Tallinn
Geographical size (km^2)	45,227
Population (million)	1.32
GDP (euro per capita)	14,300
GDP (per capita in PPS)	75
Annual net earnings average (€)	9446

Historical and Cultural Background of Sport in Estonia

Estonia is a small country, the size of the Netherlands with a population ten times smaller (1.3 million). Due to its strategically advantageous geographical location in the Baltics region the country has for several centuries been under the rules of Denmark, Sweden, Germany and Russia. As a consequence, local culture is a blend of various cultures. However, by retaining its language and borders throughout this period of history the struggle for self-government was culminated in the establishment of the independent state in 1918. From the start of the Second World War in 1939 until 1991 Estonia was occupied by the Soviet Union. After having regained its sovereign state the country has been on the fast track to catch up with the social organisation and economic capacities, and is at the moment considered a high-income economy by the World Bank (The World Bank, 2017).

Among the three economic sectors by ownership, the public sector holds the key role in the provision of sport in Estonia. Voluntary sector organisations are rare

K. Port (✉) • K. Kulbin
School of Natural Sciences and Health, Tallinn University, Tallinn, Estonia
e-mail: kport@tlu.ee; kulbin@tlu.ee

A. Laine, H. Vehmas (eds.), *The Private Sport Sector in Europe*, Sports Economics, Management and Policy 14, https://doi.org/10.1007/978-3-319-61310-9_6

despite formal appearances since publicly financed sport clubs have for historical and economic reasons the status of non-profit organisations as will be later explained in more detail. Voluntary work by itself in sport has minor, spontaneous and local impact. A number of private-sector enterprises for sport services have emerged, but they are still limited in number and effect. In order to understand the development of the contemporary sport organisations and related private business initiatives in Estonia three historically distinctive phases should be differentiated. (Port & Lusmägi, 2015.)

Beginning of the Sport Movement

The first organisational forms of sport in Estonia stem from the surge of a German gymnastics movement "*turnvereine*" in the nineteenth century. The first sport club, Revaler Turnverein (Tallinn, the capital of Estonia, was known as Reval at that time) was established in 1863 (Mainla, 2012). The first book on the correct methods of gymnastics for schoolmasters was published in 1879 (Kurrik, 1879). Recently discovered athletism coincided with the national awakening, and therefore, gained momentum that raised the need of governing the movement. Inexperienced realm of sport needed to nurture connections to financiers, connect and promote the idea to somewhat bemused and confused general public, but also to avoid internal strife and foster cooperation. The first national Sport Congress was organised in 1919, just a year after the establishment of the independent Estonian state. In 1920, Estonian first-ever national team participated in the Olympic Games in Antwerp and brought home several medals and rankings among the world top. The success in the Olympics encouraged participation in sport and increased the number of clubs to meet the demand. However, due to the amateur ideal of the Olympic movement, sport was regarded as a non-commercial, voluntary, after-work endeavour, mainly financed by the municipalities and by the state. During the period of 1918–1940, Estonians won a total of 21 Olympic medals, and there were 350 sport associations, clubs, unions and sections along with 119 sporting grounds, 63 arenas for gymnastics and 25 swimming pools in the country. (Järva, Maidlo, & Teemägi, 2015.)

World War II and Soviet Socialist Republic of Estonia

In the eve of the World War II the governments of the German Reich and of the Union of Soviet Socialist Republics (USSR) decided that the areas belonging to the Baltic States would be included in the sphere of influence of the USSR. After the annexation by the Soviet Union as the Estonian SSR in the summer of 1940, the Soviet Union regime stipulated a new organisation of sport and thus, all previous constituents of sport organisations were disbanded as "rudiments of an oppressive state". New regime saw sport as a display of the superiority of the social organisation that had the goal to achieve a scientifically proven system for the physical education of the population for the preparation of a capable workforce, soldiers for the army and highly qualified athletes. All sport-related ventures were under the central management and control of the Sports Committee, headquartered in Moscow. The economy was based on the public and collective state ownership of the means of production and thus, private ownership was abolished. All sport was based on the notion of amateurism; sport clubs were organised by the state, trade unions or institutions including, for example, the army, heavy industries and agriculture. The majority of these organisations had their own network of sport schools (mainly for competitive sport among youth), amounting to a total of 59 sport schools in Estonia. (Port & Lusmägi, 2015.)

1991 – Return to Independence and Renewal of the Sport Organisation

The third existential chapter in the Estonian sport is current and in progress. After the re-establishment of the formal independence as a sovereign state in 1991 the country started to build its political, economic and social organisations. For sport, the pre-1940 state of organisation with its formal structure of governance was re-formed.

Sport in Estonia is regulated by the Estonian Sports Act that defines a sport club as the building block of a sport organisation. The most recent Sports Act have been adopted in 2005 by the Estonian Parliament. (Spordiseadus, 2005.) By 1989, a total of 9507 various athletics collectives with approximately 300,000 members existed in Estonia, of the all registered organisations only 37 bore the name of a "sport club" regardless of being mostly built on the concept of a sport club (Port & Lusmägi, 2015). Then again the clubs did not have the characteristics of a democratic club such as the freedom of organisational judgement, self-financing and non-formal memberships because only the employees of the institution were allowed to become members.

New official status specifies that a sport club is a legal person governed by the private law. Its principal activity is the development of sport. However, for the complex of economic, social, legal, fiscal and even for cultural reasons until 2005, sport clubs were legally required to be solely non-profit entities. Their main income came from the state and municipal subsidies with a relatively small part being paid via membership fees. For example, in 2005 the total amount of membership fees was 4.5 million euros and the support from the local governments amounted to 7.2 million euros. During the period of 2007–2008, the proportion tipped and the share paid by the members had multiplied while public support had become constant. In 2013, members paid 25 million euros as compared to 10.5 million euros from the local administrations. (Port & Lusmägi, 2015.)

Public Sport Sector

Estonian public sport system is to a great extent governed by the National Olympic Committee that also fulfils an umbrella organisation for sport federations and acts as a non-governmental liaison to two main ministries that preside the field of sport.

Ministry of Culture is the primary stakeholder and has the responsibility of dealing with the matters relating to the development of sport, conduits financial support to sport federations and for different sport programmes, promotes national and international co-operation and implements sport policies. In addition, sport and physical activity related policies and finances in the schools and higher education organisations are covered by the Ministry of Education and Research. Some areas of sport are also financed and developed by the Ministry of Defence and the Ministry of Social Affairs. (Raudsepp, Ööpik, & Lusmägi, 2013.)

Estonian Sport Council that is set up by the Ministry of Culture coordinates the work between Estonian Olympic Committee and different ministries, county governments and local municipalities in the area of sport. The county governments are obliged to create conditions for sporting activities and to monitor of the use of earmarked state budget funds. Local municipalities assume responsibilities in planning, construction and maintenance of sport facilities and financial backing of sport organizations working in the public interest.

Athletes and teams in the national and international championships are controlled and represented by the sport federations, and they are in majority members of the Estonian Olympic Committee and the Estonian Paralympic Committee. Clubs and organisations advocating a specific field of sport, for example school sport, student sport, sport of the disabled and veteran sport in the national or county level, are united into the Regional Sport Associations, that are further represented in the talks with County Governments via the Regional Sport Council of Estonia.

The general role and work division between different institutions is based on The Sports Act (Spordiseadus, 2005). The Act establishes the types of sport organizations in Estonia. It also determines the division of labour and responsibilities between the Government and local municipalities in promoting sport-for-all, top-level sport, children's and youth sport, development of infrastructure of sport, financing of the voluntary sport sector, and warrants for the school physical education. (Raudsepp et al., 2013.)

The System of Sport Schools

One unique aspect of the Estonian sport organisation is the sport schools that were popular during the Soviet rule. Estonia is split into 15 administrative subdivisions (counties) that are further divided into urban (33 towns) and rural (193 parishes) municipalities. A popular approach for managing the local needs in sport was taken by the means of publicly funded sport schools that provided full day salaried jobs for coaches and maintained teams for competitions at various levels. In 1988 sport school system provided 2994 training groups for 45,606 children employing 1401 coaches. (Port & Lusmägi, 2015.)

Objectively sport schools were surrogates for a system of sport clubs with emphasis on the youth sport, and the system kicked the ball rolling for several top-level athletes. As was pointed out previously, after regaining the state of independence it was decided that sport clubs are the basic building blocks of the sport organisations and thus, majority of the sport schools were closed. The process of shutting down the sport schools was further catalysed by several social changes. For example the public school system started to work only in the morning shifts, in contrast to the previously used two-shift system in which younger children went to school after lunch. One after-effect was a cutback in coaching time as for the pupils only the second half of the day was now available for sports. This time slot became contested by several other leisure activities and with a growing selection of alternative hobbies. In addition, sport was not considered as the most important social issues at that time of change.

On the other hand, taking into consideration the local needs and opportunities not all sport schools were closed, and a few have been newly established. Today there are some 20 sport schools organised and supported by the local authorities. Sport schools are organised according to the regulations governed by two laws: Private Schools Act (Erakooli Seadus, 1998) and Hobby Schools Act (Huvikooli Seadus, 2006). Overall funding given to the sport schools by the local governments in 2014 was 5.7 million euros, which is 0.35% of the total budget of the local municipalities and 9.7% of the total funds dedicated to the support of sport (Eesti Spordiregister, 2017).

The System of Voluntarily Organised and Publicly Bankrolled Sport Clubs

The main body of the contemporary sport organisation in Estonia is a non-profit voluntary club. However, clubs are not voluntary according to the direct definition of a third sector organisation, as they function in partnership with the public sector by hiring their facilities and receiving substantial share of the funds to cover operating expenses, including the salaries. The work of the coaches is reimbursed and their time of coaching is considered as working time. Therefore, the stated body of sport clubs is partly a substitute of the public services mainly for formative years and partly an emergent business theatre for grown-ups.

Coaching Is a Regulated Profession

In Estonia sport coaching is a regulated profession as long as one is working in a publicly financed sport organisation (Spordiseadus, 2005). This means that to work it is necessary to have valid occupational accreditation, which can be obtained through a system of formalised learning and testing of skills.

The occupational qualification of coaches is awarded with the sport federations. Currently the awarding body in sport coaching is the Estonian Olympic Committee. The framework of the qualifications of coaches is administered by sectorial skills councils and the Estonian Qualifications Authority. Therefore, the tally of coaches is by law, part of the national statistics maintained by the Estonian Sport Register (Eesti Spordiregister, 2017). Individuals and representatives of sport organisations use the service in the same way as the online banking, utilising the national ID-card infrastructure.

Data from the register is used for monitoring club activities, membership and qualification of coaches. It also enables decisions about club financing and the development of various policies. The latter facilitated the initiation and utilisation of the governmental supplementary funding in Government Action Plan 2015–2019 of sport coaches according to their qualification ("Vabariigi Valitsuse tegevusprogramm 2015–2019", 2015).

Funding

Main operating funds assisting the day-to-day costs of running a registered sport organisation are provided by the state and local governments with a few exceptions acquiring sizeable support from the private sector. Last-mentioned clubs make up highest level national competitive leagues predominantly in football, basketball and volleyball where owing to visibility they attract corporate sponsorship. Commercial interest in non-profit sponsorships has been elusive despite the socially responsible products and services that are provided by the non-profits in the sport sector.

Though, one can perceive an adjustment in this picture both politically and culturally. In recent times the political parties have been warming up to the idea of incentivising physical activity and thus, there are proposals for the amendments in the tax rules to stimulate business contributions for the promotion of physical activity among the population. Culturally triggered by a few noticeable doping scandals there appears to be a shift in the viewpoints among corporate sponsors away from contributions to competitive athletes toward mass sporting events.

Developing Sport Sector for Grown-ups

Sport was for a long time considered to be the domain for youth and competition sport. There has been a positive change in the attitudes across the population towards physical activity and active forms of leisure attributable to the overall advances of the social wellbeing and recognition of physical activity in the prevention of several diseases (Tali, Lusmagi, & Unt, 2016). Hence Estonian Parliament adopted a decision agreeing that: "sport and exercise are healthy, educational, entertaining and social activities to all demographic and social target groups, diversifying cultural and youth work, increasingly contributing to the integration, economic activities and employment". Based on the State Budget Act the parliament stipulated the Estonian sport policy vision and nationwide purpose in the "The Fundamentals of the Estonian sport policy until 2030" ("Eesti spordipoliitika põhialused aastani 2030", 2015).

According to the latest Eurobarometer 2014 (European Commission, 2014) the share of the population who "never exercise or play sport at all" was 36%. Based on the same data, 39% of the respondents "participated in sport regularly or at least with some regularity". The size of the Estonian population according to the census estimates in the 2011 was 1,294,236 (Statistics Estonia, 2012). From the data of the 2014 survey of consumption of culture in Estonia, 11% of the population utilized some of the organised forms of sport (Port & Lusmägi, 2015). Therefore one can deduce that roughly every fourth person among the physically active populace participate during the study period in some forms of organised sport provided mainly by a club. Absolute majority of these services have been provided by the non-profit sector, and these entities collected the significant share of the private money allotted for sport and leisure (Eesti Spordiregister, 2017).

The private sector then has the challenge to contest the already established and at least partly publicly financed system of sport clubs for the share of a personal income that individuals are willing to spend on sport. There is a reason to be optimistic as currently the majority of the beyond mid-twenties cohorts who participate in sport accomplish it by the means of a non-organised or in a self-organised modes. Share of people, especially those who prefer less structured style of sport and just enjoy the activities remains to be self-sufficient, but there is a considerable group of potential customers of the paid-for-services. In addition, among the currently passive and non-exercising populace there are people willing to join in and willing to pay for the assistance.

The Position of the Private Sector in Sport Clubs

For the historical, political and social reasons described above private capital has remained mainly in a low-key presence and on the side-lines of the sport-related services and activities until today. Companies reaching out and filling in the gap for the services that are not provided by the mainstream sport organisations represent usually the fields of sport event management (e.g., marathon running and other mass sport events) and the private fitness facilities. Until 2005, when the Sports Act (Spordiseadus, 2005) was changed to allow profit-making entities to be registered as sport clubs the latter were not seen to be included in any form to the officially recognised organisation of sport. Their membership was often gated to a limited number of members who were prepared to pay relatively high entrance fees.

Changes in the law in 2005 did not open the floodgates of the private money into the realm of sport clubs. Mostly due to the force of habit and relatively well functioning fabric of already established coaching services the profitability outlook was kept dim for private capital investments. At that time there were other commercially lucrative business opportunities in technology, real estate and financial sectors. In 2005 the already reasonably functioning system included 1599 non-profit sport clubs that provided free or low-cost services to 152,242 members and paid rather dismal salary to 6063 employees (Port & Lusmägi, 2015).

The Period of Tax-Free Salaries

Salary was not the correct term as a non-profit organisation was allowed to purpose for reimbursement of tax exempt stipend. Also, the so-called "employee" was often a part-time member of staff who had additional means of income outside a sport organisation and was registered as a taxpayer in some other field of work. As it was pointed out earlier, the coaching services are used mainly later in the day, leaving the instructor to pursue other activities during thc first part of the day to earn complementary income for example as a teacher or a salesman. As a result, coaching has become a sideline for many.

This method of employment and clubs' financing was regarded legal and justified as an efficient means of using rationed pool of money available to sport organisations assigned to them from the limited budgets of municipalities and of the state. However, the same financial arrangement was at times in use by commercially founded sport clubs, in particularly for the salaries of the competing team athletes and other part-time workforce, such as students.

This is also a reason for the low number of employees in the official statistics of the sport organisations, as the recipient of a stipend is not an employee and therefore exempted from reporting. Nonetheless, in 2013 the Estonian Tax and Customs Board decided to clarify the intent of the law of taxation about payments made to the athletes and coaches, by essentially ruling out the payment of a stipend as a remuneration for work. At the same time the Estonian Government assigned budgetary means for the encouragement of taking up coaching in a sport organisation as a salaried employee. ("Vabariigi Valitsuse tegevusprogramm 2015–2019", 2015.)

Searching for the Paying Customers

State supported sport clubs were expected to focus on servicing youth sport since the public funding was earmarked for the children of up to 19 years of age. After the amendment of the law only a few privately held and profit-making clubs, mainly emerging from the fitness gym business, entered the sport club scene. Their proportion is still small, roughly 9% by the number of entities as we can see later in this article. However, privately held clubs have gained popularity particularly among the working population that has been previously left unattended, unaided and outside the organisation of sport. Main paid-for services include various forms of aerobics and strength training at gyms. (Port & Lusmägi, 2015.)

After 2005 non-profit club memberships saw a 10% decline, which has remained more or less stable since then. Some of the causes for the decline in the club memberships are probably associated with a world-wide financial crisis that took place at about the same time. Symptomatically the decline was most prominent among male participants, while both the share of youth under 20 years of age and female segments showed modest gains in the memberships. (Port & Lusmägi, 2015.)

Physically active adult population in Estonia pay for participation in mass events. Taavi Rõivas, contemporary prime minister of Estonia (880) going with the flow of participants in SEB Tallinn marathon in 2014. *Photo: Toomas Huik.*

At the same time sport and other leisure activities witnessed an increase in popularity and media further generated enthusiasm about participation in sport. Stereotypically this should be taken as a suggestion for the excited business development. Alas, private equity seems to be fearful that it is difficult to monetize capital investments through privately held sport clubs because of the competition from publicly funded sport clubs. Then again privately held and business-oriented entities are flexible in the development of novel value propositions and their main clientele consists of grown-ups earning a salary and looking for new and improved sport and leisure services. It will be presented later in this article that there are a few successful private entities, yet unused in the households, that provide various wellbeing, hedonism and recreation related sport services. Alas, there are also loss-making companies, some of which may be seen as an early stage funding in the expectation of growth. At the same time the majority of the private capital is utilized in the sector of retail sales and manufacturing of the sporting goods as can be seen below.

Statistical Characterisation of the Private Sport Sector

According to Eurostat the biggest share of the GDP (or gross value added) in the EU originates from the non-financial corporations (around 60%), while slightly less than one-quarter is generated by household production activities, mainly the imputed value of the services from owner-occupied dwellings, and small businesses. The government accounts for around 15% and the financial corporations for a small fraction of GDP. In 2014, the added value of the Estonian institutional sector of non-financial corporations was 11.9 billion euros, of which revenue based on a selection of directly sport-related business fields, according the Estonian equivalent (EMTAK) of the *Statistical classification of economic activities in the European Community* (NACE Rev. 2, 2008), comprised 1.7% or 207 million euros (see Table 1). In comparison, the financial and insurance activities had a revenue of 543.4 million euros, and accommodation and food service activities 285.7 million euros. (Statistical Yearbook of Estonia, 2015.)

NACE Codes, Reporting Bugs and Issues Related to Data Collection

Statistics used for the current overview has some weaknesses, of which some are due to business decisions by owners about their interpretation and selection of the codes for the compulsory reporting. For example, a handful of companies have continued to report their operations by the means of outdated codes, despite evolving the business to new areas. In addition, one cannot always exclude human errors. For example, one company (Yuma Eesti AS) among the top wholesalers of sporting goods, almost exclusively on export markets, is visible in official statistics under NACE code 46499 (Wholesale of household goods). For the current report they are counted in using NACE code 46492 (Wholesale of sports goods) as is also practiced by a local major credit rating company.

In the same vein, Estonia has several privately held indoor water parks that consist of a system of pools and saunas, commonly called spas. These are characteristically connected to hotels and therefore the separation of these services from hospitality business of hotels and similar accommodation (NACE code 5510) is often complicated. For example, there are two Olympic size pools in Estonia that meet the requirements for international competitions. Both are privatised and further expanded into spas with a hotel and statistically compiled commonly as hospitality businesses. These facilities are still used for competitions and training, but for the third party to figure out the share of the revenue originating from sport and leisure related services is hidden inside the officially reported full amount figures. Yet again, for this report the two are counted in by separating the revenue from pool related services as NACE code 93131 (Fitness facilities).

It is complicated to separate sport-related businesses from general footwear and clothing wholesales. Owing to rendered corrections in identifying companies according to their business relationship to sport, there will be potentially small divergences from other domain related reports coming from Estonia. For example, the market overview of vendors of the sporting goods by a local credit rating company limits their selection to principal players and combines retail and wholesale statistics with a few of their own corrections regarding miscoding, explained above. However, the overall validity of the data used in this article seems to be corroborated with a close match to other reports in the field. Data used for the overview is from the official database of Statistics Estonia (Statistics Estonia, 2015).

Money Favours Buying Sporting Goods Instead of Services

In accordance with the notion in the introduction the profit making business in Estonian sport scene has evolved mainly around the sales of goods and to a lesser extent around manufacturing in a few specialized areas. Directly sport-related NACE business fields in Estonia in 2014 are presented in Table 1. One can see that the main driving force behind the growth has been the demand from the internal market with the exception of manufacturing.

Table 1 Directly sport-related business fields in Estonia in 2014.

Business field	NACE code	Companies (n)	Revenue (1000 €)
Retail sale of sporting equipment in specialised stores	47641	133	88,502.1
Wholesale of sports goods (excluding sports clothing and footwear)	46492	48	55,091.6
Fitness facilities	93131	145	25,201.3
Operation of sport facilities	93111	67	13,544.3
Manufacture of sporting goods	32301	35	12,815.6
Other sport activities not classified elsewhere	93199	171	6604.6
Activities of sport clubs	93121	58	3173.6
Rental and leasing of recreational and sports goods	77211	39	1019.3
Activities related to sport and recreational fishing and hunting	93192	10	963.5
Total		**706**	**206,915.9**

Source: Statistics Estonia (2015).

The comparison of the share of the retail sales of sporting equipment in specialised stores to sales figures of the services provided by the commercial fitness facilities and sport clubs supports the findings described earlier according to which the majority of the physically active population participates in sport in a non-organised mode. Or at least they tend to remain out of the reach of the commercial service providers. The same conclusion is further supported by the study of the consumption of culture in Estonia in 2014 (Port & Lusmägi, 2015). According to this study, 11% of the physically active population participate in organised sport through training groups in sport clubs, 21% in joined groups of friends, 16% with families, whereas 51% preferred to exercise alone.

The average salary in Estonia in 2014 was 1001 euros per month. According to the 2015 statistics of the household finance and consumption (Statistical Yearbook of Estonia, 2015) monthly expenditures of a household were 395 euros, out of which a household member spent most of the money on food, in other words 92 euros per month, 65 euros on housing, 51 euros on transport, 42 euros on recreation, 26 euros on household, 21 euros on clothing and footwear, and 18 euros on communication services. The average monthly fee of a fitness club in Estonia is around 50 euros. Therefore we can conclude that joining a commercial club removes additional 5–10% from the personal budget depending on whether one consumes the services for half or full year.

As a result, out of the 145 companies in the official register that sells fitness club services 45 were profitable according their EBITDA-%[1]. Table 2 shows key 20 entities covering 96% of total revenue out of 72 companies which reported a revenue stream in 2014. The official Sport Register (Eesti Spordiregister, 2017) identified 2258 operating sport clubs during the same year. This includes all publicly funded non-profit entities, as well as the commercial ones. As shown in Table 1 there were 145 commercially run fitness facilities and 58 sport clubs at that time, comprising 9% of the number of total entities among sport clubs in Estonia.

Table 2 Key 20 private sector enterprises by revenue comprising 96% of total revenue in the sector of fitness facilities (NACE code 93131) in Estonia in 2014.

Company	Offices (n)	Revenue (1000 €)	EBITDA-%	Staff (n)
My Fitness AS	18	6793.1	29.3	n/a
Kalevi Veekeskus OÜ	1	5482.7	23.9	n/a
Audentes AS	1	2210.5	−19.6	127
Freewill OÜ	2	2194.6	6.0	126
Tondi Tennisekeskus OÜ	1	1715.4	92.5	29
Tartu Veekeskus OÜ	1	1502.1	15.8	35
Reval Sport Agency OÜ	1	1139.0	−10.3	38
Haabersti Jäähall AS	1	664.4	14.4	n/a
EGCC AS	1	588.3	16.7	10
Eesti Golfikeskus AS	1	508.7	16.9	9
Tondiraba Tennisekeskus OÜ	1	392.7	45.8	n/a
Fittest Klubi OÜ	1	291.8	2.2	4
Pirita TOP Tennis OÜ	1	192.3	8.3	10
Tervisekeskuse Halduse OÜ	1	149.4	−6.7	3
Vedru AS	1	126.7	−3.9	2
SDE OÜ	1	124.5	−12.5	4
Powerstar OÜ	1	118.9	0.8	5
Viimsi Sport OÜ	1	110.7	34.4	5
Spordimaja OÜ	1	81.3	1.8	5
Heaoluagentuur OÜ	1	55.2	3.1	n/a

Source: Statistics Estonia (2015).

[1] EBITDA stands for Earnings Before Interests, Taxes, Depreciation and Amortisation. EBITDA-% = 100 × EBITDA/revenue. EBITDA-% = EBITDA margin.

Furthermore, in 2014 there were 2649 sport facilities registered and broadly defined as buildings or parts of them that are regularly used by the public for organised sport and training (Eesti Spordiregister, 2017). The majority of these facilities were owned by the municipalities or state. There were 67 private companies making revenue from operating sport facilities (NACE code 93111) (see Table 3). Out of these, 25 companies reported profit in 2014. The list includes a few of the company names that were also indicated among the fitness facility businesses. These companies have their own sporting facilities and sport complexes consisting, for example, of a group of sport facilities, tennis courts, swimming pools and golf courses.

Table 3 Key 20 private sector enterprises by revenue comprising 95% of the total revenue in the sector of operating sport facilities (NACE code 93111) in Estonia in 2014.

Company	Revenue (1000 €)	EBITDA-%	Staff (n)
Audentes Halduse OÜ	2603.9	46.3	23
Tondi Tennisekeskus OÜ	1715.4	92.5	35
Tartu Veekeskus OÜ	1502.1	15.8	36
Piko Hobikross OÜ	741.9	−153.5	23
Haapsalu Linna Spordibaasid OÜ	735.6	8.4	36
HK Hall OÜ	734.8	14.0	12
Haabersti Jäähall AS	664.4	14.5	10
Rocca Al Mare Tenniskekskus OÜ	656.5	5.3	10
Keila Tervisekeskus OÜ	540.8	−20.4	23
TTÜ Sport OÜ	536.4	0.9	8
Eesti Golfikeskus AS	508.7	16.9	n/a
PHG Holding OÜ	412.2	−52.3	15
Tondiraba Tennisekeskus OÜ	392.7	45.8	4
Lõuna Jää OÜ	351.4	1.2	10
Dorpat Sport OÜ	310.3	44.7	10
White Beach Development AS	251.9	6.0	8
Pirita TOP Tennis OÜ	192.3	8.3	3
Bowlex OÜ	143.9	6.9	8
Saare Tennisekeskus OÜ	88.5	−70.2	3
Rapla Bowling OÜ	87.1	−5.6	1

Source: Statistics Estonia (2015).

Market size by the revenue of the retail in specialised stores and wholesale businesses of sport goods is defined by using NACE codes 46492 (Wholesale of sports goods, excluding sports clothing and footwear) and 47641 (Retail sale of sporting equipment in specialised stores). There were 256 business entities in this market in 2014, of for 180 companies the above sport-related trade being the main or core business. In 2014, the retail and wholesale market size of sport goods in Estonia was worth 153 million euros.

In general 135 businesses earned profit in the above given market, indicating that their earned revenue excluding wages, utilities and other expenses necessary for day-to-day operations had a positive year-end balance. Out of these, 25 companies generated more than 90% of the total market revenue (see Table 4). The share of export sales was 21% (32.7 million euros), two thirds of which belonged to one company whose core activity is wholesale exports (Yuma Eesti AS). Hence, the main economic driving force of the market was and continues to be domestic consumption. If we use for the informal calculation, the 39% share of physically active population as consumer base for the specialised stores in sport goods, they would have spent on average 239 euros in 2014, or approximately 20 euros per month per person on sporting goods. This is roughly the same amount of money spent by a household member either on clothing and footwear or on communication services.

Table 4 Key 25 private sector enterprises covering 91% revenue of the of Retail and Wholesale of sporting goods sector (NACE codes 46492 and 47641) in Estonia in 2014.

Company	Revenue (1000 €)	EBITDA-%	Staff (n)
Sportland Eesti AS	33,957.0	4.4	389
Jalajälg AS	23,652.0	2.5	n/a
Yuma Eesti OÜ	21,600.4	−2.3	0
Rademar OÜ	16,269.1	−4.9	202
Hawaii Express OÜ	8159.6	5.5	87
Veloplus OÜ	3763.3	12.4	13
Matkasport OÜ	3607.1	3.1	32
Table Tennis Products OÜ	2656.2	4.9	14
Surfar OÜ	2483.8	6.3	20
A & Tova OÜ	2091.5	−0.6	12
Ekstreemspordi AS	1745.5	−5.2	25
AT Sport OÜ	1716.5	−2.1	16
Fysioline Eesti OÜ	946.4	18.3	6
Schotter AS	889.7	6.1	7
Spoleman OÜ	803.2	12.8	6
Ceranos Invest OÜ	763.0	20.1	2
Seart Production OÜ	731.4	17.2	8
Maratonsport OÜ	663.5	9.3	12
Spordipartner Trading OÜ	601.6	6.9	6
Qicraft Estonia OÜ	596.8	5.3	1
Benetec OÜ	581.1	32.0	10
Darf OÜ	579.9	16.0	5
Morganstein OÜ	541.1	0.2	0
Konger & Konger OÜ	536.9	13.0	12
Paasmar OÜ	520.1	−3.0	8

Source: Statistics Estonia (2015).

Conclusions

Currently the majority of the physically active adult population in Estonia is only infrequently buying sport-related services or joining a sport club. This means that the money allotted to leisure is used mainly for obtaining sporting goods or for joining mass sport events a couple of times a year. This state of affairs is understandable in the light of the recent history and the overall organisation of sport in Estonia. However, instead of investing time and money in the new equipment for exercising, the ageing and overworked population has begun to look for services and innovations that are related to human wellbeing. Politicians have acknowledged this topic and agreed on the national sport policy to promote both participation in physical activities and in the development of service economy in the sector of sport and leisure. ("Eesti spordipoliitika põhialused aastani 2030", 2015.)

As compared to 2014, a quarter of Estonia's corporate added value came from the service companies. Service sector generated added value of 2.9 billion euros, which is 8% higher than in 2013, and 45% higher than in 2010. Slightly more than a quarter of the added value of the sector came from information and communication companies, and a little over a fifth from real estate, professional, scientific and technical activities, as well as administrative and ancillary companies. In 2014, the average labour costs continued to rise. The labour cost per employee increased by 5.7% and hourly labour costs by 6.6% as compared to 2013. In the last few years, unemployment (7.5% equals to 52,900 persons) has been decreasing rapidly in Estonia and the share of the employed persons (66.5% equals to 653,300 persons) has been increasing. (Statistical Yearbook of Estonia, 2015.) Therefore, people work more, earn more and have got accustomed to developing and using various services. However, it seems that using sport and leisure services is still in a state of wavering because consumers do not know what a good bargain is.

Estonia has a small population. Small size has a predisposition for a fast reaction to external and internal dynamics. Therefore, current state of hesitancy and probing in the private sector of sport is expected to be temporary. Demographic trends will shape the future of the economy in sport sector. Depending on the age of the country's population in the near future it is crucial to understand the direction of the development of the essential goods and services. In Estonia the ratio of children compared to older population groups is declining, as well as the ratio of workers to retired people, and therefore there is an increasing pressure on those currently in employment to work more. As a result, health and working capacity related issues are becoming more prominent and provide a topic for discussion. A noticeable share of this discussion is being associated with the prevention and rehabilitation through physical exercise and efforts towards healthier lifestyle. This has resulted in the development of various exercise and physiotherapeutic based services that have been introduced to health and general practitioner (GP) centres.

Alas, GP practices should not be functional nodes in the national organisation of sport. For example family doctors are partners in health and wellbeing. Major part of the current sport organisations in Estonia are economically frugal, non-profit entities and hence conservative. The fast responding, customer oriented, commercially funded sport clubs comprise only a small share of the existing sport organisations in Estonia, and are mainly available in bigger towns. Taking into consideration the forecast that during the next decade Estonian population is drawn to the capital Tallinn and its suburbia, it will create a high potential for the development of the commercial services in sport and leisure. However, beyond commercial foundation the majority of sport clubs are going to remain and function with the help of the state and municipal subsidies, as they provide services for the youth. This may have both favourable and detrimental effects on the commercialisation of the services, depending on the direction of political agreements. The conclusion of the current overview describes the situation as well as the full of potential for developing innovative services in the domain of sport and recreation.

References

Eesti spordipoliitika põhialused aastani 2030. (2015). [The fundamentals of the Estonian sport policy until 2030]. *Riigi Teataja* III, 20.02.2015, 2. Retrieved October 12, 2016 from https://www.riigiteataja.ee/akt/320022015002

Eesti Spordiregister. (2017). [Estonian Sport Register]. Retrieved January 17, 2017 from https://www.spordiregister.ee/

Erakooli Seadus. (1998). [Private Schools Act]. *Riigi Teataja* I 1998, 57, 859. Retrieved October 12, 2016 from https://www.riigiteataja.ee/akt/13001161

European Commission. (2014). *Sport and physical activity*. Special Eurobarometer 412/Wave 80.2. Brussels, Belgium: D-G Education and Culture.

Huvikooli Seadus. (2006). [Hobby Schools Act]. *Riigi Teataja* I 2007, 4, 19. Retrieved October 12, 2016 from https://www.riigiteataja.ee/akt/13339594

Järva, R., Maidlo, J., & Teemägi, E. (2015). *Eesti spordi aastaraamat 1918–1940* [Estonian Sport Yearbook 1918–1940]. Tartu, Estonia: Eesti Spordiajaloo Selts.

Kurrik, J. (1879). *Turnimise raamat* [Book on gymnastics]. Retrieved June 2, 2016 from http://www.etera.ee/zoom/1437/view?page=5&p=separate&view=0,0,1984,3307

Mainla, E. (2012). 100 aastat esimestest olümpiamängusest Tallinnas [100 years from the first Olympic games in Tallinn]. *Sport & Muuseum*, (1). Retrieved January 30, 2017 from www.digar.ee/arhiiv/et/download/198064

Port, K., & Lusmägi, P. (2015). Sport clubs in Estonia. In C. Breuer, R. Hoeckman, S. Nagel, & H. van der Werff (Eds.), *Sport clubs in Europe* (pp. 131–146). Cham, Switzerland: Springer International Publishing Switzerland.

Raudsepp, L., Ööpik, V., & Lusmägi, P. (2013). Estonia. In K. Hallmann & K. Petry (Eds.), *Comparative sport development: Systems, participation and public policy* (pp. 33–45). New York, NY: Springer.

Spordiseadus. (2005). [Sports Act]. *Riigi Teataja* I 2005, 22, 148. Retrieved November 20, 2016 from https://www.riigiteataja.ee/akt/1013701

Statistical Yearbook of Estonia. (2015). Tallinn, Estonia: Statistikaamet.

Statistics Estonia. (2012). *Population and housing census 2011*. Retrieved January 11, 2017 from http://estonia.eu/about-estonia/country/population-census-2011.html

Statistics Estonia. (2015). Retrieved January 17, 2017 from http://www.stat.ee/requests-and-orders-for-information

Tali, M., Lusmagi, P., & Unt, E. (2016). Leisure time physical activity in Estonian population: Adherence to physical activity recommendations and relationships with overweight. *Arch Public Health, 74*(1), 36. https://doi.org/10.1186/s13690-016-0148-6.
The World Bank. (2017). *World development indicators*. Retrieved Februry 02, 2017 from http://databank.worldbank.org/data/reports.aspx?source=world development-indicators
Vabariigi Valitsuse tegevusprogramm 2015–2019. (2015). [Government Action Plan 2015–2019]. *Riigi Teataja* III, 03.06.2015, 6. Retrieved January 11, 2017 from https://www.riigiteataja.ee/akt/303062015006

FINLAND: The Importance of the Private Sport Sector Has Increased in the 2000s

Antti Laine

Selected country facts (in 2013)	
Capital	Helsinki
Geographical size (km^2)	338,440
Population (million)	5.43
GDP (euro per capita)	37,400
GDP (per capita in PPS)	113
Annual net earnings average (€)	29,654

Finnish Sport System

Finnish sport system can be described by sectors. The public sector is considered to cover primarily the state and municipalities. The private sector comprises those persons and organizations who are seeking financial gain by offering sport products and services. The voluntary sector, which is also known as the third sector or the civic sector or the non-profit sector, in turn, includes sport clubs and other voluntary organizations that organize physical activities for the citizens.

The voluntary sector has been the most important sector of the Finnish sport system since the beginning of modern sport. Its meaning has shrunk over the years, but Finnish leisure sports continue to rely largely upon voluntary civic activities. If the number of hours worked by volunteers in the sport organizations is multiplied by the average hourly fee for employees according to the national accounts, the imputed value of unpaid work in 2010 was approximately 1.16 billion euros (Lith, 2013, 26).

A. Laine (✉)
Faculty of Sport and Health Sciences, University of Jyväskylä, Jyväskylä, Finland
e-mail: antti.laine@jyu.fi

A. Laine, H. Vehmas (eds.), *The Private Sport Sector in Europe*, Sports Economics, Management and Policy 14, https://doi.org/10.1007/978-3-319-61310-9_7

In 2010 Finland's GDP (i.e., the added value created in the production of goods and services) was 180 billion euros at current prices (Statistics Finland, 2011).

Additionally, the role of the public sector is significant in Finland. The strong position of the public sector, as well as the division of labor between the public sector and the voluntary sector, is based on the first Sports Act, which entered into force at the beginning of 1980. The Sports Act was aimed to provide a situation where the municipalities, assisted by the state, were ordered to provide their inhabitants as comprehensive and affordable sport facilities as possible. The aim was to secure sport services for the entire population, regardless of their place of residence, gender, and socio-economic status. (Ilmanen, 2015.)

After an initial stage, the Sports Act has been revised several times. In fact, it has been nicknamed "a butterfly act," referring to the fact that the act has been revised relatively often in accordance with the respective social needs (Suomi, 2015). The currently valid Sports Act dates back to 2015 (since that latest reform it is called Act on the Promotion of Sports and Physical Activity). The Sports Act is a so-called framework law. It does not contain any detailed provisions, nor does it oblige the taking of practical measures, but rather determines the general principles. Priorities have fluctuated over the years, but the basic principle of division of labor between the public and the voluntary sector has remained mainly the same.

The voluntary sector is predominantly responsible for the local level of sport club work. Clubs have organized themselves upwards into regional and national organizations. Clubs and organizations are in many respects dependent on the support of the public sector. The municipalities are responsible for creating conditions for residents' physical activity, to take care of the construction and maintenance of sport facilities, facilitating physical activities of the residents and supporting civic activities. Municipalities support the activities of the sport clubs, both directly by grants and indirectly by providing low-cost sport facilities. The state, in turn, directs and assists national-level organizational activities. State control measures include, inter alia, the laws, regulations, and conditions for grants. The support of sport and physical activities organized by the state belongs to responsibility of the Ministry of Education and Culture. (E.g., Ilmanen, 2015; Suomi, 2015.)

The private sport sector offers its services for a fee on the market basis. The Sports Act really does not take a stand on the conditions of the private sector services. The continually expanding private service provision and the growing importance of the sport industry as a provider of jobs have been referred to, but entrepreneurship is mainly seen as one of the factors for a change of the operating environment, rather than an important producer of municipal sport services. While municipalities financially support sport clubs, they do not seem to be willing to subsidize private sport services through tax revenue so that residents would have access to them at a lower cost. However, due to growth in the need for services caused by the aging of the population, the municipal decision-makers have been called upon to come up with new solutions (Lith, 2013, 2–4). During the preparation of the Sports Act, which came into force in 2015, it was hoped that changes would come about in the act according to which private companies would also be accounted for as sport service providers (e.g., Koivisto, 2011, 11–15); however, no changes of this kind were made.

The Sports Act aims to promote (1) the opportunities for various population groups to engage in physical activity and exercise; (2) well-being and health of the population; (3) the maintenance and improvement of physical performance; (4) the growth and development of children and young people; (5) sport-related civic activities, including club activities; (6) top-level sport; (7) honesty and ethical principles of sport; and (8) the reduction of inequalities in sport. The implementation of this aim is based on equality, non-discrimination, community, multiculturalism, healthy lifestyles, as well as respect for the environment and sustainable development. (Liikuntalaki 390/2015.)

In the Finnish sport system, the roles of the state and municipalities as the financier of activities are significant. When examining the public funding, it is important to note that Finnish gambling is based on the system of exclusive rights. The responsibility for the operation belongs to Veikkaus Oy, which is wholly owned by the Finnish state and is the main financier of the Finnish sport system. In 2014, sport was supported with 147.4 million euros from the lottery funds allocated by the Ministry of Education and Culture, which was 27.3% of the total number of shared lottery funds (540.8 MEUR) (Liikuntatoimi tilastojen valossa, 2016). If additional funding from the budget funds within the framework of state finances in funding is not granted, the funding allocated to sport by the state is composed almost entirely of lottery funds.

From the point of view of this article, it is important to emphasize that sport clubs operating as limited companies have no access to club support granted from lottery funds. However, they have the possibility to make cooperation agreements directly with Veikkaus Oy. Veikkaus has the exclusive right to market betting games in Finland, and because of that sport clubs cannot advertise international betting companies, for example.

The Significance of the Private Sport Sector Increases

Finnish society prospered in the 1970s and 1980s, which increased the service provision of municipal sport administration to record proportions. Even in the late 1980s, the continued growth in the Finnish economy seemed to secure the remaining service provision at a high level. However, in the early 1990s, Finland went into economic recession, and because of the ensuing government austerity policy the municipal sport services were also forced to make cutbacks. Along with the recession, the Keynesian economic policy influencing Finland after World War II was replaced by neoliberalism. While Keynesianism had stressed the controlling share of the state and the government in the national economy, according to the neoliberal economic thinking, the services provided by the public administration had to be reduced, thus making room for market-based service production in the private sector. When Finland recovered from the economic recession of the 1990s, the position of the public sector in the production of sport services strengthened again until 2008, when the downturn staggered the economy of the whole Western world. As a result, the state and municipal economy have been increasingly squeezed, which has led to a major change in the production of sport services. The main trend has been that the private sector has increased its share in the production of services. (See Ilmanen, 2015.)

According to the national sport survey the share of adult exercisers (19–65 years old) using private sport facilities rose during the first decade of the 2000s from 4 to 15% ("Kansallinen liikuntatutkimus 2009–2010", 2010, 45). Despite the economic downturn, the sport industry has been in a strong upward trend for many years (Kosonen, 2014, 5–7). The number of sport industry companies and personnel employed by them increased clearly between 2002 and 2011. In 2002 there were 3952 companies in the sport sector in Finland employing 11,853 people. In 2011, the corresponding figures were 5317 companies and 17,039 employees. (Gholamzadeh Fasanov, 2016, 79–83[1].) It seems that the production of sport services is to a large extent independent of short-term cyclical fluctuations. Some explanations are at least the changes in the leisure consumption structure, tax-free sport vouchers, and a positive trend in consumer purchasing power. Sport vouchers are payment tools exempt from VAT that employers can obtain for their employees. The precondition for the voucher system, based on the Income Tax Act, is that the benefits must be organized by the employer and offered to the entire staff. (Lith, 2013, 2, 10.) Many employers feel that sport vouchers are more cost-effective than investing in their own sport facilities and simpler to operate than drafting bilateral agreements with service providers. From the employee's point of view, the important benefit of the vouchers is that they provide variety in the options for engaging in physical activities.

The positions of the private sector have also been reinforced by the changes in the nature of voluntary activities. Voluntary work has obtained market-based and consumer-like features. Customer-oriented thinking has started to become more common. People do not commit to their activities in the same manner as before. The services previously produced by volunteers are currently settled by payments.

Directly Sport-Related Business Fields

The private sport sector is complex and fragmented. Definition of the sector is difficult, because the sport industry companies do not constitute a coherent and clearly demarcated sector (Koivisto, 2010, 8). Its characteristics take shape by taking advantage of the Finnish equivalent (TOL 2008) of the *Statistical classification of economic activities in the European Community* (NACE Rev. 2, 2008). Classifications of economic activities are used as the data collection and description framework for the statistics describing economic activities. TOL 2008 includes ten directly sport-related classes. Table 1 summarizes the key figures in those classes in 2013. The source used is Enterprises by Industry 2013–2015 section in Structural Business and Financial Statement Statistics (Statistics Finland, 2016).

[1]The classification has been made in a slightly different way than in this article, so the figures are not comparable with the figures for 2013 presented in the article.

Table 1 Directly sport-related business fields in Finland in 2013.

Business field	NACE code	Companies (n)	Staff (n)	Revenue (1000 €)	Revenue/ Company (1000 €)	Av. salary (1000 €)
Retail sale of sport equipment and bicycles	47641	931	3857	1,030,778	1107.2	25.8
Wholesale of sport goods	46493	365	1100	549,008	1504.1	39.2
Operation of sport facilities	93110	605	2731	285,029	471.1	27.4
Other sport activities	93190	1747	2016	240,039	137.4	28.2
Manufacture of sport goods	32300	136	847	164,487	1209.5	36.6
Fitness facilities	93130	353	1677	162,234	459.6	25.1
Skiing centre activities	93291	63	870	82,466	1309.0	25.7
Sport and recreation education	85510	594	895	67,711	114.0	17.9
Activities of sport clubs	93120	148	548	43,464	293.7	32.5
Renting and leasing of sporting goods	77210	71	87	12,167	171.4	23.7
Total		**5013**	**14,628**	**2,637,383**	**526.1**	**27.7**

Source: Statistics Finland (2016).

A total of 5013 companies operated and 14,628 people were employed in those business fields in 2013. The total revenue of the fields was approximately 2.64 billion euros. The annual average gross earnings of employees working in the fields (EUR 27,000) were well below the average of Finnish employees. (Table 1.) According to Statistics Finland's Structure of Earnings statistics in 2013, Finnish employees' average gross earnings were 39,400 euros per year (Statistics Finland, 2014).

When making a comparison based on the Structural Business and Financial Statement Statistics, a few things should be kept in mind. First of all, some of the companies operate in several fields but are placed in only one class. For example, the *operation of sport facilities* and *activities of sport clubs* are often run within a single company. Clubs may own their premises, in this sense sport facilities, and be in charge of running them as well as other club activities. The statistics are mainly based on the company's own declaration of what field its economic activity is primarily focused upon. Secondly, not all companies are placed in the "right" business field. For example, one of the major fitness centers is placed in the class *activities of sport clubs*, and one of the major sport clubs is placed in a retail sub-category unrelated to sport. Some of the companies classified in the sport sector, in turn, conduct their business predominantly outside of the sport sector.

Despite such factors, Table 1 gives a fairly good picture of the key financial figures of the directly sport-related business fields. However, they do not reveal the magnitude of business for the entire sport sector, as there are numerous companies classified into other business fields but operating partly in the sport sector. These include manufacturers of sport clothes and sport footwear, sport-related products offered by the food and beverage industry, sport-related financial and insurance operations, as well as companies engaged in sport communications. Since the vast majority of businesses in such sectors are directed elsewhere and not just to the sport industry, they have not been taken into account in the review of the statistical key figures of the sport sector based on the economic activities.

In Finland, there are no so-called satellite accounts which could collect statistics specifically on the economic and employment effects of sport, but the information may be collected from other statistics (HE 190/2014 vp, 13). On the basis of the report of the Ministry of Economic Affairs and Employment published in 2014, the revenue from sport businesses is estimated to be at least 5.5 billion euros. The figure consists of the above-presented directly sport-related business fields, although they are somewhat more broadly defined (€2.93 bn)[2], of diverse equine sector entities (€1.00 bn), Veikkaus sport bets (€0.40 bn), communication, entertainment and the lifestyle sector (€0.25 bn), the wellness and health services sector (€0.50 bn), the sport tourism sector (€0.12 bn), and other individual companies manufacturing products for the sport industry (€0.40 bn). As part of the wellness and health sector is included in directly sport-related business fields, the overall estimates have been rounded 0.1 billion downwards. (Kosonen, 2014, 7–14.) In 2014 Finland's GDP was 205 billion euros at current prices (Statistics Finland, 2015).

Next, I will look in greater detail at four of the directly sport-related business fields. I have chosen to review the biggest fields in terms of revenue, namely *retail sale of sport equipment and bicycles* (NACE code 47641) and *wholesale of sport goods* (NACE 46493), as well as one very profitable business field on the basis of the EBITDA-%[3] of the field's largest companies (NACE 93130 / *fitness facilities*) and one poorly profitable business field (NACE 93120 / *activities of sport clubs*).

Sporting Goods Retail and Wholesale Trade

In examining the Finnish private sport sector, special attention must be directed to the sporting goods group Amer Sports Corporation. The company owns a number of global consumer brands, and in terms of foreign sales it is a major Finnish company

---

[2] *Retail sale of boats and boating accessories* (NACE code 47642) is included, as well as *amusement and recreation activities with no existing category* (NACE 93299).

[3] EBITDA shows how much of the company's revenue remains uncovered after the reduction of the company's operating costs (EBITDA-% = 100 × EBITDA/revenue). EBITDA-% = EBITDA margin.

conducting consumer business. The airline Finnair and gaming company Supercell are in the same size range (see Saarinen, 2015).

Amer Sports Corporation's roots are in a tobacco factory founded in 1950. Before focusing on sport, the company had been working in a number of other business areas. It has, inter alia, published books, imported cars, and operated as a shipowner. The company acquired its first sport brand in the mid-1970s and the sport business unit was founded in 1986. This was followed by a series of major acquisitions made every five years (Wilson 1989, Atomic 1994 and Suunto 1999). In 2004, the company sold its tobacco business to Philip Morris. At the same time, a turnaround was sealed: the company changed from a tobacco manufacturer to a trader of sport products. (See Amer Sports, 2016.)

Along with abandonment of the tobacco business, the company's name was changed from Amer Group to Amer Sports. The following year (2005) the company made a major acquisition when it acquired Salomon and a few other brands from Adidas for 485 million euros. At the same time, Amer expanded its operations from sport to outdoor activities. The price was kept high, but the deal proved to be profitable. Today, Salomon is the main brand of Amer Sports. Other significant brands are Atomic, Arc'teryx, Mavic, Precor, Suunto, and Wilson. (See Amer Sports, 2016.)

The main product categories of Amer Sports are now clothing and footwear. The company's products are sold around the world each year for more than two billion euros. Amer Sports' revenue and operating profit have grown steadily since 2009. At that time, revenue totaled 1.5 billion euros and operating profit 44 million euros. In 2015, the corresponding figures were 2.5 billion and 212 million euros. Amer Sports' center of gravity is sporting goods wholesale, but in recent years direct consumer sales have also grown rapidly, due to the enlargement of the store chain and the addition of e-commerce. (Amer Sports, 2015.)

About half of Amer Sports' share ownership is in Finland, and the company's headquarters is located in Helsinki, the capital of Finland. However, considering the size of the company, the company's business in its home country is minor. For example, out of the company's approximately 8000 employees, only slightly less than 500 work in Finland, and the share of Finland's sales is just over 1%. Suunto, which manufactures sport instruments (e.g., heart rate monitors and wrist computers) is the only one of the main brands that was born in Finland. (Amer Sports, 2015.)

Amer Sports Corporation is a special case among the Finnish companies engaged in sporting goods wholesale and retail trade. Its parent company's main business is registered as *activities of holding companies* (NACE 64200). The parent company's revenue is not included in the above-presented report of the Ministry of Economic Affairs and Employment (see Kosonen, 2014). This is logical to the extent that the parent company owns dozens of companies residing in different parts of the world.

The business field of Amer Sports International Oy, one of the companies operating under the parent company, is registered as a wholesale trader (NACE 46493), and Amer Sports Suomi Oy is registered as a manufacturer of sport goods (NACE 32300). Only a small part of the total revenue of the parent company is focused on these two companies, which should be considered when making business field comparisons. In terms of its revenue, for example, Amer Sports International Oy does not reach the ranks of the biggest Finnish companies that are engaged in the wholesale and retail trade in the sport field. (See Suomen Asiakastieto, 2016.)

In 2013, there were 931 companies in Finland engaged in the *retail sale of sport equipment and bicycles* business, with a total revenue of 1.03 billion euros. The number of staff employed by the companies was by far the largest of the directly sport-related business fields, reaching 3857 people. In 2013, the number of companies in the *wholesale of sport goods* was 365, and their combined revenue 549 million euros. (Table 1; Statistics Finland, 2016.) Table 2 lists Finland's biggest sporting goods retail and wholesale trade companies by revenue on the basis of the 2013 financial statements (Suomen Asiakastieto, 2016). In addition to the revenue, the table shows the EBITDA-% and the number of employees of the companies.

Table 2 The biggest retail sale of sport equipment and bicycles (NACE code 47641) and wholesale of sport goods (NACE code 46493) companies by revenue in Finland in 2013.

Company	NACE code	Revenue (1000 €)	EBITDA-%	Staff (n)
Intersport Finland Oy	46493	190,439	6.0	242
Stadium Oy	47641	77,779	6.5	380
Oy Sultrade Ltd	46493	39,821	3.4	76
SGN Sportia Oy	46493	34,814	0.4	11
Adidas Suomi Oy	46493	33,758	2.7	n/a
Oy Finn-Tack Ltd	46493	30,886	4.6	31
Reebok-CCM Hockey Oy	46493	30,211	−8.7	15
After Sports Oy	47641	26,480	−10.5	228
Oy Patrol Ab	46493	24,673	7.3	23
Partioaitta	47641	22,790	6.9	169
Halti Oy	46493	22,545	−2.0	51
Normark Logistics Europe Oy	46493	21,944	2.7	n/a

Source: Suomen Asiakastieto (2016).

Intersport Finland and SGN Sportia are companies serving the retailers of the chains, which are among other things responsible for the management, marketing, and joint purchasing of the chains. The retailers of the chains are independent companies. At the end of 2016, there were 57 Intersport and 54 Sportia stores in Finland. Intersport Finland is also responsible for the Budget Sport chain, encompassing ten stores across Finland. Stadium traders are not independent companies. At the end of 2016, there were 26 Stadium stores in Finland.

Intersport is a big international company (the parent company is Intersport International Corporation), and Stadium is a Nordic company originally from Sweden. In 2014, a new large Nordic player arrived on the Finnish sport retail market, when the first store of Norwegian XXL Sports & Outdoor Group was opened in Finland. The company's revenue in Finland in the first year of operation was already 34.9 million euros (Suomen Asiakastieto, 2016), although it opened its first shop only in April and the other three at the end of the year. The volumes of the stores and the sales have increased rapidly thereafter. In 2015, the company's revenue in Finland amounted to more than 90 million euros (EBITDA-% 2.3). At the end of 2016, the company had 13 stores in Finland. In terms of revenue, XXL Sports & Outdoor is Scandinavia's largest sporting goods retailer. In 2015, the entire Group's revenue amounted to approximately 714 million euros (EBITDA-% 11.2). As of the end of 2016, there were 31 stores in its country of origin, Norway, and in Sweden 21 stores. The stores are large department stores averaging about 3900 square meters in size, and in addition, the company has invested heavily in the online store. (About XXL, 2016; XXL ASA Annual Report, 2015.) XXL Sports & Outdoor Group's arrival in Finland caused competition in the sport retail market to tighten significantly, which should be considered in the examination of the 2013 data (Table 2). An example of this is After-Sports Oy, which is a subsidiary of the short-term owners of long-term loss-making Top Sport store chain, acquired at the company's reorganization in 2013. Even After-Sports Oy failed to make Top Sport profitable and sold it. At the end of 2016, Top Sport was acquired by L-Fashion Group Oy.

Fitness Facilities

The fitness center business has grown strongly in recent years in Finland. In 2007, the industry classification for *fitness facilities* (NACE 93130) covered 179 companies, with a total revenue of 69.5 million euros. At the time, the companies employed 829 people. By 2015, the number of companies had more than doubled (426) and their revenue almost tripled to 197.7 million euros. The number of employees in companies increased during this period of time by nearly one thousand (1807). (Statistics Finland, 2013, 2016.) The data for 2007–2015 has been summarized in Table 3.

Table 3 Fitness facilities (NACE code 93130) in Finland in 2007–2015.

Year	Companies (n)	Staff (n)	Revenue (1000 €)
2007	179	829	69,485
2008	219	1045	91,447
2009	267	1244	114,461
2010	285	1368	122,202
2011	314	1507	134,634
2012	337	1487	148,365
2013	353	1677	162,234
2014	388	1631	184,043
2015	426	1807	197,705

Sources: Statistics Finland (2013; 2016).

In the 2000s, the number of fitness center users has more than tripled (Lith, 2013, 2). Growing use of the tax-free sport voucher system has been especially beneficial to fitness centers. The growth can also be explained by the diversification in the range of services and by the fact that membership system become common in the early 2000s.

In recent years, growth has been concentrated among the industry's biggest players. In 2014, a giant was born in the Finnish market, as the major Nordic companies, Swedish-owned Elixia and Danish-owned Sats, merged. With the merger, they are part of the Health & Fitness Nordic Group, which is owned by Nordic private equity investors. Until the merger, Sats had made heavy losses in the Finnish market. From its founding year in 2003, it did not make a profit in any single year. The losses that it managed to accumulate over ten years amounted to around 24 million euros. On the other hand, the profitability of Elixia in the Finnish market was very good. (Ojanen, 2014.) In Sweden the situation before the merger was the exact opposite: Elixia was much smaller and unprofitable, while Sats was larger and more profitable (Laine, 2015). At present, the corporate symbol of the company used in Finland is Elixia and in Sweden Sats.

Finland's biggest *fitness facilities* (limited companies) by revenue in 2013 are listed in Table 4. The staff amounts are not comparable in all respects, as the reporting practice of part-time and fixed-term employees varies. Some of the companies listed in the table are registered to NACE classes *operation of sport facilities* (93110) and *activities of sport clubs* (93120), but as significant players in the fitness industry, they have been taken into consideration. Accordingly, one company has been excluded (Roque Fitness Europe Oy), because it is focusing on the manufacture and sale of fitness equipment. Subsidiaries have not been considered. For example, the figures of GoGo Liikuntakeskus Oy do not include the GoGo Express fitness centers, as they belong to a different company (GoGo Express Oy).

Table 4 The biggest fitness facilities by revenue in Finland in 2013.

Company	NACE code	Offices (n)	Revenue (1000 €)	EBITDA-%	Staff (n)
Oy Elixia Finland Ab	93130	15	28,690	29.6	204
Fysioline Fressi Oy	93130	12	12.910	11.4	354
Sats Finland	93110	11	10,178	−11.7	88
Kuntokumppanit Oy	93130	5	5006	1.7	45
GoGo Liikuntakeskus Oy	93120	3	2828	26.6	24
Forever Helsinki Oy	93130	3	2744	21.4	33
Hukka Oy	93110	1	2508	20.2	n/a
Forever Varisto Oy	93130	1	2354	30	23
Ab Sports Gym Wasa Oy	93130	1	2254	19	35

Sources: Suomen Asiakastieto (2016); office information from companies' websites.

The profitability of several fitness centers has been excellent in recent years (Table 4). Revenue of the companies has increased significantly. For example, in 2012 the average company's revenue grew by 10% and in the following year by 12.5%. In the economic activity comparison, the figures are in a class of their own, as the median growth of Finnish companies in 2013 increased by only a half per cent. (Ojanen, 2014.)

After the merger of Sats and Elixia the figures listed in Table 4 changed. Under the merger, Sats sold four offices to a Finnish-owned Fysioline Fressi Oy. Fysioline Fressi Oy's revenue has risen since then considerably: in 2015 it was already 19.5 million euros (Lähteenmäki, 2017). At the end of 2016, the merged Sats Elixia had 23 offices in six different cities, and Fysioline Fressi Oy had 18 offices in ten different cities. The activities of both are heavily concentrated in the metropolitan area, where at the end of 2016 Sats Elixia had 16 offices, and Fressi had seven offices. Out of the offices of Kuntokumppanit Oy (Motivus), in turn, only one is located outside of Helsinki. Focusing on the metropolitan area is quite natural, since out of about 5.5 million inhabitants in Finland, over a fifth is currently residing in the metropolitan area (Helsinki, Espoo, and Vantaa).

Forever can be found in Table 4 in several places, as the centers of Forever's parent company (FD-Group) are legally independent companies. The business operations of some of the companies in the table are not limited to mere fitness center activities. For example, Liikuntakeskus Hukka Oy located in Oulu offers in addition sport facilities targeted for practicing ball and racquet sports. A similar operator is also Esport, located in the metropolitan area, which advertises itself as the largest indoor sport center in the Nordic countries. Its fitness centers (Esport Fitness and Esport Bristol) are some of the largest in Finland. However, the financial data of Esport is not available and therefore not included in the table.

In recent years, the provision of fitness centers has diversified significantly in Finland. Alongside the big chains with a comprehensive range of services, there are now plenty of more affordable, so-called unmanned gyms that are always open. The largest such operator is the Fitness24Seven chain, which has grown rapidly in popularity (see Lähteenmäki, 2017). Fitness24Seven, originally from Sweden, opened its first gym in Finland in 2012. Even in 2013 the company's revenue in Finland was less than a million euros, and operation suffered from heavy losses (EBITDA-% −21.6), but since then numbers have turned to strong growth. In 2014, revenue amounted to 2.9 million euros, and the EBITDA-% was 19.3. In 2015, the corresponding figures were 5.1 million and 15.5%. (Suomen Asiakastieto, 2016.) At the end of 2016, there were 38 Fitness24Seven gyms in Finland, of which exactly half (19) were located in the metropolitan area.

Sport Clubs Operating as Limited Companies

Elite sport has globally commercialized and professionalized. Organizing the activities in the associated form has been found difficult, which is why part of the elite sport clubs have incorporated their operations. During the season that ended in

2016, all of the Finnish highest league men's ice hockey teams (15) and highest league men's football teams except one (11/12) were limited companies. With few exceptions, the men's second highest league ice hockey (10/12) and football teams (9/10) were also limited companies, but otherwise the company form was uncommon even in elite sport. For example, out of all men's basketball, handball, volleyball, baseball, floorball and bandy highest league teams, only six were limited companies. No women's highest league team was a limited company.

In 2013, 148 companies were placed in the industry classification to class *activities of sport clubs* (NACE 93120) in Finland (Table 1; Statistics Finland, 2016). Not all companies in that class are sport clubs in the truest sense of the word, but among them are also several companies that would belong to some other class of economic activity (e.g., fitness centers, ski centers, and sport facilities). In any case, the total number of clubs shows that only a small number of sport clubs are operated as commercial companies, as according to different estimates, there are around 7000–9000 active sport clubs in Finland. The vast majority of sport clubs are registered non-profit organizations who enjoy broad tax exemption. The activities of these should not focus on business, and they are not allowed to produce economic benefit for those involved, for example dividends or a larger than reasonable salary. There are about 6000–7000 sport clubs within the municipal grant system in Finland (HE 190/2014 vp 11).

In Finland, the markets for running sport club activities aimed at financial gains are narrow. With the exception of men's highest league ice hockey and football, average attendance figures are modest, and the income derived from media rights is marginal. In addition, sponsor incomes are tight. The marching order of the two most popular sports in Finland are distinct, and at the same time exceptional in the whole of Europe: based on the average attendance figures, the amount of television audience and incomes from media rights, football is not the sport moving masses the most. The most followed sport in Finland throughout the year is clearly ice hockey (see Laine, 2011, 120–132). For example, the average attendance of the men's highest league (for the regular season that ended in 2016) in ice hockey were 4250 (Liiga, 2016) and in football 2551 (Kuntopuntari, 2016).

The men's highest league in hockey is Finland's only sport league, which can be considered a pure professional league. In the season that ended in 2016, the annual average salary of the players, according to Jarmo Saarela, Executive Director of Suomen jääkiekkoilijat ry, was 76,000 euros (Saarela, personal communication December 7, 2016). The previous salary survey of the Finnish Football Players Association is from the year 2011. According to Markus Juhola, Executive Director of the Association, the annual average salary of the highest football league at the time was about 17,500 euros. The share of full-time players was about 75%. (Juhola, personal communication December 7, 2016.) In other sports the number of professionals at the national level is small.

Next, I will look at the profitability of Finnish sport clubs, using the key financial figures for the men's highest league hockey teams as a case-by-case example. The men's highest hockey league (Liiga) is Finland's most important sport brand. The activities of the league are maintained by Jääkiekon SM-Liiga Oy. There are currently 15 teams playing in the league, each of which had to acquire a league share.

In 2009, the price of one share was 1.6 million euros (SM-liiga, 2009). The league is closed; it is not possible to drop out of it to a lower level.

During the 2012–2013 season, the league had 14 teams. One of those operated as an association (HPK incorporated its operations in 2015) and the business activities of one were part of the managing company's business (Jokerit/Helsinki Halli Oy). Table 5 shows the revenue, the EBITDA-%, and the staff of the clubs, with the exception of HPK and Jokerit, according to the financial statements of 2013 (Suomen Asiakastieto, 2016). The staff numbers are not comparable in all respects, as the reporting practice of part-time and fixed-term employees in the financial reporting varies.

Table 5 Finnish Liiga ice hockey clubs revenue, EBITDA-% and staff in 2013.

Company	NACE code	Revenue (1000 €)	EBITDA-%	Staff (n)
Oy HIFK-Hockey Ab	93190	9098	4.0	54
Oulun Kärpät Oy	47114	8180	3.9	64
Rauman Lukko Oy	93120	8162	−10.9	80
JYP Jyväskylä Oy	93120	7424	4.1	53
Kalpa Hockey Oy	93120	7281	−7.9	66
Lahden Pelicans Oy	93120	6659	−0.6	84
HC Ässät Pori Oy	93190	6494	6.7	107
Tamhockey Oy (Tappara)	93190	6352	0.7	49
HC TPS Turku Oy	93120	5073	−3.5	49
Ilves Hockey Oy	93120	4876	−0.1	104
Liiga-Saipa Oy	93120	4829	17.0	111
Jääkiekko Espoo Oy (Blues)	93120	4261	−30.7	45

Source: Suomen Asiakastieto (2016).

League clubs run significant revenues, but operating profitability is weak. In 2013, the revenue of the clubs recorded in the table ranged between 4.3 and 9.1 million euros. The EBITDA-% of six clubs was positive and that of six clubs was negative. Some of the clubs suffered heavy financial losses. (Table 5.) There are annual variations in the totals; for example, Porin Ässat won the Finnish championship in the 2012–2013 season, which contributed significantly to HC Ässät Pori Oy's financial result (EBITDA-% 6.7). In 2014, HC Pori Ässät Oy's EBITDA-% was 2.3 positive and in 2015, 5.6 negative. (Suomen Asiakastieto, 2016.) Financial losses are common for the league's clubs.

Finnish public service broadcaster YLE published a report in 2016 on the economy of the league's clubs. Based on the report, the majority of the clubs suffer losses one year after another. They remain alive only because their owners or background actors support the operation financially. Only a small number of clubs are profitable. For example, during the 2013–2014 season the total loss for the teams was about 8.2 million euros, and during the 2014–2015 season the loss was more than six million euros. Out of 14 clubs involved in the report, the operation of only three clubs was truly profitable. (Hänninen & Kössö, 2016.)

For some of the clubs, the net result, that is the result from ordinary operations, was a loss year after year. One of these is Rauman Lukko, which is from the small town of Rauma with about 40,000 inhabitants. The net loss of Rauman Lukko Oy, the club's background company during 2011–2015, was a total of 6.34 million euros (Kössö, 2016). The club, however, has a financially strong owner, whose group contribution helps to achieve a positive balance sheet each year. Between 2011 and 2015, the annual group contribution received by Rauman Lukko ranged between 0.8 and 1.6 million euros and the total amount was 6.7 million euros (Kössö, 2016). Tampereen Ilves (Ilves Hockey Oy) in turn last had a positive result in 2008 and has since amassed a cumulative loss of over four million euros. Losses have been covered by investing more capital, and the majority owner has given the club an interest-free loan. (Elo & Rajala, 2016.)

The most followed sport in Finland is ice hockey. The men's highest ice hockey league is the only truly professional sport league in the country. League clubs run significant revenues, but in many clubs operating profitability is weak. Photo from a playoff game between Espoo Blues and Rauman Lukko in March 26, 2014. Espoo Blues has gone bankrupt since that and Rauman Lukko has made net losses year after year. *Photo: Jussi Eskola.*

Not all clubs have been able to solve their financial problems. Out of the clubs in Table 5, Jääkiekko Espoo Oy, the background company of Espoo Blues, went bankrupt at the end of the 2015–2016 season and operation of the club ended along with it. Fresh bankruptcies can also be found in other of the men's highest league team sports. For example, in 2015 bankruptcy was applied for by football (MyPa) and basketball clubs (Namika Lahti) that played in the men's highest league during the preceding season.

The loss-making activities of Jokerit (Jokerit Hockey Club Oy) from Helsinki is in its own class. Jokerit moved in 2014 from the highest league of Finnish ice hockey to the multinational Russian highest league, KHL (Kontinental Hockey League). Jokerit is one of the seven foreign teams of KHL. The other 22 are Russian.

Before moving to KHL, the event activities for the home arena of Jokerit (Helsinki Halli Oy), combined with the activities of the hockey team Jokerit, were strongly loss-making throughout the 2000s. The aggregate net loss in the 2000–2012 period was approximately 28 million euros. The bulk of the losses were made by the hockey team. (Rajala & Vanhanen, 2013.) In 2013 the team's home arena was sold to Arena Events Oy, which a few months later acquired 49% of the shares of Jokerit Hockey Club Oy. Arena Events is owned by the Finnish-Russian Rotenberg family and Russian billionaire Gennady Timchenko, who also has Finnish citizenship. In connection with the transaction, it was announced that Jokerit would move to play in KHL as of the 2014–2015 season. (Hakola, 2013.)

KHL has sought to expand to the west, and Jokerit has been seen as an important partner. This has required the new owners to make large financial investments. The revenue of Jokerit has not substantially increased compared to the times in the Finnish league, but the costs have soared and the equation has been economically unsustainable. Income has not even been sufficient for salaries. During the first two seasons in KHL, the losses amounted to as much as 28.8 million euros. The investment worth more than ten million euros in equity was rapidly spent to cover the losses. It has been possible to continue the loss-making activities only with the help of a capital loan of 21.4 million euros. (Rajala, 2016.)

However, it should be pointed out that the magnitude of Jokerit's economic losses is an exceptional case in the Finnish team sport business. It should equally be stressed that there are a number of financially healthy Finnish sport clubs. Some of the clubs have even been able to pay dividends to their shareholders. However, this is rare, which in turn is telling of the essential nature of the sport clubs business in Finland: investors do not expect a return on capital, and the avoidance of financial losses is often considered an acceptable financial statement.

Conclusions

The private sport sector has become a major player in Finland. Out of the sport service providers, it is the private companies that have increased their market share the most. For example, according to the National Sport Survey 2009–2010, 15% of adults (19–65 year olds) engaged in fitness activities in private companies. This proportion was already higher than those engaged in sport clubs (14%). Compared to 2005–2006, the relative growth in the number of people exercising in private companies was almost 80%. In the same period of time, sport clubs had increased their relative popularity by around 4%. ("Kansallinen liikuntatutkimus 2009–2010",

2010, 45.) More recent data are not available, but it is likely that private companies have increased their share further, and the same trend is likely to continue in the coming years. However, this is significantly affected by how the purchasing power of consumers is changing. Additionally, the lifestyle choices made by people have a key effect. Currently, there is a rampant fitness boom, but an adverse reaction to this trend can be expected.

The Finnish sport industry is moving from the production of goods towards the production of services (Gholamzadeh Fasanov, 2016, 140–141). Lucrative business based on customer encounters requires the focus of a sufficient amount of the population to a sufficiently small area. In Finland, business activities in the sport sector focus on the Helsinki Metropolitan Area and other regional centers, which lead to regional segregation. In the declining out-migration areas, opportunities to run businesses are weak.

The business field analysis of sporting goods trade and fitness facilities shows that large foreign companies have taken over the market in Finland. On the other hand, looking at the matter more broadly, the sport sector is characterized by the nature of small business. In SSS, about half of companies in the sector had no paid staff, and nearly 30% employed fewer than two persons (Lith, 2013, 19).

Out of the business fields introduced in this article, fitness facilities have in recent years been economically profitable. Overall, the profitability of the companies in the sport sector – in spite of the positive growth in demand and revenue – however, is quite weak, when the profitability is measured by relating the companies operating profit to the operating income (Lith, 2013, 64–72). The sector has grown rapidly, and the business commencement threshold has been especially low in small businesses. In many of such companies operational profitability has not been achieved. The sport clubs who have incorporated their operation are their own story, many of which are heavily loss-making. This reflects the fact that the Finnish market is still quite limited for professional sport.

References

About XXL. (2016). Our business. Retrieved December 10, 2016 from http://www.xxlasa.com/corporate/about/our-business/

Amer Sports. (2015). *Financial review*. Retrieved November 24, 2016 from https://s3-eu-west-1.amazonaws.com/amersports/uploads/20160621134135/amer-sports-financial-review-2015.pdf

Amer Sports. (2016). Our history. Retrieved November 24, 2016 from https://www.amersports.com/about-us/our-business/our-history/

Elo, E., & Rajala, A. (2016). Liigassa jälleen kriisijoukkue - tilintarkastaja epäilee kykyä jatkaa toimintaa [Crisis team again in the League – The auditor has doubts regarding the ability to continue operations]. *Kauppalehti* November 17, 2016. Retrieved December 4, 2016 from http://www.kauppalehti.fi/uutiset/liigassa-jalleen-kriisijoukkue-tilintarkastaja-epailee-kykya-jatkaa-toimintaa/Q9rVVSYE

Gholamzadeh Fasanov, H. (2016). *Sport as an industry in Finland. Exploring the economic significance, contributions, and development of the sport sector as an industry* (PhD dissertation). University of Jyväskylä. Studies in Sport, Physical Education and Health 240.

Hakola, T. (2013). Harkimo myi 49 prosenttia Jokereista – KHL-siirto varmistui [Harkimo sold 49 per cent of Jokerit – switch to KHL confirmed]. *Helsingin Sanomat* October 20, 2013. Retrieved December 4, 2016 from http://www.hs.fi/urheilu/art-2000002684805.html

HE 190/2014 vp. *Hallituksen esitys eduskunnalle liikuntalaiksi* [Government proposal to Parliament for a Sports Act]. Retrieved October 14, 2016 from http://www.finlex.fi/fi/esitykset/he/2014/20140190.pdf

Hänninen, J., & Kössö, T. (2016). Laaja selvitys paljastaa SM-liigaseurojen surkean tilan – paikoin surkuhupaisaa huseeraamista [An extensive report reveals the sorry state of the SM-league clubs – at times, it's not clear whether to laugh or cry]. *Yle* March, 1, 2016. Retrieved December 4, 2016 from http://yle.fi/urheilu/3-8706628

Ilmanen, K. (2015). Liikuntapalvelujen muutos 1800-luvun lopulta 2000-luvulle [The change of sport services from the end of 19th century to 21st century]. In H. Itkonen & A. Laine (Eds.), *Liikunta yhteiskunnallisena ilmiönä* (pp. 19–37.) University of Jyväskylä. Department of Sport Sciences. Studies 1/2015.

Kansallinen liikuntatutkimus 2009–2010. (2010). [National sport survey 2009–2010]. SLU:n julkaisusarja 6/2010. Helsinki, Finland: SLU.

Koivisto, N. (2010). *Liikunta-alan yrittäjyyden kehittämisstrategia 2020* [The Development Strategy 2020 for sports industry entrepreneurship]. Helsinki, Finland: Diges ry.

Koivisto, N. (2011). *Liikunta-alan yrittäjyyden toimenpideohjelma 2020* [Operational Programme 2020 for the sports industry entrepreneurship]. Helsinki, Finland: Diges ry.

Kosonen, H. (2014). *Liikuntaliiketoiminnan ekosysteemin muutokset* [Changes in the sports business ecosystem]. Tem raportteja 20/2014.

Kuntopuntari. (2016). Veikkausliigan yleisömäärät 2016 [Veikkausliiga attendance 2016]. Retrieved November 27, 2016 from https://kuntopuntari.wordpress.com/2016/04/18/veikkausliigan-yleisomaarat-2016/

Kössö, T. (2016). Tappiollisen Lukon omistaja ylläpitää liigayhtiötä – tavoite saada seura kannattavaksi [The owner of the loss-making Lukko to maintain the league company – the aim is to make the club profitable]. *Yle* March, 1, 2016. Retrieved December 4, 2016 from http://yle.fi/urheilu/3-8706657

Laine, A. (2011). *Urheilujournalismin Suomi-Ruotsi-maaottelu: Vertaileva tutkimus suomalaisten ja ruotsalaisten iltapäivälehtien Ateenan 2004 ja Torinon 2006 olympiauutisoinnista* [A Match in Sports Journalism Between Finland and Sweden. A Comparative Study of Finnish and Swedish Tabloid Coverage of the Athens 2004 and Turin 2006 Olympic Games] (PhD dissertation). Helsinki, Finland: Edita.

Laine, A. (2015). Liikunta- ja urheilualan yrityskenttä [Sport business field]. In H. Itkonen & A. Laine (Eds.), *Liikunta yhteiskunnallisena ilmiönä* (pp. 77–98). University of Jyväskylä. Department of Sport Sciences. Studies 1/2015.

Liiga. (2016). Joukkuetilastot 2015–2016 [Team statistics 2015–2016]. Retrieved November 27, 2016 from http://liiga.fi/tilastot/2015-2016/runkosarja/joukkueet/?stats_type=yleisomaara&home_away=&sort=

Liikuntalaki 390/2015. [Finnish Sports Law 390/2015]. Retrieved Retrieved October 4, 2016 from http://www.finlex.fi/fi/laki/alkup/2015/20150390

Liikuntatoimi tilastojen valossa. (2016). [Sport services in the light of statistics]. Opetus- ja kulttuuriministeriön julkaisuja 2016:11.

Lith, P. (2013). *Urheilu- ja liikuntaklusteri. Raportti liikuntapalveluiden kysynnästä ja tarjonnasta, yritystoiminnasta ja yritysten taloudellisesta asemasta* [Sports and exercise cluster. The report on supply and demand of sports services, sports business, and financial position of the companies]. Ilmiöselvitys 5/2013. Verohallinto. Harmaan talouden selvitysyksikkö.

Lähteenmäki, P. (2017). Halpasalit kiristävät kuntokisaa [Budget-friendly fitness facilities tighten fitness competition]. *Talouselämä, 1*, 34–35.

Ojanen, L. (2014). Kuntobisnes sykkii vahvaa kasvua [The fitness business is bustling with strong growth]. *Kauppalehti* August, 20, 2014. Retrieved November 16, 2016 from http://www.kauppalehti.fi/uutiset/kuntobisnes-sykkii-vahvaa-kasvua/VAKU3BEQ

Rajala, A. (2016). Jokereille jättitappiot viime pelikaudesta [Huge losses to Jokerit from last season]. *Kauppalehti* December 14, 2016. Retrieved December 16, 2016 from http://www.kauppalehti.fi/uutiset/jokereille-jattitappiot-viime-pelikaudesta/LmPRM3nu

Rajala, A., & Vanhanen, H. (2013). Harkimon areenan tappiohistoria synkkeni [Harkimo arena loss history darkened]. *Kauppalehti* December 14, 2013. Retrieved December 4, 2016 from http://www.kauppalehti.fi/uutiset/harkimon-areenan-tappiohistoria-synkkeni/jh2zMwP5

Saarinen, J. (2015). Suomalainen tupakkayhtiö muuttui vaivihkaa maailmanlaajuiseksi urheilujätiksi ja kasvaa vahvasti [Finnish tobacco company turned quietly into a worldwide sports giant and is growing strongly]. *Helsingin Sanomat* December 7, 2015. Retrieved October 24, 2016 from http://www.hs.fi/talous/a1449384755887

SM-liiga. (2009). SM-liigaosakkeen hinta on 1 593 533 euroa [Price for SM-league stock is 1 593 533 euros]. Retrieved November 27, 2016 from http://liiga.fi/uutiset/2009/04/09/sm-liigaosakkeen-hinta-on-1-593-533-euroa

Statistics Finland. (2011). Gross domestic product grew up by 3.1 per cent in 2010. Retrieved September 2, 2016 from http://www.stat.fi/ajk/tiedotteet/2011/tiedote_003_2011-03-01_en.html

Statistics Finland. (2013). Data on statistics on Finnish enterprises. Retrieved September 2, 2016 from http://www.stat.fi/til/syr/tau.html

Statistics Finland. (2014). Median monthly earnings of wage and salary earners were EUR 2928 per month in 2013. Retrieved September 2, 2016 from http://www.stat.fi/til/pra/2013/pra_2013_2014-10-14_tie_001_en.html

Statistics Finland. (2015). Gross domestic product contracted by 0.4 per cent last year. Retrieved September 2, 2016 from http://www.stat.fi/til/vtp/2014/vtp_2014_2015-07-09_tie_001_en.html

Statistics Finland. (2016). Structural business and financial statement statistics. Retrieved September 2, 2016 from http://www.stat.fi/til/yrti/tau_en.html

Suomen Asiakastieto. (2016). Voitto+ -yritystalouden CD 1/2016 [Voitto+ business economy CD 1/2016]. Helsinki, Finland: Suomen Asiakastieto.

Suomi, K. (2015). Valtion liikuntapolitiikan linjauksia 1980–2014 [National sports policy guidelines 1980-2014]. In H. Itkonen & A. Laine (Eds.), *Liikunta yhteiskunnallisena ilmiönä* (pp. 59–76.) University of Jyväskylä. Department of Sport Sciences. Studies 1/2015.

XXL ASA Annual Report. (2015). Retrieved December 10, 2016 from http://www.xxlasa.com/wp-content/uploads/2015/04/XXL-ASA-Annual-Report-20151.pdf

FRANCE: A Market Dominated by Sport Goods Retailers

Nicolas Delorme

Selected country facts (in 2013)	
Capital	Paris
Geographical size (km^2)	633,187
Population (million)	65.60
GDP (euro per capita)	32,100
GDP (per capita in PPS)	109
Annual net earnings average (€)	26,396

Organisation of Sport in France

After the importation of the 'English Sport' during the 1870s, the 'sport model' has developed rapidly in France (Terret, 2016). The activism of Pierre de Coubertin, and his role in the implementation of the modern Olympic Games, has significantly contributed to the development of sport and physical activities in France (Weber, 1970). Very quickly, sport and physical activities were seen as a strategic domain by various stakeholders who tried to arrogate the exclusive control and organisation of these practices. The consequences were an institutionalisation in three different sectors: public, voluntary and private (Gasparini, 2000). In France, if the public and voluntary sectors were originally dominant both in terms of power and legitimacy, the private sector has evolved considerably over the last thirty years (Gayant, 2016).

N. Delorme (✉)
University of Bordeaux, Bordeaux, France
e-mail: nicolas.delorme@u-bordeaux.fr

A. Laine, H. Vehmas (eds.), *The Private Sport Sector in Europe*, Sports Economics, Management and Policy 14, https://doi.org/10.1007/978-3-319-61310-9_8

The Public Sport Sector

In the public sector, sport is mainly regulated by the Ministry of City, Youth and Sports (Ministère de la Ville, de la Jeunesse et des Sports – MVJS) through its State Secretariat for Sport. Some other Ministries are also marginal actors in the regulation of sport such as the Ministry of National Education and Ministry of Defence. The MVJS has the responsibility to define the aims of the national policy of sport and to fix its legal framework, notably through the sport's code.

Nowadays, the national sport policy is structured around four main goals: (1) the development of sport for everyone, (2) the organisation of high level sports, (3) the prevention and protection of sports people and fight against doping, violence, racism and all forms of discrimination, and (4) the promotion of the jobs issued from sport and the development of sport employment (MVJS, 2016a). To implement these actions, the MVJS rely on a centralised administration, decentralised services as well as on a network of public institutions such as the French anti-doping agency. In 2016, the budget devoted to sport in the MVJS was 497 billion euros, which was 0.14% of the state budget (MVJS, 2016b).

More recently, the MVJS targeted the development and the structuration of the private sector as a new strategic priority. In June 2016, the Ministry launched an Observatory of Sports Economics, which aims to develop the best analysis tools in order to accurately measure the impact of sport on French economy (MVJS, 2016a). Observatory of Sports Economics also makes recommendations to adapt the public policies in this domain. Beyond the state level, the French public sector also includes various territorial communities, in particular the municipalities and the local authorities who spend each year more than ten billion euros for local sport policies and sport facilities (MVJS, 2016a).

The Voluntary Sport Sector

The voluntary sector is very dynamic in France, especially in form of sport associations (Ferrand-Bechmann, 2004; Tchernonog, 2007). The voluntary sport sector is organised according to a pyramidal structure, which replicates the French administrative divisions: national federations, regional sport bodies, local sport bodies and clubs. The French voluntary sport model is specific due to the position held by the state (Gasparini, 2000). Indeed, the organisation of the voluntary sector relies on the official recognition of sport federations by the state. Operating as non-profit organisations defined originally by the '1901 Act' on associations, the sport federations are placed under the supervisory authority of the MVJS. Most of them, while keeping their autonomy, are given a mission of public service by the MVJS such as the development and democratisation of sport and physical activities. Once this status is granted, the state provides support to the federations in terms of annual subsidies and human resources such as technical sports advisors (Chifflet, 2005). This support is also seen as an efficient means to keep control over the sport voluntary sector (Chifflet, 2005; Honta & Julhe, 2015; Julhe & Honta, 2016). On the other hand, clubs are mainly funded by the local authorities through subsidies and free provision of sport equipment (Charrier & Durand, 2005).

The voluntary sector is usually divided into three types of sport federations: Olympic single sport federations, non-Olympic single sport federations and multi-sport federations. In 2015, France counted 33 Olympic single sport federations, 65 non-Olympic single sport federations and 25 multi-sport federations. During the same year, all together, these federations represented a total of 16,102,957 licensees (with individual multi-licensees included) distributed among 165,859 sport clubs. The five most important single sport federations in terms of licensees were the football federation (2,135,193 licensees), the tennis federation (1,052,127 licensees), the horsing federation (673,026 licensees), the judo federation (552,815 licensees) and the basketball federation (513,727 licensees). In terms of amount of the voluntary clubs, the five most important federations were the football federation (16,972 clubs), the tennis federation (7854 clubs), the petanque federation (5873 clubs), the judo federation (5408 clubs) and the karate federation (4788 clubs). In France, some federations include both voluntary clubs and private businesses such as the horsing federation with 2840 private clubs and 6165 private businesses. (MVJS, 2016a.)

As mentioned above, sport volunteering is very dynamic in France. Indeed, it represents about 3.5 million out of 14.2 million volunteers in total. Volunteers in sport invest 453 million hours per year. The voluntary engagement represents on average 93 hours of volunteering per year per volunteer for associations relying entirely on volunteers, and 108 hours for associations employing staff. The sport sector has an estimated 275,400 full-time equivalent (FTE) volunteers. This represents 29% of the total amount of voluntary work in France (935,400 FTE volunteers) and 79% of the total volume of work in the sport sector. (MVJS, 2016a.)

The Private Sport Sector

In France, a macroeconomic indicator, defined as the "gross domestic sport expenditure", is published annually. It aggregates the amounts spent by residents and households in sporting goods and services with state government sport budget, sport expenditures by local authorities, sport sponsorship expenses and TV broadcasting rights paid (Andreff, 2008). This indicator has risen from 0.5% of the gross domestic product in 1971 to 1.77% in 2005, which means 30.4 billion euros (Andreff, 2008). In 2013, it reached 38.1 billion euros which was 1.8% of the gross domestic product (MVJS, 2016c). In the same year, the private sport sector represented a share of 16.7 billion euros (43.8%) of the "gross domestic sport expenditure" (see Table 1). As mentioned earlier, the MVJS recently targeted the development and the structuration of the private sector as a strategic priority. Indeed, the French private sport sector has resisted the 2008 economic crisis particularly well (MVJS, 2016c). Consequently, it is seen as an important lever of the French economy growth (MVJS, 2016a). However, until very recently, national accounting of the sport economy has not really developed in France (Andreff, 2008; MVJS, 2016a), apart from some basic data from the National Institute of Statistics and Economic Studies (Institut National de la Statistique et des Etudes Economiques – INSEE). As a result of the cooperation between the MVJS and the Ministry of Economy, a first study focusing on the sport retail industries was recently published by the Observatory of Sports Economics (MVJS, 2016b). The retail sale of sport equipment is one of the most important business fields in the private sport sector (see Table 1), which explainsss why the Observatory of Sports Economics started with a study of this specific market.

Directly Sport-Related Business Fields

Based on the French equivalent (NAF Rev. 2) of the *Statistical classification of economic activities in the European Community* (NACE Rev. 2, 2008), Table 1 presents directly sport-related business fields in France in 2013. A total of 68,855 companies are included in these business fields. In terms of amount of companies the three largest business fields are the sport and recreation education (34,394 companies), the activities of sport clubs (10,131 companies) and the retail sale of sport equipment and bicycles (7524 companies). The smallest business field is the manufacture of sport goods (553 companies).

These companies employ over 89,000 individuals. The three largest business fields based on the number of employees are the retail sale of sport equipment and bicycles (41,624 employees), the operation of sport facilities (15,470 employees) and the activities of sport clubs (10,075 employees). The smallest employers' are the fitness facilities (3110 employees) and the other sport activities (7501 employees). One can note that the employee numbers are generally not positively correlated with the number of companies. For example, the retails of sport equipment and bicycles and the operation of sport facilities are the biggest employers with a moderate/small number of companies. On the contrary, the sport and recreation education business field has the biggest number of companies whereas it has a relatively small number of employees. In fact, many of these are one-person businesses and do not have any employee. (INSEE, 2016.) Indeed, in this case, according to the French law, it is possible to earn dividends instead of a salary. Consequently, individuals opting for this solution are not counted as employees in the official statistics of the National Institute of Statistics and Economic Studies.

As mentioned above, the private sport sector has generated a total revenue of 16.7 billion euros in 2013. However, a detailed analysis shows an important heterogeneity between the various business fields. With 8.6 billion euros of revenue, the retail sale of sport equipment and bicycles represents 51.5% of the total revenue in the French private sport sector. This performance sets it apart from other significant business fields, namely the activities of sport clubs with 2.4 billion euros (14.4% of the total revenue), the sport and recreation education with 1.8 billion euros (10.7% of the total revenue) and the operation of sport facilities with 1.5 billion euros (9.2% of the total revenue). At the opposite, the renting and leasing of recreational and sport goods (0.52 billion euros – 3.1% of the total revenue), the other sport activities (0.46 billion euros – 2.8% of the total revenue) and the fitness facilities (0.32 billion euros – 1.9% of the total revenue) are the smallest business fields in terms of revenue. (See Table 1.)

Considering the "revenue/number of companies" ratio as an indicator of business sizes, the three biggest business fields are the manufacture of sport goods (average of 1.9 million euros per company), the retail sale of sport equipment and bicycles (average of 1.1 million euros per company) and the operation of sport facilities (average of 0.6 million euros per company). At the opposite, the renting and leasing of recreational and sport goods (average of 0.11 million euros per company), the other sport activities (average of 0.06 million euros per company) and the sport and recreation education (average of 0.05 million euros per company) are the smallest business fields in terms of efficiency. (See Table 1.)

Finally, some significant discrepancies in terms of average salary according to the business field can be found from Table 1. The average salary in the French private sport sector was 33,200 euros per year in 2013. It was nevertheless above the French average salary, which was at 28,900 euros per year the same year (INSEE, 2016). The average salary in the sport and recreation education business field was twice as high with 69,100 euros per year. This high salary level is undoubtedly linked to the aforementioned poor performance level in terms of efficiency noticed in this business field. At the opposite, some business fields were significantly below the average salary in the private sport sector (but also below the French average salary): the fitness facilities (22,900 euros per year), the renting and leasing of recreational and sport goods (22,800 euros per year) and the retail sale of sport equipment and bicycles (22,500 euros per year). According to the INSEE (2016), these business fields have a significantly higher proportion of employees who just earn the guaranteed minimum salary according to the French law (i.e., 17,600 euros per year in 2013).

Table 1 Directly sport-related business fields in France in 2013.

Business field	NACE code	Companies (n)	Staff (n)	Revenue (1000 €)	Revenue/Company (1000 €)	Av. salary (1000 €)
Retail sale of sport equipment and bicycles	4764	7524	41,624	8,599,500	1142.90	22.5
Activities of sport clubs	9312	10,131	10,075	2,407,100	237.6	27.5
Sport and recreation education	8551	34,394	7138	1,790,800	52.1	69.1
Operation of sport facilities	9311	2511	15,470	1,532,400	610.3	32.2
Manufacture of sport goods	3230	553	4254	1,068,400	1932.00	35.9
Renting and leasing of recreational and sport goods	7721	4342	5098	519,200	119.6	22.8
Other sport activities	9319	7501	2232	463,600	61.8	32.7
Fitness facilities	9313	1899	3110	315,100	165.9	22.9
Total		**68,855**	**89,001**	**16,696,100**	**242.5**	**33.2**

Source: INSEE (2016).

Beyond these main characteristics collected by the National Institute of Statistics and Economic Studies, a review of the scientific literature devoted to the French private sport sector brings to light the scarcity of research on this topic. The few available studies are outdated (e.g., Andreff, 2006; Calvet & Gerbier, 1992; Desbordes, Ohl, & Tribou, 2004; Malenfant, 1991; Ohl & Taks, 2008; Ohl & Tribou, 2004). As mentioned above, this observation led the MVJS to establish the Observatory of Sports Economics in 2016. This organisation has recently published a study focusing on the French sport retail industries (MVJS, 2016b). To my knowledge, it is the only available study with updated data in relation to the French private sport sector. As discussed previously, the retail sale of sport equipment is the most important business field in terms of revenue and employment. It is also one of the most efficient and one of the biggest in relation to the number of companies. It is thus an important business field for the sport economy and more broadly for the French economy. For all these reasons, the next part of this chapter will focus on the French sport goods retailers together with sport goods manufacturers.

The Main Characteristics of Sport Goods Retailers and Manufacturers

Sport goods retailers are obviously strongly linked to the manufacturers of sport goods, even if nowadays some French companies are both manufacturers and retailers (e.g., Decathlon – see below). Consequently, a quick overview of the French sport goods market will provide some elements of contextualisation to link with the retail industries.

After the United Kingdom, France is the second largest European sport goods market with a 17% market share (Gerke & Benson-Rea, 2017). In 2013, manufacture of sport goods (NACE code 3230) generated over one billion euros revenue in France, but had a negative balance trade of -651.9 million euros and a coverage rate of 76% (MVJS, 2015). Imports are thus more important than exports in the French case. The same tendency was noted between 2010 and 2015 (MVJS, 2016c).

According to MarketLine (2015 – cited by Gerke & Benson-Rea, 2017), the three largest French market segments are the winter sport goods (24% of market share), the ball sport goods (23%) and the fitness equipment (19%). According to Desbordes et al. (2004), the best-known French sport goods manufacturers worldwide are Gitane (bicycles), Oxbow (snowboards and surfboards), Beneteau (boats), Salomon (skis), Petzl (climbing equipment) and Millet (backpacks). However, the three main French manufacturers in terms of revenue in 2013 were Amer Sport France (410.2 million euros), Rossignol (198.1 million euros) and Babolat (128.2 million euros) (MVJS, 2016b).

According to the Observatory of Sports Economics (MVJS, 2016b), a typology including six categories could be formed in relation to the French sport goods retailers and manufacturers. This typology was built taking into account three main dimensions. First, it was done by making a distinction between the companies that have an activity of conception and/or manufacturing and those that are only dedicated to retailing. Second, in making a distinction between those that have at least a part of the production process in France (such as conception, manufacturing and/or assembling) and those that only realise the production process abroad. And third, in taking into account the existence of their own retail network and the fact that this network only distributes the manufacturer's brand or also those of other manufacturers. (See Table 2.)

By applying this segmentation, the six categories are: 1) sport goods manufacturers, 2) sport goods manufacturers – retailers, 3) sport goods retailers – manufacturers, 4) sport goods importers, 5) sport goods importers – retailers and 6) sport goods retailers. Table 2 provides an overview of this typology with the main characteristics for each category.

Table 2 Typology of French sport goods retailers and manufacturers.

Retailing		Conception, manufacturing and/or assembling in France	
Own brand	Other brands		
		Manufacturer Ex: Petzl	Part of the conception/manufacturing/assembling in France
			Do not have an own retail network
			Brands are distributed by other stores
x		**Manufacturer – Retailer** Ex: Quiksilver	Part of the conception/manufacturing/assembling in France
			Have their own retail network but its brand(s) are mainly distributed by other stores
x	x	**Retailer – Manufacturer** Ex: Decathlon	Part of the conception/manufacturing/assembling in France
			Have their own retail network where its brand(s) are solely distributed
			Also distribute other brands
Retailing		Conception, manufacturing and/or assembling abroad	
Own brand	Other brands		
		Importer Ex: Asics	Conception/manufacturing/assembling abroad
			Do not have their own retail network
			Brands are distributed by other stores
x		**Importer – Retailer** Ex: Adidas	Conception/manufacturing/assembling in France
			Have their own retail network but its brand(s) are mainly distributed by other stores
Retailing		No conception, manufacturing and/or assembling	
Own brand	Other brands		
	x	**Retailer** Ex: Sport 2000	Do not design/manufacture/assemble any product
			Only distribute brands that do not belong to it

Source: Adapted from MVJS (2016b).

With companies, which are manufacturers, retailers or both at the same time, this typology shows the complexity of the French private sport sector. According to the Observatory of Sports Economics (MVJS, 2016b), the main difference between the "manufacturer – retailer" and the "retailer – manufacturer" categories is the distribution of their own brands (see Table 2). In the first case, even if the companies have their own retail network, their brands are mainly distributed by other stores/retailers (e.g., Quiksilver). In the second case, the companies have their own retail network where their brands are solely distributed. They also distribute other brands (e.g., Decathlon). The complexity arises from the fact that the "manufacturer – retailer" or the "retailer – manufacturer" companies could have a different NACE code (3230 – manufacture of sport goods or 4764 – retail sale of sport equipment and bicycles), independently of their main activity. Most of the time, this choice is linked to the history of the companies which were originally pure manufacturers or pure retailers. These hybrid companies show the limit of the NACE classification and should be taken into account in sport economics studies.

According to the recent study by the Observatory of Sports Economics (MVJS, 2016b), the sport goods manufacturers and the sport goods retailers are experiencing opposite growth dynamics. The first ones have been subject to a decrease of 7% of their revenue in 2013. According to the aforementioned study, this was the result of a slowdown in demand, but also the increasingly tough international demand in this business field. This trend ran over the next years (MVJS, 2016a).

On the contrary, the sport goods retailers have been subject to an increase of 3.5% of their revenue in 2013. This result was obtained through the development of their own brands and the delocalisation of their production (MVJS, 2016b). Here again, this trend ran over the next years (MVJS, 2016a). A more detailed analysis however shows a decrease of the revenue for the sport textiles (-1.8% in 2013). This trend is a consequence of two phenomena. First, a decrease of the sportswear demand. Second, an increased competition from the ready-to-wear stores and their very developed networks of distributions, which have diversified their offers with the inclusion of sportswear products in their collections.

Sport goods retailers dominate the French private sport sector. Decathlon is clearly the biggest sport goods retailer in terms of revenue and with 37.2% market share. *Photo: Decathlon.*

Sport Goods Retailers: A Concentrated Market

Table 3 presents the seven biggest companies according revenue among French sport retail industries in 2013 (i.e., manufacturers – retailers, retailers – manufacturers and retailers – see the above typology). All together, these actors represent 70.9% of the total revenue in this business field (MVJS, 2016b).

The French sport goods retailers market has a clear oligopolistic structure. Indeed, 53.5% of the total revenue in this business field is generated by only two companies: Decathlon (37.2%) and Intersport (16.3%). Behind these two dominant companies, the other five main actors generate 17.4% of the total revenue in this concentrated market, each having small market shares: Go Sport (5.8%), Sport 2000 (5.8%), Foot Locker (2.2%), Courir (2%) and Au Vieux Campeur (1.6%).

Apart from Go Sport (−4.2%), all the companies had a positive EBITDA (Earning Before Interest, Taxes, Depreciation and Amortisation) margin in 2013. EBITDA-% indicator is seen as a proxy for a company's current operating profitability. It allows a comparison of profitability between companies by neutralising the effects of (1) interest payments from the various form of financing (by ignoring interest payment), (2) political jurisdiction (by ignoring taxes), (3) collection of assets (by ignoring depreciation of assets) and (4) different takeover histories (by ignoring amortisation often stemming from goodwill). Among the largest French sport goods retailers, the positive EBITDA-% (excluding Go Sport) range from 1.4% (Intersport) to 9% (Au Vieux Campeur). The negative EBITDA-% of Go Sport is solely due to a decline in sales (BFM Business, 2014).

Taking the "revenue/number of stores" ratio as an indicator of efficiency, Decathlon is the most efficient company with an average revenue of 10.5 million euros per store. While it is the second company in terms of market shares, Intersport is only the fourth in terms of efficiency with an average revenue of 2.3 million euros per store, behind Go Sport (average revenue of 3.9 million euros per store) and Au Vieux Campeur (average revenue of 2.8 million euros per store). It is also interesting to note that Intersport has twice as many stores than Decathlon (600 versus 304), but half as many employees (7000 versus 14,647). Interestingly, the data show a nearly perfect positive linear correlation between the number of employees and the revenue ($r = 0.98$, $P<.001$) whereas there is no significant correlation between the number of stores and the revenue among the seven biggest sport goods retailers in France ($r = 0.32$, $P<.48$). Consequently, it seems that the number of employees is a determinant factor related to the revenue, rather than the number of stores. One should however remain cautious with this interpretation because of the small size of the sample and the fact that numerous other factors are not measured and/or controlled.

Table 3 Biggest sport goods retailers by revenue in France in 2013.

Company	Stores (n)	Revenue (1000 €)	EBITDA-%	Staff (n)
Decathlon	304	3,200,000	6,7	14,647
Intersport	600	1,400,000	1,4	7000
Go Sport	127	500,000	-4,2	5000
Sport 2000	600	495,000	n/a	n/a
Foot Locker	131	192,000	5,3	924
Courir	197	172,000	2,4	910
Au Vieux Campeur	48	135,000	9	350

Sources: MVJS (2016b) and companies' websites.

Decathlon: An Uncontested Polyvalent Leader in Sports Goods Retailing

As mentioned above, Decathlon is the leader of the sport goods retailers in France with 37.2% market share. It is well ahead of Intersport, which market share is more than half smaller (16.3%). Additionally, Decathlon is the tenth largest sport goods retailer in the world (Kapferer, 2012).

This leading position has been obtained after a shift from a pure retailer to a retailer – manufacturer (Les Echos Business, 2013). Indeed, the company has decided to take a way of "intrapreneurial" expansion consisting in carrying out an upstream vertical integration through the creation of independent and autonomous specialised brands (Gerke & Benson-Rea, 2017; Hillairet, Richard, & Bouchet, 2009). This strategic shift has been accompanied by the setup of a dual management system of innovation and creativity (Abdourazakou, 2016). There are currently 20 brands (called "Passion Brands"), each representing a 'sport universe' relating to one or more sport families (Table 4). These brands are only available in Decathlon stores and are positioned as the best quality/price ratio products, becoming direct competitors for the manufacturers' brands.

Table 4 Decathlon's "Passion Brands".

Brand	Sport families
Aptonia	Sport nutrition and health
Artengo	Racket sports
Btwin	Cycling
Caperlan	Fishing
Domyos	Fitness, dance, gymnastics, combat sports
Fouganza	Horse riding
Geologic	Darts, archery, boules
Geonaute	Electronics
Inesis	Golf
Kalenji	Running
Kipsta	Team sports
Nabaiji	Swimming
Newfeel	Walking
Orao	Sport optics
Oxelo	Urban skate sports
Quechua	Mountain sports
Simond	Climbing and mountaineering
Solognac	Nature and hunting
Tribord	Water and nautical sports
Wed'ze	Skiing and snowboarding

Source: Gerke and Benson-Rea (2017).

More recently, Decathlon has continued the diversification of its activities by proposing different services that complement the product and retail departments (Gerke & Benson-Rea, 2017). These services cover a broad spectrum of activities ranging from funding solutions to ski renting (see Table 5). Similar to their own products with their "Passion Brands", each service offered is represented by a specific brand. According to Abdourazakou (2016), thanks to its strategy of diversification and to its international expansion, Decathlon "is now a direct challenger for world sport leaders".

Table 5 Decathlon's service brands.

Brand	Sport families
Alsolia	Funding solutions
Atelier	Servicing, repairs, customisations
Decathlon Sport Insurance	Insurance
Hockey Community	Hockey social network
Jiwok	MP3 personal coach
Skimium	Ski renting
Sowego	Active mobility
Sporeka	Gift cards

Source: Gerke and Benson-Rea (2017).

Conclusions

The French private sport sector has resisted the 2008 economic crisis particularly well and it has been seen as an important lever for the French economy growth. Consequently, the development and the structuration of this sector have become strategic priorities for the French Government. Indeed, a quantitative survey of sport participation in France found that 'omnivority' – defined as the simultaneous practice of different sports – and massification of activities are major phenomena (Lefèvre & Ohl, 2012). New sport needs have emerged such as quick access to sensations, greater autonomy, low time constraints or logistical limitations (e.g., Augustin, 2011; Gaubert, 2012; Lebreton, 2010; Lefèvre & Ohl, 2012; Tlili & Delorme, 2014). Most traditional sport federations currently fail to meet these needs (Tlili & Delorme, 2014). For example, five-a-side football has been establishing itself as one of the most prominent activities in the French physical and sport landscape. By introducing numerous innovations, this specific variation of the game of football has quickly managed to create a form of sport consumption which runs parallel to federal provision and attract many consumers (Gaubert, 2015).

These new sport needs, added to the current lack of federal offer, provide significant business opportunities for the private sport sector. This is all the more true since this sector remains significantly under-developed in France (MVJS, 2016b; Tlili & Delorme, 2014). Thus, it represents an important potential source of employment. These employment opportunities should not be neglected in a country where the unemplSSoyment rate stagnates for a long time (INSEE, 2017). This is one of the reasons why the French government decided that the development and the structuration of this sector have become strategic priorities (MVJS, 2016a). Consequently, one should expect a significant development of private sector in the coming years.

However, as discussed in this article, national accounting of the sport economy is still not really developed in France, apart from some basic data from the National Institute of Statistics and Economic Studies. Furthermore, a review of the scientific literature devoted to the French private sport sector brought to light the scarcity and the obsolescence of research on this topic. It was one of the main reasons for the implementation of an Observatory of Sports Economics in 2016. This recent initiative will undoubtedly be very useful both for the companies of the private sport sector and for the scholars interested in this research field. It will help us to improve our understanding of this sector.

As rightly pointed by Andreff (2008), the last important issue to underline is the fact that the relevant market for many companies in the French sport economy is no longer a domestic market but rather a global-wide one. As deplored by the author, there is no accurate accounting of the sport economy at a global level. Consequently, "the first concern for those economists interested in the sport economy should be able to find ways through which data collection and data creation on all aspects of globalization in the sporting industry can be improved" (Andreff, 2008). Here again, it will definitely help us to improve our understanding of the sector.

References

Abdourazakou, Y. (2016). Managing innovation in the sport equipment industry: Upstream process management. *Management Studies, 4*(1), 1–8.

Andreff, W. (2006). The sports goods industry. In W. Andreff & S. Szymanski (Eds.), *Handbook on the economics of sport* (pp. 27–39). Cheltenham, UK: Edward Elgar Publishing.

Andreff, W. (2008). Globalization of the sport economy. *Rivista di Diritto ed Economia dello Sport, 4*(3), 13–32.

Augustin, J. P. (2011). Qu'est-ce que le sport? Cultures sportives et géographie [What is sport? Sport cultures and geography]. *Annales de la Géographie, 680*(4), 361–382.

BFM Business. (2014). *Groupe GO Sport: Résultats Annuels 2013* [GO Sport Company: 2013 Annual Results]. Retrieved September 17, 2015 from http://bfmbusiness.bfmtv.com/bourse/groupe-go-sport-resultats-annuels-2013-710780.html

Calvet, J., & Gerbier, B. (1992). La restructuration de l'industrie des articles de sports d'hiver [The restructuration of winter sport goods industry]. *Revue de Géographie Alpine, 80*(1), 21–35.

Charrier, D., & Durand, C. (2005). Le financement des politiques sportives locales: sport pour tous, sport professionnel, une dualité à réinventer [Financing of local sport policies: Sport for all, professional sport, a duality to be reinvented]. *Annuaire des collectivités locales, 25*(1), 65–75.

Chifflet, P. (2005). *Idéologie sportive et service public en France. Mythe d'un système unifié* [Sport ideology and public service in France. Myth of a unified system]. Grenoble, France: Presses Universitaires de Grenoble.

Desbordes, M., Ohl, F., & Tribou, G. (2004). *Marketing du Sport* [Sport marketing]. Paris, France: Economica.

Ferrand-Bechmann, D. (2004). *Les bénévoles et leurs associations* [Volunteers and their associations]. Paris, France: L'Harmattan.

Gaubert, V. (2012). Vers une ludisation des pratiques sportives… quand jouer au football (re) devient plaisir [Towards recreational sporting activities… when football is back in the game]. *Géographie et Cultures, 84*, 43–61.

Gaubert, V. (2015). Le cycle de vie d'une pratique ludo-sportive: le cas du football indoor en France [Life cycle of a recreational sporting practice: the case of five-a-side football in France]. *Loisir et Société, 38*(1), 37–54.

Gasparini, W. (2000). *Sociologie de l'organisation sportive* [Sociology of sport organisation]. Paris, France: La Découverte.

Gayant, J. P. (2016). *Economie du sport* [Sport economics]. Paris, France: Dunod.

Gerke, A., & Benson-Rea, M. (2017). The expansion of the sport good industry. In U. Wagner, R. K. Storm, & K. Nielsen (Eds.), *Wh€n sport m€€ts busin€ss: Capabilities, challenges, critiques* (pp. 11–29). London, UK: Sage.

Hillairet, D., Richard, G., & Bouchet, P. (2009). The dual management of innovation by the Decathlon Group. A distinctive strategic system on the sport goods market. *Journal of Innovation Economics & Management, 3*(1), 189–210.

Honta, M., & Julhe, S. (2015). Serving the state and the private sector: the paradoxical effects of the reconstruction of public action on the career paths of Sports Ministry agents in France. *International Review for the Sociology of Sport, 50*(2), 179–195.

INSEE. (2016). *Caractéristiques comptables, financières et d'emploi des entreprises en 2013* [Accounting, financial and employment characteristics of the companies in 2013]. Retrieved September 15, 2016 from http://www.insee.fr/fr/statistiques/2020132?sommaire=2020369

INSEE. (2017). Taux de Chômage en France [Unemployment rate in France]. Retrieved January 30, 2017 from https://www.bdm.insee.fr/bdm2/affichageSeries?idbank=001688526&page=tableau&request_locale=fr

Julhe, S., & Honta, M. (2016). Les conseillers techniques du ministère des Sports. Création et contrôle d'un corps d'agents de l'État (1960–1987) [The technical advisors of the Ministry of Sports. Establishment and control of public employees (1960–1987)]. *STAPS, 113*(3), 21–36.

Kapferer, J. N. (2012). *The new strategic brand management. Advanced insights and strategic thinking*. London, UK: Kogan Page.

Lebreton, F. (2010). *Cultures urbaines et sportives "alternatives". Socio-anthropologie de l'urbanité ludique* [Alternative urban and sport cultures. Socio-anthropology of fun urbanity]. Paris, France: L'Harmattan.

Lefèvre, B., & Ohl, F. (2012). Consuming sports: Distinction, univorism and omnivorism. *Sport in Society, 15*(1), 44–63.

Les Echos Business. (2013). *Decathlon: quand les marques propres montrent la voie* [Decathlon: When own brands show the way]. Retrieved September 14, 2015 from http://business.lesechos.fr/directions-generales/strategie/business-model/decathlon-une-marque-propre-qui-montre-la-voie-5408.php?sizXK60UzOZLVBPw.99

Malenfant, C. (1991). Economics of sport: The French case. *World Leis Recreat, 33*(1), 29–31.

MVJS. (2015). *Les chiffres-clés du sport* [Factsheet on sport]. Paris, France: MVJS.

MVJS. (2016a). *Enjeux de l'économie du sport* [Issues in sport economics]. Retrieved October 10, 2016 from http://www.sports.gouv.fr/organisation/organisation-du-sport-en-france/sporteco/

MVJS. (2016b). *Enjeux et perspectives des industries du sport en France et à l'international* [Issues and perspectives in French and international sport industries]. Paris, France: Pipame.

MVJS. (2016c). Le poids économique du sport en 2013: la dépense sportive nationale croît plus vite que le PIB [The economic weight of sport in 2013]. *Stat-Info, 16*, 1–8.

Ohl, F., & Taks, M. (2008). La consommation sportive: état des lieux [Sport consumption: State of affairs]. *Revue Française du Marketing, 219*(4-5), 27–46.

Ohl, F., & Tribou, G. (2004). *Les marchés du Sport* [Sport markets]. Paris, France: Armand Colin.

Tchernonog, V. (2007). *Le paysage associatif français. Mesures et évolutions* [The French associative landscape]. Paris, France: Juris Editions.

Terret, T. (2016). *Histoire du sport* [Sport history]. Paris, France: Presses Universitaires de France.

Tlili, H., & Delorme, N. (2014). *Pourquoi les jeunes filles ne pratiquent pas d'activités physiques et sportives ? Une recherche-action dans les Zones Urbaines Sensibles françaises* [Why young women do not practice physical and sport activities? A research-action in French Sensitive Urban Areas]. Paris, France: UFOLEP.

Weber, E. (1970). Pierre de Coubertin and the Introduction of Organized Sport in France. *Journal of Contemporary History, 5*(2), 3–26.

GERMANY: Transformation Towards a More Private Sport Sector

Christoph Breuer, Thomas Giel, and Kirstin Hallmann

Selected country facts (in 2013)	
Capital	Berlin
Geographical size (km²)	633,187
Population (million)	80.52
GDP (euro per capita)	35,000
GDP (per capita in PPS)	124
Annual net earnings average (€)	27,075

Introduction

Germany is considered as a social market economy. A social market economy can be described as an economic system, which assigns the state to undertake socio-political corrections and work towards social balance within a 'capitalist competition' (Schubert & Klein, 2011); i.e., the provision of goods and services is coordinated by the for-profit organisations. However, an economy is a complex system and functions through the coexistence of organisations stemming from private, voluntary, and public sectors (Weisbrod, 1988). Following the principle of the social market economy, the state (i.e., the public sector) subsidises the voluntary (non-profit) sector.

Voluntary sport organisations have been dominating the German sport system for several years (Breuer, Feiler, & Wicker, 2015). Interestingly, sport courses organised

C. Breuer (✉) • T. Giel • K. Hallmann
Institute of Sport Economics and Sport Management, German Sport University Cologne, Cologne, Germany
e-mail: Breuer@dshs-koeln.de; T.Giel@dshs-koeln.de; K.Hallmann@dshs-koeln.de

A. Laine, H. Vehmas (eds.), *The Private Sport Sector in Europe*, Sports Economics, Management and Policy 14, https://doi.org/10.1007/978-3-319-61310-9_9

by public sport organisations (e.g., in swimming pools and on ice rinks) are rare. Most often, public sport organisations own the facilities, which are used by voluntary organisations. Sport has become more commercialised and private sport organisations, which are especially represented by the sport goods sector and commercial sport providers, have emerged nowadays challenging the voluntary sport organisations (Gratton & Taylor, 2000). The private sport sector has already overtaken the voluntary sport sector in some metropolitan areas. This has led to more people being active at private sport organisations than in voluntary sport organisations in those areas.

This chapter is structured as follows: First, the emergence of the private sport sector will be explained theoretically. Thereafter the position of the private sport sector in Germany will be quantified followed by a description of structural characteristics of the private sport sector. Thereby, the most powerful sport business fields in Germany will be highlighted.

Public, Private, and Voluntary Sport Sector: Explaining the Transition from a Voluntary to a Private and Voluntary Sport System in Germany

An understanding of the growth of the private sport sector in Germany requires (1) an understanding why voluntary sport organisations were able to dominate the sport market for many years and (2) which societal changes have occurred since then. Both phenomena will be explained by using the standard model of sociological explanation (see Fig. 1; Esser, 1993). The core element of this model is the logic of selection, which follows the rational choice approach. Individuals have different options. They usually select the option from which they expect the greatest utility; i.e., it is assumed that individuals want to maximise their utility. According to Lindenberg (1996), individuals strive in particular for well-being and social recognition. This *logic of selection* consists of six basic elements: alternatives, consequences, reviews, expectations, evaluation of alternatives, and selection (Esser, 1999). Specifically, the selection process is as follows: The individual considers all possible alternatives ($A_1, A_2, \ldots, A_i, \ldots, A_m$) and reflects the expected utility of each alternative. The subjective utility ($U_1, U_2, \ldots, U_j, \ldots, U_n$) is composed of the objective expected consequence of the action ($O_1, O_2, \ldots, O_n$) and the subjective evaluation of this consequence ($V_1, V_2, \ldots, V_n$). It should be noted that any action can lead to multiple utilities. Expectations p_{ij} ($p_{11}, p_{12}, \ldots, p_{ij}, \ldots, p_{mn}$) indicate the likelihood that an action A_i will be converted into a subjective utility U_j. Expectations p_{ij} consist of the product of control c_i and efficiency e_{ij} of a mean to achieve the objective: $p_{ij}=c_i*e_{ij}$. The control c describes the degree of control over the resources ($X_1, X_2, \ldots, X_n$) that is necessary for achieving these goals and the efficiency e of the suitability of a resource ($X_1, X_2, \ldots, X_n$) for achieving these goals (Esser, 1999). The higher the control and the higher the efficiency of a resource are for the achievement of the objectives, the higher is the expectation that the action leads to the subjective utility.

In a next step, the expected utility-weights for each of the alternatives of A_i will be evaluated: $EU(A_i)=\Sigma p_{ij}U_j=p_{11}U_1+p_{12}U_1+\ldots+p_{mn}U_n$. Finally, that alternative with the biggest EU-weight will be selected (Esser, 1999).

Individual's selection is always framed by the social situation (*logic of situation*; Esser, 1999). Hereby it has to be differentiated between opportunities, for example the supply of goods and services to certain prices, and social norms and values. Opportunities do function as a constraint of alternatives, whereas social norms and values influence the valuation of an alternative's expected utility. Thus, both have an effect on the selection of alternatives.

Depending on the number of people who share the same social situation or the same ranking of alternatives, a certain collective phenomenon will arise (*logic of aggregation*; Esser, 1999). In the simplest case – if individuals' decisions are not interconnected (e.g., through social contagion) – the collective effect is just the sum of all individual effects.

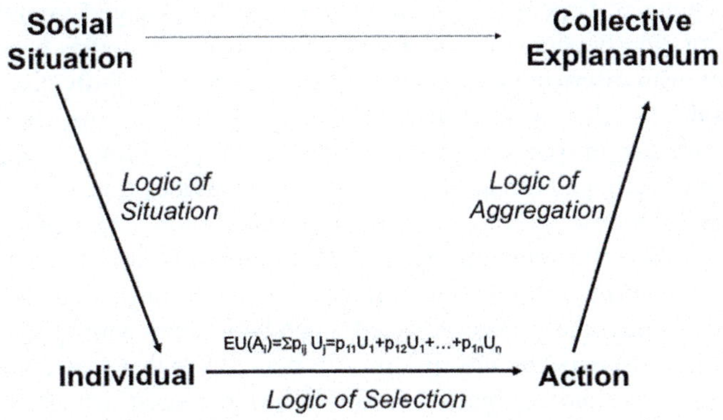

Fig. 1 Model of sociological explanation. Adopted from Esser (1993).

Sport has been played and exercised by a large number of individuals in Germany. The standard rule has been to exercise and play in a voluntary sport club (besides physical education). Consequently, the collective phenomenon was a sport market with a dominant market position of voluntary sport clubs. The question arises why this was the case. At first the social situation in the 1970s and 1980s has to be understood (Breuer, 2004). There were different predominant age and gender norms in those times. Playing sport was considered as something for children and adolescents but not as a serious activity for adults or even the elderly. This can be emphasised by looking at a traditional German term for 'senior citizen residence' which is called "Altersruhesitz". This term contains the word "Ruhe" (which means "rest") indicating that having a rest was seen as more reasonable for the elderly than being active. Classical gender roles reinforced this effect especially for the female population. At the same time body norms were different from today. In the 1970s and 1980s slim and sporty bodies were not as much socially admired as today. The shape of one's own body was not part of the concept of identity. Moreover, being physically active was not considered being health-conscious. Additionally, the society was not a thrill-seeking society at those times (Breuer, 2004).

This corresponds with a constraint of sport opportunities. The sport courses available were predominantly run by voluntary clubs. A close network of sport functionarics with politicians and bureaucrats guaranteed clubs a favoured access to public sport facilities as well as tax advantages for clubs, which worked as a market entry barrier for private sport providers.

Thus, there were only a few alternatives for being active at a private sport organisation. The expected utility of participating in sport was significantly lower and consequently also the willingness to pay for sport. The average willingness to pay for sport was so low that private sport organisations easily might have failed to break even.

A key precondition for the transition into a private and voluntary sport market was a change in the social situation at the end of the 1980s. The starting point was an elevator effect in education. People got better educated and with that attitudes and values changed. Especially age and gender norms changed tremendously. An active adult or elderly person together with slim and sporty bodies became societal ideals. Sport was discovered as an important medium for individual and public health promotion. Also, a thrill-seeking society emerged. Thus, the individual's decision to take part in sports, to choose a sport and a sport provider, and how much he or she is willing to pay for sport goods and sport services was now framed differently. As a consequence, average expected utilities of sport selections have become influenced by the following aspects: (1) Well-being and social recognition have always been important utilities. But with the changed norms, values, and education levels, these utilities can be accomplished much better now with sports than in former times. Thus, the expectations ($p_{11}, p_{12}, \ldots, p_{ij}, \ldots, p_{mn}$) that a sport-related action A_i will be converted into a subjective utility U_j has increased strongly. (2) The economic development in Germany led to higher wages and thus to a higher control over (monetary) resources (X_m) that are necessary to achieve these goals. (3) In contrast, an increase in working hours yielded to a decrease in time resources (X_t) to achieve these goals. This resulted in higher expected utilities of sport programmes which focus (a) either on health promotion, fitness, body-shaping, or thrill and (b) can be used following a flexible schedule. At the same time this led to a higher willingness to pay for sport services. From an economic point of view health, fitness, and experience goods and services share the characteristic of non-existing complete need satisfaction (Rittner, 1988). There is no point of total health, fitness, or experience. Thus, even people who consume those goods already intensively are willing to spend more money for it. This is the main reason why health, fitness, and experience goods and services are so-called superior goods. The demand for superior goods grows disproportionately higher to the income or monetary budget of a person (Rittner & Breuer, 2000).

Since the described programme elements are the main features of private sport services in Germany, a certain demand for sport services has raised. More and more private sport providers are able to break even. And this again has changed the social situation in terms of sport opportunities. More choices in the form of private sport alternatives have become available to the consumers and more consumers decided in favour of commercial sport providers. The transition from a former purely voluntary sport system to a private and voluntary sport system has occurred.

Position of the Private Sport Sector

As outlined in the previous section, the sport sector in Germany has changed over the last years. Due to several also earlier mentioned reasons especially commercial sport providers have gained in importance. Although these providers are not integrated in the German national sport structure (Petry & Hallmann, 2013), they are not only well-established in the market and accepted by the society, but also valued by many people as a further opportunity to work out and stay healthy or to fulfil other needs in a customised way. Already in 1990, researchers, focusing on commercial sport providers in Germany, argued that the commercial providers are able to motivate new customer groups to become active in sport participation with new kinds of sport programmes (Dietrich, Heinemann, & Schubert, 1990). These programmes offered by the private sport sector go beyond the ones of the voluntary and the public sport sector and additionally increase the quality of sport supply through the increased competition (Kaiser, 2014; Thieme, 2015).

There is a positive development of the private sport sector in Germany. Notwithstanding the importance of private sport providers such as fitness centres, together with the coexistence of private, public and voluntary sport supply for the society are key factors when one-size-fits-all approach is not able to meet all the individuals' needs. *Photo: German Sport University Cologne.*

Especially all kinds of fitness sports are predominantly offered by commercial sport providers (Hallmann, Feiler, & Breuer, 2015) and it is generally possible to assign the different kinds of sports to different organisational sport structures in Germany. While dancing, yoga, and pilates classes are usually provided by private sport organisations, sports such as cycling, running, and swimming are rather non-organised. On the other hand soccer, gymnastics, or volleyball are typically sports that are practised in non-profit sport clubs (Petry & Hallmann, 2013).

According to Hallmann et al. (2015) typical private sport sector's customers are predominantly female, well-educated, who work longer hours, and are not disabled, while for migration background and age no effect was found. Interestingly, these individual characteristics differ to some extent from the typical 'user' of non-profit sport clubs who tend to be male, young, German, working fewer hours, spending only few or no time at all with upbringing children or caring for relatives, living in multi-person households, and not disabled.

Investigating characteristics of the participants who are active in the private sport sector, a selection effect due to the price level of commercial sport providers cannot be observed based on data from the German Socio-Economic Panel (SOEP)[1]. This means that in this case adolescents coming from wealthier families are not over-represented in the programmes of commercial sport providers (Thieme, 2015).

Focusing on youth sport participation in Germany, every fifth female adolescent as well as every third male adolescent informs to regularly use offers of commercial sport providers. Beyond that, about 10% of sportive 17-year olds indicate that private sport organisations are most important for their sport activities. Additionally, male adolescents use especially the fitness and strength training programmes offered by commercial sport providers, while female adolescents (rather) focus on dancing (Thieme, 2015).

Another interesting demographic aspect is the gender difference regarding the organisational form of sport participation. Especially older females choose to be active in 'differently organised sport'; i.e., neither self-organised nor organised in a sport club. This category also includes commercial sport providers (Alfs, 2014).

Several differences exist between the various kinds of private sport organisations as for example the form of organisation, the structure, focus, or also range of its services, as well as the structure of its revenues or personnel (Kaiser, 2014). However, all private sport organisations generally correspond to the growing service orientation of the society by offering services to people treated as its customers. Moreover, the positive German macroeconomic development has led to people increasing their economic welfare, but having less time available. This also supports the positive development of private sport organisations as people prefer to pay for individual services instead of participating as members in eventually time-consuming activities in traditional sport clubs that require more commitment for the club's common welfare (Deloitte, 2015). Furthermore, the demographic trend of the population getting older and therefore more and more health-conscious as well as the changes in values focusing on fun, health, individual well-being, and experiences

[1] The SOEP is a yearly representative longitudinal study of over 10,000 German private households.

promote the current success of organisations located in the private sport sector, too. Private sport organisations are able to adapt to the changing needs and utility preferences of the society because they represent rather customised services and thereby differentiate themselves from voluntary and public sport organisations (Deloitte, 2015; Kaiser, 2014). However, experts stress the importance of the coexistence of the three organisational types of sport supply for the society as a one-size-fits-all approach is not able to meet all the individuals' needs. The demand of modern society is more flexible and therefore people need choices to fulfil their individual needs (e.g., Skinner, Zakus, & Cowell, 2008).

Although the private sport sector has already been described in the 1990's as an "unknown entity" (Dietrich et al., 1990, 7), research on commercial sport providers has mostly been neglected in Germany so far in contrast to for example voluntary sport clubs, which are regularly analysed by the extensive Sport Development Reports (Breuer, 2007; 2009; 2011; 2013; 2015) commissioned by the German Olympic Sports Confederation and the Federal Institute for Sport Science. This is true even though sport clubs began to lose their central position in the German sport system already decades ago (Dietrich et al., 1990) and even though the majority of the sporting activities nowadays takes place outside of the sport clubs mainly in informal sports (Alfs, 2014). This was confirmed in a study in 2009. While 67% of the Germans who play or exercise sport did sport self-organised, 22% specified to be active in a sport club and 11% were organised differently, including commercial sport providers (Preuss, Alfs, & Ahlert, 2012). Even the classification of commercial sport providers in a category called "organised differently" shows the minor importance of the private sport sector in a lot of research studies up to the present.

A survey conducted with the residents in the city of Munich in 2008 dedicated itself to the organisational structures of the German sporting system and analysed if substitution effects among sport programmes offered by the voluntary, the public, and the private sport sector exist. Results indicated that in certain sports commercial providers are able to complement the supply of the voluntary sport sector by targeting other groups at different times of the day. The study also revealed that the availability of private sport organisations' programmes has a negative effect on the participation in non-profit sport clubs (Hallmann et al., 2015). Thus, it looks like private sport organisations are not negatively affected by the existence of the voluntary and the public sport sector. In contrast, Hallmann et al. (2015) could show that for-profit sport organisations have the capability to push non-profit sport organisations aside. The more commercial sport programmes are offered in a local area, the lower is the probability that a citizen joins a sport club.

Another study (Nowy, Wicker, Feiler, & Breuer, 2015) with data collected in 2013 concentrated on a comparison of non-profit and for-profit sport organisations in regard of their organisational performance. The results suggested that non-profit sport organisations outclass for-profit sport organisations in terms of the price structure, but are clearly inferior regarding to the overall financial performance of for-profit sport organisations, which also put more emphasis on programme quality, employee qualifications, as well as strategies compared to non-profit sport organisations. On the other hand, the legal structure of a sport institution has been found to impact the sponsorship income significantly as the income received by member associations is significantly higher than those of private firms indicating a financial benefit for non-profit sport organisations (Wicker, Weingaertner, Breuer, & Dietl, 2012).

Structure and Characteristics of the Private Sport Sector – Particular Focus on the Fitness Sector and Professional Football Clubs

Key Figures Indicating the Development of the Private Sport Sector

The continuously increasing importance of the private sport sector in Germany can be well illustrated by the steady growth of members and facilities in the fitness sector. Out of 4.4 million Germans holding memberships in fitness centres in 2003 (Statista GmbH, 2016b), the number rose to 7.3 million in 2010. In 2014, as many as 9.1 million people – and therewith every 10th German – have been registered in fitness centres (Deloitte, 2015). This corresponds to a 6.1% growth compared to 2013 (8.6 million people) respectively nearly a one fourth growth compared to 2010. It also means that in Germany fitness centres have more members than any other sports underlining their high significance in the country. Disregarding the different organisational structures and socio-demographics of the target groups, the sport with the second most members is football with a total of 6.9 million in the same year (Deloitte, 2015). Members of fitness facilities are identified to be predominantly female (55%) and more than one fourth (28%) of the members are at least 50 years old (Deloitte, 2015).

Together with the enduring growth of fitness facilities in Germany (from 7114 fitness centres in 2010 to 8026 in 2014) and their total revenues (from 3.8 billion euros in 2010 to 4.7 in 2014), the member growth can be traced back to a stable economic situation in Germany and an increased health consciousness of the society as already mentioned earlier as decisive factors for the success of the private sport sector in general. Especially the circumstance of people becoming more health-conscious has led many fitness facilities to position themselves rather as health providers than just a possibility for some leisure activity (Deloitte, 2015).

Compared to other European countries, the German fitness market was the biggest in 2014 accounting for nearly 20% out of the overall 50.1 million members of fitness centres in Europe. However, the German penetration rate (11.2%) is only average compared to some other European countries. Especially Norway (19.6%), Sweden (16.6%), and The Netherlands (16.0%) have more members relatively to their population in their fitness facilities. Regarding the revenues, Germany is ranked only second with its 4.7 billion euros following Great Britain's 5.1 billion euros (Deloitte, 2015).

Based on data provided by the Federal Statistical Office as well as data from the statistic company Statista, information about the development of the sport sector can be provided. Several directly sport-related classes following the the *Statistical classification of economic activities in the European Community* (NACE Rev. 2, 2008) respectively its German equivalent classification *"Klassifikation der Wirtschaftszweige"* (WZ 2008) are subsequently considered in more detail.

Analysing data of the directly sport-related class *manufacture of sport goods* (code number 3230) for businesses with 20 and more working people from the years 2008 to 2014, the available categories showed a steady increase over the years, namely amount of companies (2008: 48; 2014: 69), number of people working in the field (2008: 4072; 2014: 5710), and total remuneration (2008: 115.4 million euros; 2014: 176.8 million euros). Only the category of total revenues declined from 2008 to 2009, but rose again continuously from 2009 onwards (2008: 616.8 million euros; 2009: 585.1 million euros; 2014: 756.5 million euros).

A different impression can be conveyed by analysing the data from the two directly sport-related country specific classes *wholesale of sport goods* (NACE code 47642) and *retail sale of bicycles* (47641). Numbers fluctuate and the trends change nearly annually in both classes. But generally the development is slightly negative for the former and slightly positive for the latter class in the categories amount of companies, number of employees, as well as total revenues. Regarding the total revenues of the two directly sport-related classes *retail sale of bicycles, sporting, and camping equipment* (4764) and *renting and leasing of recreational and sport goods* (7721), fluctuations also occur from one year to the next, but the overall development is positive for both classes with a slight increase from 6.8 billion euros (2008) to 6.9 billion euros (2013) in the former, and a large increase from 35.8 million euros (2008) to 70.1 million euros (2013) in the latter (Statista GmbH, 2016d; 2016f). Hence, all these numbers underline the overall positive development of the private sport sector in Germany since many years.

Key Information About Sport Business Fields

The classification presented in Table 1 is based on the *Statistical classification of economic activities in the European Community* (NACE Rev. 2, 2008) respectively its German equivalent classification *"Klassifikation der Wirtschaftszweige"* (WZ 2008). Data of the national sport businesses for the year 2013 have been provided by the Federal Statistical Office. Data is available for three different NACE sections containing directly sport-related classes, including *manufacturing* (letter C), *wholesale and retail trade* (G), as well as *administrative and support service activities* (N).

Data of two directly sport-related classes, namely *manufacture of sport goods* (3230) and *renting and leasing of recreational and sport goods* (7721), as well as two directly sport-related country specific classes, namely *wholesale of sport goods* (46492) and *retail sale of bicycles* (47641), are available in Germany for the year 2013. While for the two directly sport-related classes data about the number of companies, staff, revenues, and average salary exist, the two directly sport-related country specific classes lack information of the average salary (see Table 1).

Table 1 Directly sport-related business fields in Germany in 2013.

Business field	Companies (n)	Staff (n)	Revenue (1000 €)	Revenue/Company (1000 €)	Av. salary (1000 €)
Manufacture of sport goods[a]	64	5287[b]	726,185	11,346.6	31.1[c]
Wholesale of sport goods[d]	875	9875[e]	4,850,000	5542.9	n/a
Retail sale of bicycles	5523	20,141[f]	2,719,000	492.3	n/a
Renting and leasing of recreational and sport goods[g]	520	1965[h]	70,566	135.7	7.7[i]
Total	**Σ=6982**	**Σ=37,268**	***M*=8,365,751**	***M*=4379.4**	***M*=19.4**

[a]Only businesses with 20 and more working people are included in the data of the Federal Statistical Office.
[b]The number represents the number of working people in this business field.
[c]The average salary is calculated by dividing the total remuneration by the number of working people.
[d]In the German classification it is called *wholesale of bicycles, sporting, and camping equipment.*
[e]The number represents the number of employees (10,551 individuals in emploeyment) in this business field.
[f]The number represents the number of employees (25,962 individuals in employment) in this business field.
[g]Only businesses with total revenues of at least 17,500 euros are included in the data of the Federal Statistical Office.
[h]The number represents the number of employees in this business field. Additionally 545 working owners or unpaid contributing family members result in 2510 working people.
[i]The average salary is calculated by dividing the total labour costs by the number of employees. The amount is remarkably low for an annual salary. A potential reason might be a lot of part-time workers employed in this directly sport-related class earning low salary.

Comparing these four NACE classes with each other, the highest total revenues are gained in the class *wholesale of sport goods* (46492) with nearly five billion euros earning nearly twice as much as the class *retail sale of bicycles* (47641) following second with 2.7 billion euros. However, the companies in the class *manufacture of sport goods* (3230) are considered most efficient as the revenues per company are clearly the highest with on average 11.3 million euros. This is in so far surprising as the two largest German sport goods manufacturers Adidas and Puma apparently are not included in the 64 companies of this class as both their total revenues extend the specified class' total revenues. The directly sport-related class *renting and leasing of recreational and sport goods* (7721) seems to be the economically least decisive out of the four presented classes with only 135,700 euros total revenues per company. Still, this class employs nearly 2000 people in Germany (see Table 1).

Moreover, further details of other directly sport-related NACE classes could be found via the statistics company Statista. For example, the number of individuals in employment in the directly sport-related country specific class *retail sale of sporting and camping equipment* (47642) in 2013 constituted 37,625 people (Statista GmbH, 2016a), so that a total of 63,587 individuals in employment worked in the directly sport-related class *retail sale of bicycles, sporting, and camping equipment* (4764). Furthermore, this directly sport-related class' revenues for the year 2013 amount to 6.875 billion euros (Statista GmbH, 2016f).

For the directly sport-related class *manufacture of sport goods* (3230), which is also already mentioned in Table 1, revenues of 898 million euros are noted for 2013, when all companies are considered and not only the ones with 20 and more working people (Statista GmbH, 2016c).

In contrast, the revenues of the German sport clubs are subject to the turnover tax and amounted to 4.1 billion euros in 2013 (Statista GmbH, 2016e). Therewith the sport clubs approach the amount of total revenues of the organisations which have been classified into the class *wholesale of sport goods* (46492) displayed in Table 1.

Key Information About Companies of the Most Significant Sport Business Fields

In addition, further information about company specific statistics from the most significant German sport business fields is provided according to the NACE Rev. 2 codes and based on the Amadeus database (produced by Bureau van Dijk) containing comprehensive information of more than 20 million European companies. Two of the most important German sport business fields are presented in the Tables 2 and 3 with some key facts and key financial figures of their largest companies. First, Table 2 contains information about companies, which are classified in NACE into the directly sport-related class *fitness facilities* (9313) as its main or additional business. Second, Table 3 incorporates company details classified in NACE into the directly sport-related class *activities of sport clubs* (9312) as its main business only.

Then, some further large companies from other sport-related business fields are discussed textually. Indicator used to measure companies' financial performance is EBITDA (Earnings Before Interest, Taxes, Depreciation and Amortization) margin (i.e., EBITDA-%).

Table 2 Largest companies based on revenue and classified in NACE into the class fitness facilities as their main or additional business in Germany in 2013.

Company	Brands	Gyms (n)[a]	Revenue (1000 €)	EBITDA-%	Staff (n)	Business
McFIT GmbH	McFIT	169	226,218	33.3	297	Additional
Fitness First Germany GmbH	Fitness First	85	149,210	2.8	2314	Additional
JK-HOLDING GmbH		0	111,762	20.2	362	Additional
Grau Fitness GmbH	KIWI Fitness	1	46,423	10.6	232	Main
Life Fitness Europe GmbH		0	39,539	4.0	92	Additional
Holmes Place Lifestyle Clubs GmbH	Holmes Place	11	35,396	-4.8	382	Main
MeridianSpa Hamburg GmbH	MeridianSpa	5	23,528	15.9	227	Main
FitX Deutschland GmbH	FitX	44	13,820	-20.2	224	Main
Kieser Training GmbH	Kieser Training	115	11,248	5.3	n/a	Additional
Jopp AG	Hard Candy Fitness, SUPERWOMEN Fitness	11	10,922	-5.9	n/a	Main
CCB HERZWERK GmbH	CCB HERZWERK	1	6400	n/a	26	Main
Sport-Park Group GmbH & Co. KG	SPORT-PARK	4	5000	n/a	n/a	Main
Wellness und Fitness Park Schwetzingen GmbH	Pfitzenmeier	1	4748	22.9	138	Main
Benefit Fitness & Wellness KG	beneFit	6	4742	37.3	n/a	Main
MeridianSpa Berlin GmbH	MeridianSpa	1	4560	n/a	n/a	Main

[a]The amount of gyms is based on own research in early 2016 and therefore not necessarily equal to the number in 2013.

The inclusion of the companies that have been classified into the class *fitness facilities* (9313) not as its main business, but only as an additional business in Table 2 is due to the overall methodological difficulty of clearly assigning a company's main business into one specific NACE class. In the Amadeus database this classification is made by the respective information provider and therefore the two biggest fitness centres in Germany, namely McFIT and Fitness First, would be neglected in this overview of fitness facilities when considering only main businesses.

Another difficulty is that the Amadeus database gives information only about the legally independent businesses. Therefore, subsidiaries as for example the MeridianSpa Berlin GmbH and the MeridianSpa Hamburg GmbH are presented as two separate companies and are not combined to the MeridianSpa Deutschland GmbH representing all German facilities together. Additionally, out of the several facilities of Werner Pfitzenmeier in the German fitness sector only the Wellness und Fitness Park Schwetzingen GmbH is included in Table 2, because the different facilities are all legally independent companies. The JK-HOLDING GmbH as well as the Life Fitness Europe GmbH are both included in Table 2 without having their own gyms, because they are mainly occupied with the production of fitness equipment and therefore classified also into the class *fitness facilities* (9313) as their additional business.

Table 3 Largest companies based on revenue and classified in NACE into the class activities of sport clubs as their main business in Germany in 2013.

Company	Brands	Revenue (1000 €)	EBITDA-%	Staff (n)
FC Bayern München AG	Bayern München	432,763	22.1	486
Borussia Dortmund GmbH & Co. KGaA	Borussia Dortmund	307,817	28.4	524
FC Gelsenkirchen-Schalke 04 e.V.	FC Schalke 04	215,618	21.3	1,337
Hamburger Sport-Verein e.V.	Hamburger SV	131,532	9.1	249
Volkswagen Motorsport GmbH	Volkswagen Motorsport	97,604	3.2	162
Borussia VfL 1900 Mönchengladbach GmbH	Borussia Mönchengladbach	91,173	22.2	225
Eintracht Frankfurt Fußball AG	Eintracht Frankfurt	86,475	10.8	290
Hannover 96 GmbH & Co. KGaA	Hannover 96	78,040	15.9	156
TSG 1899 Hoffenheim Fußball-Spielbetriebs GmbH	TSG Hoffenheim	76,719	-4.7	205
1.Fussball- und Sportverein Mainz 05	1.FSV Mainz 05	66,700	n/a	n/a

Contrary to Table 2, only companies that are classified into the NACE class *activities of sport clubs* (9312) as their main business are listed in Table 3, which is clearly dominated by the football teams playing in the German Bundesliga. It has to be noted that again not every professional football team has been classified into this class based on the main business by the respective information provider.

However, most and especially the biggest teams are included into the class. Table 3 disregards only two exceptions which are missing in the clubs' top ten based on revenues, because they have been classified into the class *activities of sport clubs* (9312) only as an additional business. These two teams are the VfB Stuttgart 1893 e.V. and the SV Werder Bremen GmbH & Co. KGaA. While the former had a total revenue of 114.8 million euros in 2013 and therewith the fifth highest from the football teams in Table 3, the latter directly followed with revenues of 93.6 million euros ranked after the Volkswagen Motorsport GmbH, which is the only business outside of football in Table 3. No further information is available for the VfB Stuttgart 1893 e.V., but the SV Werder Bremen GmbH & Co. KGaA had an EBITDA of 3.7 million leading to an EBITDA-% of 3.9 and employed 482 people in 2013. As in the real sporting performance the biggest German football team Bayern Munich is undisputed leading in this class regarding the total revenues and only Borussia Dortmund is more or less able to keep pace with the Bavarian superiority (see Table 3).

The General German Automobile Association (ADAC) is also classified into the directly sport-related class *activities of sport clubs* (9312) by the Amadeus database, but only as an additional business. Including the ADAC, which incorporates sport in terms of motorsports, into the overview shown in Table 3, this registered association surpasses the above mentioned sport clubs by far in regard of total revenues. In 2013, the ADAC had a revenue of 949.7 million euros and thereby more than twice as much as the football club of Bayern Munich. Its EBITDA and number of employees were not reported. However, it has to be noted that sport plays only a minor role in the ADAC.

Obviously there are larger and more significant companies in Germany from other sport business fields. Especially the two sport goods manufacturers, namely adidas AG and Puma SE should be mentioned at this point. While the adidas AG is uncatchable leading the class *manufacture of other wearing apparel and accessories* (code number 1419) based on the revenues (14.7 billion euros), EBITDA (1.5 billion euros leading to an EBITDA-% of 10.4), as well as staff (48,518 employees) in 2013, the Puma SE follows second in all these three categories in the same class with a revenue of three billion euros, an EBITDA of 176.6 million euros (leading to an EBITDA-% of 5.9) and 10,750 employees.

In the directly sport-related class *manufacture of sport goods* (3230) Heinz Kettler GmbH & Co. KG is the leading company generating revenues of 202.9 million euros in 2013 and therefore more than twice as much than the next best company Jako AG in this class with 76.6 million euros. Kettler, which is especially producing fitness equipment, employed 1046 people and achieved an EBITDA-% of 2.2 in 2013. Two companies of the directly sport-related class *retail sale of bicycles, sporting, and camping equipment* (4764) exceeded the threshold of 200 million euros, namely Karstadt Sports GmbH (243.5 million euros) and Globetrotter Ausrüstungs GmbH (201.2 million euros). While the former employed 928 people and achieved an EBITDA-% of 0.4, the latter had an EBITDA-% of 2.4 and 1326 employees in 2013.

Conclusions

The private sport industry has developed into an important market player in Germany. Its further perspective looks quite good. It is estimated that its revenues and market share will grow. On the one hand, this can be traced back to the competitive advantages that have emerged from the structure and institutions of for-profit organisations such as financial incentives for owners, pressure to innovate (Heinemann, 1995) as well as higher financial performances, and more emphasis on programme quality, employee qualifications and strategies (Nowy et al., 2015). Relative competitive advantages of for-profit sport organisations do also emerge from non-profit sport clubs' continuing and rising problems of recruiting volunteers, referees, coaches, and especially board members (Breuer & Feiler, 2015). On the other hand, an ongoing social and economic change with more spending power but less leisure of the population may also influence the market position of for-profit sport organisations in Germany. This could harm the voluntary sport clubs since they can barely offer flexible training hours and financial constraints of members and customers will be less important. Moreover, it must not be forgotten that sport- and body-related values and norms also play a crucial role how the private sport sector will develop.

References

Alfs, C. (2014). *Sportkonsum in Deutschland: Empirische Analysen zur Allokation von Zeit und Geld für Sport* [Sport consumption in Germany: Empirical analysis of the allocation of time and money for sports]. Wiesbaden, Germany: Springer.

Breuer, C. (2004). Zur Dynamik der Sportnachfrage im Lebenslauf [The dynamics of sport demand in a life cycle]. *Sport und Gesellschaft, 1*(*1*), 50–72.

Breuer, C. (2007). *Sportentwicklungsbericht 2005/2006 – Analyse zur Situation der Sportvereine in Deutschland* (Vol. 2) [Sport Development Report 2005/2006 – Analysis of the situation of sports clubs in Germany]. Cologne, Germany: Sportverlag Strauß.

Breuer, C. (2009). *Sportentwicklungsbericht 2007/2008 – Analyse zur Situation der Sportvereine in Deutschland* [Sport Development Report 2007/2008 – Analysis of the situation of sports clubs in Germany]. Cologne, Germany: Sportverlag Strauß.

Breuer, C. (2011). *Sportentwicklungsbericht 2009/2010 – Analyse zur Situation der Sportvereine in Deutschland* [Sport Development Report 2009/2010 – Analysis of the situation of sports clubs in Germany]. Cologne, Germany: Sportverlag Strauß.

Breuer, C. (2013). *Sportentwicklungsbericht 2011/2012 – Analyse zur Situation der Sportvereine in Deutschland* [Sport Development Report 2011/2012 – Analysis of the situation of sports clubs in Germany]. Cologne, Germany: Sportverlag Strauß.

Breuer, C. (2015). *Sportentwicklungsbericht 2013/2014 – Analyse zur Situation der Sportvereine in Deutschland* [Sport Development Report 2013/2014 – Analysis of the situation of sports clubs in Germany]. Cologne, Germany: Sportverlag Strauß.

Breuer, C., & Feiler, S. (2015). *Sport development report 2013/2014: Analysis of the situation of sports clubs in Germany. Abbreviated Version*. Cologne, Germany: Sportverlag Strauß.

Breuer, C., Feiler, S., & Wicker, P. (2015). Sport clubs in Germany. In C. Breuer, R. Hoekman, S. Nagel, & H. van der Werff (Eds.), *Sport clubs in Europe: A cross-national comparative perspective* (pp. 187–208). Cham, Switzerland: Springer International Publishing Switzerland.

Deloitte. (2015). *Der deutsche Fitnessmarkt - Studie 2015* [The German fitness market – Study 2015]. Düsseldorf, Germany: Deloitte & Touche GmbH Wirtschaftsprüfungsgesellschaft.

Dietrich, K., Heinemann, K., & Schubert, M. (1990). *Kommerzielle Sportanbieter* [Commercial sport suppliers]. Schorndorf, Germany: Hofmann.

Esser, H. (1993). *Soziologie – Allgemeine Grundlagen* [Sociology – General basics]. Frankfurt/Main, Germany: Campus.

Esser, H. (1999). *Soziologie – Spezielle Grundlagen* [Sociology – Special basics]. Frankfurt/Main, Germany: Campus.

Gratton, C., & Taylor, P. (2000). *Economics of sport and recreation*. London, UK: E & FN Spon.

Hallmann, K., Feiler, S., & Breuer, C. (2015). Design and delivery of sport for all programmes: Should it be market, non-profit, or state-run? *International Journal of Sport Policy and Politics, 7*(4), 565–585.

Heinemann, K. (1995). *Einführung in die Ökonomie des Sports* [Introduction to sport economics]. Schorndorf, Germany: Hofmann.

Kaiser, S. (2014). Markt und Sportentwicklung - die Rolle der kommerziellen Sportanbieter [Market and sport development – The role of commercial sport suppliers]. In A. Rütten, S. Nagel, & R. Kähler (Eds.), *Handbuch Sportentwicklungsplanung* (pp. 245–252). Schorndorf, Germany: Hofmann.

Lindenberg, S. (1996). Die Relevanz theoriereicher Brückenannahmen [The relevance of theoretical bridging assumptions]. *Kölner Zeitschrift für Soziologie und Sozialpsychologie, 48*(1), 126–140.

Nowy, T., Wicker, P., Feiler, S., & Breuer, C. (2015). Organizational performance of nonprofit and for-profit sport organizations. *European Sport Management Quarterly, 15*(2), 155–175.

Petry, K., & Hallmann, K. (2013). Germany. In K. Hallmann & K. Petry (Eds.), *Comparative sport development. Systems, participation and public policy* (pp. 75–86). New York, NY: Springer.

Preuss, H., Alfs, C., & Ahlert, G. (2012). *Sport als Wirtschaftsbranche: Der Sportkonsum privater Haushalte in Deutschland* [Sport as an economic sector: The sport consumption of private households in Germany]. Wiesbaden, Germany: Springer.

Rittner, V. (1988). Sport als ökonomisches Interessenobjekt [Sport as an object of economic interest]. In H. Digel (Ed.), *Sport im Verein und Verband* (pp. 158–187). Schorndorf, Germany: Hofmann.

Rittner, V., & Breuer, C. (2000). *Kommunale Sportpolitik. Wege aus dem Dornröschenschlaf* [Municipal sport policy. Ways out of the deep slumber]. Cologne, Germany: Sport und Buch Strauß.

Schubert, K., & Klein, M. (2011). *Das Politiklexikon* [Encyclopaedia of politics]. Bonn, Germany: Dietz.

Skinner, J., Zakus, D. H., & Cowell, J. (2008). Development through sport: Building social capital in disadvantaged communities. *Sport Management Review, 11*(3), 253–275.

Statista GmbH. (2016a). Anzahl der Beschäftigten im Einzelhandel in Deutschland nach Branchen im Jahr 2013 [Number of retail employees in Germany sorted by industry sector in 2013]. Retrieved March 18, 2016 from http://de.statista.com/statistik/daten/studie/378672/umfrage/beschaeftigte-im-einzelhandel-in-deutschland-nach-branchen/

Statista GmbH. (2016b). Mitgliederzahl der Fitnessstudios in Deutschland von 2003 bis 2014 (in Millionen) [Number of gym members in Germany from 2003 to 2014 (in million)]. Retrieved March 15, 2016 from http://de.statista.com/statistik/daten/studie/5966/umfrage/mitglieder-der-deutschen-fitnessclubs/

Statista GmbH. (2016c). Umsatz der Branche Herstellung von Sportgeräten in Deutschland von 2008 bis 2013 und Prognose bis zum Jahr 2020 (in Millionen Euro) [Sales numbers of the sport equipment manufacturing industry in Germany from 2008 to 2013 with forecasts until 2020 (in million Euros)]. Retrieved March 18, 2016 from http://de.statista.com/prognosen/400326/herstellung-von-sportgeraeten-in-deutschland---umsatzprognose

Statista GmbH. (2016d). Umsatz der Branche Vermietung von Sport- und Freizeitgeräten in Deutschland von 2008 bis 2013 und Prognose bis zum Jahr 2020 (in Millionen Euro) [Sales numbers of the sport and leisure equipment rental industry in Germany from 2008 to 2013 with forecasts until 2020 (in million Euros)]. Retrieved March 18, 2016 from http://de.statista.com/prognosen/400521/vermietung-von-sport--und-freizeitgeraeten-in-deutschland---umsatzprognose

Statista GmbH. (2016e). Umsatz der umsatzsteuerpflichtigen Sportvereine in Deutschland von 2009 bis 2013 (in 1.000 Euro) [Sales numbers of sports clubs liable to tax on sales in Germany from 2009 to 2013 (in 1000 Euros)]. Retrieved March 18, 2016 from http://de.statista.com/statistik/daten/studie/422168/umfrage/umsatz-deutscher-sportvereine/

Statista GmbH. (2016f). Umsatz im Einzelhandel mit Fahrrädern, Sport- und Campingartikeln in Deutschland von 2008 bis 2013 und Prognose bis zum Jahr 2020 (in Millionen Euro) [Sales numbers of the retail industry offering bicycles, sport and camping gear in Germany from 2008 to 2013 with forecasts until 2020 (in million Euros)]. Retrieved March 18, 2016 from http://de.statista.com/prognosen/400430/einzelhandel-mit-fahrraedern-sport--und-campingartikeln-in-deutschland---umsatzprognose

Thieme, L. (2015). Kommerzieller Sport [Commercial sports]. In W. Schmidt, N. Neuber, T. Rauschenbach, H. P. Brandl-Bredenbeck, J. Süßenbach, & C. Breuer (Eds.), *Dritter Deutscher Kinder- und Jugendsportbericht* (pp. 162–178). Schorndorf, Germany: Hofmann.

Weisbrod, B. A. (1988). *The nonprofit economy*. Cambridge, MA: Harvard University Press.

Wicker, P., Weingaertner, C., Breuer, C., & Dietl, H. (2012). The effect of a sports institution's legal structure on sponsorship income: The case of amateur equestrian sports in Germany. *International Journal of Sport Finance, 7*(4), 340–357.

GREECE: The Impact of Economic Crisis on the Private Sport Sector

Kostas Alexandris and Panagiota Balaska

Selected country facts (in 2013)	
Capital	Athens
Geographical size (km²)	131,957
Population (million)	11.00
GDP (euro per capita)	16,500
GDP (per capita in PPS)	72
Annual net earnings average (€)	15,397

Introduction: The Greek Economy

For the last eight years (2009–2016) Greece has been in the middle of the economic crisis, which has affected all parts of the economy. Therefore, brief information about the economy of the country will be presented. Greek economy is mainly based on the service sector (85%), industry sector (12%) and agriculture (3%) (Passport to Trade: A Bridge to Success, 2016). One of the most important industries within the service sector is tourism. According to Greek Tourism in 2015 (2015) Greece attracts approximately 26 million visitors per year, who contribute to more than 14.2 billion euros to the Greek economy.

Since 2009 severe economic crisis has affected all the elements of life and society in Greece. Summarizing economic indicators, Theodorou (2015) reported that in the beginning of 2008 the country lost about 25% of its economic activities. In 2015 the GDP of the country was 176 billion euros and the GDP per capita 16,028

K. Alexandris (✉) • P. Balaska
Department of Physical Education and Sport Sciences, Aristotle University of Thessaloniki, Thessaloniki, Greece
e-mail: kalexand@phed.auth.gr

A. Laine, H. Vehmas (eds.), *The Private Sport Sector in Europe*, Sports Economics, Management and Policy 14, https://doi.org/10.1007/978-3-319-61310-9_10

euros, compared to 2008, when the GDP of the country was 242 billion euros and the GDP per capita 22,500 euros. The amount of taxes that the employees and retirees had to pay in 2009 was seven times more than in 2004. The percentage of the population who lived in danger of poverty was 23% in 2015. Almost 70 billion euros have gone out of the Greek banks during the last five years. One out of four of the small and medium size companies have closed down since 2008 (230,000 companies). About 77 billion loans are considered as non-performing or "red loans" (33.5% of all loans). (Theodorou, 2015.) Non-performing loans are those that the borrower has delayed more than three months to pay the interest or the principal (Papadoyiannis, 2016). The unemployment rate of the country has reached to 24.1%, when back in 2008 it was 7.3% (Greece Economic Indicators, 2016). In June 2016 the Greek government reached an agreement with its creditors that 10.3 billion euros will be lent to cover the upcoming debts in order to finance and support the Greek economy in the near future. As an exchange for this money more austerity measures have been imposed by the Greek government. The question regarding the sustainability of the Greek debts remains unanswered. (Greek Economic Outlook, 2016.)

Economic Impact of Sport

According to the "Study on the Contribution of Sport to Economic Growth and Employment in the EU" (2012) the share of the sport-related gross value added, which shows the direct effects of the sport sector in Greece, was 0.36% of overall gross value added according to the *statistical definition of sport*. This is one% by the *narrow definition of sport* and 1.44% by the *broad definition of sport*. The statistical definition includes only sport activities. Thus, the share of the organized sport sector such as sport clubs, public sport venues and sport event organizers is included in the statistical definition. The narrow definition is broader than the statistical definition and it covers sport activities plus all other activities that are direct inputs of sport, such as all goods and services which are necessary for participation in sport. Finally the broad definition includes everything defined in the statistical and narrow definitions plus all activities which require sport as an input (i.e., all goods and services which are related to any sport activity but without being necessarily directly related to sport participation). This includes for example the hotel industry, sport medicine and sport journalism. (Study on the Contribution of Sport to Economic Growth and Employment in the EU, 2012.)

These shares of the sport-related gross values added in Greece are below the EU average, which is 1.13% by the narrow definition and 1.76% by the broad definition. The sport-related value added, which shows the direct effects of the Greek sport sector, amounts to 1.74 billion euros according to the narrow definition, 2.52 billion euros according to the broad definition and 0.63 billion euros according to the statistical definition. It has to be emphasized that these figures represent economic activities of all sport sectors (public, private and non-profit). Sport-related employment (direct effects) amounts to 56,226 persons according to the narrow definition and 70,878 persons with respect to the broad definition. For the statistical definition sport-related employment reported in this study was 19,594. (Study on the Contribution of Sport to Economic Growth and Employment in the EU, 2012.)

More specific information about the economic activities in sport is provided in the Table 1, which has been drawn from the Hellenic Statistical Authority (2011). The latest information available is from 2011. Different business fields, numbers of businesses and revenues are presented in the Table 1, based on the Greek equivalent (STAKOD 08) of the *Statistical classification of economic activities in the European Community* (NACE Rev. 2, 2008). As it can be seen, the largest field is the sport retailing category which includes 2497 businesses with a revenue of 410 million euros.

The rest of the categories include sport facilities and variety of sport services. Out of those, facilities is the largest category, in which both Sport facilities (NACE code 9311) and Gymnastics facilities (9313) can be added. This field is a mixture of private (e.g., private swimming pools and gymnasiums) and public (sport stadiums) businesses. These facilities are used both for providing opportunities for sport participation and for sport spectatorship.

Fitness/health related businesses/programs (9604) is the next biggest category, including private health and fitness clubs. Other sport programs (9319) and Sport clubs (9312) categories follow. In these two categories are included for example professional or semi-professional football, basketball and volleyball clubs, but also private golf clubs, fitness programs and other sport clubs that operate as limited companies. Some of the sport clubs provide opportunities for sport spectatorship since they participate in international, national, regional and local sport leagues. Football and basketball are currently the only professional sport leagues in Greece. Sport and recreation education (8551) involves sport camps and professional sport schools at the vocational level (Institutes of Vocational Training, IVT). Finally, in the Outdoor/theme parks (9321) category mainly outdoor leisure and entertainment parks are included.

Table 1 Directly sport-related business fields in Greece in 2011.

Business field	NACE code	Companies (n)	Revenue (1000 €)
Sport goods retailing	4764	2497	410,445.1
Sport facilities	9311	638	108,091.0
Fitness/health related businesses/programs	9604	1083	89,104.0
Other sport programs	9319	629	78,292.0
Gymnastic facilities	9313	1018	52,049.0
Sport clubs	9312	308	23,342.0
Sport and recreation education	8551	839	22,845.0
Outdoor and theme parks	9321	160	17,925.0
Total		**7172**	**802,097.1**

Source: Hellenic Statistical Authority (2011).

The Sport Administration System

The Hellenic Ministry of Culture and Sports is responsible for developing the central government's sport policy in Greece. This is done in co-operation with the General Secretariat of Sports, which is one of the four Secretariats of the Ministry. The other three Secretariats are The Secretariats of Tourism, Culture and Infrastructure. The General Secretariat of Sports is financed by the Central Government budget, the Greek Organization of Football Prognostics (O.P.A.P.), the Hellenic Horse Racing Organization and the National Investment Program. (Alexandris & Balaska, 2015a.)

As seen in Fig. 1, sport federations are directed by the General Secretariat of Sports, which decides the amount of financial support that sport federations receive every year. Sport federations are non-profit organizations, which are managed by elected committees. These committees are elected by the sport clubs which are members of the federations. Each federation is responsible for promoting the sport that it represents. Each federation is also responsible for supervising its sport clubs and associations, who deliver the sport services and programs. Local authorities play also an important role in the Greek sport administration system. Their sport departments manage sport facilities and deliver "Sport for All" programs. These programs aim to promote public welfare by providing opportunities for local residents to participate. "Sport for All" programs are financed by the members' fees and the General Secretariat of Sports. (Alexandris & Balaska, 2015a.)

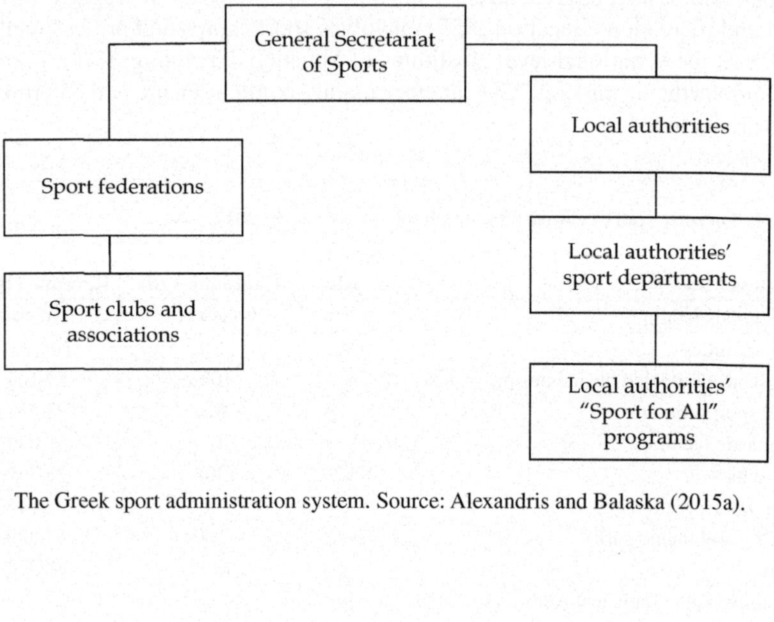

Fig. 1 The Greek sport administration system. Source: Alexandris and Balaska (2015a).

Consumer Demand for Sport Products

Sport consumer demand is influenced by several factors, which are discussed in detail by Funk, Alexandris and McDonald (2016). Some of these factors are relevant to the sport market in Greece within the current economic situation. *Price* of the sport product is the first factor that can have positive or negative effect. Competition between companies can lead to reduced prices, especially in periods of limited demand. This is the case with health and fitness clubs in Greece, as will be discussed later.

The second factor proposed by Funk et al. (2016) relates to the *communication and advertising campaigns*. Advertising has two main objectives: to increase consumer awareness and to build the product brand, in order to differentiate it from the competition. Strong brands tend to spend more money on advertising campaigns. They are also involved in sponsorship programs. During the last eight years (2009–2016) the money spent on sport advertising and sponsorship in Greece has been significantly reduced (Alexandris & Balaska, 2015b).

The third factor proposed by Funk et al. (2016) relates to the influence of the *socio-cultural environment*. This includes influence of several reference groups, such as family, age, social class, culture and sub-culture groups. There have been several changes in the Greek society during the last twenty years. Some of the most prominent ones are the changing role of women in the Greek society (more financially independent), the increase in the life-expectancy, the economic pressure of the middle class (due to austerity measures), and the increased understanding of the value of active lifestyle. (Alexandris & Balaska, 2015b; Balaska & Alexandris, 2014.) Most of these changes with the exception of the negative financial situation have had positive impact in the demand of sport products in Greece.

The fourth factor proposed by Funk et al. (2016) relates to the *consumer power*. According to the report Greek Economic Indicators (2016), the total consumer spending in Greece in January 2016 was 30.3 million euros, while in January 2009 it was more than 42 million euros. Furthermore, consumer confidence in April 2016 was -72, while it was -30 in January 2015. The consumer confidence is measured on a scale of −100 to +100, where −100 indicate extreme lack of confidence, 0 neutrality and +100 extreme confidence. (Greek Economic Indicators, 2016.) The last factor proposed by Funk et al. (2016) relates to the *socio-cultural trends and lifestyles*, which typically influence sport consumer behavior. It can be argued that participating in sport and caring about personal fitness have been taken more seriously by the Greeks during the last five years (Alexandris & Balaska, 2015a; Balaska & Alexandris, 2014).

Public and Voluntary Sport Sectors

Sport in Greece is provided by the public (state and local authorities), voluntary (sport clubs and non-profit associations) and the private sectors. The public sport sector includes "Sport for all" programs and sport facilities provided and managed by local authorities and by the General Secretariat of Sports. (Fig. 2.) "Sport for all" programs in Greece are provided by the local authorities and their sport departments, with the aim to promote sport in society and contribute to the quality of life of the residents of local communities (Alexandris & Balaska, 2015a; 2015b).

These programs usually have low enrollment fees, in comparison with the private sport sector and they target also to the "disadvantaged" groups of the population (e.g., elderly, disabled and individuals with chronic diseases). Traditionally these sport programs have been financially supported by the General Secretariat of Sports. Although there have been financial reductions in the financial support of the General Secretariat of Sports, local authorities are still financially supported to run these programs. The central government has recognized the value of the recreational sport for the quality of life of the local communities. However, it has to be noted that local authorities have started to explore alternative sources of finance (e.g., sponsorships, higher membership fees and renting of the facilities) in their efforts to become as much as possible financially independent. (Alexandris & Balaska, 2015a; 2015b; Balaska & Alexandris, 2014.)

Local authorities manage also indoor and outdoor sport facilities, such as gyms, swimming pools, basketball, football and volleyball courts. These sport facilities are for the use of citizens in general and also used by the local amateur sport teams and sport clubs. The state that it is represented by the General Secretariat of Sports, also manages indoor and outdoor sport facilities. The sport facilities are administered by the committees that are assigned by the General Secretariat of Sports. These sport facilities are used by both amateur and professional sport teams, as well as by the sport clubs that promote elite sport.

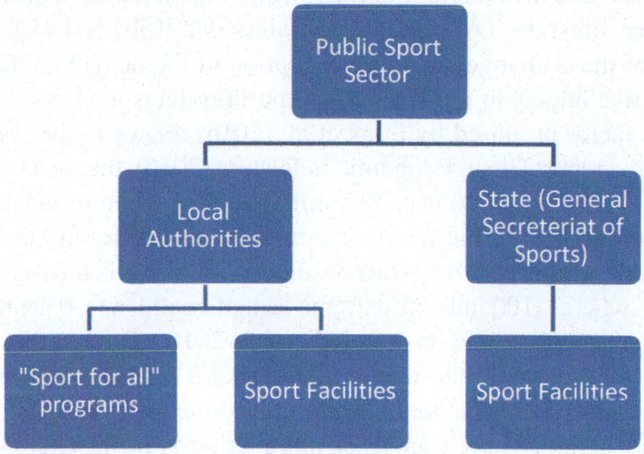

Fig. 2 The administration of the public sport sector in Greece. Source: Alexandris and Balaska (2015a).

The voluntary sport sector consists of sport clubs. According to the General Secretariat of Sports (2016a), there are 11,846 sport clubs in Greece that are registered in the General Secretariat of Sports. The prefecture of Attiki has the largest number of sport clubs (2536), followed by the prefectures of Thessaloniki (961), Achaia (425) and Larissa (396). There is a positive correlation between the population of each prefecture and the number of clubs, as well as between the financial situation of each prefecture (local GDP) and the number of sport clubs. On average, one sport club corresponds to 764 residents. It is estimated that 1% increase in the population is associated with 0.44% increase in the number of clubs. Considering the demographic trends, as analyzed before, the total number of sport clubs is not expected to increase during the following years. Increases however might take place in specific sports which are developing. According to the General Secretariat of Sports (2016b), football has the highest number of sport clubs (2438), followed by basketball (737), volleyball (376), swimming (326) and athletics (320). Football also has the highest number of certified coaches (5346), followed by basketball (3902), volleyball (1936), athletics (1601) and swimming (1407). Water skiing has the highest ratio of coaches per club (45), followed by taekwondo IDF (11.1) and mountain skiing (8). In total 7103 certified coaches work today in sport clubs in Greece. (General Secretariat of Sports, 2016b.)

As Alexandris and Balaska (2015a) point out, sport clubs have traditionally targeted at youth, providing opportunities for training of young athletes and promoting elite sport. However, during the last couple of years there have emerged also sport clubs and associations that provide sport and recreation opportunities for adults, mainly in outdoor sports (e.g., running, biking and triathlon). Sport clubs are financed by the membership fees and the General Secretariat of Sports, through which funds have been allocated by their sport federations. The amount of financial help that the sport clubs are given depends mainly on the success of the club in promoting "sports for excellence", as measured by the number of elite athletes. Due to the dramatic reductions in the budget of the sport federations during the last seven years (2009–2015) in Greece, the clubs have started to cut down their operation costs and at the same time looked for similar alternative financial sources as the local authorities. (Alexandris & Balaska, 2015a; 2015b; Giannoulakis, Papadimitriou, & Alexandris, 2016.)

Sport tourism is developing quickly in Greece. Windsurfing picture illustrates the outdoor recreation opportunities in the country and why tourists travel to Greece.

One of the fast developing areas within the non-profit sector is the outdoor running sport events, which have been growing fast in Greece during the last five years (Alexandris, 2016a; 2016b; 2016c). According to Polatidou (2015), the number of mountain running races increased from 16 to 85 between the years 2008 and 2013, and the number of participants in these events increased from 2220 to 12,000 during the same years. In 2012 the mountain races accounted for almost 33% of the total number of running events (Petridis, 2015). The vast majority of the outdoor running sport events are mainly organized by non-profit sport organizations, in co-operation with local authorities. Tourism and economic impact of these events for local communities is significant. For example according to Alexandris (2016a) mountain running events, such as the Metsovo Race and the Olympus marathon, have direct economic impacts in the local communities of around 200,000 euros. It is a significant amount for the local communities. Considering that there are currently more than one hundred such mountain sport events, the total economic activity generated in this area exceeds to two million euros. Other than the mountain marathons, there are also two big city marathons in Greece, The Athens Classic Marathon and the Alexander the Great Marathon, which take place in Thessaloniki. Both of these marathons have evidenced an impressive growth during the last five years. In The Athens Classic Marathon the number of 20,000 runners in 2010 increased to 50,000 in 2016. In the Alexander the Great Marathon, the number of runners increased from 11,000 in 2013 to 20,000 in 2015. (Alexandris, 2016d.) The economic impact of the 2016 Athens Classic Marathon for the city was more than 15 million euros (Assimakopoulos, 2016).

Private Sport Sector

The private sport sector in Greece can be defined as consisting of three business fields. These are the participatory sport field, the sport goods field and the sport / recreation education field. The participatory sport field include sport and gymnastic facilities (NACE codes 9311 and 9313), health/fitness clubs (9604), sport clubs (9312), other sport programs (9319) as well as outdoor and theme parks (9321). The sport goods field includes sport goods retailing (4764) and manufacturing. However, sport goods manufacturing has no separate NACE category in Greece. The sport / recreation education field has separate category (8551), as presented earlier in the Table 1.

The Participatory Sport

Since there is no published information about the specific activity of all NACE categories in the participatory sport field in Greece, focus is on the fitness business (NACE codes 9604 and 9313), which is probably the most dynamic field. According to Alexandros Batrakoulis, scientific coordinator of the Greek Aerobics and Fitness Training School, it is estimated that there are about 1250 private health and fitness clubs in the country (A. Batrakoulis, personal communication, September 15, 2016). This brings Greece to the tenth place among the European countries. Germany is the number one country in Europe with altogether 8322 health and fitness clubs, followed by the United Kingdom (6312 clubs). In Greece private health and fitness clubs have about 625,000 members, who nowadays pay an average fee of 20–25 euros per month. (Rodriquez, 2016.) These low fees result from the economic crisis; many of the health and fitness clubs managers reduced their monthly and annually fees as a defensive strategy to survive. As a comparison, the average monthly fee three years earlier (in 2013) was 50 euros (Ablondi, 2014). In general, the average monthly fee is relatively low in Greece, in fact among the lowest in Europe. This can be illustrated for example by a comparison with Switzerland, where the average monthly fee is 61 euros (Ablondi, 2014). The fee in the Greek fitness clubs varies according to the type of the club and the services that they offer. For instance personal training studios are generally more expensive. Also the location of the clubs has an impact on the fees. Clubs in Athens and Thessaloniki tend to be more expensive than in the other parts of the country.

It is estimated that the economic activities produced by health and fitness clubs in Greece value approximately 187 million euros per year. This brings Greece into the last position among the European countries. It is still a small market when compared for example to the UK, which has the biggest market in Europe, worth 6.2 billion euros. (Rodriguez, 2016.) Nevertheless, it needs to be noted, that there are also economic activities related to the personal training services in Greece in which many of the services are informal. This implies that the activities are not always recorded.

The health and fitness club sector provides an indicative example of what has been the influence of the economic crisis on the participatory sport field in Greece. While the economic crisis has had a dramatically negative effect in almost all types of businesses in Greece, the fitness club sector seems to have managed to survive in some ways. According to a recent study that was conducted during June-July 2016 (Alexandris, 2016c) on a sample of 60 fitness clubs in Thessaloniki and Athens, 43 of the clubs reported a decrease in the number of their membership as a result of the economic crisis. Despite this, another 33% reported an increase and 24% reported no changes in their club memberships. The negative impact, however, is more intense and evident in the profits of the clubs. The majority (67%) of the clubs reported a decrease in their profits. However, there was another 12% that reported an increase and 17% that reported no changes in their profits. The average decrease in the number of memberships was 20% and in the profits 27%. (Table 2.)

Table 2 Economic crisis and health/fitness clubs (n = 60) in Thessaloniki, Greece in 2009–2016.

The influence of economic crisis in the number of members of health/fitness clubs		
Decrease	Increase	No change
43%	33%	24%
Average decrease in number of members: 20%	Average increase in number lof members: 21%	
The influence of economic crisis in the profit of health/fitness clubs		
Decrease	Increase	No change
67%	12%	17%
Average decrease in profit: 27%	Average increase in profit: 22%	

Source: Alexandris (2016c).

These negative effects on the profits of the clubs were mainly due to the decrease in the membership fees. The vast majority (86%) of the clubs reported that they had reduced their monthly and annual fees. As expected, reductions in the operating costs (84%), in the number of employees (62%) and in the salaries (62%) were typical defensive strategies adopted. However, enriching the fitness programs (84%) and improving the existing ones (74%) were also popular strategies adopted by the clubs. Finally, it is worth mentioning that despite the negative economic environment, 48% of the club managers saw the future of the fitness industry as positively developing, 27% as neutral and only 27% as negative. This relatively positive profile of the fitness sector in Greece relates to the changing values and lifestyles of the Greek population towards a more active way of living. It might also relate to Greeks' understanding of the positive psychological benefits of sport and recreation in an otherwise pessimistic and stressful environment that Greeks have been living for the past eight years, as a result of the economic crisis. (Alexandris & Balaska, 2015b; Balaska & Alexandris, 2014.)

Other than health and fitness clubs, economic activity within the participatory sport field is also generated for example by tennis and golf clubs, five-a-side football court businesses, outdoor parks and several other sport clubs which operate as limited companies. There is very little statistical information available for each of such economic activity. Some estimation can be made about tennis clubs. According to George Makatsis, tennis professional and freelance writer, it is estimated that there are about 80 tennis clubs in Greece, with a variety of number of members ranging from 100 to 1000. The monthly fees vary between 50–100 euros. (G. Makatsis, personal communication, June 8, 2016.) It is estimated that the economic activity produced by the private tennis clubs is about two million euros per year.

The Sport Goods

According to the ICAP Group's(2014) study (ICAP is a business consulting company) the sport goods field in Greece is categorized into two different parts. These are the sport goods manufacturers and businesses that import sport goods. The sport goods manufacturers can be categorized into a) businesses that produce sport clothes and have their own trademark (e.g., Bodytalk) and into b) businesses that produce sport clothes for foreign brands (under the trademark of the foreign brands). In the first mentioned group clothes are manufactured either in Greece or abroad, and they are either distributed in the Greek market through retailing or they are exported. The latter case is however rare, because Greek sport brands are not strong enough to compete with the international brands. In the second group companies have only export activities as they export these clothes. There used to be also two product-specific sport goods manufacturing categories: manufacturers of sport shoes and manufacturers of sport clothes, but currently there are no more real activities on sport shoes manufacturing. This field has declined because Greek shoes were not competitive enough in comparison with imported sport shoes. The import sport businesses on the other hand are categorized into a) businesses which import international brands (e.g., Nike, Adidas and Puma) sport goods and sell them in the Greek market and into b) businesses that import sport goods which are manufactured abroad and sold in the Greek market with their local trademark. (ICAP Group, 2014.)

According to the ICAP Group's (2014) study, the total sales of the manufacturing sport companies in Greece was17.7 million euros in 2013. There was a 1.2% decrease from 2012 (17.9 MEUR). As can be seen in Fig. 3, in 2009 (the year when the economic crisis started in Greece), this field had the highest sales (18.1 MEUR). By far the biggest sport manufacturer in Greece is Bodytalk, which had a sales volume of 15.2 million euros in 2013. The company produces sport clothes and has 33 retail shops in Greece. Other Greek sport manufacturers are rather small.

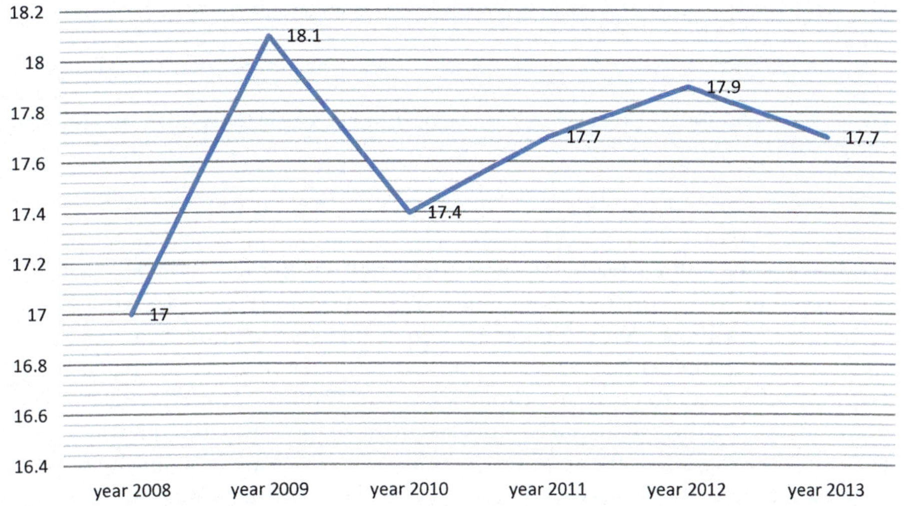

Fig. 3 Total sales (in MEUR) by manufacturing sport companies in Greece in 2008–2013. Source: ICAP Group (2014).

According to the ICAP Group's (2014) report the import sport businesses sales in 2013 were around 452 million euros, which shows a decrease of almost 50% in comparison to the 2012 (894,9 MEUR). The influence of the economic crisis is very clear in this field. As seen in the Fig. 4, the volume of the sales in 2009 was almost 1.2 billion euros, and there has been a continuous decrease since then. (ICAP Group, 2014.) It has to be noted that ICAP Group's data is not based on the data provided by the Hellenic Statistical Authority, as previously presented in Table 1. The difference between the amount of sport retailing sales reported in Table 1 and the amount reported in ICAP Group's study is mainly due to the definition of what is considered as "sport good". In ICAP Group's study businesses which are not pure sport ones (e.g., Notos Com) have been included. These businesses sell also casual and lifestyle clothes and shoes.

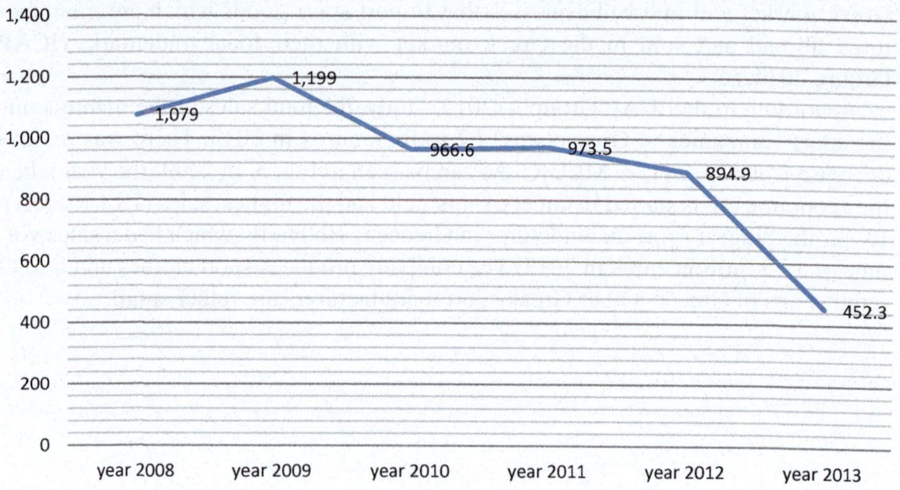

Fig. 4 Total sales (in MEUR) by Greek import sport businesses in 2008–2013. Source: ICAP Group (2014).

The six biggest import sport businesses by revenue are presented in the Table 3. As shown, Folli-Follie which represents Nike and Converse in Greece had the highest income in 2013 (176.7 MEUR), followed by Adidas Hellas (94.8 MEUR) and Intersport (72 MEUR). Sport Equipment Hellas, Intersport and International Sports (representing Admiral) had increases in their revenues in 2013 compared to the previous year. According ICAP Group's statistics Follie - Follie had a dramatic decrease, but it is difficult to draw a conclusion about that since the company's businesses include on top of the sport products also jewelry, travel equipment and lifestyle clothes and shoes. It is not clear what has been included with the 2012 and 2013 revenues.

Table 3 Biggest import sport businesses by revenue (in MEUR) in Greece in 2008–2013.

Company	2008	2009	2010	2011	2012	2013
Follie - Follie	268.2	397.5	379.0	406.5	407.9	176.7
notos com	310.2	301.4	242.2	201.4	158.4	n/a
Adidas Hellas	81.6	86.7	60.6	95.3	99.9	94.8
Intersport Athletics	64.0	68.0	63.1	66.6	67.6	72.0
Sport Equipment Hellas A.E. (ex Puma Hellas)	78.0	64.4	37.2	28.3	27.7	60.3
International Sports (Admiral)	30.4	34.4	37.5	38.5	39.4	40.6

Source: ICAP Group (2014).

The number of retail stores of the sport import businesses is presented in the Table 4. Some of these businesses have expanded through franchising, while some others have expanded their corporate store network.

Table 4 Number of retail stores of the import sport businesses in Greece in 2012.

Company	Retail stores
Follie - Follie	29 stores under names "Nike" and "Nike exclusive" and 3 under name "Converse"
Adidas Hellas	10 corporate stores under name "Adidas" and 11 more franchising shops
Intersport Athletics	42 stores in Greece under name "Intersport"
Sports Wind	10 stores under name "PUMA"
International Sports	140 stores under name "Admiral"

Source: ICAP Group (2014).

Sport/Recreation Education

As previously discussed, the sport and recreation education field (NACE code 8551) involves summer sport camps and professional sport schools at the vocational level (Institutes of Vocational Training, IVT). Published information about the economic activity in this sector does not exist. In terms of private sport schools, it has to be noted that private sport education in Greece does not have a legal accreditation at the higher education level due to the restrictions from the Greek constitution. However, private schooling is possible at the professional and vocational levels. There are today six private fitness schools (four national and two local) in Greece, which give professional certificates at vocational level (e.g., yoga and pilates certificates) (A. Batrakoulis, personal communication, September 15, 2016). It is estimated that these schools register in total about 2000 students per year. There are no fixed fees that the students need to pay, but instead the tuition fees depend upon the teaching hours and the types of courses that they include. It is estimated that the total economic activities of all of these schools equals to about one million euros per year. Private sport education is an increasing market, which will probably be developing in the following years in the numbers of students and subjects, especially in the area of fitness. In terms of the sport camps it is estimated that there are about 40 private summer children camps in Greece today. These operate during the summer months (June-August) and have the capacity to host 300–2000 children. There is no published information about the economic activity of these sport camps. Obviously, since the total revenue of sport and recreation education is almost 23 million euros (see Table 1), there is a lot more economic activity in this category which is not discussed in this chapter.

Conclusions

Based on the presented data it is estimated that sport businesses in Greece produce an economic activity of around one billion euros per year. The private sport sector in Greece is therefore a small part of the total Greek economy, around half per cent of the GDP of the country (in 2015 195 billion euros). It is also clear that it is one of the smallest sport sectors within the European Union. However, private sport sector can in future grow, especially with the developments in sport tourism, which can take several forms related to the provision of winter and summer sport services. Examples can be found in skiing resorts, some of which will become private in the near future, but also mountain activities provided by outdoor sport companies in co-operation with hotels and other tourism bodies. Sport tourism has a strong perspective to also develop in line with summer tourism. Hotels and resorts invest today on sport activities in order to enhance their products and improve guests' experiences. Some resorts have also started to organize their own sport events. The case of the "Navarino Challenge", which in 2016 took place for the fourth time and is organized by Costa Navarino Resort in Peloponnese, is an indicative example. This event includes several sport competitions for example in running, climbing, swimming and kick-boxing. There are also several sport and recreation businesses that organize and sell individual summer sport activities, such as scuba diving, yachting and water sports. The case of the island of Kalymnos is an indicative example. Climbing has traditionally been their main tourism product, and there are several companies, which do business based on this sport activity.

On finishing this article, it should be noted that any discussion about the future of sport businesses in Greece should be made within the context of the current and future economic situations. The influence of the economic crisis has been dramatic in the field of sport goods, where the volume of sales has been significantly decreasing since 2009, the year when the economic crisis started in Greece. However, the economic crisis has had a milder effect on businesses that provide sport participation services such as health and fitness clubs. Despite the reduced consumer purchasing power, there has been a recent increase in the percentage of the Greeks who participate in sport and recreational activities (European Commission, 2014). This gives an optimistic view of the future .When the economic climate improves, also the sport industry, both the participatory services and the sport goods field is expected to grow and develop. That is why most of the health club managers report positive perspectives about the future of the health and fitness sector.

References

Ablondi, J. (2014). *The IHRSA global report 2014*. Boston, MA: International Health, Racquet and Sports Club Association.

Alexandris, K. (2016a). Small-scale sport events and local tourism development. In P. Lytras & P. Tsiartas (Eds.), *The epitome of Greek tourism* (pp. 19–28). Athens, Greece: Papazisis.

Alexandris, K. (2016b). Testing the role of sport event personality on the development of event involvement and loyalty: The case of mountain running races. *International Journal of Festivals and Event Management, 7*(1), 2–20.

Alexandris, K. (2016c). *The impact of the economic crisis on health and fitness clubs in Greece* (Working Paper). Thessaloniki, Greece: Aristotle University of Thessaloniki, School of PE and Sport Sciences.

Alexandris, K. (2016d). The economic impact of city marathons. Paper presented at the 1st conference of the Alexander the Great Marathon, 2–3 April, Thessaloniki, Greece.

Alexandris, K., & Balaska, P. (2015a). Sport clubs in Greece. In C. Breuer, R. Hoekman, N. Siegfried, & H. van der Werff (Eds.), *Sport clubs in Europe* (pp. 209–220). Cham, Switzerland: Springer International Publishing Switzerland.

Alexandris, K., & Balaska, P. (2015b). The future of "sport for all" programs in Greece: Issues and challenges. Paper presented at the 12th European Association for sociology of sport conference, 10–13 June, Dublin, Ireland.

Assimakopoulos, M. (2016). Πως φτάσαμε στο θαύμα του Μαραθωνίου της Αθήνας [How we reached at the miracle of the Athens Classic Marathon]. *Business News*. Retrieved February 21, 2017, http://www.businessnews.gr/article/47895/pos-ftasame-sto-thayma-toy-marathonioy-athinas#.V7YI1rEyW1k.email

Balaska, P., & Alexandris, K. (2014). Examining recreational sport participation in a period of economic crisis: The case of Greece. Paper presented at the EASM Conference, 9-12 September, Coventry, UK.

European Commission. (2014). *Sport and physical activity*. Special Eurobarometer 412/Wave 80.2. Brussels, Belgium: D-G Education and Culture.

Funk, D., Alexandris, K., & McDonald, H. (2016). *Sport consumer behavior*. London, UK: Routledge.

General Secretariat of Sports. (2016a). *Γεωγραφική Ταξινόμηση των Αθλητικών Σωματείων* [Geographical taxonomy of Greek Sport Clubs]. Report by the Department of Sport Development, Promotion, International Relations and Scientific Support for Sports. Retrieved June 15, 2016 from http://gga.gov.gr/

General Secretariat of Sports. (2016b). *Ανάλυση του Αριθμού των Προπονητών ανά Άθλημα και του Αριθμούν των Αθλητικών Σωματείων σε κάθε Άθλημα* [Analysis of number of coaches per sport and the number of sport clubs of each sport]. Report by the Department of Sport Development, Promotion, International Relations and Scientific Support for Sports. Retrieved June 15, 2016 from http://gga.gov.gr/

Giannoulakis, C., Papadimitriou, D., & Alexandris, K. (2016). Implications of austerity measures on National Sport Federations: Evidence from Greece. *European Sport Management Quarterly*. https://doi.org/10.1080/16184742.2016.1178795.

Greece Economic Indicators. (2016). Retrieved June 2, 2016 from http://www.tradingeconomics.com/greece/indicators

Greek Economic Outlook. (2016). *Focus economics*. Retrieved June 2, 2016 from http://www.focus-economics.com/countries/greece
Greek Tourism in 2015. (2015). [Ο Ελληνικός Τουρισμός το 2015]. Retrieved June 2, 2016 from http://www.newmoney.gr/palmos-oikonomias/oikonomia/item/247498-rekor-kai-to-2015-ston-tourismo-me-26-ekat-afikseis-kai-14,5-dis-eiro-esoda
Hellenic Statistical Authority. (2011). Clusters of sport businesses in Greece. Retrieved July 6, 2016 from http://www.statistics.gr/
ICAP Group. (2014). *Sector study ICAP group: Sport goods*. Athens, Greece: ICAC Group.
Passport to Trade: A Bridge to Success. (2016). Greek business culture. Retrieved December 7, 2016 from http://businessculture.org/southern-europe/business-culture-in-greece/
Papadoyiannis, Y. (2016). Greece by far the eurozone's champion in nonperforming loans. Retrieved December 15, 2016 from http://www.ekathimerini.com/207902/article/ekathimerini/business/greece-by-far-the-eurozones-champSion-in-nonperforming-loans
Petridis, L. (2015). Greece: Mass running: A new trend from ancient Greece. In J. Scheerder & K. Breedveld (Eds.), *Running across Europe* (pp. 140–160). London, UK: Palgrave and MacMillan.
Polatidou, P. (2015). *Διερεύνηση των παραγόντων που επηρεάζουν την επανάληψη της συμμετοχής σε διεθνής διοργανώσεις υπαίθριων δραστηριοτήτων υψηλών απαιτήσεων* [Investigating the factors that influence repeated participation in international high level outdoor events] (Unpublished Doctoral Dissertation). Aristotle University of Thessaloniki, School of PE and Sport Sciences, Thessaloniki, Greece.
Rodriguez, M. (2016). *The IHRSA global report 2016*. Boston, MA: International Health, Racquet and Sports Club Association.
Study on the Contribution of Sport to Economic Growth and Employment in the EU. (2012). Study commissioned by the European Commission. D-G Education and Culture. SpEA.
Theodorou, S. (2015). *Η Ελληνική Κρίση σε Αριθμούς* [The Greek crisis in numbers]. Retrieved June 1, 2016 from http://www.thetoc.gr/oikonomia/article/wsj-i-elliniki-krisi-se-arithmous

HUNGARY: Filling the Gaps in the Strategic State Sector

Szilvia Perényi, Mihaly Szerovay, and Ilona Bodnár

Selected country facts (in 2013)	
Capital	Budapest
Geographical size (km^2)	93,011
Population (million)	9.91
GDP (euro per capita)	10,300
GDP (per capita in PPS)	67
Annual net earnings average (€)	6430

Introduction

The development of the private sport sector in Hungary reaches back to times before the development of the civil sport sector. Documents dated to as early as the 1800s indicate that the first sport organizations operated as private companies established by trainers with high societal prestige in sports such as fencing and gymnastics (Bodnár and Perényi, 2012). This process was supported by the reform movement

S. Perényi (✉)
Department of Sport Management, University of Physical Education, Budapest, Hungary
e-mail: sperenyi@hotmail.com

M. Szerovay
Faculty of Sport and Health Sciences, University of Jyväskylä, Jyväskylä, Finland
e-mail: mihaly.szerovay@jyu.fi

I. Bodnár
Faculty of Primary and Pre-School Education, Eötvös Loránd University, Budapest, Hungary
e-mail: bodnar.ilona@tok.elte.hu

A. Laine, H. Vehmas (eds.), *The Private Sport Sector in Europe*, Sports Economics, Management and Policy 14, https://doi.org/10.1007/978-3-319-61310-9_11

of the epoch aimed at the renewal of the Hungarian society as a whole, and initiated changes in political and cultural life as well as in the area of sport. Aristocrats leading the reform movement felt responsible to make sport more popular in the country. They used their private funds to establish horse-riding stables, fencing clubs and boating houses. The memberships in these establishments were exclusive in terms of access; mainly aristocrats could join. After the 1830s, the founders opened up their organisations to lower segments of the society due to their will of using sport in the forming of national cohesion and identity. Sport as a leisure activity reached new segments of society and the privately run sport companies were re-incorporated as joint-stock companies targeting the young bourgeoisie generations to become members. (Zeidler, 2006a; 2006b.) The appearance of sport clubs as civil organisations, as opposed to private sport organisations in sport, was delayed by political breaks to prevent the re-formulation of Hungarian independence movement following the revolution in 1848. As a result, club-based sport developed only after 1870s, and the first sport club, the Hungarian Athletic Club, was founded in Budapest in 1875 with the aim to reach the middle segments of society. (Bodnár & Perényi, 2012; Zeidler, 2012.)

Interest in sport and physical exercise was continuously growing and it reached a level where a necessity for physical education in schools emerged. In addition, from the 1920s the number of sport clubs increased and new sport facilities were constructed, especially for football (Perényi & Bodnár, 2015). After lengthy political discussions, the first professional league started in Hungarian football in 1926 (Dénes, Sándor, & B. Bába, 2014), nevertheless, official professionalism lasted only for a few years and did not return until 1990. All these elements demonstrated that both the social (civil) and the political (governmental) support for sport increased during this period, which consequently pushed the share of the private sector back in sport.

Furthermore, the defeat in the World War I was followed by an economic crisis, which restricted possibilities for both for the state and on the market. Following the crisis the public sector expanded through the introduction of the physical education classes in schools, and through the launch of the physical education teachers training in higher education in 1925.[1] Sport clubs covered the increasingly popular elite-oriented competition sport. Within this expanding space for sport and physical exercise, the private sector could find its role and place only in certain gaps left by the public policy and civil sectors. For example, in those sports, which were not part of the physical education curriculum in schools, such as fencing and rowing, the private sport companies continued their operation and provided training opportunities. (Perényi & Bodnár, 2015.) Because of the demand for such services, the existence of these companies was not only justified, but a need for the formulation of additional private companies emerged. For example, in the case of girls and young women this

[1]The first higher education institution, Hungarian University of Physical Education, was established in 1925 in Budapest.

need was reinforced by their delayed offer of school physical education classes, and by the delayed eligibility of women for PE teachers' training programs. Consequently, the request for training and sporting opportunities for girls and young women were possible to be offered to female by the so called movement artists running their private movement companies in art gymnastics and dancing. These trainers offered graceful movement opportunities for young girls and women from the early 1900s, which became increasingly popular during this period, and later laid the foundation for the rhythmic gymnastics of today. (Bodnár & Perényi, 2015.)

The expansion of the civil sport sector continued during the time up until World War II with an increase of sport clubs predominantly in capital city Budapest. In addition, continental and world events were organized in Hungary. The private sector also gained space; its competency areas were maintained on those previously mentioned gaps that were not covered by the public and civil sectors. The communist transformation after the World War II changed the Hungarian political and economic systems fundamentally. The state sector became highly dominant without giving space to the civil and private sectors in all areas of society. During this period, a centrally articulated sport policy defined the directions of sport development and the activities in sport were accompanied by centrally provided funding as well. As sport in Hungary became part of the central control of the party in power, sport organisations also became part of the political engine. Besides the civil sector's dominant dependency of and influence by the state (Földesi, 1996), private initiatives not only lacked space for existence, but most of them were taken over by the state. Thus, it is reasonable to say that within sport also the private sport sector had the fingerprints in the periodical transitions that were influenced by macro levels of political and economic transitions. Consequently, the period of state control made the private sector of sport to shrink even more significantly. After admitting the failures and dysfunctional operations of the state socialist system, a slow shift occurred in the 1980s in which the civil and private sector gained more significance. Nevertheless, sport and physical activities were hardly involved.

Following the political and economic changes in 1989–1990, the previously "automatically" allocated state funding was withdrawn from sport (Földesi, 1996). This transition resulted in new ways of organizing sport in the public, private and voluntary sectors in Hungary (András, 2011; Bakonyi, 2004; Földesi & Egressy, 2005; Perényi, 2013; Perényi & Bodnár, 2015; Szabó, 2012), and left more space for the formulation of private sport entities as well. In this transition, the private sector took over roles, functions, and activities both from the state and from the sport clubs. A multidimensional transition characterised the state-civil-private triangle following the 1989–1990 period, in which the mix of elements can be described by three main changes (1) from state to voluntary, (2) from state to private, and (3) from voluntary to private sectors (Bodnár & Perényi, 2012; Perényi & Bodnár, 2015).

The aforementioned threefold transition was repeatedly influenced in 2010, when the modification of the sport structure in addition to the new legal environment gave more space for the state involvement.[2] The new regulations in structure and funding indirectly influenced the private sport sector as well. Consequently, the private sport sector went through similar transition to the years in the beginning of the twentieth century, as again, it could only compensate the deficits of the public policy and take advantages of the opportunities outside of the direct reach or interest of sport federations or clubs.

Private Sport Sector in the New Democracy

There are three main areas identified in which the private sport sector has had space to emerge in Hungary. First, as previously mentioned, the priorities and areas of state sport policies have influenced the development and the functions of the private sector in sport, thus the private sport sector has found its playing field in segments, which were not included in the central sport policy or funding. Accordingly, it was demonstrated that with some exceptional periods such as the state socialist era, the private sport sector in Hungary has always been present, but its scope and forms of function have been adapted to the actual social, political, and economic environments. Therefore, its share in the public-civil-private triangle has changed under those influences. For example, the previously mentioned joint-stock companies in fencing or gymnastics and movement artist studios for women around 1930s, together with leisure sport activities offered by fitness clubs and development of running and running events were launched by the 1990s to demonstrate the paths taken by private companies.

Street running events, for example, were initially organised by individuals connected to both civil organisations and municipality sport committees. As Perényi (2015) states, during the first era of the development of running in the beginning of the 1980s, clubs and municipalities remained the centre organizers and promoters of running and running events in Hungary with the focus on the capital of the country. Accordingly, the first marathon race was organized in 1984 in Budapest by the Sports Committee of the Budapest Municipality, and the event's title sponsor was also a state-owned travel agency. However, following the political and economic changes and part of the privatisation processes, in 1991, the exclusive rights of organising the Budapest marathon was incorporated into a private event management firm, to a sport business named Budapest Sport Office, one of the first of its own kind. The role of the private sector in this event was influenced by the with-

[2] Act CLXXII of 2011 on the amendment of Act I of 2004 on Sport (2011) appointed the Hungarian Olympic Committee as the main organization governing the civil sector of sport and distributing all state funding.

drawal of state funding from operating state businesses and their privatization causing their withdrawal from supporting sport. In the commercialisation of such events, this process created space for international companies entering the Eastern European market, such as Nike or Ikea; thus, the private sector's related share has grown in leisure sports.

From the new millennium onwards, the number of events and event organizers has grown in running and the profit making logic has become present with growing extent. On one hand, private event management firms were formed with the focus on running or on other leisure sport events such as fitness or aerobic. On the other hand, civil organisations (clubs and federations) also use event organisation as a tool for generating income to supplement with funding their core sport services offered to members and to cover expenses of daily operation or wages of administrative staff and coaches. (Perényi, 2015.) Other areas of leisure sport, such as the fitness clubs, fitness trainers' training, mass fitness, and aerobics events were also open for the private sport sector, which clearly created opportunities for companies (Szabó, 2012).

Municipalities have increasingly outsourced certain activities in recent years, which may be identified as a second area that has strengthened the private sport sector. As the legal regulations delegated state responsibilities to local municipalities in different areas such as culture, tourism, and sport, opportunities for the private sector emerged in connection to municipalities as well. In most municipalities, a department or a sub-department was formed to oversee these state responsibilities. However, an independent organisational unit is dedicated to sport only in the case of large municipalities. The law, however, defines neither the measures for the degree of this support, nor the resources for the delegated sport-related tasks. Municipalities shall fulfil their legally allocated responsibilities in connection to sport by their own resources. (Földesi, 1996; Gyömörei, 2014; Kozma, Bába, & Perényi, 2016.) Consequently, the private sector has gained a bigger role in the process as municipalities have recently used outsourcing practices in relation to their lawful sport-related responsibilities. Accordingly, a growing number of municipalities have formed non-profit limited liability companies or shareholder companies for the operation of sport facilities or for managing grassroots sport. (Bács, 2011; Becsky & Dékán, 2014; Perényi, Kozma, Bács, Lente-Puskás, & Bartha, 2015.) In 2012, close to 200 such non-profit, municipality or higher education related, companies were founded. For example, the Debreceni Sport Centrum functions as a non-profit public benefit limited liability company with a prominently public benefit organization status, and it manages several sport facilities in the city such as ice rinks, swimming centre, track and field courses, and football fields all with the ownership of the city. The organisation receives its partial funding from the municipality, but over two-thirds of its budget must be earned with its services and market oriented activities (Becsky & Dékán, 2014). Another example of such outsourcing activity is the Pécs Sport non-profit private company limited by shares employing over 110 persons, which demonstrates its magnitude and the diversity of its activities. Kozma et al. (2016) found, however, that the degree of the municipality support for sport is largely dependent upon the personal preferences and attitudes of the municipality leaders towards sport. Municipalities in agreement with the governmental sport policy directions handle sport as high priority contemplated with higher frequency of sport activities and higher amount of allocated local funding. In municipalities, however, where this preference and priority for sport is not present, sport life seems to be less active. (Kozma et al., 2016.)

The third area in which the private sector of sport has emerged is the field of professional sport. In addition to the influences of domestic sport policies, European and global processes have also driven the development of the private sport sector in Hungary. Along with national political and economic changes, the regulatory framework formulated by European and international federations have increasingly shaped the field of professional sport in Hungary as well. For example, many clubs in ball games operate as business entities nowadays.

Facts About the Private Sport Sector

In order to compare statistically different sport business fields in Hungary, statistical data obtained from the Hungarian Central Statistical Office (2016) was utilized. Table 1 introduces the statistical information of the directly sport-related business fields in Hungary in 2013, according to the Hungarian equivalent (TEÀOR Számok '08) of the *Statistical classification of economic activities in the European Community* (NACE Rev. 2, 2008).

Table 1 Directly sport-related business fields in Hungary in 2013.

Business field	NACE code	Active enterprises	Persons employed	Revenue (1000 €)	Gross operating surplus (1000 €)	Gross operating surplus / Company (€)	Av. Salary (€)
Other sport activities	9319	2455	4612	127,944	−45,694	−18,612	7961
Retail sale of sporting equipment in specialised stores	4764	971	2275	95,636	913	940	3424
Manufacture of sport goods	3230	127	1093	94,940	10,324	81,288	7664
Operation of sport facilities	9311	408	1507	41,262	979	2398	5247
Activities of sport clubs	9312	78	477	21,220	−4108	−52,671	11,984
Sport and recreation education	8551	847	1150	18,885	1162	1372	2402
Fitness facilities	9313	575	1161	17,029	646	1124	2472
Renting and leasing of recreational and sport goods	7721	245	433	10,776	1456	5944	2289
Total		**5706**	**12,708**	**427,692**	**−34,322**	**−5952**	**5755**

Source: Hungarian Central Statistical Office (2016).

According to Table 1, the number of active companies operating in the Hungarian sport field amounted to 5706, employing close to 13,000 people. In comparison, the sport civil sector is present with 11,000 registered sport clubs, and less than 3000 full-time employees (Perényi et al., 2015). The revenue of the field was 427,7 million euros. It needs to be highlighted that the sport industry as a whole made a loss in 2013. However, when examining Table 1, it reveals that the loss resulted from the operations of the classes 'activities of sport clubs' and 'other sport activities'. Professional sport clubs typically belong to these classes. At the same time, employees in these categories had the highest income on average. Companies in other classes operated profitably. The numbers below average salary imply that in the categories 'fitness facilities', 'sport and recreation education', and 'retail sale of sporting equipment in specialized stores' a large number of employees worked part-time.

It needs to be mentioned that there are also sport-related products offered by businesses that are not specifically formed or registered under directly sport-related NACE codes. Many companies operate in different fields, but belong to only one class in the database. Furthermore, multinational companies have entered the area of sport facility or event management, marking the presence of the globalization processes. It needs to be also noted that the expansion of sport in Hungary was initiated by the governmental decision of choosing sport as a strategic area, which has created a need for professionals with new competencies. Therefore, it has been necessary, for example, to rethink university courses on offer. Programs in sport law and sport economy have been established, while new programs have been launched in sport management and recreation management.

The cooperation between the former state socialist countries was based upon the division of industries and production. Hungary did not have a considerable role in producing sport equipment in that division of labour. Therefore, after the transition in 1990 and with the start of the privatization, there were no private enterprises founded in this field. Accordingly, private and civil sector developed mainly in the service sector, for example in leisure sport, which was neglected in the sport policies of the state socialist system (Perényi et al., 2015).

The Influence of the Regulatory Framework on the Private Sector

The different 'generations' of sports acts provide a revealing aspect of the development of the private sport sector. There have been a number of versions and amendments of the sports acts during the past twenty years (Perényi, 2013). The evolution of their contents since 1996, when the first sports act was passed, has reflected a shift towards market-orientation in the top-level sport, including the acceptance of athlete as a profession and the creation of the necessary regulative framework for this new environment. It is reasonable to say that the transition in the Hungarian sport began later than in other fields of society in the 1990s (Dénes, 1997; Földesi, 1996). In addition, the attitudes of the government in power towards the status of sport may also be interpreted through the different versions of these acts.

Considering the status of top-level athletes, they were typically employed by large state-owned corporations during the era of state socialism between 1949 and 1990. Officially amateur players were professionals in practice. This system may be called shamateurism or hidden professionalism (Földesi, 1999; Szerovay & Itkonen, 2015). Development of the status of professional athletes in Hungary appeared for the first time in the Act LXIV of 1996 on Sport (1996) within the Hungarian legal framework. Nevertheless, the notion of a professional player was defined more precisely in the 1998 amendment of this statute (Act XXXI of 1998 on the Amendment of Act LXIV of 1996 on Sport, 1998). Prior to 1996, professional athletes were able to have numerous statuses. They could have been employed in the form of limited partnerships and limited liability companies (Legal commentary on Act I of 2004 on Sport, 2004). The Act CXLV of 2000 on Sport (2000) went further to regulate the context of market-based sport and defining the status of professional and amateur players (Hungarian Telegraphic Office, 2000) in order to clear up the situation of the sport clubs, federations, and amateurs as well as professional athletes. However, until 2004, players could have been self-employed or in sole proprietorship, which allowed them to minimize or avoid paying taxes and allowances. Requirement of working contracts for employing professional athletes had been a common practice internationally at that time in accordance with UEFA and FIFA regulations (András, 2003). In 2011, the notion of a professional athlete was defined even more precisely (Act CLXXII of 2011 on the amendment of Act I of 2004 on Sport, 2011). It is reasonable to say that the environment has gradually become more favourable for the employment of professional players (Szerovay & Itkonen, 2015).

Concerning the regulations of the organizational framework of professional and amateur sport, an example from football is revealing: the 1998 amendment of the Act LXIV of 1996 on Sport specified that all clubs as a prerequisite of participation in the highest division need to formulate corporations (András, 2003). Subsequently, the Act I of 2004 on Sport (2004) allowed Hungarian sport clubs to choose from a number of legal forms. As Perényi and Bodnár (2015) state, diversification of the organizational forms of function in sport took place. In addition to the classical sport clubs, different and previously non-existing organizational forms were accepted for the diverse functions in sporting practices. For example, foundations, non-profit limited companies, and limited companies emerged based on the changes in the new legal environment. Limited companies, limited partnerships, and independent sole-traders started to appear both in competition sport as well as in leisure sport. The new regulations allowed non-profit private companies to provide sporting services, and thus enabling additional sources of income.

Further relevant points that emerged regarding the 'development path' of sports acts include commercial contracts, as well as the concepts of sponsorship and merchandising, which were clarified in 2004 (Legal commentary on Act I of 2004 on Sport, 2004). These measures underpin the shift towards a more market-oriented mind-set in the Hungarian sport market. The 2011 amendment has given a more important role to sport schools as a venue for practicing amateur sport as well as to academies that undertake grassroots development. In addition, the development of access control in certain sport events (e.g., football matches), club card system for fans, and compulsory liability insurances for athletes were added to the expansion of the business section connecting to sport. (Act CLXXII of 2011 on the amendment of Act I of 2004 on Sport, 2011.)

The balance of the 'state-civil-private' triangle in the Hungarian sport was non-existent before the political changes in 1989–1990. In fact, the dominance of the state sector remained high even after efforts were made to raise the share of the private sector's role. An example for such efforts is the creation of the corporate tax benefit scheme (TAO), which was established to channel additional resources to sport. The TAO program, supported by a new legal environment, has targeted companies to give financial support to sport projects in the five biggest team sports (football, handball, basketball, water polo, ice hockey), while receiving tax-benefits (Perényi & Bodnár, 2015). The funds given were regulated to be used, among other things, for wages of sport professionals, such as coaches, trainers, masseuses, and administrators. As a result, a pulling effect was experienced in clubs and non-profit sport companies in the number of employees, and this framework has created a certain level of transparency in the payment of allowances and taxes. The scheme has also enabled the flow of private money into the construction of new and rehabilitation of old sport facilities. (Perényi, 2013.) In addition, the so-called horizontal cluster co-operations emerged behind the management and maintenance of these new sport units. A good example for such cluster function is the Hungarian Sport and Lifestyle Cluster, which with the participation of the city, the local university and football team along with several local businesses undertakes the management of several sporting services including a new stadium, built in 2014 with twenty thousand seating capacity in the city of Debrecen (Becsky & Dékán, 2014).

Team Sports Reflect the Local and Global Contexts of the Private Sport Sector

As mentioned earlier, the private sector found market opportunities in segments where the state policies did not define high governmental priories or where the operation of civil organisations did not raise their interests. On the other hand, the formulation of the private sector has been also influenced by the European practices introduced by the European sport umbrella organisations through recommendations or requirements for modifications in national regulations. In order to make further analysis of the privatization processes in sport in Hungary, a case study is presented to describe the transitions in football and other team sports supported by data in relation to number of employees and key financial figures. Statistical data and three semi-structured interviews with Hungarian football experts were used for this purpose. Team sports in Hungary, especially football, experienced both the process of functional discrepancies merging from civil organisational forms and the need for complying with regulations stemming from the continental or world umbrella organisations, such as UEFA regulations. High participation rates, among which football is the first, are another reason for choosing team sports as the focus of the case study. In addition, their development is among the main priorities of the central governmental and sport policy. Furthermore, private companies of these sports indirectly benefit from the governmental financial support mechanisms such as the aforementioned TAO (corporate tax benefit scheme).

The Increasing Economic Significance of Football and Other Team Sports

The emergence of profit and non-profit companies can be demonstrated by the shift that took place in the Hungarian football market. The transition of the first league football clubs from their function as sport clubs into limited companies is revealing, because football has been considered as the most important sport in the Hungarian public and political discourses, in addition to its leading position in sport participation and spectatorship. Molnar (2007, 313) argues, that football in Hungary has always been a "part of wider socio-historical processes in various forms". Consequently, football has highly attracted several stakeholders, such as leisure and professional participants (players), commercial actors, fans, and the political field. In addition, changes in Hungarian football have been driven by the global processes, such as commercialization and professionalization.

The economic power of the sport companies in football is shown in Table 2. In addition to the seven biggest football clubs measured by their revenue in 2015, the stadium management company operating the Groupama Aréna, stadium of Ferencváros football team[3], two handball teams, and two football academies were included in order to widen the scope of our analysis to sport companies functioning in areas other than professional football. Football academies refer to the elite youth development by the top clubs. Football clubs have to apply to the Hungarian Football Federation for an academy licence, which consist of numerous requirements to comply with, including player education and facilities. (Hungarian Football Federation, 2012.) For the selection of the mentioned sport enterprises, we extracted data from the Amadeus database (Bureau van Dijk Electronic Publishing, 2016), which contains comparable financial information for public and private companies across Europe. The analysis begun by filtering Hungary and subsequently for NACE group 931, with the focus on sport-related activities.

The exceptional economic appearance of the sport enterprises in Hungarian football especially in comparison to other sports is represented in Table 2. For example, in case of the number of employees this data shows that Ferencváros football team has three times more full-time employees in comparison to clubs with similar success profile, such as Veszprém or Pick Szeged, in handball. This is even more revealing in comparison to other forms of organisations in sport such as municipality owned non-profit sports companies. For example, the Debrecen Sport Centrum LLC, operating a multisport structure in 10–15 sport disciplines with over one thousand youth athletes, has less than 20 full-time employees while most of the coaches would be part-time. (Becsky & Dékán, 2014.)

[3] Named as *FTC Football Ltd* in Table 2.

Table 2 Economic power of Hungarian football clubs, handball clubs, and football academies.

Company name	City	Type	No of recorded shareholders	Operating revenue (1000 €) 2015	Operating revenue (1000 €) 2014	Operating revenue (1000 €) 2013	Number of employees 2015	Number of employees 2014	Number of employees 2013
FTC FOOTBALL LTD	Budapest	Football	1	13,007	12,787	10,021	145	139	130
FEHÉRVÁR F. C. LLC	Székesfehérvár	Football	1	n/a	5789	7857	n/a	116	104
HONVÉD FOOTBALL CLUB LLC	Budapest	Football	3	4043	3382	3451	110	118	99
DVSC FOOTBALL MANAGEMENT LTD	Debrecen	Football	1	n/a	5081	2448	n/a	67	47
MTK BUDAPEST FOOTBALL LTD	Budapest	Football	2	2902	1594	1616	62	106	62
PUSKÁS FOOTBALL CLUB LLC	Felcsút	Football	1	4775	2410	1200	64	58	54
VASAS FOOTBALL CLUB LLC	Budapest	Football	1	1863	806	268	37	31	28
LAGARDÈRE SPORTS LLC	Budapest	Stadium management	1	9513	3567	n/a	12	9	n/a
VESZPRÉM HANDBALL TEAM LTD	Veszprém	Handball	1	6894	4413	1792	39	28	16
PICK HANDBALL LTD	Szeged	Handball	2	3558	3138	2524	67	60	50
DEBRECEN FOOTBALL ACADEMY NON-PROFIT LLC	Debrecen	Football academy	3	n/a	301	893	n/a	8	24
VASAS ACADEMY LLC	Budapest	Football academy	5	1080	1090	1189	51	46	47

Source: Bureau Van Dijk Electronic Publishing (2016).

As Table 2 demonstrates, the changes in the operating revenues and the number of employees reflect the favourable environment for top-level sport in Hungary since 2010. The number of employees shows a slight increase in the period of 2013–2015. The operating revenues have also grown in almost all cases. Increasing revenues can be explained by growing broadcasting and commercial revenues as well as by the aforementioned TAO (corporate tax benefit scheme). The biggest sport enterprises have been typically football clubs, but we can also identify some handball clubs such as Veszprém and Pick Szeged men's teams and Ferencváros women's team that have reached several million euros in annual revenue. Such high figures for handball can be explained partly by successful participation in the European platform. In addition to participating in the Hungarian national league, Veszprém participates in a top-level transnational league called SEHA (South East Handball Association League). The legal forms of the clubs included in Table 2 are either limited liability companies or private limited companies. In addition, Debrecen football academy operates as a non-profit limited liability company.

Some football academies reached revenues of a million euros, which is considerable even in the international level (see European Club Association, 2012). Football has greatly benefited from the already mentioned corporate tax benefit scheme (TAO), which came into force in 2011. This framework has permitted clubs to cover competition costs and travelling for youth players. (Perényi & Bodnár, 2015.) TAO has been utilized for youth activities, personnel and investment in sport infrastructure (European Commission, 2011). In addition, the simplified entrepreneurial tax and contribution regime (EKHO) was introduced to simplify the employment of sport professionals. TAO and support from the Hungarian Football Federation have contributed to the greatest part of their incomes of elite youth clubs in the last couple of years (Szerovay, Perényi, & Itkonen, 2016).

As mentioned previously, the Hungarian government has taken an active role in supporting sport through a number of channels since 2010. For instance, numerous stadium construction and development projects have been launched recently. The National Stadium Development Programme, which was reinforced by a government decree in 2013, has indicated strong political support for elite football (Hungarian Journal, 2013). Among the largest clubs, the brand new stadiums of Ferencváros and Debrecen were opened in 2014. According to the government's plans, the stadiums of all clubs playing in the first league will be renewed. In addition, many second and third tier clubs are included in the development programme. (Csepregi, 2016.) Stadium operation shows a diversity of the forms in Hungary from clusters of organisations such in the case of Debrecen stadium to municipality maintenance in case of Paksi FC and the Rudolf Illovszky stadium owned and run by Vasas Sport Club.

The globalization processes can be identified in the stadium management in Hungary as well. A specialized multinational stadium management company, Lagardère Group, through its Hungarian branch, Lagardère Sports Hungary, has operated the Groupama Aréna, home stadium of Ferencváros since its inauguration in 2014. (Lagardère, 2014.) Groupama Aréna is a facility staging altogether over 150 events a year. Apart from football matches, the stadium hosts a large number of other events and conferences (C. Siklósi, managing director, interview, 25 April, 2016), which create additional revenue streams. The Hungarian national team in football has played the majority of its games in this stadium since autumn 2014, due to the reconstruction of the national stadium (Ferenc Puskás Stadium) at the time of the writing. The cooperation with Lagardère Sports Hungary is the first of this kind in Hungary and will last at least for ten years.

Hungarian football fans preparing for the UEFA EURO 2016 qualifying match against Finland in front of the Groupama Aréna in Budapest in November 14, 2014. *Photo: Jussi Eskola.*

Team sports, especially football, serve to illustrate the evolution of the private sport sector in a global and local context. Football clubs have enjoyed a favourable environment since 2010, as new facilities have been built and revenues from the Hungarian Football Federation have grown considerably. Also the resources available for football academies have greatly increased. Changes in the sector were demonstrated by the international dimension of the stadium management. However, football clubs' situation has been diverse, as some of them suffered from serious financial difficulties, even bankruptcy.

Conclusions

The private sector in the Hungarian sport has emerged quite early, dating back to the beginning of the 1800s. Its development, however, was fragmented by the political and economic transitions storming through the national, European and global historical scenes. Hungary in this flow of events has taken predetermined paths that have been influenced by the powers leading out of its own perimeters. In general, however, the private sector in Hungarian sport has been developed in areas that were not in the focus in the politics of central government. Consequently, sport companies were founded for those functions, purposes, and target groups that were not covered by governmental, municipality programs or sports clubs. These opportunities have encouraged sport professionals with entrepreneur's capacities to form companies, use market-oriented business logic, and establish new businesses.

This article has illustrated the recent changes of the private sport sector by looking at the evolution of the legal framework in sport through 'the development paths' of sports acts in Hungary since 1996. The changes have reflected the shift towards an increasingly market-oriented environment, and a relatively late transformation in sport compared to other branches in society. Another revealing example comes from team sports. The development of professional football has been driven by the global-local interactions, including the economic and political changes in Hungary and global influences of the sport. As a result "a hybrid formation of organizing the sport market" (Molnar, 2002, 72) emerged. The resources available for professional football clubs and other team sports have risen considerably since 2010. Facility development, increased revenues from the federation, and tax schemes have contributed to a favourable environment for professional clubs. On the other hand, sponsorships have often lacked financial logic, and sport economists have argued that broadcasting rights are overpriced for the Hungarian top division (M. Muszbek, sport economist, interview, June 4, 2014; G. Szabados, sport economist, interview, January, 29, 2014).

Sport in Hungary is an impulsively changing and developing sub-system of the political and economic life and of the society more broadly. Its importance is emphasised by the constantly changing legal environment that it called upon to serve its functions. For example, a new amendment of the sports act was approved by the Hungarian Parliament in November 2016. As the goals of Hungarian sport were not completely fulfilled in the Olympic Games in Rio de Janeiro, the sport structure and funding mechanisms are repeatedly being reorganized. According to the new framework, which came into force in the beginning of 2017, the allocation of state funding was re-shifted from the Hungarian Olympic Committee to the state-secretary in charge of sport under the Ministry of Human Capacities. (Hungarian Telegraphic Office, 2016.) The consequences of these modifications are expected to be experienced mainly by the organisations' functions in the civil sector of sport. However, as mentioned earlier, any change affecting any players of the state-civil-private triangle of sport may generate indirect effects to all. Effects of the impulsive transitions in state-civil relations on private organisations of sport remain to be seen in the future. Nevertheless, the trends of the municipalities' outsourcing activities in relation to the management of the newly built sporting facilities, and the use of private organisations as forms of function in team sports or by team sport academies, for example, is expected to continue.

References

Act CLXXII of 2011 on the amendment of Act I of 2004 on Sport [*2011. évi CLXXII. törvény a sportról szóló 2004. évi I. törvény módosításáról*]. (2011). Retrieved October 13, 2016 from http://njt.hu/cgi_bin/njt_doc.cgi?docid=139772.203174

Act CXLV of 2000 on Sport [*2000. évi CXLV. törvény a sportról*]. (2000). Retrieved October 13, 2016 from http://www.magyarkozlony.hu/dokumentumok/e94550d6d25d6a0f26cc5bb6e672e9d44fa616ec/megtekintes

Act I of 2004 on Sport [*2004. évi I. törvény a sportról*]. (2004). Retrieved October 13, 2016 from http://net.jogtar.hu/jr/gen/hjegy_doc.cgi?docid=a0400001.tv

Act LXIV of 1996 on Sport [*1996. évi LXIV. törvény a sportról*]. (1996). Retrieved October 11, 2016 from http://www.fsz.bme.hu/mtsz/torveny/sport.htm

Act XXXI of 1998 on the Amendment of Act LXIV of 1996 on Sport [*1998. évi XXXI. törvény a sportról szóló 1996. évi LXIV. törvény módosításáról*]. (1998). Retrieved October 16, 2016 from http://mkogy.jogtar.hu/?page=show&docid=99800031.TV

András, K. (2003). *Üzleti elemek a sportban, a labdarúgás példáján* [Business elements in sports – A case study in football] (Doctoral dissertation). Retrieved March 3, 2015 from http://phd.lib.uni-corvinus.hu/150/1/andras_krisztina.pdf

András, K. (2011). A hivatásos labdarúgás működési modellje [Functional model of professional football, competition of sport disciplines]. In T. Sterbenz & G. Szőts (Eds.), *MSTT füzetek: Sportágak versenye III* (pp. 8–42). Budapest, Hungary: Magyar Sporttudományi Társaság.

Bakonyi, T. (2004). *Civil álom és politikus állam: Adalékok a civil sportszervezetek státuszának legújabb-kori politikatörténetéhez Magyarországon* [Civil dream and political state: Comments on the modern political history of the status of sport organizations in Hungary]. Budapest, Hungary: Semmelweis University, Faculty of Physical Education and Sport Sciences.

Bács, Z. (2011). A magyar sport működési szerkezetének lehetséges szegmense: A felsőoktatási sportszervezetek [New dimensions in Hungarian sport: Sport organisations in higher education institutions]. *Magyar Sporttudományi Szemle, 12*(47), 21–23.

Becsky, A., & Dékán, T. (2014). Verseny és együttműködés a sport és az életmód különböző területein. Klaszterszemlélet a sportban [Competition and cooperation in sport and lifestyle. Cluster approach in sport]. In S. Perényi (Ed.), *A mozgás szabadsága: A szabadidősport társadalmi, gazdasági és egészségügyi megközelítései* (pp. 243–251). Debrecen, Hungary: Debreceni Egyetem.

Bodnár, I., & Perényi, S. (2012). A socio-historical approach to the professionalization of sporting occupations in Hungary during the first decades of the twentieth century: The coach. *International Journal of the History of Sport, 29*(8), 1097–1124.

Bodnár, I., & Perényi, S. (2015). Movement artists and female teachers of physical education: Women's body culture at the beginning of the last century in Hungary. In R. Diketmüller (Ed.), *Inspirational women in Europe making a difference in physical education, sport and dance* (pp. 63–73). Juiz de Fora, Brazil: Universidade Federal de Juiz de Fora.

Bureau van Dijk Electronic Publishing. (2016). *Amadeus. A database of comparable financial information for public and private companies across Europe*. Retrieved April 7, 2016 from https://amadeus.bvdinfo.com/version-20161125/home.serv?product=amadeusneo

Csepregi, B. (2016). *Stadionláz, 2. rész* [Stadium fever, part 2]. Retrieved November 15, 2016 from https://atlatszo.hu/2016/05/03/stadionlaz-2-resz-legalabb-215-milliard-forintba-fogfajni-a-koznek-orban-stadionos-bogracsgulyasa/

Dénes, F. (1997). Lövésből lesz… A hivatásos magyar labdarúgás átalakulásának közgazdasági alapjai [If you shoot, it may be a goal… The economic foundations of the transition of Hungarian professional football]. *Replika, 27*, 143–151.

Dénes, T., Sándor, M., & É. B. Bába, (2014). *A magyar labdarúgás története II.: Profikorszak vb-ezüsttel (1926–1944)* [The history of Hungarian football II.: Professional period with a silver medal from the World Cup (1926–1944)]. Debrecen, Hungary: Campus K.

European Club Association. (2012). *Report on youth academies in Europe*. Retrieved September 17, 2016 from http://www.ecaeurope.com/Research/ECA%20Report%20on%20Youth%20Academies/ECA%20Report%20on%20Youth%20Academies.pdf

European Commission. (2011). *SA.31722 – Hungary. Supporting the Hungarian sport sector via tax benefit scheme*. Retrieved July 25, 2015 from http://ec.europa.eu/competition/state_aid/cases/240466/240466_1271180_52_3.pdf

Földesi, S. G. (1996). Sport policy in Hungary. In L. Chalip, A. Johnson, & L. Stachura (Eds.), *National sports policies: An international handbook* (pp. 187–211). Westport, CT/London, UK: Greenwood Press.

Földesi, S. G. (1999). *Félamatőrök, félprofik* [Semi-professionals, semi-amateurs]. Budapest, Hungary: Magyar Olimpiai Bizottság.

Földesi, S. G., & Egressy, J. (2005). Post-transformational Trends in Hungarian Sport (1995–2004). *European Journal for Sport and Society, 2*(2), 85–96.

Gyömörei, T. (2014). *Az önkormányzatok sportfinanszírozása Magyarországon* [Sport financing of municipalities in Hungary]. Budapest, Hungary: IDResearch Kutatási és Képzési Kft.

Hungarian Central Statistical Office. (2016). *Labour and performance indicators. Enterprises classified in national economic sections B to J, L to N, P to S*. Retrieved September 25, 2016 from http://statinfo.ksh.hu/Statinfo/haViewer.jsp

Hungarian Football Federation. (2012). *Tájékoztató a labdarúgó akadémiai licence minősítési eljárásról* [Handout on the football academy license qualification process]. Retrieved September 15, 2015 from http://www.mlsz.hu/szovetseg/

Hungarian Journal. (2013). *1638/2013. (IX. 11.) Kormányhatározat a Nemzeti Stadionfejlesztési Programmal kapcsolatos feladatokról* [1638/2013. (11.9) Government Decree on tasks related to the National Stadium Development Program]. Retrieved January 5, 2017 from http://www.kozlonyok.hu/nkonline/MKPDF/hiteles/MK13148.pdf

Hungarian Telegraphic Office. (2000). *Elfogadták a sporttörvényt* [The Sports Act was passed]. Retrieved October 15, 2016 from http://archiv1988-2005.mti.hu/Pages/HirSearch.aspx

Hungarian Telegraphic Office. (2016). *A sportirányítás és az ágazat finanszírozásának átalakításáról döntött kedden az Országgyűlés* [The Parliament approved the reform of sport governance and sport financing on Tuesday]. Retrieved December 20, 2016 from http://mti.hu/Pages/Default.aspx?lang=hun&menuid=

Kozma, G., Bába, É. B., & Perényi, S. (2016). A magyarországi helyi önkormányzatok sporttal kapcsolatos kiadásainak vizsgálata [Analysis of sport-related expenditures of local municipalities in Hungary]. *Hungarian Review of Sport Science, 17*(67), 32–38.

Lagardère. (2014). *Press release: Lagardère Unlimited Stadium Solutions strengthens its portfolio with Ferencváros Stadium in Budapest, Hungary*. Retrieved November 20, 2015 from http://www.lagardere.com/press-room/press-releases/press-releases-363.html&idpress=6502

Legal commentary on Act I of 2004 on Sport [*2004. évi I. törvény a sportról indoklása*]. (2004). Retrieved December 15, 2016 from http://www.mgysz.hu/2009/jogszab/sporttorveny2004_ertelmezes.pdf

Molnar, G. (2002). *Globalization: The structural changes of the Hungarian sport life after the Communist Regime* (Master's thesis). Miami University. Physical Education, Health, and Sport Studies

Molnar, G. (2007). Hungarian Football: A socio-historical overview. *Sport in History, 27*(2), 293–317.

Perényi, S. (2013). Hungary. In K. Hallmann & K. Petry (Eds.), *Comparative sport development. Systems, participation and public policy* (pp. 87–100). New York, NY: Springer.

Perényi, S. (2015). Hungary. The popularisation and expansion of amateur running culture. In J. Scheerder, K. Breedveld, & J. Borgers (Eds.), *Running across Europe. The rise and size of one of the largest sport markets* (pp. 63–86). Basingstoke, UK: Palgrave Macmillan.

Perényi, S., & Bodnár, I. (2015). Sports clubs in Hungary. In C. Breuer, R. Hoekman, S. Nagel, & H. van der Werff (Eds.), *Sport clubs in Europe: A cross-national comparative perspective* (pp. 221–247). Cham, Switzerland: Springer International Publishing Switzerland.

Perényi S, Kozma G, Bács Z, Lente-Puskás A,& Bartha É (2015). *A sporttal foglalkozó magyar nonprofit szervezetek tevékenységprofil és szervezeti forma szerinti elemzése – területi jellemzők figyelembevételével* [Analysis of sport-related non-profit organisations according to their organisation forms and activity type – Taking regional characteristics into consideration]. Debrecen, Hungary: University of Debrecen.

Szabó Á. (2012). *A magyar szabadidősport működésének vizsgálata. Piacok, értékteremtés, feladatok a szabadidősportban* [Analysis of the functions of Hungarian leisure sports. Markets, values, tasks in leisure sports] (Doctoral dissertation). Budapest, Hungary: Corvinus University.

Szerovay, M., & Itkonen, H. (2015). Suomalaisten ja unkarilaisten huippujalkapalloilijoiden aseman muutokset 1980-luvulta nykypäiviin [The development of the role of Finnish and Hungarian top-level football players since the 1980's]. In H. Roiko-Jokela & E. Sironen (Eds.), *Urheilun toinen puoli. Suomen urheiluhistoriallisen seuran vuosikirja* (pp. 109–127). Porvoo, Finland: Bookwell.

Szerovay, M., Perényi, S., & Itkonen, H. (2016). Glocal processes in peripheral football countries: Elite youth football clubs in Finland and Hungary. *Hungarian Review of Sport Science, 17*(65), 26–33.

Zeidler, M. (2006a). English influences on modern sport in Hungary 1. *The Hungarian Quarterly, 47*(181), 36–54.

Zeidler, M. (2006b). English influences on modern sport in Hungary 2. *The Hungarian Quarterly, 47*(182), 27–47.

Zeidler, M. (2012). Clair Ignác testgyakorlati iskolája [Ignác Clair's school of physical practice]. In M. Zeidler (Ed.), *A labdaháztól a Népstadionig: Sportélet Pesten és Budán a 18-20. században* (pp. 105–130). Bratislava, Slovakia: Kalligram.

ITALY: Dichotomies Between Professionalism vs. Voluntarism and Commercialisation vs. Non-profit in the Sport Sector

Antonio Borgogni, Simone Digennaro, and Emiliano Mazzoli

Selected country facts (in 2013)	
Capital	Rome
Geographical size (km²)	302,073
Population (million)	60.80
GDP (euro per capita)	26,500
GDP (per capita in PPS)	99
Annual net earnings average (€)	20,675

Introduction

Italy is a parliamentary republic and one of the most populated nations in the European Union with almost 61 million inhabitants (Istituto Nazionale di Statistica [ISTAT], 2015). During the last decades, not differently from the majority of the European countries, it has developed a dynamic and efficient sport system based on around

A. Borgogni (✉)
Department of Human Sciences, Society and Health, University of Cassino and Southern Lazio, Lazio, Italy
e-mail: a.borgogni@unicas.it

S. Digennaro
Department of Human Sciences, Society and Health, University of Cassino and Southern Lazio, Lazio, Italy
e-mail: s.digennaro@unicas.it

E. Mazzoli
School of Health and Social Development, Faculty of Health, Deakin University, Geelong, Australia
e-mail: emiliano.mazzoli@deakin.edu.au

A. Laine, H. Vehmas (eds.), *The Private Sport Sector in Europe*, Sports Economics, Management and Policy 14, https://doi.org/10.1007/978-3-319-61310-9_12

65,000 organisations and a work force of more than 860,000 people[1] (Centro Studi Investimenti Sociali [CENSIS], 2008).

The sport system did not attain mass dimensions until after the World War II. The first analysis of the level of participation in sport activities in Italy was, in fact, carried out in 1959 (ISTAT, 2005). At that time, individuals who formally engaged in sport activities were no more than 1.3 million and the number of sport clubs was 17,800. Ten years later, in 1970, there were 25,800 sport organisations providing services to 2.6 million people (Lolli, 1997). In the early 1980s researchers estimated that there were 7.2 million active people who supported activities of the 53,000 sport organisations (Porro, Bizzaglia, & Conti, 1999).

The following decades witnessed a further increase in the level of participation and an enlargement of the access to various groups of population: women, people with disabilities and senior citizens. Recent official statistics (ISTAT, 2013a) report that sport participation in Italy has observed a phase of stagnation, remaining almost unvaried over the last ten years. In particular, data from 2013 show that, 21.3% of the population engaged in regular physical activities or sport, whilst 8.7% practiced sport only occasionally (ISTAT, 2013a). According to these data, people participating in some physical activity, such as walking (for at least two kilometres), gardening, swimming or cycling, figured 27.7%. The proportion of the inactive people in Italy, who are not involved in any sport or physical activities during their spare time, was 42.0%; elderly people showed a decreased interest in participating in sport, and a growing appeal for other forms of physical activity (such as walking and swimming) that reached its highest percentage (38.1%) among the 60-64 age group. Larger differences appeared when looking at gender, where the percentage of men practicing sport and physical activity, regularly or occasionally was two times higher than women (ISTAT, 2013a).

Italy is subdivided into 21 regions that have a direct effect on the policy and strategy concerning sport and other related sectors such as health. Thus, the rate of active population, influenced of other things by the regional policy, has remarkable regional differences within the country (Digennaro, Borgogni, & Sterchele, 2016). In particular, southern regions have the highest rate of inactive people: Campania, for instance, in 2012 registered a 57.8% of inactive inhabitants; on the contrary regions such as Veneto and Trentino Alto Adige, situated in the north-east, show 77.0% and 84.6% of active people respectively, percentages that are aligned with the level of participation of the Scandinavian countries. Notable differences can be also detected in the regional financial policies. A study conducted by CENSIS (2008) showed that regions like Lazio and Veneto allocated more than 20 million euros to the sport system, whereas regions such as Marche and Calabria assigned less than one million euros in the same year. This study also shows that, nationally, the average budget per person allocated by the regions to support the sport system is 5.37 euros. Again, the gap is eloquent: Calabria in the other end allocated a budget

[1] Estimation made by CENSIS; the value includes the total number of sport administrators, coaches and referees who were registered as members of National Sport Federations and/or Sport Governing Bodies. Athletes were not included.

of 0.49 euros per person and Trentino Alto Adige in the other allocated 25.69 euros per person (CENSIS, 2008).

Despite the overall almost unchanged Italians' sport participation over the last years with huge differences among the regions, the increasing professionalization of the sport industry, substantially affected by the globalization and the application of business techniques to the sport sector, has led to important changes in the way people consume, produce and manage sport (Hoye, Smith, Nicholson, & Stewart, 2015). It is estimated that almost all 12,867,000 Italians who participate regularly in sport activities are members of some sport organisations (Borgogni, Digennaro, & Sterchele, 2015). Borgogni et al. (2015) highlight that sport organisations play a fundamental role in the Italian sport system, which is strongly underpinned by the voluntary-based associations. In the same vein, these organisations have a pivotal role in the growth of the private sport sector that appears to be consistently developing among the regions. Although the northern regions count a noticeable larger number of sport clubs compared to central and southern regions, when observing the number of clubs per capita this difference fades away, and some of the central and southern regions rank higher than many northern ones. Moreover, the rate at which new clubs were founded between 2001 and 2008 was higher in the south than elsewhere in the country (Borgogni et al., 2015).

The Organisation of the Italian Sport System

In Italy, there is not a National Act ruling specifically sport matters, although a specific legislation on sport recognizes the Italian National Olympic Committee (CONI) as the National Governing Body for Sport (through Law 426/1942 and later amendments in Laws 242/1999, 138/2002 and 15/2004). Differently from other European countries, the sport sector is governed by CONI, as a result, according to Porro (1995), of the processes of the authoritarian modernisation that were steered by the Fascism during the regime (1922-1943) with the aim to turn CONI into a control apparatus of the population. As Porro further explains, during the Fascist regime, the Italian sport system became more structured with the implementation of a more modern organisational system that was controlled by CONI. In this way, the governing body of sport was turned into an apparatus of the regime through which the government could maintain a direct control over all the activities carried out by sport associations and, broadly, over the entire population. As an effect of this configuration, until recently, this system gave CONI a sweeping responsibility over the entire sport attributing, de facto, to the organisation the functions elsewhere exercised by the Ministry of Sport (Porro, 1995).

The peculiar role played by CONI along with the distinctive features of some of the actors operating in the system — such as the Sport Promotion Bodies (Enti di Promozione Sportiva) that represent one of the most innovative experiences of sport for all organisations in Europe — has determined an almost unique form of sport system. This particular configuration remained substantially unchanged until the 1990s that witnessed the beginning of a slow process of re-organisation of the system, and still in process today. As an effect of the Legislative Decree 242 (1999), CONI was attributed with a legal personality under the public law and put under the supervision of the Ministry of Heritage and Culture. In parallel, sport federations were turned into non-profit organisations with legal personality (the possession of legal rights and obligations by a person/organisation) under the private law. They get economic resources for their activities partly from governmental grants received from CONI (around 40% on average) and partly through self-financing assets deriving from institutional activities (e.g., memberships, television contracts and sponsorships), but the specifics of each federation are highly heterogeneous (Andreotti, 2014).

In 2001, the reform of the Constitution saw the transferal of the sport affairs to the regions and local authorities. They received assignments to the promotion of sport and recreational activities in the sphere of people and community services. A direct participation in sport activities was recognised as a right that must be equally ensured to all the segments of the population (United Nations Educational Scientific and Cultural Organization [UNESCO], 2015). Thus, the system was substantially presented as a combination of the two different subsystems: one related to the Olympic Movement in which the main actors are CONI, acting as reference point, and the Federations that play a crucial role in promoting and supporting, above all, elite and competitive sport; and the other linked to the realm of the sport for all that has a regional/local dimension and is inspired by the principles of subsidiarity, adequacy and differentiation (Digennaro et al., 2016).

The role played by the state in the regulation of the sport system is partially limited. CONI acts under the supervision of the state as the body in charge in promoting sport activities at all levels, and supervising the sport movement throughout the nation. Differently from the state level, each region has a specific law that is regarded to structure a regional framework and set the overall strategy in the promotion of sport. The degree of coordination among the state, CONI, the regions and others actors (e.g., the sport federations) appears to be weak (Blando, 2009). However, the Italian Parliament is recently debating about the necessity to reduce the responsibilities of the regions and reallocate the entire responsibility of administering the national sport system to CONI. In this light, different configurations of the sport system might emerge in the near future, but at the present it is difficult to predict what direction the system will evolve in the upcoming years.

The Italian sport system's financing is based on four pillars: householder expenditures, local authorities' sport budgets, government budgets and enterprises' finance (such as media and sponsors). In 2012, the overall household expenditure for sport was around 22 billion euros (ISTAT, 2012), which was the 2.3% of the total expenditure. Sportswear was the main item of consumption (6.7 billion euros) followed by the expenditures directly related to the access to sport activities and services (3.3 billion euros), and sport tourism (2.9 billion euros). The value of the production directly related to the sport activities was 53.2 billion euros (CONI, 2012). Regardless the difficulties linked with the economic crisis, the production registered growing trends since the 2009.

The Italian state supports the sport system through a yearly budget of around 410 million euros allocated to CONI, which oversees the distribution of the available financial resources to the national and local levels (CONI, 2015). Local authorities further support sport with financial resources that are distributed at local level. The majority of the local financial resources come from the municipalities (74%), followed by the regions (15%) and the provinces (11%). Compared to other European countries, the public finance for sport in Italy is lower. For example, the United Kingdom and Germany provide 50% and France 65% more than Italy (Banca Nazionale del Lavoro [BNL], 2013).

With regard to the enterprise contribution, sponsorship has usually been the biggest source of funding, followed by broadcasting right fees (Andreff & Szymanski, 2006). However, this kind of contribution is suffering from the effects of the economic crisis that has gripped the country.

The Private Sector and the Economic Value of Sport

In Italy, the sport sector creates about the 1.6% of the Gross Domestic Product (CONI, 2012), which includes 3% of the satellite activities (BNL, 2013). The private sector plays a crucial role with an economic contribution that can be estimated in 53.2 billion euros (CONI, 2012). A rather similar figure is reported by a European study conducted by the Austrian Institute for Sports Economics (SpEA, 2012). In this study sport represented 0.76% of the Italian Gross Value Added and provided employment to 239,881 people, relative to the Vilnius' narrow definition of sport (i.e., all products and services that are necessary as inputs for producing sport as an output). These figures rise to 1.21% and 329,860 people respectively when sport activities and services are defined according to the Vilnius' broad definition of sport (i.e., all product and services that have a direct or indirect relation to sport without being necessary to do sport) (SpEA, 2012).

The first systematic analysis of the private sport sector in Italy was carried out in 1999 by the Italian Institute of Statistics in collaboration with CONI (Garofalo, Lorenzi, & Zamaro, 2002). At that time, the authors counted 77,145 sport organisations (10.7% public bodies, 73.8% non-profit organisations and 15.5% professional organisations), providing occupation to around 43,000 people (15%, 21% and 64% respectively). Unfortunately, no similar studies have been conducted over the following years, so more recent figures are not available at the moment. Notwithstanding, the comparison of different sources give possibilities to draw a picture of the economic dimension of the sport sector and, in particular, of the private sector (e.g., CENSIS, 2008; CONI, 2014; ISTAT, 2013b; Nomisma, 1999).

According to CONI (2014), there was an overall increased proportion of the actors operating in the sport sector between 2003 and 2013, including registered athletes (+31.8%), sport associations (+3.6%) and other sport operators (+1.6%). Community-based associations and clubs, largely belonging to the non-profit sector, play a key role in the dissemination of sport, active lifestyle and culture, as they are the organisational units in direct contact with the broader population on a daily basis. They provide sport facilities and equipment, supporting staff and coaches as well as training opportunities for athletes. In this regard, it is useful to make some considerations about the relationship between sport and the labour market: a study conducted by the European Observatory of Employment in Sport (Le Roux, Chantelat, & Camy, 1999) reported that the "hard-core" sport sector (NACE rev. 1.1 – group 92.6) counted a number of 55,000 workers, who had sport as their main occupation, although not always full time. However, this value is quite different from what was reported by the national statistics in 2002, with a number of 26,964 people working in the NACE rev. 1.1 class 92.6 (ISTAT, 2002), and in 2013, when 40,118 people operated in the same sector (NACE rev. 2 – classes 85.51 and 93.1) (ISTAT, 2013b).

According to Madella (2002), the access to the sport professions is not regulated by law, except for a limited number of cases, such as skiing instructors and mountain guides. The author outlines that the Italian labour market comprises both full-time professionals and individuals who operate on a voluntary base. The types of contracts vary greatly: full-time and part time contracts tend to be more adopted in professional sport or in high level organisations and in general, in the private sector. However, there is a consistent number of employees with fixed-term contracts; self-employment and freelance work were, and still are, very common, especially in the fitness sectors (Digennaro, Colella, Morano, Vannini, & Borgogni, 2012; Madella, 2002).

With some exceptions, private sport organisations tend to have a small size configuration and a limited number of employees. A standard model of the organisation size determination (see e.g., Lucas, 1978) suggests that the reason for an organisation being small is that their managers have low entrepreneurial ability. This model can be used to partially explain the Italian situation: an efficient training and education system focussing specifically on the managerial area was in fact not developed until the mid-1990s. However, other factors can also be considered: the fragmentation of the system is certainly an element that influences directly the size of the organisations. The fitness sector for example, is typified by a large number of small and medium organisations that provide their services to a limited number of customers (Madella & Digennaro, 2009). We believe that the crisis of the sport system during the 1990s, followed by the economic recession in 2008–2013, have forced organisations to reduce their sizes to survive with limited resources.

In 2011, ISTAT (2014) ran a census on the size of the non-profit sport sector. This revealed that in December 2011, there were 92,838 non-profit sport organisations in Italy, which was 63% more than in 1999. CENSIS (2008) conducted another analysis of the economic value of volunteering based on a sample of 11,000 non-profit sport organisations. Data showed that on average, every organisation can count on the assistance of 1012 volunteers, who provide voluntary work for five hours a week. Considering an estimated total number of 95,000 non-profit sport organisations operating in Italy in 2008, the contribution of the voluntary work can be valued around 3.4 billion euros per year (based on 39 working weeks per year and an hourly salary of 15 euros per hour) (CENSIS, 2008). A less recent study (Nomisma, 1999) estimated that in 1999 the volume of the voluntary services offered to non-profit sport organisations was equal to 190 million hours. If these working hours had been rewarded a salary of 15 euros per hour, the economic contribution of the volunteers in sport in 1999 could have been valued approximately 2.85 billion euros (GHK, 2010).

The private sector is largely composed by the public liability companies, cooperatives and limited liability companies. These companies have great impact in the society as they have the capacity to convey a wider media exposure, as well as important revenues from sponsors, copyrights, merchandising and event attendances. The main operating national laws in the private/professional sport sector are: Law 91 (1981), which provides a general outline of the professional sport sector and define boundaries of their operators; and Law 586 (1996). The latter is subsequent to the "Bosman ruling", according to which the incorporation Act must provide that a portion of the profits, not less than 10%, has to be destined to youth training and technical-sport training (Art. 10.3). This rule enables professional sport clubs to become capital profit making companies and allows them to pursue profits. Thanks to sport's direct, international and emotionally power language, there is a relevant number of satellite activities and organisations, besides the professional sport clubs, that benefit from the overall interest generated by the sport industry. From the authors' point of view, their operative sub-sectors include event management, media, sporting garments production and sale, gambling, equipment manufacturing, major sport facilities building and operation and major fitness clubs. Excluding a limited number of large organisations, sport organisations in Italy are undergoing a deep transformation, which is linked to a dichotomy between professionalism and voluntarism, commercialisation and non-profit.

Structural and Economic Data

Available structural and economic data on the Italian private sport sector have been collected and made available by the ISTAT and Bureau van Dijk Electronic Publishing. Overall, in 2013 the private sport sector in Italy generated revenues for over ten billion euros, largely influenced by the manufacture (12%) and the retail sale (43%) of sport goods, and which provided occupation to around 103,300 people (ISTAT, 2013b). Table 1 provides an outline of the size and the economic value of the directly sport-related business fields in Italy in 2013, according to the Italian equivalent (Ateco, 2007) of the *Statistical classification of economic activities in the European Community* (NACE Rev. 2, 2008).

Table 1 Directly sport-related business fields in Italy in 2013.

Business field	NACE code	Companies (n)	Revenue (1000 €)	Staff (n)	Revenue/ Company (1000 €)	Av. salary (1000 €)
Retail sale of sport equipment and bicycles	47.64	9859	4,350,298	32,605	441.25	20.37
Manufacture of sport goods	32.30	625	1,165,688	4756	1,865.10	23.71
Operation of sport facilities	93.11	2866	1,019,610	11,218	355.76	17.91
Other sport activities	93.19	5089	938,904	9124	184.50	76.45
Activities of physical well-being institutes	96.04	5706	728,221	17,563	127.62	16.08
Activities of sport clubs	93.12	868	719,645	6115	829.08	175.75
Fitness facilities	93.13	3563	436,347	7544	122.47	14.21
Operation of recreation areas and parks	93.21	1172	368,067	4663	314.05	18.58
Renting and leasing of recreational and sport goods	77.21	2057	227,495	3564	110.60	20.38
Sport and recreation education	85.51	2497	158,975	6117	63.67	12.18
TOTAL		**34,302**	**10,113,250**	**103,269**	**294.83**	**36.45**

Source: ISTAT (2013b).

The data in Table 1 evidently show that in 2013 the manufacture of sport goods was, on the average, the most profitable business field, showing an annual revenue per company of almost two million euros, whereas smallest revenues were registered in the field of sport and recreational education. The retail sale of sport equipment and bicycles had, by far, the largest number of companies, almost one third of the total, and also provision of employment to the highest number of people. The activities of sport clubs seem to provide the most valuable conditions for their workers, with an average salary of around 176,000 euros per year, considerably higher than those available in other sectors. This remarkable difference is mainly due to the profitable turnover generated by football clubs operating in this area. Second business field by average salary is other sport activities (ISTAT, 2013b).

Between 2008 and 2013, all business fields experienced variations. The number of active companies decreased in the fields of manufacture of sport goods (-6.86%), retail sale of sport goods (-4.76%), sport recreation and education (-26.52%), fitness facilities (-3.34%) and activities of physical well-being institutes (-3.53%). On the contrary, a significant increase was registered in the renting and leasing of recreational and sport goods (+87.68%), operation of sport facilities (+9.81%), activities of sport clubs (+73.25%), other sport activities (+62.74%) and operational and recreational areas and parks (+13.90%) fields (ISTAT, 2013b). The number of employees followed the same trend except for sport and recreation education that, despite the reduction of the total number of companies operating in the national territory by almost one thousand units in just a five-year time, registered an increased percentage of people operating in this sector by around 40% (ISTAT, 2013b).

An interestingly growing business is the renting and leasing of recreational and sport goods that, besides the number of companies, increased continuously the employment opportunities (+73.43%) and tripled the overall revenues (+149.55%), showing higher rates of increase between 2011 and 2013 (ISTAT, 2013b). Similarly, the data also show that the activities of sport clubs grew remarkably over a five-year span, especially as they provided employment opportunities to more than 6100 people, which is 116.8% more than in 2008. The highest growth was registered between 2010 and 2011, an explosive phenomenon that duplicated the number of workers in this sector in only one year (ISTAT, 2013b). Other sport activities showed comparable growths, even though they appeared much smoother. Despite the general negative trend in the number of companies, occupation and average salaries, fitness clubs showed higher revenues per company in 2013, compared to what observed in 2008 (ISTAT, 2013b).

Apparently, in 2013, the manufacture of sport goods was not a growing economy anymore, as it showed a constant decrease in the revenues (-15.18%) and occupation (-26.45%), despite the constantly increasing average salary (+14.75%) (ISTAT, 2013b). However, it still has an important economic impact in the society as its overall revenues amount to over one million euros per year (Table 1).

Overall, the majority of the analysed fields show an ongoing growth in the number of companies, as well as their revenues and occupation opportunities. Generally, the positive rates of the differences exceeded by far the negative trends (ISTAT, 2013b). Thus, even in this period of European crisis, professional sport in Italy seems to be a growing sector.

Sport and Fitness Companies: Goods, Facilities and Clubs

With regard to the manufacture of sport goods (NACE code 32.30), the top three companies operating in Italy in 2013 were Technogym S.p.A., Decathlon Produzione Italia S.r.l. and Tecnica Group S.p.A., which generated an income of 284 million euros, 227.7 million euros and 166 million euros respectively. Technogym, the leader company in this field, produces fitness and biomedical rehabilitation equipment, based on medical research in health and wellness. According to Bureau van Dijk (2016), Technogym has supplied more than 27,000 fitness and wellness centres and 30,000 private homes in more than 80 countries, with approximately 15 million regular users. It is also by far the company providing occupation to the largest number of people (no. of staff 706), followed only by Sparco S.p.A. (no. of staff 460), which ranked fourth by revenue, and Tecnica

Group S.p.A. (no. of staff 427). However, the most profitable activities in this area are led by Technisub S.p.A., Elite S.r.l. and La Sportiva S.p.A., with an EBITDA-%[2] of 28.52, 24.30 and 15.46 respectively. A common characteristic of these companies is that they produce highly technical clothing and equipment for some specific sport disciplines, such as scuba diving, archery and rock climbing, suggesting that a specialised manufacture of sport goods might be more profitable than a more general production. (Table 2.)

Table 2 Largest private companies operating in manufacture of sport goods (NACE code 32.30) in Italy in 2013.

Company	Revenue (1000 €)	EBITDA-%	Staff (n)
Technogym S.p.A.	284,002	9.35	706
Decathlon Produzione Italia S.r.l.	227,658	2.55	69
Tecnica Group S.p.A.	166,081	-5.13	427
Sparco S.p.A.	49,108	6.01	460
La Sportiva S.p.A.	46,052	15.49	218
Rossignol Lange S.r.l.	39,285	7.44	98
Elite S.r.l.	27,334	24.30	38
Technisub S.p.A.	25,104	28.52	36
Brunswick Marine in Italia S.p.A.	22,705	3.80	30
Mizuno Italia S.r.l.	18,375	8.24	18

Source: Bureau van Dijk (2016).

Looking at the retail sales of sport equipment and bicycles (NACE code 47.64), in 2013 Decathlon Italia S.r.l. produced the largest profits in Italy, almost one billion euros, positioning itself far above its competitors. This company, part of a French-based group, started its activities in 1993, first as a retail store in Milan with engagements in the design, production and sale of sport goods and sportswear. Decathlon Group operates over 350 stores that retail clothing and equipment covering around 65 sport disciplines, in more than a dozen of countries (Bureau van Dijk, 2016). The second ranked company, Cisalfa S.p.A., produced 310.2 million euros of revenues, whilst all the other companies obtained figures under 91 million euros. In line with the differences in revenues, Decathlon is the company providing occupation to the largest number of people (i.e., 6369) followed by the other companies consistently, with the only exception for F.lli D'Amato S.p.A., company, which despite a rather small number of staff (i.e., 43 people), is ranked third by its revenue in this business field. Conversely, the most profitable company is Manifattura Mario Colombo & C. S.p.A., which produced an EBITDA-% of 11.89 in 2013 and whose revenue was not particularly significant when compared to those of the first two ranked companies. Manifattura Mario Colombo & C. S.p.A., better known as Colmar, is mainly involved in the retail trade of ski, golf and beach apparel. (Table 3.)

[2] EBITDA stands for Earnings Before Interests, Taxes, Depreciation and Amortisation. EBITDA-% = 100 × EBITDA/revenue. EBITDA-% = EBITDA margin.

Table 3 Largest private companies operating in retail sale of sport equipment and bicycles (NACE code 47.64) in Italy in 2013.

Company	Revenue (1000 €)	EBITDA-%	Staff (n)
Decathlon Italia S.r.l.	962,501	6.82	6369
Cisalfa Sport S.p.A.	310,215	2.29	2062
F.lli D'Amato S.p.A.	90,924	6.30	43
Game 7 Athletics S.p.A.	64,761	1.46	461
Manifattura Mario Colombo & C. S.p.A.	64,211	11.89	236
DF Sport Specialist S.p.A.	60,460	3.27	275
Universo Sport S.p.A.	42,617	-5.25	244
Nencini Sport S.p.A.	32,458	2.63	167
Safra Motor S.r.l.	24,247	2.51	78
King S.p.A.	22,312	9.34	72

Source: Bureau van Dijk (2016).

The Giro d'Italia is one of the most popular Italian international events. It generates income in several economic fields such as retail sale of sport equipment and bicycles (NACE 47.64), manufacture of sport goods (NACE 32.20) and tourism. In the photo Italian Ivan Basso arrives in the Verona Arena as a winner of the 93rd Giro d'Italia in May 30, 2010.

According to Bureau van Dijk (2016), the leading company within the operations of sport facilities (NACE code 93.11) is Società Incremento Turistico Canazei (SITC) S.p.A., founded in 1947, mainly operating the ski lifts in Italy and, more broadly, promoting winter and summer tourism in Canazei and high Val di Fassa areas (Dolomiti Alps). Besides this, the company also operates a swimming pool in Canazei, a wellbeing centre, and owns the mountain shelter *Maria al Sass Pordoi*.

Data shows that, in 2013, it provided occupation to 170 people and generated almost 22.2 million euros in revenue. Out of the top ten organisations operating in this business field, also Sport Management S.p.A. stands out for the large number of staff members (i.e., almost 800 people) (Bureau van Dijk, 2016). Overall, the operation of ski lifts, race tracks and swimming pools seem to be the most profitable activities, with SITC and Funivie Valdaora S.p.A. being by far at the lead of this business field, showing the remarkable results of more than 41% and almost 50% EBITDA margin respectively. (Table 4.)

Table 4 Largest private companies operating sport facilities (NACE code 93.11) in Italy in 2013.

Company	Revenue (1000 €)	EBITDA-%	Staff (n)
Società Incremento Turistico Canazei (SITC) S.p.A.	22,190	41.41	170
Hippogroup Cesenate S.p.A.	20,636	7.96	78
Sport Management S.p.A.	16,017	8.92	799
Milano Sport S.p.A.	15,292	-6.73	148
Forumnet S.p.A.	12,186	12.83	24
Funivie Valdaora S.p.A.	11,188	49.12	32
San Virgilio R.E. S.p.A.	9159	26.80	45
Gestisport S.C.A.R.L.	9091	8.41	35
Platinum Hotels & Resorts S.r.l.	8859	6.63	40
Santa Monica S.p.A.	8599	10.51	15

Source: Bureau van Dijk (2016).

Unsurprisingly, most of the top ten companies operating in the field of sport clubs (NACE code 93.12) are football clubs: Juventus F.C., A.C. Milan, A.S. Roma, F.C. Internazionale, S.S.C. Napoli, A.S. Livorno, S.S. Lazio, A.C.F. Fiorentina are all among the top ten companies in 2013 (Bureau van Dijk, 2016). However, the leader company is Scuderia Toro Rosso S.p.A., established in 1975 and operating in the construction and assembly of racing cars. The company is a Formula One racing team owned in a 50/50 partnership between the drinks company Red Bull and former F1 driver Gerhard Berger. Interestingly, the football clubs show controversial data regarding the profitability. For example, whilst S.S.C. Napoli S.p.A. and ACF Fiorentina S.p.A. showed very positive results in EBITDA-%, A.S. Roma S.p.A. and F.C. Internazionale Milano S.p.A. exhibit quite negative ones, highlighting that the profitability of this business field might be characterised by a high variability and instability. (Table 5.)

Table 5 Largest private companies conducting activities of sport clubs (NACE code 93.12) in Italy in 2013.

Company	Revenue (1000 €)	EBITDA-%	Staff (n)
Scuderia Toro Rosso S.p.A.	78,443	8.12	304
Juventus F.C. S.p.A.	38,051	19.64	214
A.C. Milan S.p.A.	30,277	6.48	200
A.S. Roma S.p.A.	21,240	-11.57	144
F.C. Internazionale Milano S.p.A.	19,612	-7.10	212
S.S.C. Napoli S.p.A.	15,134	32.42	28
A.S. Livorno Calcio S.r.l.	15,095	5.28	11
Gresini Racing S.r.l.	11,409	8.42	25
S.S. Lazio S.p.A.	11,262	11.22	146
ACF Fiorentina S.p.A.	9771	26.67	121

Source: Bureau van Dijk (2016).

The leading fitness centre operating in Italy in 2013 was Virgin Active Italia S.p.A., with generated revenues of 96.7 million euros and 871 staff members. The company is a firm operating in many countries all around the world. It was incorporated in Italy in 2002, has placed its headquarters in Milan, and provides a wide range of services related to health and fitness through its vast national and international network of clubs. The second ranked company in this field is Healthcity Italia S.p.A., established in 2000, also based in Milan. The company runs a number of gyms and other recreation facilities that include swimming pools, parks, tennis courts, cinema and theatres, bowling complex and others. In 2013, Healthcity Italia S.p.A. produced an income of almost 13.6 million euros and gave occupation to 140 people. The other leading companies operating in this field showed smaller dimensions, if compared with their top two competitors; overall, their revenues were 6.4-2.2 million euros and the number of staff members varied between two and 73 people. Similarly to what observed with the activities of sport clubs (NACE code 93.12), the profitability of companies operating fitness facilities showed high variable results. For example the EBITDA margin of Club Milano Corso Como S.r.l. was 27% whilst Helthycity Italia obtained -3% in 2013. (Table 6.)

Table 6 Largest private companies operating fitness facilities (NACE code 93.13) in Italy in 2013.

Company	Revenue (1000 €)	EBITDA-%	Staff (n)
Virgin Active Italia S.p.A.	96,725	5.69	871
Healthcity Italia S.p.A.	13,583	2.98	140
Aria di Fitness SSDaRL	6392	0.45	2
Peperoncino Verde S.r.l.	6345	3.50	73
Club Milano Corso Como S.r.l.	5257	27.04	2
Primefitness SSDaRL	4368	8.93	n/a
Grand Hotel Parker's S.r.l.	3479	-1.01	73
Il Gladiatore S.r.l.	2877	15.39	2
Orange Torino SSDaRL	2784	0.67	13
La Wellness SSDaRL	2284	6.69	13

Source: Bureau van Dijk (2016).

Conclusions

The analysis of the available data shows that in 2013, the private sport sector in Italy generated revenues for over 10 billion euros and gave occupation to more than 103,000 people (ISTAT, 2013b). The predominant market is the retail sale of sport goods that in Italy counted around 10,000 companies and almost 4.5 million euros of revenue in 2013. Broadly, the private sport sector is a growing economy, representing 0.62% of Gross Domestic Product in 2013 (calculation based on the available data from ISTAT, 2013b and Eurostat, 2015).

The recent reorganisation of the Italian sport system along with the changes in laws and regulations have prompted renewed attention to the knowledge of what works in terms in getting the private sector further growing. As a consequence of the global economic and financial crisis, the Italian economy and public finance situation deteriorated significantly with negative effects also for the sport system. The combination of the global crisis with the changes in the legal framework has put the Italian sport system in a period of profound transformation. Therefore, sport organisations are reshaping their missions, their organisational structures and the way they interact with the main actors of the sector such as CONI and national sport federations. The magnitude and inherent tensions associated with these changes have created a context that many consider to represent a climate of crisis in the private sport sector. In this light, the Italian government has tried to indirectly support the growth of the sport system through a fiscal policy in favour of the sport organisations through the provision of different forms of fiscal exemptions. However, there is the necessity for further interventions, especially in the private sectors that, regardless of the potential, in terms of absolute numbers (e.g., revenues and number of employees), still represent a small fraction of the Italian businesses in general. A growth potential can be foreseen for instance in the labour market. In Italy, the number of people employed in the sport sectors is still limited compared to the other

European Countries (Kleissner & Grohal, 2015). An enlargement of the labour market, if supported, might offer new opportunities for growth both for the private sector and the sport sector in general with positive effects expected for the entire Italian economic system.

From the scientific perspective, there is a need to further analyse this sector in the Italian context from the social and economic points of view. The available literature mainly focuses on legal, management, marketing and corporate social responsibility aspects. Despite their importance, they are not sufficient to fully understand the impact of such a relevant sector on the society. Until recently, rigorous analyses of the sport sector have been rare in Italy. Although there is no question about the importance of profit making sport actors, this sector has received less attention in the sport-related research. This is particularly apparent in the area of finance, private sector and labour market development. The quantification of private sport activity in Italy by number of businesses, employees, turnover, beneficiaries of services and other similar parameters represents an important analytical step to measure the fundamental aspects of the sector and at the same time to understand the main trends.

Contributions
Antonio Borgogni was the scientific coordinator of the study, conceptualized the research and led the writing of the article. He was the author of the section "The organisation of the Italian Sport System". Simone Digennaro designed the research and organized and supervised data collection. He was the author of the section "The private sector and the economic value of sport". Emiliano Mazzoli carried out the data research and completed data analysis. He was the author of the sections "Structural and economic data" and "Italian sport and fitness companies: goods, facilities and clubs". The authors jointly wrote the "Introduction" and the "Conclusions" and edited the draft of the article.

References

Andreff, W., & Szymanski, S. (2006). *Handbook on the economics of sport.* North Hampton, MA: Edward Elgar.

Andreotti, M. (2014). *La Dimensione Economica delle Federazioni Sportive Nazionali* [The Economic Dimension of National (Italian) Sports Federations] (Master's thesis). Retrieved July 20, 2016 from http://dspace.unive.it/bitstream/handle/10579/4891/826933-1181428.pdf?sequence=2

Blando, F. (2009). Evoluzione e prospettive del rapporto tra Stato, Regioni e CONI in materia di sport [Evolution and perspective of the relation between the state, regions and CONI in the field of sport]. *Istituzioni del federalismo: rivista di studi giuridici e politici, 30*(1), 21–76.

BNL. (2013). Lo sport in Italia: economia, passione e business [Sport in Italy: Economy, passion and business]. *Focus settimanale di studi BNL,* 16 maggio 2013.

Borgogni, A., Digennaro, S., & Sterchele, D. (2015). Sport clubs in Italy. In C. Breuer, R. Hoekman, S. Nagel, & H. van der Werff (Eds.), *Sport clubs in Europe: A cross-national comparative perspective* (pp. 249–270). Cham, Switzerland: Springer International Publishing Switzerland.

Bureau van Dijk. (2016). Company level data NACE classification [Data file]. Retrieved February 9, 2016 from AIDA database https://aida.bvdinfo.com/version-2016727/home.serv?product=aidaneo

CENSIS. (2008). *1° Rapporto Sport & Società* [1st report sport and society]. Retrieved January 30, 2016 from http://www.coni.it/images/documenti/ReportSport_e_Societ_2008_01.pdf

CONI. (2012). *Sport – Italia 2020 Il Libro Bianco dello Sport Italiano* [Sport – Italy 2020, The White Paper on the Italian Sport]. Retrieved August 4, 2016 from http://www.coni.it/images/Libro_Bianco_-_Sito.pdf

CONI. (2014). *Lo sport in Italia. Numeri e contesto* [Sport in Italy. Numbers and context]. Retrieved February 7, 2016 from http://www.coni.it/images/numeri_dello_sport/Lo_Sport_in_Italia.pdf

CONI. (2015). *Bilancio di esercizio 2015* [Financial statement 2015]. Retrieved August 10, 2016 from http://www.coni.it/images/documenti/Bilancio-CONI-2015.pdf

Digennaro, S., Colella, D., Morano, M., Vannini, E., & Borgogni, A. (2012). Nuovi profili professionali per gli operatori sportivi [New professional profiles for sport employees]. *Educazione Fisica e Sport nella Scuola, 223*, 18–22.

Digennaro, S., Borgogni, A., & Sterchele, D. (2016). Un analisis de la participacion deportiva en Italia desde el advocacy coalition framework [The analysis of sport participation in Italy through the advocacy coalition framework]. In R. Llopis-Goig (Ed.), *Participacion deportiva en Europa. Politicas, culturas y practicas* (pp. 359–383). Barcelona, Spain: Oberta UOC Publishing.

Eurostat. (2015). Table 1: GDP at current market prices, 2003-04 and 2012-14 YB15 [Data file]. Retrieved August 29, 2016 from http://ec.europa.eu/eurostat/statistics-explained/index.php/National_accounts_and_GDP

Garofalo, G., Lorenzini, F., & Zamaro, N. (2002). *Lo sport, le organizzazioni sportive e il valore economico del sistema: la struttura e i dati del censimento non-profit* [Sport, sport organisation and the economic values of the system: The structure and the data of the survey]. Proceedings of the 5th Italian National conference on statistics, 2012. ISTAT.

GHK. (2010). Volunteering in Sport - Italy. Annex of *Volunteering in the European Union*. European Commission. D-G Education and Culture. Retrieved February 9, 2016 from http://edz.bib.uni-mannheim.de/daten/edz-b/gdbk/10/ksj/volunteering-in-sport-italy_en.pdf

Hoye, R., Smith, A. C., Nicholson, M., & Stewart, B. (2015). *Sport management: Principles and applications*. London, UK: Routledge.

ISTAT. (2002). Tavola di dati: Statistiche nazionali sulla struttura delle imprese [Table: National statistic on the enterprices] [Data file]. Retrieved August 27, 2016 from http://dati.istat.it/

ISTAT. (2005). *Lo sport che cambia – I comportamenti emergenti e le nuove tendenze della pratica sportiva in Italia* [The sport the change: Emerging behaviours and new sport practice tendencies]. Rome, Italy: ISTAT.

ISTAT. (2012). Aspetti della vita quotidiana [Aspects of the daily life] [Data file]. Retrieved February 3, 2016 from http://www.istat.it/it/archivio/96427

ISTAT. (2013a). *Aspetti della vita quotidiana* [Aspects of the daily life]. Rome, Italy: ISTAT.

ISTAT. (2013b). Tavola di dati: Imprese e risorse umane: selected years 2008–2013 [Table: Enterprises and human resources] [Data file]. Retrieved January 12, 2016 from http://dati.istat.it/

ISTAT. (2014). *9° Censimento dell'industria e dei servizi e Censimento delle istituzioni non profit: il non profit nello sport* [9th survey on industry and services and survey on the non-profit institutions: Non-profit in the sport sector]. Retrieved January 12, 2016 from http://www.istat.it/it/files/2014/07/Il-non-profit-nello-sport_fascicolo.pdf

ISTAT. (2015). *Italia in cifre 2015* [Italy in digits 2015]. Retrieved August 29, 2016 from http://www.istat.it/it/files/2015/08/ItaliaInCifre2015It.pdf

Kleissner A., & Grohal, G. (2015). *Research for Cult Committee – The economic dimension of sport*. D-G for Internal Policies, Policy Department B: Structural and cohesion policies culture and education. Brussels, Belgium: European Commission.

Law 586. (1996). *Conversione in legge, con modificazioni, del decreto-legge 20 settembre 1996, n. 485, recante disposizioni urgenti per le societa' sportive professionistiche* [Conversion into law, with amendments, of Decree-Law of 20 September 1996 n. 485 laying down urgent measures for professional sports companies] (Italian Republic). Retrieved July 18, 2016 from http://www.gazzettaufficiale.it/eli/id/1996/11/20/096G0616/sg

Law 91. (1981). *Norme in materia di rapporti tra società e sportivi professionisti* [Rules on the relationship between society and sports professionals] (Italian Republic). Retrieved January 15, 2016 from http://www.gazzettaufficiale.it/atto/serie_generale/caricaDettaglioAtto/originario?atto.dataPubblicazioneGazzetta=1981-03-27&atto.codiceRedazionale=081U0091&elenco30giorni=false

Le Roux, N., Chantelat, P., & Camy, J. (1999). *Sport and employment in Europe*. Final report. Brussels, Belgium: European Commission.

Legislative Decree 242. (1999). *Riordino del Comitato olimpico nazionale italiano – CONI, a norma dell'articolo 11 della legge 15 marzo 1997, n. 59* [Reorganization of the Italian National Olympic Committee - CONI, in accordance with article 11 of the law 15 March 1997 n. 59] (Italian Republic). Retrieved February 19, 2016 from http://www.gazzettaufficiale.it/eli/id/1999/07/29/099G0324/sg

Lucas, R. E. (1978). On the size distribution of business firms. *Bell Journal of Economics, 9*, 508–523.

Lolli, S. (1997). Un approccio alle professioni dello sport in Italia [An approach to the sport professions in Italy]. In G. P. Prandstraller (Ed.), *Guardare alle professioni* (pp. 152–161). Milano, Italy: Franco Angeli.

Madella, A. (2002). *Le professioni dello sport. Il mercato del lavoro nello sport in Italia: caratteristiche e tendenze* [Sport professions. Labour market in Italy: Characteristic and trends]. Rome, Italy: Scuola dello Sport.

Madella, A., & Digennaro, S. (2009). *Manuale di sociologia dello sport. Analisi del fenomeno e studio delle organizzazioni sportive* [Handbook on sport sociology. Analysis of the phenomena and study of the sport organisations]. Rome, Italy: SdS edizioni.

Nomisma. (1999). *Sport ed economia. Studio sugli aspetti economici del sistema sportivo italiano negli anni 1994–1998* [Sport and economy. Analysis on the economic aspects of the Italian sport system in 1994–1998]. Bologna, Italy: Nomisma.

Porro, N. (1995). *Identità, nazione, cittadinanza: sport, società e sistema politico nell'Italia contemporanea* [National identity and citizenship: Sport, society and sport system in Italy]. Rome, Italy: Seam.

Porro, N., Bizzaglia, G., & Conti, D. (1999). The sport system and sports organisations in Italy. In K. Heinemann (Ed.), *Sport clubs in various European countries* (pp. 33–70). Stuttgart, Germany/New York, NY: Schattauer.

SpEA. (2012). *Study on the contribution of sport to economic growth and employment in the EU*. Study commissioned by the European Commission, D-G Education and Culture (Final Report). Retrieved June 14, 2016 from http://ec.europa.eu/sport/library/studies/study-contribution-spors-economic-growth-final-rpt.pdf

UNESCO. (2015). *Revised international charter of physical education, physical activity and sport*. SHS/2015/PI/H/14 REV. Retrieved August 29, 2016 from http://unesdoc.unesco.org/images/0023/002354/235409e.pdf

LATVIA: On Its Way to Developing the Private Sport Sector

Signe Luika

Selected country facts (in 2013)	
Capital	Riga
Geographical size (km^2)	64,573
Population (million)	2.02
GDP (euro per capita)	11,300
GDP (per capita in PPS)	62
Annual net earnings average (€)	6487

The Organization of Sport Sector in Latvia

The sport sector in Latvia consists of three components: governmental and local authorities; societies and foundations; and merchants. It is regulated by more than 40 regulatory enactments. For operating efficiently, four types of resources, namely labour, financial, material and information resources are seen necessary for the functioning of the sport sector.

The development of the sport sector in Latvia is ensured by a large number of institutions and organizations with different legal statuses. The Ministry of Education and Science of the Republic of Latvia is divided into an organizational model of the sport sector that includes governmental and non-governmental organizations, and enterprises. Each of these have particular tasks and objectives. The organizational model of the sport sector is illustrated in Fig. 1.

S. Luika (✉)
Latvian Academy of Sport Education, Riga, Latvia
e-mail: signe.luika@lspa.lv

A. Laine, H. Vehmas (eds.), *The Private Sport Sector in Europe*, Sports Economics, Management and Policy 14, https://doi.org/10.1007/978-3-319-61310-9_13

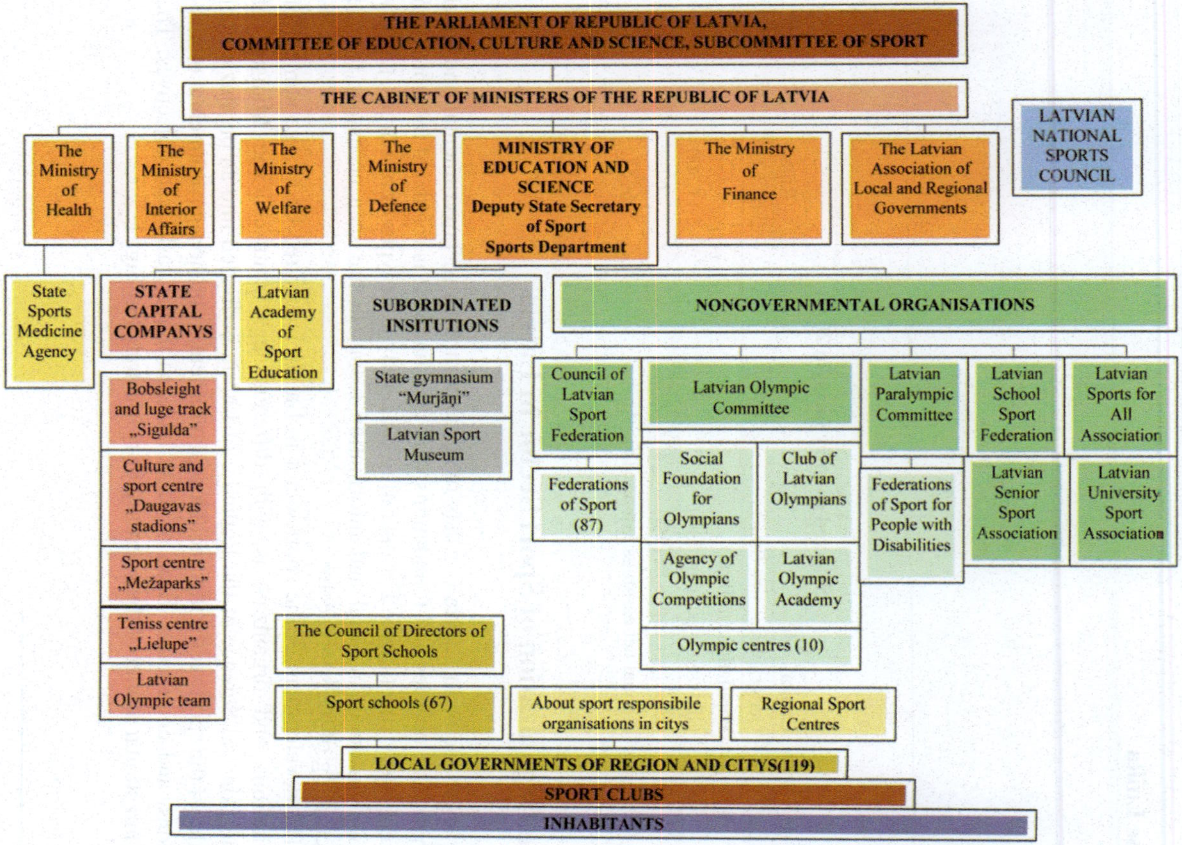

Fig. 1 The organizational model of the sport sector in Latvia. Source: The Ministry of Education and Science of Latvia (2016a).

Governmental Sport Sector

According to the Latvian Constitution Article 64 the right of the legislation belongs to the parliament – Saeima. Saeima is the leading institution in the sport sector, which develops and submits proposals to the legislation. Saeima has adopted the Sports Law, which defines the organization and development of sport in general together with the legal framework for sport organizations, the state and local authorities and the basic tasks in the development of sport and sport funding foundations. Sports Law also includes the principles related to taking part in the international sport movement. (Latvijas Vēstnesis, 2002.)

The Ministry of Education and Science is responsible for the sport sector. According to the Sports Law it shall: implement a unified state policy; develop drafts for regulatory enactments; implement purposeful international cooperation and ensure Latvian representation in international sport organizations; and perform other functions and tasks that are specified in regulatory enactments. (Latvijas Vēstnesis, 2002.)

The Cabinet of Ministers of the Republic of Latvia, as it is determined by the Sports Law, is established by the Latvian National Sports Council, which is a public, advisory body consisting of ministers and heads of national sport organizations. The Cabinet of Ministers establishes ministries. The sport sector, together with education and science is under the governance of the Ministry of Education and Science. (The Ministry of Education and Science of Latvia, 2016a.) The Cabinet also implements executive power, which includes a wide range of competences, such as the right to decide relevant issues in the sport sector. The most important competences are first, the right to approve the Latvian National Sports Council and its Chairman, and the regulation of the Latvian National Sports Council, and second, the right to define the procedure for allocating and assigning monetary prizes for outstanding achievements in sport. (Latvijas Vēstnesis, 2002.)

Moreover, according to the Sports Law, the Latvian National Sports Council has several responsibilities. It shall participate in the development of the national sport policy; draw up proposals for the state budget funds in the field of sport and submit them to the Ministry of Education and Science. It shall also provide the cabinet with recommendations in relation to the awarding of the monetary prizes for outstanding achievements in sport; provide opinions about the conformity and statutes of sport facilities; advise the Ministry of Defence and the Ministry of Interior about the types of sports to be supported in the institutions of the ministries; and provide the Ministry of Welfare with opinions about support programmes for outstanding sport veterans of Latvia. (Latvijas Vēstnesis, 2002.)

The sport organization system in Latvia also includes ministries of other sectors, which, according to the Sports law, have particular competences for reaching the goals in the sport sector. These are the Ministry of Health, Ministry of Welfare, Ministry of Defence and Ministry of Internal Affairs.

The Ministry of Education and Science has extended their activities also closer to the profit-making sector as it has shares in five capital companies. These are Bobsleja un kamaniņu trase "Sigulda" Ltd. (Bobsleigh and Luge track "Sigulda"); Kultūras un sporta centrs "Daugavas stadions State Ltd." (Culture and Sports Centre "Daugava"); Sporta centrs "Mežaparks Ltd." (Sports Centre "Mežparks"); Tenisa centrs "Lielupe" Ltd." (Tennis Centre "Lielupe") and Latvijas Olimpiskā vienība Ltd. (Latvian Olympic Team) (The Ministry of Education and Science of Latvia, 2016a.)

According to the Law on Governance of Capital Shares of a Public Person and Capital Companies the state capital company is a capital company whose all capital shares or voting stocks belong to the state. In such organizations, the representatives of the holders of the capital shares or local government capital companies shall promote the implementation of the objectives and tasks laid down in laws, cabinet regulations, and approved sectoral development concepts and strategies, and other documents governing the development of the sector. (Latvijas Vēstnesis, 2016.)

For example, the Latvian Academy of Sport Education, the Latvian Sports Museum and the Murjani Sports Gymnasium are under the supervision of the Ministry of Education and Science. According to the constitution of The Latvian Academy of Sport Education (approved on April 26, 2007 in Saeima), it provides students with the highest academic and professional education and qualification to develop sport science and improve culture. (Latvijas Vēstnesis, 2013.) The aim of the Latvian Sports Museum is to collect, maintain, investigate, exhibit and popularize material evidences connected with Latvian sport history. It includes also intangible assets that possesses historical, scientific and memorial meaning, and information connected with Latvian sport history. (Latvijas Vēstnesis, 2012.) The Murjani Sports Gymnasium on the other hand is a sport educational institution established by the state that is entitled to implement basic education, general secondary educational programmes and professional sport education programmes (Murjani State Gymnasium, 2009).

The Ministry of Health is responsible for an important sport sector organization, namely the State Sports Medicine Centre. The aim of the centre is to carry out research about residents (especially children and adolescents) by collecting and analysing data about their physical development and fitness, capacity for work, movement and motor ability. Moreover, the collected data has to be comparable with the similar data from other countries. Additionally, the centre has to provide recommendations for residents (especially children and adolescents) about their improvements in the physical fitness and for example about the formation of correct standing postures. (Latvijas Vēstnesis, 2014.)

Role of Local Governments in the Sport Sector

An important role in the organization of sport in Latvia belongs to the local governments (authorities). The role of the local governments is defined by the Article 7 of the Sports Law according to the following main aspects. First, the local governments, when promoting healthy lifestyles and sport development in their administrative territories, are entitled to specify an employee or institution responsible for sport; build and maintain sport facilities and ensure the necessary equipment; promote the formation and operation of sport organizations, including sport clubs; support the further education of sport specialists and other sport employees; finance sport competitions; and finance licensed sport education programmes and sport events, which are implemented by sport clubs in the administrative territory thereof. Second, local governments are entitled to finance sport education programmes in the accredited sport educational institutions under their supervision. (Latvijas Vēstnesis, 2002.)

The local governments have the right to establish sport education institutions – sport schools, which are financed by the budget of local government or the state. In 2014 there were 72 sport schools operating in Latvia, and 32,803 people in age of 6–25 years were engaged in those sport schools. (The Ministry of Education and Science of Latvia, 2016b.)

Main Non-governmental Organizations in the Sport Sector

The largest part of the organizations in the Latvian sport organization system consist of non-governmental organizations that are societies and foundations. According to the Law of the Societies and Foundations, an association is a voluntary union founded by persons for achieving the goals that are specified in the articles of association, and which shall not have a profit-making nature. A foundation, or a fund, is an aggregate of property that has been set aside for the achievement of a goal specified by the founder, which shall neither have a profit-making nature. (Latvijas Vēstnesis, 2003.) In most cases non-governmental organizations have been created to satisfy the needs of the society where they are not fulfilled by the government, local government or businesses. Non-governmental organizations provide opportunities for people to improve their quality of life, self-assertion in a professional way and personal growth. (Luika, 2012.) In 2014, there were 749 associations and foundations in the field of sport in Latvia (The Ministry of Education and Science of Latvia, 2016b.)

Many non-governmental organizations are part of the organizational structure formed by the Ministry of Education and Science. One of the leading organizations is the Latvian Sports Federation Council. According to the Sports Law, the Latvian Sports Federation Council shall coordinate, represent and implement the shared interests of the recognized sport federations in Latvia. (Latvijas Vēstnesis, 2002.)

Another important non-governmental organization in Latvia is the Latvian Olympic Committee, which is established by the representatives of the Olympic sport federations. Its aim is to ensure the representation of Latvia in the International Olympic Movement and the participation of Latvian athletes and sport teams in the Olympic Games. (Latvian Olympic Committee, 1991.) Latvian Olympic Committee plays an important role in establishing also other non-governmental sport organizations. Organizations such as Olympians Social Fund, Olympic competition agency, Latvian Olympian Club and ten Olympic centres have been founded by the Latvian Olympic Committee. (The Ministry of Education and Science of Latvia, 2016a.)

Sport federations for people with disabilities are united under the Latvian Paralympic Committee. Its operations are regulated by the Sports Law by defining that Latvian Paralympic Committee is responsible for the activities of sport federations of disabled people recognised in Latvia in respect with the types of sports represented in the International Paralympic Committee. This organization also coordinates other types of disabled sports and it represents and implements sport interests of the disabled people. (Latvijas Vēstnesis, 2002.)

The Latvian School Sports Federation (LSSF) is a non-governmental organization, which unites general education schools and sport school clubs in Latvia to promote the development of sport and youth engagement in sport activities (Latvian School Sport Federation, 2008). Latvian Sports for All Association is also placed in the non-governmental organization sector. The association aims to create necessary conditions for grassroots sport in Latvia and find possibilities for all residents to engage in physical activities. (Latvian Sports for All Association, 2013.)

The main objectives of the Latvian Veteran/Senior Sports Association are to lead, coordinate and organize the movement of sport veterans/seniors in Latvia in collaboration with sport federations, government, local authorities, and public and private organizations. This organization also promotes the participation in international sport veteran/senior events. (Latvian Sport – Veteran Senior Association, 2010.)

In addition, an important role in the sport organization system belongs to the Latvian University Sport Federation. Its main objective is to promote and popularize sport activities and healthy lifestyle among Latvian university students and employees. (Latvian University Sport Association, 2016.)

Regulation and Resources of the Sport Sector

The sport sector in Latvia is regulated by more than 40 regulatory enactments in different directions regarding the sport facilities, the organization of sport events, doping, National sport council, national sport federations, sport awarding, medical care, information about budget funding, sport team funding, certification of sport specialists, foundation and operation of non-governmental organizations, foundation and operation of enterprises, and donations (Luika, 2012).

The necessity of the Sports Law was initiated by the society already in 1998, but obtained only in 2002. The purpose of the Sports Law is to specify the general and legal basis for the organization and development of sport, mutual relationship of sport organizations, state and local government institutions and the basic tasks in sport development. In addition the Sports Law aims to specify the basis for the financing of sport and the principles that shall be taken under consideration when taking part in the international sport movement. The Law also determines basic principles in the sport sector: the principle of equality, the principle of fair play and the principle of safety. (Latvijas Vēstnesis, 2002.)

Each sector including the operations of the sport sector requires labour, financial, material and information recourses. Regulatory resources of the sport sector are demonstrated in Fig. 2.

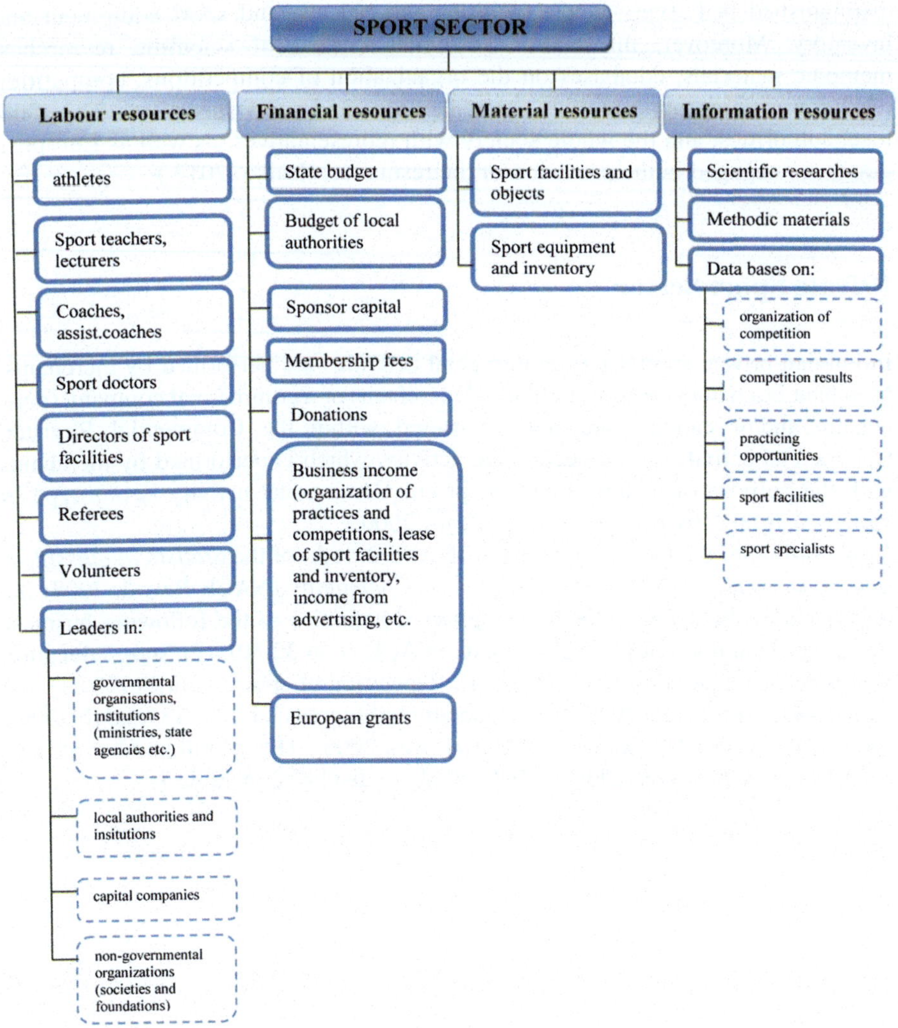

Fig. 2 Resources of the sport sector. Source: Luika (2012).

Sport labour resources in Latvia consist of the following components: athletes, sport teachers, lecturers, coaches and assistant coaches, sport physicians, directors of sport facilities, referees, volunteers, leaders of the sport sector in governmental organizations, institutions (e.g., ministries and state agencies), local authorities and institutions, capital companies and non-governmental organizations (e.g., societies and foundations). Financial resources come from the state budget, budget of local authorities, sponsor capital, membership fees, donations, business income (e.g., organizing competitions), leasing of sport facilities, inventory and income from advertising, and European foundations. Two types of material resources are distinguished in Latvia – sport facilities and objects, and sport equipment and inventory. Moreover, information resources consist of scientific researches, methodic materials, databases on the organization of competitions, competition results, practicing opportunities, sport facilities and sport specialists. The state, local authorities, and the whole society with representatives, as well as European grants are engaged in the provision of the resources. (Luika, 2012.)

Private Sport Sector

In Latvian private sport sector commercial activities are performed by merchants. Merchant is a natural person (individual merchant) or a commercial company (partnership and/or capital company) registered within the Commercial Register. Commercial activity is open economic activity, which is performed by merchants with the purpose of gaining financial profit. Commercial activity is one type of entrepreneurial activity. (Latvijas Vēstnesis, 2000.)

According to the Latvian equivalent (NACE 2. red.) of the *Statistical classification of economic activities in the European Community* (NACE Rev. 2, 2008) the merchants of the sport sector have registered activities in the following business fields: (1) Manufacturing of sport goods (NACE code 32.30), (2) Sport education and extracurricular education (85.51), (3) Operation of sport facilities (93.11), (4) Operation of sport clubs (93.12), (5) Operation of fitness clubs (93.13) and (6) Other sport activities (93.19) (Register of Enterprises, 2006). The overall number of merchants in these business fields in 2000–2014 are displayed in Table 1.

Table 1 **The number of sport merchants in Latvia in 2000–2014.**

Business field	NACE code	2000	2001	2002	2003	2004	2005	2006	2007	2008	2009	2010	2011	2012	2013	2014
Manufacturing of sport goods	**32.30**	11	13	15	18	18	19	20	20	26	29	33	40	45	49	56
Sport education and extracurricular education	**85.51**	8	9	10	9	12	17	19	22	36	37	45	59	71	86	92
Operation of sport facilities	**93.11**	35	41	51	63	78	91	103	111	139	145	148	157	166	174	175
Operation of sport clubs	**93.12**	46	62	69	81	96	100	119	113	137	145	147	160	172	173	169
Operation of fitness clubs	**93.13**	8	9	10	11	14	18	23	26	32	37	40	50	58	73	75
Other sport activities	**93.19**	14	17	24	24	32	40	53	59	83	90	107	140	168	216	223

Source: Information of business database Lursoft (2016).

The overall number of the sport merchants increased in Latvia from 122 merchants in 2000 to 790 merchants in 2014. The highest number of merchants was registered in “Other sport activities”. In 2014 there were 223 merchants operating in that business field. Moreover, this field experienced the highest increase from 22 companies in 2000 to 223 companies in 2014. Thereby, during the period of 14 years the number of companies increased 15 times. (Information of business database Lursoft, 2016.)

The lowest increase was noticed in “Operation of sport clubs” from 46 companies in 2000 to 169 in 2014. As a result, the increase was “only” nearly four times more. Very similar business field by the content is “Operation of fitness clubs”, in which there were eight merchants registered in 2000, but as many as 75 merchants in 2014. As a consequence, the increase was more than nine times. (Information of business database Lursoft, 2016.)

In order to evaluate the efficiency of the sector it is important to take into the account the revenue and the profit. The revenue of sport merchants is displayed in Fig. 3.

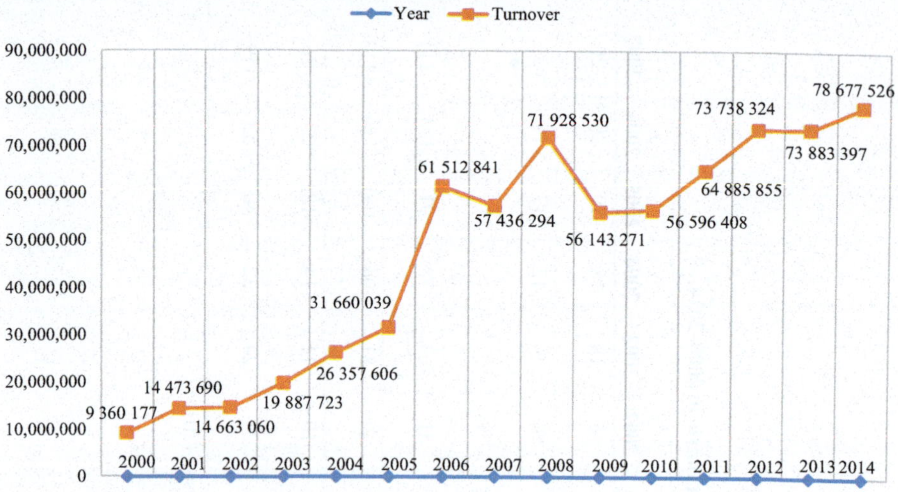

Fig. 3 The revenue (in euros) of merchants in the sport sector in 2000–2014. Source: Information of business database Lursoft (2016).

The total revenue of merchants in the sport sector increased from 9.4 million euros in 2000 to 78.7 million euros in 2014. Figure 3 displays a rapid growth of the revenue in 2006, which is more than two times higher than in 2005. (Information of business database Lursoft, 2016.) These significant changes can be explained by the improvement of the economic situation of the state and the gross domestic product (GDP). In 2006 GDP increased by 11% in comparison with 2005, and Latvia demonstrated one of the highest growth tempos of national economy in Europe. (The Central Statistical Bureau of Latvia, 2007.)

By the analysis of the sport-related NACE business fields during 2000–2014 the highest total revenue was discovered in “Operation of sport clubs” (313.3 million euros). The lowest total revenue in the same period was in “Sport education and extracurricular education” (13.5 million euros). In order to get a clear understanding about the sector of the merchants in 2000–2014, it is necessary to analyse their profits. The profit dynamics of sport merchants are displayed in Fig. 4.

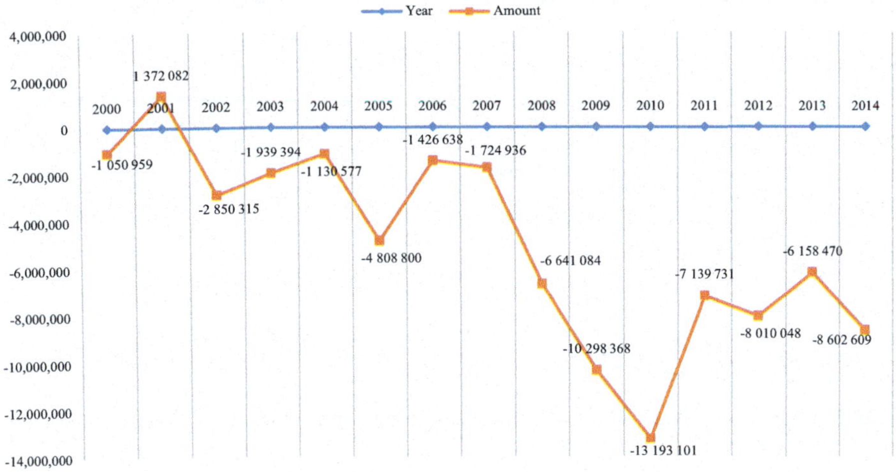

Fig. 4 The profit of sport merchants during 2000–2014. Source: Information of business database Lursoft (2016).

In 2000–2014 the sport sector operated at a loss, except in 2001, when the total profit of the sector was around 1.4 million euros. The profit decrease of the sport organizations was initiated in 2007 and finished with the highest loss record approximately 13.2 million euros in 2010. This downfall of the profit can be explained by the rapid deterioration of the economic situation within the state that took place in 2008–2010. During this period, particularly in 2009, the GDP experienced a major downfall from 18% in 2008 to 0.3% in 2009. The profit of the sport sector during 2000–2014 did not reach the same economic indicator levels as before the crisis. (Information of business database Lursoft, 2016.)

By analysing separately the different business fields, it can be concluded that during 2000–2014 there were organizations making profit in “Manufacturing of sport goods” as they gained total profit around 1.2 million euros. On the other hand, the highest loss was detected in “Operation of sport facilities”, which operated with a total loss around 4.3 million euros.

Sector capacity and efficiency can be characterized by the labour capacity and mobility. The labour capacity in the sport merchant sector during 2000–2014 is demonstrated in Fig. 5.

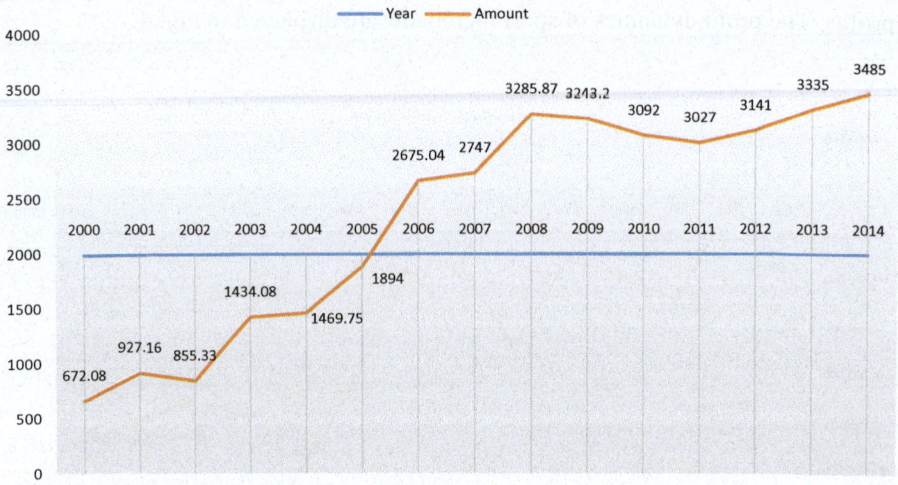

Fig. 5 Dynamics of the labour in sport merchant sector during 2000–2014. Source: Information of business database Lursoft (2016).

During 2000–2014 the total labour capacity increased more than five times. However, in comparison with 2010, the year of 2011 experienced a decline, but already in 2012 the level of 2010 was overachieved again. Nonetheless, these differences are not crucial in the sector's existence. By analysing separately the sport-related NACE business fields it can be concluded that during 2000–2014 the highest number of employees was in "Operation of sport clubs" – approximately 1012 employees. On the contrary, the lowest number of employees was detected in "Sport education and extracurricular education", in which during the same time approximately 96 employees were employed.

Private Sport Sector: In Hope for the Better Future

The private sport sector and the popularity of sport and healthy lifestyle are slowly increasing in importance in Latvia. In 2009 for example, 44% of the Latvians informed that they never exercise or participate in sport activities. In 2014, however the percentage of the physically inactive population has decreased as 39% of the Latvians informed that they never exercise or participate in sport. (European Commission, 2010; 2014.)

The interest of the citizens in engaging in sport has been influenced by several factors. These include among others the developed non-governmental sector, rise of the living standards, popularity of the healthy lifestyle and high Olympic achievements. During 2000–2014 Latvia got three gold medals, six silver medals and three bronze medals in the summer Olympic Games and four silver and three bronze medals in the winter Olympic Games (Latvian Olympic Committee, 2016).

In spite of the slowly growing popularity of sport, grassroots sports such as cycling, orienteering, running, Nordic walking and other free time activities have become very popular and gathered considerable number of participants. One successful example, which characterizes interest in grassroots sport is the SEB MTB marathon in mountain biking. This event has been organized since 2002 by a capital company called Igo Japiņa sporta aģentūra. The competition is organized every year in six or seven stages in several locations, and the participants have the opportunity to participate in all of them. SEB MTB mountain biking marathon takes place in three distances – marathon distance (60–70 km), medium distance (30–45 km), health distance (30–35 km) and children's distance (400–1000 m). The competition takes place in rural and forest roads added with obstacles of water. The total number of participants in 2003–2014 is shown in Table 2.

Table 2 Number of participants in all rounds of SEB MTB Marathon in 2003–2014.

Round	2003	2004	2005	2006	2007	2008	2009	2010	2011	2012	2013	2014
Cēsis-Valmiera	358	892	1131	1665	1834	2117	2261	2310	2051	2439	2695	2345
Sigulda/Krimulda	502	707	1074	1344	1554	1895	2154	2092	1830	2302	2566	1980
Kandava	437	725	988	1238	1431	1701						
Kuldīga	423	698	760	1024		1682			1734			1806
Cēsis					1457	1552	2025	2115	2059	2290	2341	1880
Ērgļi	451	659	882	1141	1319	1451	1849					
Vietalva								1732	1719	2031	2236	1934
Smiltene	500	673	932	1204	1333		1748	1694	2185	1963	2266	2020
Tukums							1948	1863	1731	2061	2329	1727

Source: Information of capital company "Igo Japiņa sporta aģentūra" (2016).

As shown in Table 2, the SEB MTB marathon is growing in different aspects. In 2000–2014 the number of rounds increased from six to seven. Also the number of participants increased more than five times in this period.

Riga Marathon is another important event, which supports the developments of the citizens' growing interest in sport activities. It is also an important event in creating economic impact to the country. The Riga City Council has been organizing this event already since 1991. In 2007 however, a capital company Nords Event Communications took over the organizing of the event. Further on, with growing number of partners, sponsors and supporters from 2007 until 2014, Riga Marathon was named Nordea Riga Marathon according to its main sponsor Nordea bank. The number of participants in the Nordea Riga Marathon increased five times in 2008–2014. Participants have been offered to participate in several distances: the classic marathon distance of 42 km, half-marathon distance of 21 km, 10 km distance and 3–6 km distance. The total number of participants in 2008–2014 is shown in Table 3. (Lattelecom Riga Marathon, 2016).

Table 3 Number of participants in Riga Marathon in 2008–2014.

Year	2008	2009	2010	2011	2012	2013	2014
Number of participants	4500	8600	8728	16,350	18,180	20,020	23,193

Source: Lattelecom Riga Marathon (2016).

In 2007 Riga Marathon certified its racing route according to the Association of International Marathons and Distance Races (AIMS) standards, and since 2012, the event has received an annual prestigious International Association of Athletics Federations (IAAF) bronze quality mark (Bronze Label). Such an international evaluation provides an opportunity to attract marathon participants from different parts of the world. So far the largest number of participants from foreign countries in Riga Marathon was in 2013, when there were runners from 65 different countries. Since 2015 the event has been called Lattelecom Riga Marathon according its new main partner. (Lattelecom Riga Marathon, 2016.)

Riga Marathon is creating economic impact to Latvia. From 2007 to 2014 the event was called Nordea Riga Marathon according to its main partner Nordea bank. Since 2015 the event has been called Lattelecom Riga Marathon. The photo shows the moments before the start of the 2016 event. *Photo: Edmuns Brencis/Picture Agency.*

Riga Marathon is an important event not only because it promotes sport and healthy lifestyles, but also because of socio-economic importance. First, the event has created employment opportunities. For example, in 2013 there were more than one thousand people working in the organization. This included police, medical staff, artists, service staff and more than 600 volunteers. (Lattelecom Riga Marathon, 2016.) Second, income is generated by the participants and their supporters from the spending in cafeterias, restaurants and hotels. The calculations of the expenditures have not been made yet. Third, the event promotes tourism to Riga and Latvia. Unfortunately, Riga Marathon is the only annual sport event in Latvia, which brings together a great number of people from different age groups and countries.

When realizing the importance of sport, people afford to spend more money for it. Together with the growing participation in sport activities Structure analysis of the citizen expenses (2000) reveals that in 2000 people spent 4% of their personal income for health. In 2014 the expenditure level was already 6.3% of the personal income. Nevertheless, this statistical data indicates that sport goods and services in Latvia certainly are not the most essential goods. (The Central Statistical Bureau of Latvia, 2015b.)

In 2000–2014, apart from the traditional challenges of high taxes, lack of qualified employees and altering legislation, merchants were confronted also with the economic crisis. During 2008–2010 Latvia underwent economic crisis that harshly affected the whole population, especially due the fact that the market economy is relatively young and has operated in Latvia only since the restoration of the independence in 1991. Latvia was obviously not prepared for the crisis. The GDP rapidly decreased from −3.2% in 2008 to −14.2% in 2009 and further to −2.9% in 2010. In addition, the unemployment promptly increased by 7% in 2008, to 17.5% in 2009 and further to 19.5% in 2010. (Eurostat, 2015; The Central Statistical Bureau of Latvia, 2015a). The population of Latvia is currently recovering from the crisis and the main lesson has been taught – people have become more cautious in operations with money (Kruks, 2016).

Nevertheless, there have been entrepreneurs who have established commercial companies during the times of the economic crisis. For example, in 2008 a joint stock company called Dinamo Rīga with start-up capital of around 2.92 million euros was established. It operates in sport-related business fields "Operation of sport facilities" and "Operation of sport clubs". The revenue of the company was around 13 million euros in 2014 and it operated with a total loss of 1.6 million euros. (Firmas.lv, 2016.)

Conclusions

Sport is undoubtedly an important and integral part of the Latvian society as it serves education, health, social, cultural, political and economic related functions for the public good (Luika, 2012). The Ministry of Education and Science is responsible for sport in Latvia. The Ministry has created an organizational model of sport sector in Latvia, which includes mainly governmental sport organizations, state capital companies, a few non-governmental sport organizations, but no merchants in the field of sport (The Ministry of Education and Science of Latvia, 2016a). This kind of model signalises a distance between the Ministry of Education and Science and the business of sport.

The sport sector, both governmental and private is regulated by more than 40 different laws and regulations. Such amount of regulations makes presume that sport is governed very comprehensively. However, at the same time unfortunately, the private sport sector faces imperfections in regulation. (Luika, 2012.)

The private sport sector of Latvia has a tendency to grow – all sport-related business fields in the period of 2000–2014 have demonstrated a growth. In general, there is also growth of revenues in the private sport sector. However, the economic crises that hit Latvia in 2008–2010 made a significant slipping of the revenues and not until in 2012, the level of 2008 was reached again. Unfortunately, the private sport sector, with the exception of the year 2001, has been operating at a loss. Losses began to rise in 2007 and they reached the highest point in 2010. Until 2014 the private sport sector had not gotten the return in same level as in 2007. Despite all those aspects, the number of liquidated companies is still small. (Information of business database Lursoft, 2016.)

People understand more and more about the importance of sport in their lives. The number of physically active people in Latvia has had a tendency to grow. However, in 2014 still 39% of the Latvians informed that they never exercise or participate in sport activities (European Commission, 2014). This data is not a compliment to the development of sport, but at least it shows some positive progress in the physical activity of the Latvians.

People have become more socially active and aware of their possibilities to influence the processes in sport. It is confirmed by the fact that the dynamics of the number of associations and foundations during 2000–2014 increased from 533 organizations to 749 (The Ministry of Education and Science of Latvia, 2016b). Hopefully, the number of associations and foundations also will go up together with the future data on physically active people.

It is clear that the private sport sector is important in Latvia – it secures jobs, pays taxes and provides public with goods and services that the state is unable to provide. Although the private sport sector faced many obstacles during 2000–2014 it has a tendency to grow. After the complete recovery of the economic crises, hopefully, citizens' interest in sport will still grow, which will also increase the amount of physically active people that all together will enhance the development of sport.

References

European Commission. (2010). *Sport and physical activity*. Special Eurobarometer 334/Wave 72.3. Brussels, Belgium: D-G Education and Culture.

European Commission. (2014). *Sport and physical activity*. Special Eurobarometer 412/Wave 80.2. Brussels, Belgium: D-G Education and Culture.

Eurostat. (2015). *Real GDP growth rate – Volume*. Retrieved October 12, 2016 from http://ec.europa.eu/eurostat/tgm/table.do?tab=table&init=1&plugin=1&language=en&pcode=tec00115

Firmas.lv. (2016). Dinamo Rīga, Corporation. Retrieved October 12, 2016 from https://www.firmas.lv/profile/dinamo-riga-as/010316201

Information of business database Lursoft. (2016). *Private sport sector (Lursoft publication No 1514)*. Government Printing Office.

Information of capital company "Igo Japiņa sporta aģentūra". (2016). SEB MTB mountain biking competitions year 2002–2014. Igo Japiņa sporta aģentūra database.

Kruks S. (2016). *Ekonomiskā krīze Latvijā: veiksmes stāsta pēcgarša* [Economic crises in Latvia: The aftertaste of success story]. Riga, Latvia: Rīgas Stradiņa universitāte.

Lattelecom Riga Marathon. (2016). Rīgas Maratons – jau kopš 1991.gada [Marathon of Riga – already since year 1991]. Retrieved November 16, 2016 from http://www.lattelecomrigasmaratons.lv/lv/par-maratonu/vesture/

Latvian Olympic Committee. (1991). *Biedrības "Latvijas Olimpiskā komiteja" statūti* [Statutes of Latvian Olympic Committee]. Retrieved October 26, 2016 from http://olimpiade.lv/lv/lok/statuti

Latvian Olympic Committee. (2016). Olimpiskās spēles [Olympic games]. Retrieved October 13, 2016 from http://olimpiade.lv/lv/olimpiskas-speles

Latvian School Sport Federation. (2008). *Biedrības "Latvijas Skolu sporta federācija" statūti* [The Statutes of Latvian School Sport Federation]. Retrieved October 12, 2016 from http://lssf.lv/wp-content/uploads/2014/03/LSSF-statuti.pdf

Latvian Sport for All Association. (2013). *Biedrības "Latvijas Tautas sporta asociācija" statūti* [The Statutes of Latvian Sport for All Association]. Retrieved October 12, 2016 from http://sportsvisiem.lv/statuti/

Latvian Sport Veteran – Senior Association. (2010). *Biedrības "Latvijas Sporta veterānu - senioru savienība" statūti* [The Statutes of Latvian Sport Veteran – Senior Association]. Retrieved October 12, 2016 from http://www.lsvs.lv/docs/1295/2013/LSVS_statuti_2011-lv.pdf

Latvian University Sport Association. (2016). *LASS statūti* [The Statutes of Latvian University Sport Association]. Retrieved September 12, 2016 from http://www.studentusports.lv/26/Statuti/

Latvijas Vēstnesis. (2000). *Komerclikums* [Commercial Law]. Retrieved September 12, 2016 from http://likumi.lv/doc.php?id=5490

Latvijas Vēstnesis. (2002). *Sporta likums* [Sports law]. Retrieved May 20, 2016 from http://www.likumi.lv/doc.php?id=68294

Latvijas Vēstnesis. (2003). *Biedrību un nodibinājumu likums* [Law of Associations and Foundation]. Retrieved October 20, 2016 from http://likumi.lv/doc.php?id=81050

Latvijas Vēstnesis. (2012). *Latvijas Sporta muzeja nolikums* [Regulation of Latvian Sport Museum]. Retrieved September 12, 2016 from http://likumi.lv/doc.php?id=253573

Latvijas Vēstnesis. (2013). *Par Latvijas Sporta pedagoģijas akadēmijas Satversmi* [About Constitution of Latvian Academy of Sport Pedagogy]. Retrieved September 12, 2016 from http://likumi.lv/doc.php?id=157192

Latvijas Vēstnesis. (2014). *Uzdevumi un funkcijas* [Regulation of National Sports Medicine Center]. Retrieved September 21, 2016 from http://www.vsmc.gov.lv/par-mums/uzdevumi-un-funkcijas/

Latvijas Vēstnesis. (2016). *Par valsts un pašvaldību kapitāla daļām un kapitālsabiedrībām* [Law on governance of capital shares of a public person and capital companies]. Retrieved September 12, 2016 from http://m.likumi.lv/doc.php?id=67363

Luika, S. (2012). *Inovatīvs Latvijas sporta nozares stratēģiskās plānošanas modelis* [Innovative model of sport strategical planning in Latvia] (Doctoral dissertation). Retrieved September 20, 2016 from https://www.lspa.lv/files/2012/25.12/Luika_Signe_2013.pdf

Murjani State Gymnasium. (2009). *Murjāņu sporta ģimnāzijas nolikums* [Regulations of Murjani State Gymnasium]. Retrieved October 20, 2016 from http://www.msg.edu.lv/lv/ziņas_par_iestādi_murjāņu_sporta_ģimnāzijas_nolikums

Register of Enterprises. (2006). NACE klasifikators [Nace clasificator]. Retrieved December 2, 2015 from http://www.ur.gov.lv/?a=938

The Central Statistical Bureau of Latvia. (2007). Iekšzemes kopprodukts [Gross domestic product]. Retrieved September 26, 2016 from www.csb.gov.lv/.../iekszemes-kopprodukts-2006-gada-pieaudzis-par-119-26065.html

The Central Statistical Bureau of Latvia. (2015a). Iekšzemes kopprodukts – *galvenie rādītāji* [Main indicators of gross domestic product]. Rerieved October 12, 2016 from www.csb.gov.lv/statistikas-temas/iekszemes-kopprodukts-galvenie-raditaji-30248.html

The Central Statistical Bureau of Latvia. (2015b). Mājsaimniecības patēriņa izdevuma struktūra [Household consumption expenditure structure]. Retrieved October 12, 2016 from http://data.csb.gov.lv/pxweb/lv/Sociala/Sociala__ikgad__mb/MB0010.px/table/tableViewLayout2/?rxid=f909528e-a219-4efe-8824-5f2becc527c4

The Ministry of Education and Science of Latvia. (2016a). *Sporta nozares struktūra* [The structure of sport]. Retrieved August 12, 2016 from http://www.izm.gov.lv/lv/sports/sporta-nozares-struktura

The Ministry of Education and Science of Latvia. (2016b). *Statistika par sportu, sporta organizācijas (2014.gads)* [Sport organizations in Latvia (year 2014)]. Retrieved October 12, 2016 from http://www.izm.gov.lv/lv/publikacijas-un-statistika/statistika-par-sportu

LITHUANIA: Towards Professionalization of the Private Sport Sector

Vilma Čingienė and Kristina Kalašinskaitė

Selected country facts (in 2013)	
Capital	Vilnius
Geographical size (km^2)	65,286
Population (million)	2.97
GDP (euro per capita)	11,800
GDP (per capita in PPS)	73
Annual net earnings average (€)	5955

Organization and Management of Sport: The Public, Non-governmental and Private Sectors in Lithuania

Sport in Lithuania is organized at the national, regional and local levels, and it covers governmental, intermediate and non-governmental structures. The Constitution of the Republic of Lithuania adopted in 1992 states that "The State shall promote physical culture of the society and shall support sport". Lithuanian Parliament adopted the Sport Development Strategy (2011–2020 m. Valstybinė sporto plėtros strategija, 2011) and Lithuanian Government approved the Inter-institutional Action Plan (Valstybinės sporto plėtros strategijos įgyvendinimo tarpinstitucinis veiklos planas, 2015).

V. Čingienė (✉) • K. Kalašinskaitė
Mykolas Romeris University, Vilnius, Lithuania
e-mail: v.cingiene@mruni.eu; kristina.studies@gmail.com

A. Laine, H. Vehmas (eds.), *The Private Sport Sector in Europe*, Sports Economics, Management and Policy 14, https://doi.org/10.1007/978-3-319-61310-9_14

The latest national study on sport participation (Gyventojų apklausos ir tyrimai, 2015) shows that 37% of the Lithuanians exercise or play sport regularly. These findings are similar to the most recent Eurobarometer on sport and physical activity where according to the number of citizens exercising regularly ranked Lithuania 15th among the 28 EU member states (European Commission, 2014). In more detail the Eurobarometer showed that 22% of the Lithuanians exercise or play sport at least once a week, and 15% more than five times a week. Eight per cent are members of a sport club, but only 1% members of a health or fitness club. Six per cent are members of employees', youth, school or university related club.

At the *national governmental level* the Department of Physical Education and Sports (DPES) is responsible for sport. DPES reports to the Government of the Republic of Lithuania and is under direct supervision of the Interior Ministry. Lithuanian Olympic Sport Centre (LOSC) on the other hand is a public institution engaged in non-formal sport education programs, preparing top-level athletes for the Olympic Games, World and European championships and other international competitions. At the *regional level* there are no responsible organizations in sport. At the *local level* all 60 municipalities (12 cities and 48 districts) have the responsibility for sport. Under the responsibility of the local authorities, there are 88 public sport education centers (SEC) across the country, where 41,672 children and youth between 7 and 19 years old engage in different sports, and participate in championships at local, national or international levels (Sporto įstaigų, įmonių ir ogranizacijų veiklos rodikliai, 2014).

At the *national non-governmental level*, the three main non-profit organizations are the Lithuanian National Olympic Committee (LNOC), the Lithuanian Union of Sport Federations (LUSF) and the Lithuanian Sport for All Association (LSAA). The LNOC includes 36 national Olympic sport federations. For the four-year Olympic cycle the LNOC, together with the DPES and the Lithuanian Olympic Sports Centre, prepare the selection criteria of the candidates for the Lithuanian Olympic team. In 2015 the LUSF had 80 members in Olympic and non-Olympic sport federations. The main objectives of the LUSF are focused on the development of sport in Lithuania in partnership with sport federations, presentation their interests and initiation of the new programs (2015). In addition to the 80 member sport federations of the LUSF there are 24 federations and five national federations of disability sport that do not belong to the LUSF. There are around 1224 sport clubs in the country and about 72,000 people of all ages who attend sport clubs on a regular basis (Sporto įstaigų, įmonių ir ogranizacijų veiklos rodikliai, 2014). The LSAA unites 20 voluntary sport organizations, 521 clubs with about 25,000 members and about 1400 volunteers (Lietuvos sporto visiems asociacija, 2015). The association's main objectives are to enhance people's health and social well-being through physical education and sport, to promote healthy lifestyles and to organize physical education, grassroots sport and recreation activities for all ages

The National Physical Education and Sport Council is the intermediate sport structure in the country who aims to encourage, promote and enhance the interests of all public administration institutions and non-governmental organizations in physical education and sport. The Association of the Heads of Lithuanian Municipal Sports Divisions consists of representatives from local councils and from regional or local sport organizations who can influence or give their opinions in the strategic decision making processes. The Association of the Heads of the Lithuanian Sports Education Centers unites the Directors of sport education centers and has the responsibility to supervise the organization of sport activities and discuss various issues related to the development of sport education centers.

The development of the *private sport sector* essentially began from the independence restoration of Lithuania in 1991. It is rather difficult to exactly analyze and evaluate the development of the private sport sector, because it is affected by both the factors of external economic, political and social environment, and the features of the internal sport system organization. In dominance of the sport as a public wellbeing perception, the aspect of sport and business is traditionally hard to comprehend – sport is not an aim, but rather used as a tool for the business development, the investment promotion, the innovation development and the stimulation of productivity. However, due to the socio-economic transformation the situation has changed towards an emergence of the understanding that sport is an important economic development factor in assessing the added value and new jobs.

Private Sport Sector in the Light of a Sport Market Structure

There is generally lack of information, research, analysis and assessment about the Lithuanian private sport sector. The first academic investigations, in assessing different aspects of the private sport sector, namely the sporting goods trade, the sport sponsorship and the professionalization of basketball appeared only after 1990's. The first doctoral dissertation in the context of the country's private sport sector about football business was defended in 2009 (Karpavičius, 2009). Later on doctoral dissertations on national sport strategy issues (Gedvilaitė, 2011), sport cheating prevalence and prevention problems of match fixing or doping (Zaksaitė, 2012), and the cooperation between sport organizations and sponsors (Dilys, 2015) have been defended.

Lithuanian private sport sector can be analyzed by using the commercial sport sector as a background and a starting point. The commercial sector consists of the sport goods sector and sport services sector (Gratton & Taylor, 2002) (Fig. 1).

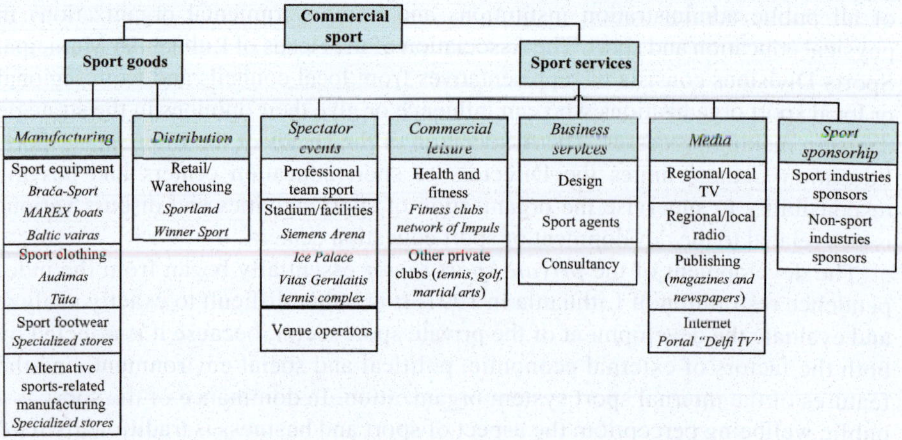

Fig. 1 Sport market structure adapted by the authors (Gratton & Taylor, 2002).

The production and marketing processes characterize the market of *sport goods*. Lithuania, like other small European countries, mainly imports sport goods. Nevertheless, there are a few main national manufacturers of sport goods: sport equipment – rowing (Brača-sport), sailing (MAREX boats), cycling (Baltic vairas), sport clothing (Audimas, Tūta), sport-related goods (orthopedic equipment for injuries prevention).

Locally produced sport goods are sold in the specialized stores or directly from the manufactures. The global brands (e.g., Nike, Adidas and Reebok) are traded in the specialized stores or in the retail network of sport goods, such as Sportland and Winner Sport.

The first group of *sport services* comprises *spectator events*. This group of sport services in the supply market makes an important part in the common sport market of the country by assessing both the professional and the sport for all segments. In the professional sport segment, team sports such as basketball and football are exceptionally dominating and attractive for the biggest part of the players and fan groups. However, it should be noted that all Lithuania's sport leagues and their members – sport clubs – are not private companies by their legal form of the activity. One application of the business system concept to the analysis of football business on national context have been analysed by Karpavičius and Jucevičius (2009). While the entitlement of the professional sport is used both in the area of individual and team sports, many clubs operate as public establishments (Lietuvos Respublikos viešųjų įstaigų įstatymas, 2015), and leagues as associations (Lietuvos Respublikos asociacijų įstatymas, 2004). It has to be stated that international sport federations more often see the potentials of the country in hosting various international events. Lithuania was proud to host the following European championships: track-and-field athletics (U18 in 2006 and U21 in 2009); men's basketball (2011); rowing (2015); World youth ice hockey championship (I division, group B, 2014 and II division, group A 2015) and 5th TAFISA (Association for International Sport for All) games in 2012.

Basketball is the most popular sport in Lithuania. Crowd watching an exhibition match between Lithuania's and Spain's men's national basket teams in Žalgiris Arena in July 18, 2016. *Photo: Fotodiena.lt.*

The question of involving cities into events has been recently discussed as municipal politicians and other responsible persons have become aware of the benefits of the events both for professional sport and for sport for all of the local residents. Compared to the organizational experiences of sport for all events for example in the Scandinavian countries, the municipalities in Lithuania still lack a clear understanding of the tangible and intangible value of sport events. Meanwhile, the attitudes of the private partners acting as sponsors are still reserved. Actively developing forms of cooperation can be more than before observed between the public and private sectors. In 2011, the Public Establishment *"Sveikas miestas"* ("Healthy city") was established as the initiative of Vilnius city Municipality. It operates in the areas of physical activity and sport, developing and promoting ideas for a healthy society and "Sports for All" movement, as well as organizing sport events in the capital. Moreover, in 2015, Vilnius Sports Festival was arranged for the fourth time, with the purpose of promotion of physical activity among various groups at the local level. It was attended by more than 4000 participants, including foreigners from different sport organizations, who introduced their services to more than 15,000 residents. This example shows common interests of co-operation of the stakeholders from public and private sectors.

A number of *sport facilities* built or reconstructed in Lithuania are based on the initiative of the private investors. Examples of these are the multi-functional Siemens arena, the Ice Palace, "Vėtra" football stadium, Vitas Gerulaitis Tennis Complex and the private sport and fitness clubs network "Impuls". By the decision of the Vilnius City Council No 1–1314 on 20th September 2006, the sport and entertainment centers development scheme of the Vilnius city was drawn up. As stated in the 2011–2020 Vilnius City Physical Education and Sports Development Strategy (2011–2020 m. Vilniaus miesto kūno kultūros ir sporto plėtotės strategija, 2011, 34) the private investments in sport infrastructure development programs and projects are not encouraged enough and no principles for the cooperation of the public and private sector in the field of sport are stated yet.

It is also important to note that the EU Structural funds 2007–2013 under the priority "Local and urban development, saving of physical education and nature and adaptation for tourism development" have been used for the development of sport infrastructure across the country. The largest multifunctional facilities have been funded by the EU and the state funds. Public establishments set up by the municipalities have been involved in the management and delivery of the various sport and physical activity services (see Table 1). Municipalities usually look for the competent staff from the private sector and demand to organize activities based on implementing of the "3 E's" principles (economy, efficiency and effectiveness). Moreover, private sport sector enterprises bring new sport business ideas and rent space in the facilities. It should be also noted that due to a great demand of the modern sport infrastructure in the country a more extensive implementation of the public-private partnership processes was launched only in 2007. Development of the legal regulation, forms of inter-institutional and inter-sectorial cooperation, partnerships and network interaction have then become necessities for the development of the whole sport sector both at national and local levels.

Table 1 Sport facilities funded by EU and State investments in Lithuania in 2007–2013.

Indicators	"Zalgiris" arena	Alytus arena	"Girstutis" swimming complex	Ignalina winter sport center	Elektrėnai ice hall
EU funding (€)	14,192,124.83	2,537,246.83	1,383,521.07	1,556,530.16	1,408,563.17
State investments (€)	34,753,658.78	5,792,493.67	1,794,769.01	1,332,252.10	2,935,737.11
Total budget (€)	41,219,586.70	5,900,482.05	4,827,921.98	2,463,977.06	2,922,460.93
Managing institution	JS[a]	PI[b]	PI	PI	PI
Number of seats	15,700	5500	569	–	1960
	basketball	basketball			
	16,500	7000			
	concert	concert			
Number of staff	400	146	17	10	49

Source: Made by authors using the official activity reports of each arena.
[a]joint-stock company.
[b]public establishment.

In Lithuania there is scarcity of the companies that specialize in organizing of sport events. This is because the national market is small and sufficiently diversified. However, there are some consistently and actively operating companies in the market who organize sport events, for example Lietuvis and Eventum group. In the sport for all events and active leisure events for over the last 5–7 years there has been an increase in the number of participants (Lietuvos sporto visiems asociacija, 2015).

The second group of sport services according to Gratton and Taylor (2002) is the *commercial leisure*. In the leisure market, especially in the health segment, a growing supply can be observed. It is influenced by the initiative of the country's suppliers and, recently, by the increasingly gaining grounds of the worldwide trends of the healthy living. Healthy lifestyle and active leisure spending's have spread significantly. Consumers are becoming more demanding of the events' quality and constantly looking for the new forms of sport and physical activity. Sports that are exceptionally distinguished in the private club activities include for example tennis, golf and martial arts.

Fitness market in Lithuania is still in its early development stages. The fitness penetration of 1.29% (i.e., the degree to which a product or service is known and/or used for) according International Health Racquets and Sports Club Association report in 2013 was far below the EU–28 average of 5.99%. According to "Impuls" CEO Vidmantas Šiugždinis the market is growing rather fast, and according to the estimation of the Lithuanian Fitness Club Association (LSKA) reached 2.7% growth in the beginning of 2016 (V.Šiugždinis, personal communication, April 28, 2016).

One important factor leading to the growth of the private sport market was the fast development of the main market player, namely "Impuls" group, which grew more than three times since it was founded by the private equity fund Baltcap in 2011. The group of companies increased their member bases from 18,000 in 2012 to 40,000 in 2016, entered Latvian and Estonian markets and are planning to achieve 15.7 million euros revenue in 2016 (V.Šiugždinis, personal communication, April 28, 2016). This fast growth was possible with the launch of the LEMON GYM brand which was the first low-cost fitness brand in the Baltic markets and has so far proved to be a success story. This budget brand which offers affordable fitness services for only 19 euros a month has attracted new target audiences such as students and seniors to exercise. "Impuls" group has the plans of the fast roll-out in Lithuania and abroad. Although the private sport and fitness market is growing, the legislation of the business activities does not provide any tax benefits to their owners, except for the sport centres that are registered as public establishments' institutions (2011–2020 m. Vilniaus miesto kūno kultūros ir sporto plėtotės strategija, 2011, 34).

The third group of sport services is *business services* (Gratton & Taylor, 2002). In Lithuania's private sport market this can be seen in the companies that begin to provide a variety of sport services related to the design solutions and legal, economic, management and other consultations issues. Three main circumstances have led to the development of the various sport services: (1) the recognition of sport as a significant business activity; (2) the growing demand for such services by the sport organizations that become more professional; (3) the sufficient experience and expertise of the individuals who are creating and providing sport and active leisure services.

It is important to highlight that the increased demand of the health-related physical activity services have led to a significant problem of coaches', trainers', and managers' competences (Beleckienė et al., 2008; Gedvilaitė, 2011; Gedvilaitė-Moan & Laskienė, 2010). Not all private health facilities provide society or customers with high-quality services, including the testing of the physical fitness, scientifically based exercise prescription or the care of the personal physical fitness changes. According to Gedvilaitė (2011), the improvement of the physical activity conditions in Lithuania is mainly a prerogative of the private sector organizations which mostly invest in major cities of the country and deliver services to the middle and upper-middle-income people. The dominance of the private business in the field of physical fitness has created an impression that Lithuania, by fostering physical activity, tends to follow not the best experience of the EU but a very much individualized approach that is also seen in the United States market (Jankauskienė, 2008).

As Gratton and Taylor (2002) indicate the fourth group of sport services is the *media*. Sport media services group, especially television and radio of the country is the least studied in the context of the private sport sector. In 2014 a survey assessing the sport press production of 2010 was accomplished (Bartusevičiūtė, 2015). It was found out that prints related to sport created a production value equal to 1.55% of the total printing market. It can be assumed that the sport press market operates on a relatively small local market in Lithuania with a strong competition for readers' attention. Traditional sport media is also strongly influenced by the rapidly growing competition with the electronic media, which reduces the popularity of the traditional press. In recent years on the webcast market, a significant breakthrough in sport events, sport competitions and health services has been evident and delivered to the specific target groups and the general public. Since 2012 the portal "Delfi TV" has been the leader in this market.

The fifth group of the private sport services is *sport sponsorship* (Gratton & Taylor, 2002). Sport sponsorship services are an important segment of the private sport sector in Lithuania. Sponsorship is relevant for sport organizations' development and for businesses seeking commercial goals. During the last years sport sponsorship issues have received attention of the researchers who have analyzed the practices of the developing sponsorship packages (Čingienė, Komskienė, & Atraškevičienė, 2013), the structural business models of cooperation between sports organizations and sponsors (Dilys & Gargasas, 2014) and the influence of sport sponsorship in the economics of the sport industry (Komskienė, Garastaitė, & Bradūnas, 2015). The National Statistics Office of Lithuania publishes data on charity and sponsorship. Assessing the period 2006–2014 it should be noted that the majority of the country's generated charity and sponsorship goes to arts, entertainment and recreation activities (29–44%) (Fig. 2).

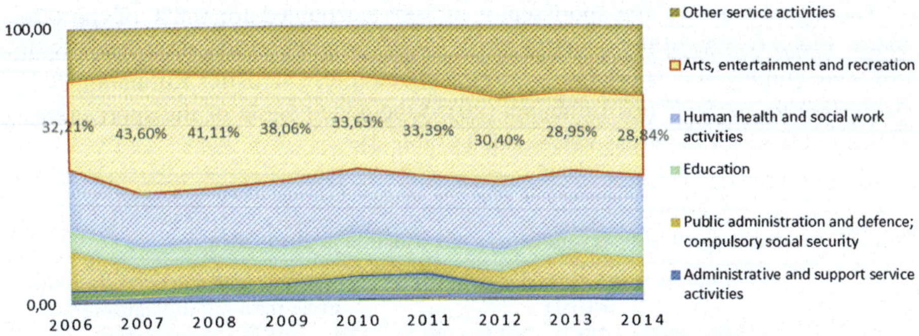

Fig. 2 The structure of the generated charity and sponsorship in Lithuania by economic activities in 2006–2014 (%). Source: Official Statistics Portal. Database of Indicators. Statistics Lithuania (2014).

Sport club activities are most receptive to the private sponsorship. The sponsorships have started to grow again from 2012, but with significantly lower sums than the amount before the economic recession in 2008–2009 (Fig. 3).

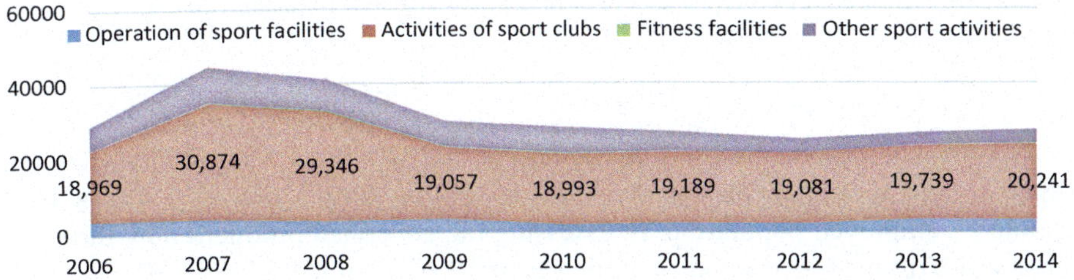

Fig. 3 The structure of the sponsorship for legal entities in Lithuania by economic activity R93 "Sport activity" in 2006–2014 (1000 €). Source: Official Statistics Portal. Database of Indicators. Statistics Lithuania (2014).

Economic Indicators of the Sport Sector

The economic role and importance of sport to the national economy was first presented by Laurinavičius and Čingienė (2011) and Čingienė and Laskienė (2013). In 2012, by the initiative of the Department of Physical Education and Sports in collaboration with the National Statistics Office the decision was taken to collect sport economic indicators and measures the economic importance of sport. The impetus of these processes was given due to the Lithuanian Presidency of the EU Council in the second half of 2013. One of the two selected topics proposed by the European Commission and agreed upon the implementations of the EU sport policy, was the economic impact of sport on the economy in general (Čingienė, 2013).

The added value of the sport sector in 2008 accounted for 0.8% of the Gross Value Added (GVA) of the country, and 1.2% the country's total employed population were employed in sport and sport-related activities (Statistics Lithuania, 2013). According to the Statistics Lithuania (2015) the added value of the sport industry was about 0.8% of the gross value added (Table 2).

Table 2 **Economic sport industry indicators of Lithuania in 2010–2014.**

	Total by sport-related economic activity					Compared with the corresponding gross national indicators (%)				
	2010	2011[a]	2012[a]	2013[a]	2014[a]	2010	2011[a]	2012[a]	2013[a]	2014[a]
Sport-related value added, MEUR	205.8	229.9	225.8	239	254.5	n/a	0.82	0.75	0.75	0.77
Sport-related production, MEUR	344.4	382.6	389.2	413.1	436.5	n/a	0.68	0.65	0.66	0.71
Sport-related total employment, thousand	17.29	18.03	18.53	17.82	18.93	n/a	1.44	1.45	n/a	n/a

Source: Official Statistics Portal. Database of Indicators. Statistics Lithuania (2015).
[a] Preliminary data.

Sport-related production during the period of 2010–2014 was slightly growing. Sport-related employment was stable as 18,000 persons, which is 1.4% of total country's employed population. In assessing the generated production by the sport sector in 2014 the biggest contribution was of the educational activities (27%), gambling and betting activities (16%), the sport activities (14%) and the retail and wholesale trade (14%) (Fig. 4).

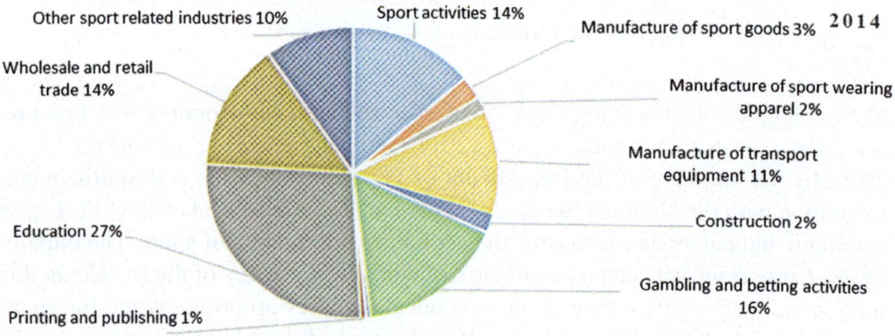

Fig. 4 Sport-related production of Lithuania in 2014. Source: Official Statistics Portal. Database of Indicators. Statistics Lithuania (2014).

The same tendencies of the same economic activities in 2014 are essentially repeated in assessing the number of employed persons in the field. People are mostly employed in the educational activities (45%), in the sporting activities (26%), in the gambling and betting activities (7%), and the retail and wholesale trade (10%) (Fig. 5).

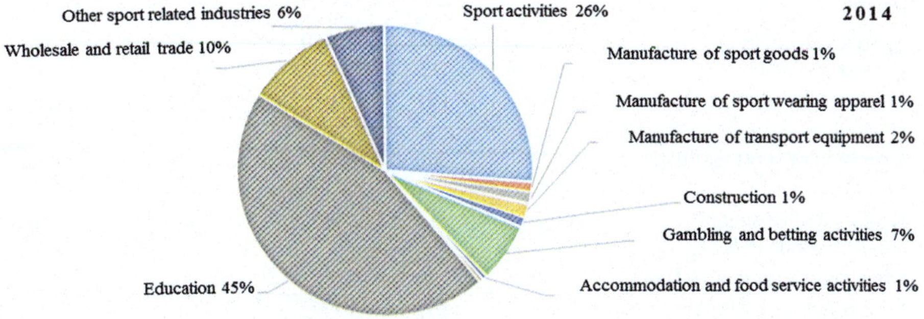

Fig. 5 Sport-related total employment of Lithuania in 2014. Source: Official Statistics Portal. Database of Indicators. Statistics Lithuania (2014).

Private sport sector in Lithuania comprises a significant part of the country's economy. The development of this sector is an engine of inclusive growth as it generates jobs, creates revenues and provides goods and services that are needed and demanded in the country. The business activities in the sub-sectors of sport and recreation education, retail sale of sport equipment bicycles and activities of sport clubs generate the main fields of the private business sector. Table 3 introduces, according to the Lithuanian equivalent (EVRK) of the *Statistical classification of economic activities in the European Community* (NACE Rev. 2, 2008), how the major parts of the private companies are concentrated, and how they generate jobs and flows of revenue.

Table 3 Directly sport-related business fields in Lithuania in 2013.

Business field (NACE code)	Companies (n)	Staff (n)	Revenue (1000 €)	Revenue/ company (1000 €)	Average salary (1000 €)
Retail sale of sport equipment & bicycles (4764)	231	1106	35,354	153	4724
Activities of sport clubs (9312)	147	849	15,692	107	4165
Sport and recreation education (8551)	1850	1197	11,759	6	656
Manufacture of sport goods (3230)	39	191	11,029	283	1042
Operation of sport facilities (9311)	23	200	6689	291	1674
Renting and leasing of sporting goods (7721)	377	312	5465	14	385
Other sport activities (9319)	49	130	2388	49	523
Fitness facilities (9313)	24	167	1952	81	720

Source: Official Statistics Portal. Database of Indicators. Statistics Lithuania (2013).

Firm level financial reporting (2013) introduces the largest companies in the private sport sector in Lithuania that are divided into production, services and retail (Table 4). In the sub-sector of production, the most significant company is a joint-stock company "Audimas", which has established 526 jobs, and generated main flows of the revenue, namely 26.4 million euros. In the field of services, the market leader is a joint-stock limited company "Impuls" which is a network of the fitness sport clubs in Lithuania that has generated the largest numbers in creating jobs and flows of revenue.

Table 4 **Largest private limited sport industry companies in Lithuania in 2013.**

Sector	**Production**				**Services**					**Retail**		
Companies	**AB "Audimas"**	**UAB "Brača sport"**	**UAB "Swix Sport Baltic"**	**UAB "Tuta"**	**UAB "Impuls"**	**UAB "VS Fitness"**	**VŠĮ "Krepšinio rytas"**	**UAB "Forum Fitness"**	**UAB "Universali arena" (Siemens arena)**	*UAB "Sportland"*	*UAB "Briedžiukas" (Winner sport prekyba)*	*UAB "Vasarė"*
Revenue (1000 €)	26,413	1962.8	7451.7	402.44	8525	374.08	2244.5	2244.5	2244.5	17,457	4834.8	1122.3
Staff (n)	526	61	43	14	207	29	20	50	24	244	115	15

Source: Firm level financial reporting (2013). Database ORBIS.

Lithuanian fitness market is developing in quite a few directions, and many world fitness trends can be seen in the country. Since 2013 there have been new openings of the low cost gyms, cross fit boxes, studios including offerings such as hot yoga, personal training and functional training studios, and group exercise community – movements. The growing popularity of the social networks has made it possible even for the smallest operators to successfully reach the final consumers. Majority of the fitness market is private, only the swimming pool services are mostly offered by the public facilities. Also the quality of the fitness services is increasing. One of the reasons for that was the launch of the EREPS (European Register of Exercise Professionals) based trainings with Europe Active certified training provider. There are still no clear initiatives from the government of Lithuania to increase the popularity of exercise and sport participation. Establishment of the Lithuanian Health and Fitness Clubs Association in 2013, participation in the Europe Active organization and other European projects may change this in the future. Some of the joint projects have started already. For example, ALCIS project is targeted to offer exercise for children in the schools and in 2015 it attracted more than 3000 children. The project aims to at least double its numbers in 2016 (V.Šiugždinis, personal communication, April 28, 2016).

The data about the expenditure on sport consumption in Lithuania was necessary in order to assess the development of the private sport sector in the forms of new sports, new service providers and changing habits of the current and potential customers. The surveys, initiated by the Department for Physical Education and Sports, are regularly conducted to find out the scopes and tendencies about participation in sport and physical activity (Gyventojų apklausos ir tyrimai, 2002; 2007; 2011). In the completed surveys there was only one question about sport consumer expenditure. According to the data in 2011 Lithuanians spent no more than 14.5 euros on the sport services per month and sought to exercise free of charge (Table 5). Only 13% of the Lithuanian population spent more than 29 euros per month for sport and only 6% of those who engaged in sport spent more on sport services. The outcome of the 2007 survey showed that sport participation is not linked with expenditures on sport activities. More than half of the respondents (61.6%) did not spend on sport at all, and 18.7% spent only 14.5 euros per year. Every tenth of the respondents (9.7%) spent up to 29 euros and 4.6% who engaged in sport spent more than 29 euros. Only 38% of the sport participants exercised for free, 37.4% spent up to 14.5 euros and 18.3% up to 29 euros per year. In general, it can be concluded that the average monthly expenditure per year of the country's sport consumer was 14.5 euros per month which is 145–175 euros per year.

Table 5 **Monthly expenditure of the Lithuanian consumers in sport activities in 2001–2011.**

Year	Number of respondents	No money spent on sport (%)	Up to EUR 14,5 (%)	Up to EUR 29 (%)	< than EUR 29 (%)
2001	7512	38	37.4	18.3	7.1
2007	3974	61.6	18.7	9.7	4.6
2011	4007	–	81	13	6

Source: Gyventojų apklausos ir tyrimai (2002; 2007; 2011).

In 2015 a public opinion and market research company *Sprinter Research* conducted a survey called *The Spending of Lithuanian Residents on Sports* contracted by the Government of the Republic of Lithuania. The goal of this survey was to gather data on the annual expenditure of the Lithuanian citizens on active and passive sport in 2014. The analysis of the survey results was conducted in the research project *Evaluation of the Economic Importance of Sport for Lithuania* funded by the Physical Education and Sport Promotion Fund. The analysis introduced a range of relationships between socio-demographic factors and sport consumption. The national sport consumer profile was identical both for active and passive sport participation in all aspects except for the age. The survey revealed that a typical Lithuanian sport consumer is a woman, aged 26–30 years (active participation) or aged 18–20 years (passive participation), an urban dweller, having a university education, employed as a specialist or a public officer, with monthly family income of 300–500 euros per person. The survey revealed also that 1.45 million euros by active sport participants and over 0.29 million euros by spectator sport participants was spent on sport goods and services in 2014 (Čingienė, 2015).

The Changes in the Private Sport Sector During the 2000's

In 2000–2010 the Lithuanian private sport sector development was characterized by the establishment of the private sport and fitness clubs, creation of the local production and well-known foreign brand sport goods stores, formation of the mutually beneficial relations with private companies as potential sponsors and the creation of TV sport programs. An important fact in 2004 was the country's accession to the European Union and the participation in the *European Year Education through Sport* activities promoted by the European Commission. Active participation of the national sport experts in the EC funded joint projects made it possible to present the achievements of the country's sport development in various aspects to the international community, for example within the project VOCASPORT (2005). A new evolution stage of the sport nurture was indicated in the period of 2005–2010. The creation of the Physical Education and Sport Promotion Fund in 2007 was a concrete example of the agreements among the main stakeholders: the government, sport organizations and private enterprises. The Department of Physical Education and Sports took an active role in the implementation of the European Union policies by appointing national experts in the three working groups: human resources, good governance and sport statistics. This understanding shows an important match of the interests between the government and private sector.

The first EU Work Plan for Sport 2011–2014 and especially the second plan for the period 2014–2017 highlight the importance of sport in contributing to the overall goals of the Europe 2020 strategy. The sport sector has strong potential in offering economic growth and new jobs. The economic benefits and innovations in sport were the main priorities of the EU sport policy in 2013–2014. Conclusions of the Council (2014) on sport innovations stated that professional sport is a natural driver of innovation. Football and motor racing for instance attract considerably financial resources through sponsorship and the sales of the media rights, and are thus able to invest heavily in the development of innovative equipment and materials. Innovations have made sport technology a leader in several fields of the applied sciences. For example in textile technology company *Audimas* and in mechanics human motion company *Brača sport* made great progress towards professionalization. In addition, the high tech equipment and advanced materials developed for sport can have relevant spill-over effects to other sectors of the economy.

EU policy promotes the support and creation of the cross-border clusters (geographically proximate groups of interconnected companies and associated institutions in a particular field), especially through the European Strategic Cluster Partnerships under the Europe's programme for small and medium enterprises (COSME). Study on clusters (Klasterių studija, 2012) indicates two clusters in Lithuania in sport industry: iVita and International Wellness Cluster. Ivita introduces high quality and high value added wellness products and services that can improve human well-being, add efficiency to person's activities, contribute to the public education and promote healthy lifestyle habits. Ivita promotes and uses the latest and most effective production and management technologies, business and science cooperation in research and development activities, as well as youth entrepreneurship and public awareness of wellness. International Wellness Cluster on the other hand focuses on health and life quality by viewing these not as separate aspects of individual and social existence, but as integrated tasks covering all elements of human life: nutrition, physical, emotional and spiritual health, sport and activeness, hygiene and beauty, perception of the needs, potential and personal responsibility for themselves and self-education (Table 6).

Table 6 Sport clusters in Lithuania.

Name of the Cluster	iVita	International Wellness Cluster
Number of companies	13	10
Revenue (MEUR)	66 (in 2014)	25 (in 2015)
Number of employees	1600	1800

Source: Klasterių studija (2012).

According to the EU sport policy trends intellectual and industrial property rights in the area of sport represent important sources of income for sport. In April 2016, a regional conference on *Intellectual property and sports* was held in Lithuania. Sport's impact in the economy, the value of intellectual property for the sport industry and abuse and misuse of intellectual property in sport issues were presented. Intellectual property rights intensive industries (2013) study from the Office for Harmonization in the Internal Market (OHIM) shows that the sales of sport equipment, not including sportswear, dropped by 6.5% across the 28 EU member states due to counterfeiting. The sales of the fake sport equipment, such as footballs, sport helmets, tennis rackets, skis, gym equipment and skateboards, costs legitimate EU manufacturers 500 million euros every year. Approximately 2800 jobs are lost in this sector throughout the EU.

Future Challenges of the Private Sport Sector

The future challenges of the Lithuanian private sport sector will depend on the closer public and private partnerships that are based on mutual understanding, trust and agreed values. The consistent dialog with the government and efforts to find the most appropriate forms of co-operation remain an important aspect for many private sport organizations, especially at the local level. The municipalities try to explore sport events to improve their image and at the same time to discover better operational links between sport event organizers and sponsors. The supply of the non-traditional, thematic events and the multi-sports competitions is growing. This enables to create stakeholders' manifold networks and alliances for the better satisfaction of the growing expectations of the segmented market.

The benefits and added value created by the private sport and sport-related companies need to be more attributed and communicated to the society. The understanding of the importance of sport as an economic activity and its potential to new job offerings has become more evident. The European Commission policy towards the development of sport and active leisure sector is significant for Lithuania both for the financial contribution up to the year 2020 as well as for the exchanges of the best practices within different countries.

The investments of the business entities or individuals to sport should be also more visible and publicly recognized. More creative sponsorship packages are expected as sponsors will look for the new visibility forms during sport events. At the same time the development of the social corporate responsibility is steadily gaining significance in the country's business environment. Sport as a socio-cultural tool becomes more and more attractive to the private companies.

More systematic analysis of the development of the private sport sector in Lithuania is assumed to create demand for specific theoretical knowledge applications into the national context. The findings of the scientific investigations should be properly elaborated and more closely targeted to the responsible persons for the evidence based decision making. Finally, further development of the private sport sector in Lithuania is conditioned by the size of the national market, the scarcity of the resources, the growing demand for the quality services and the competences of the service providers.

References

Bartusevičiūtė, R. (2015). *Sports press market assessment evaluating the economic significance of sport in Lithuania* (Unpublished master's thesis). Lithuanian Sports University, Kaunas, Lithuania.

Beleckienė, G., Murphy, C., Dienys, V., Kaminskienė, B., Motiekaitienė, V., Šlekys, A., … Vaitkutė, L. (2008). *Study on sports sector: Research report on skill needs*. Methodological Centre for Vocational Education and Training. Vilnius, Lithuania. Retrieved April 25, 2016 from http://www.kpmpc.lt/Skelbimai/SEK_EN/EN-Sporto%20sekt.%2008.07.30.pdf

Conclusions of the Council. (2014). *Conclusions of the council and of the representatives of the governments of the member states, meeting within the council, on sport as a driver of innovation and economic growth*. 2014/C 436/02. Retrieved March 10, 2016 from http://eur-lex.europa.eu/legal-content/EN/TXT/?uri=celex%3A52014XG1205(01)

Čingienė, V., Komskienė, D., & Atraškevičienė, V. (2013). Kas lemia paramos pasiūlymo sporto sektoriuje sėkmę? Paramos pasiūlymo kūrimo teorija ir praktika [What makes sponsorship proposal in sport sector successful? Sponsorship proposal development theory and practice]. *Ekonomika ir vadyba: aktualijos ir perspektyvos, 1*(29), 166–176.

Čingienė, V., & Laskienė, S. (2013). Ekonominio sporto rinkos poveikio šalies ūkiui analizės turinys ir aktualumas [Analysis of the economic impact of sport: Content and relevance]. *Sporto mokslas, 3*(73), 8–12.

Čingienė, V. (2013). *Is the contribution of sport significant to the Lithuanian economy and to what extent?* Paper presented on October 1, 2013 at the Informal sport ministers' meeting, Lithuania. Retrieved June 21, 2016 from http://www.eu2013.lt/en/events/political-meetings/informalmeetingsofministers/informal-meeting-of-ministers-for-sport

Čingienė, V. (2015). *Lietuvos gyventojų vartojimo išlaidų sporto sektoriuje tyrimo rezultatų ataskaita* [Report on the results of the survey into the spending on sports among Lithuanian consumers]. Vilnius, Lithuania.

Firm level financial reporting. (2013). Database ORBIS. Retrieved April 5, 2016 from http://www.orbis.org/

Dilys, M. (2015). *Managerial factors of the sustainable cooperation between sports organizations and sponsors* (PhD dissertation). Vilnius University, Vilnius, Lithuania.

Dilys, M., & Gargasas, A. (2014). Structural business model based on cooperation between sports organizations and sponsors. *Engineering Economics, 25*(1), 94–102.

European Commission. (2014). *Sport and physical activity*. Special Eurobarometer 412/Wave 80.2. Brussels, Belgium: D-G Education and Culture.

Gedvilaitė-Moan, A., & Laskienė, S. (2010). Organisational management peculiarities of the public sector referring to sports as a public sector example. *Engineering Economics, 21*(1), 90–98.

Gedvilaitė, A. (2011). *Physical education and sports strategy formation in Lithuania* (PhD dissertation). Vytautas Magnus University, Kaunas, Lithuania.

Gratton, C., & Taylor, P. (2002). *Economics of sport and recreation*. London, UK: Spon Press.

Gyventojų apklausos ir tyrimai. (2002). 2002 m. Lietuvos 7–80 metų amžiaus gyventojų požiūris į kūno kultūros pratybas ir dalyvavimas jose [The attitude of 7–80 year old Lithuanian population towards physical exercise and participation]. Retrieved April 10, 2016 from http://kksd.lt/index.php?1590309353

Gyventojų apklausos ir tyrimai. (2007). 2007 m. Lietuvos 7–80 metų amžiaus gyventojų požiūrio į kūno kultūros pratybas, sportą ir sportavimo įpročių tyrimo ataskaita [The attitude of 7–80 year old Lithuanian population towards physical exercise, sport and the report of exercise habits survey]. Retrieved April 10, 2016 from http://kksd.lt/index.php?1590309353

Gyventojų apklausos ir tyrimai. (2011). 2011 m. Lietuvos 7–80 metų amžiaus gyventojų požiūrio į kūno kultūros pratybas, sportą ir sportavimo įpročių tyrimo ataskaita [The attitude of 7–80 year old Lithuanian population towards physical exercise, sport and the report of exercise habits survey]. Retrieved April 10, 2016 from http://kksd.lt/index.php?1590309353

Gyventojų apklausos ir tyrimai. (2015). 2015 m. gruodžio mėn. Lietuvos gyventojų fizinio aktyvumo tyrimas [Survey on physical activity of the Lithuanian population 2015]. Retrieved March 15, 2016 from http://kksd.lt/index.php?1590309353

Intellectual property rights intensive industries. (2013). *Intellectual property rights intensive industries: Contribution to economic performance and employment in the European Union*. Industry-Level Analysis Report, September 2013. Retrieved April 10, 2016 from http://ec.europa.eu/internal_market/intellectual-property/docs/joint-report-epo-ohim-final-version_en.pdf

Jankauskienė, R. (2008). Lietuvos gyventojų fizinio aktyvumo skatinimo strategija: kūno kultūra ar kūno kultas? [Lithuanian physical activity strategy: the culture of the body or the body cult?]. *Medicina, 44*(5), 346–355.

Karpavičius, T. (2009). *The football business system: A structural dimension* (PhD dissertation). Kaunas Technological University, Kaunas, Lithuania.

Karpavičius, T., & Jucevičius, G. (2009). The application of the business system concept to the analysis of football business. *Engineering Economics, 4*(63), 86–95.

Klasterių studija. (2012). [Study on clusters]. Vilnius, Lithuania. Retrieved April 15, 2016 from http://www.klaster.lt/uploads/documents/Klasteriu_studija_2012.pdf

Komskienė, D., Garastaitė, L., & Bradūnas, A. (2015). The influence of sports sponsorship on the economy of national sports industry. *Laisvalaikio tyrimai, 2*(6), 1–14. Retrieved April 10, 2016 from http://laisvalaikiotyrimai.lsu.lt/images/Straipsnis_Nr_6/Komskien%C4%97.pdf.

Laurinavičius, A., & Čingienė, V. (2011). Ekonominių dėsnių ir analizės metodų pritaikymo sporte, kaip ūkio šakoje, aktualumas [The relevance of economic laws and methods of analysis for application in sports as an industry]. *Sporto mokslas, 4*(66), 32–39.

Lietuvos Respublikos asociacijų įstatymas. (2004). [Lithuanian Republic Law on Associations]. Retrieved December 14, 2016 from https://www.e-tar.lt/portal/en/legalAct/TAR.FF00B0EA2F0E/aYICcDjePH

Lietuvos Respublikos viešųjų įstaigų įstatymas. (2015). [Lithuanian Republic Law on Public Establishments]. Retrieved December 14, 2016 from https://www.e-tar.lt/portal/en/legalAct/TAR.1E52802BE548/WtMUskoNPR

Lietuvos sporto federacijų sąjunga. (2015). [Lithuanian Union of Sports Federations]. Retrieved April 10, 2016 from http://www.lsfs.lt/

Lietuvos sporto visiems asociacija. (2015). [Lithuanian Sport for All Association]. Retrieved April 15, 2016 from http://www.sportasvisiems.lt/

Sporto įstaigų, įmonių ir ogranizacijų veiklos rodikliai. (2014). Lietuvos sporto informacijos centras [Lithuanian Sports Information Centre]. Retrieved February 24, 2017 from http://sportinfo.lt/bendrieji-rodikliai

Statistics Lithuania. (2013; 2014; 2015). Sport-related production and employment in Lithuania. Retrieved March 15, 2016 from http://osp.stat.gov.lt/

VOCASPORT. (2005). *Vocational education and training in the field of sport in the European Union*. Retrieved April 15, 2016 from http://eose.org/wp-content/uploads/2014/03/vocasport-Final-Report-English-Version.pdf

Zaksaitė, S. (2012). *Cheating in sports: prevalence and prevention problems* (PhD dissertation). Vilnius University, Vilnius, Lithuania.

2011–2020 m. Valstybinė sporto plėtros strategija. (2011). [2011–2020 National Sports Development Strategy]. Vilnius, Lithuania. Retrieved March 15, 2016 from https://www.e-tar.lt/portal/lt/legalAct/TAR.5149504F601C

2011–2020 m. Valstybinės sporto plėtros strategijos įgyvendinimo tarpinstitucinis veiklos planas. (2015). [Inter-institutional action plan for the implementation of the National Sports Development Strategy 2011–2020]. Vilnius, Lithuania. Retrieved March 15, 2016 from https://www.e-tar.lt/portal/en/legalAct/79300c30a88b11e4a82d9548fb36f682

2011–2020 m. Vilniaus miesto kūno kultūros ir sporto plėtotės strategija. (2011). [2011–2020 Vilnius city physical education and sports development strategy]. Vilnius, Lithuania. Retrieved March 15, 2016 from http://www.vilnius.lt/lit/Vilniaus_miesto_kulturos_strategijos_gai/1731478

THE NETHERLANDS: A Joint Venture of Clubs, Businesses, Municipalities and Schools in Sport

Koen Breedveld and Andries Kuipers

Selected country facts (in 2013)	
Capital	Amsterdam
Geographical size (km^2)	41,542
Population (million)	16.78
GDP (euro per capita)	38,900
GDP (per capita in PPS)	134
Annual net earnings average (€)	33,162

Introduction

In 2010, Maurits Hendriks, the Dutch head of sport ('technisch directeur') at the Dutch Olympic Committee/National Sport Federation NOC*NSF, calculated that a gold medal costs the Dutch considerably less than a comparable medal would cost for example the UK or any other leading sport country (NOC*NSF, 2010). This finding had great appeal to the Dutch people. First, because the Dutch, like the Scotch, are known to be quite keen on keeping their money in their pockets. And second, because traditionally, the Dutch have never favoured government spending large sums of money on prestigious national 'projects'.

K. Breedveld (✉)
Mulier Institute, Utrecht, Netherlands
e-mail: k.breedveld@mulierinstituut.nl

A. Kuipers
Statistics Netherlands, The Hague, Netherlands
e-mail: ad.kuipers@cbs.nl

A. Laine, H. Vehmas (eds.), *The Private Sport Sector in Europe*, Sports Economics, Management and Policy 14, https://doi.org/10.1007/978-3-319-61310-9_15

How can we explain the fact that a gold medal is cheaper in the Netherlands than it is in some other countries? The answer behind this question is, needless to say, complex. Part of it has to do with the way sport is organized in the Netherlands. Sport clubs are still an important and significant pillar of the sport sector in the Netherlands. Outside of the formal economy, a great amount of volunteers dedicate their precious time to organizing sport activities and maintaining sport facilities. In addition, quite some time and money is invested in sport through the school system and through municipalities, keeping costs for sport for the consumers low.

What does this imply for the private sport sector then? Can there be a viable private sport sector in a system where sport clubs, schools and municipalities make up for such a large share of the sport sector? In this article, we will first highlight some general characteristics of the way sport is organized in the Netherlands: its history, main players and the way sport is funded. Next, we will provide a general overview of the Dutch sport economy: its contribution to the total economy, and the main parts that it consists of. In addition, we will describe in greater detail the specific sub-branches of the Dutch sport economy, focussing especially on the private sector. We will end this article with a short summary of our main findings.

Sport in the Netherlands: History, Organization and Main Players

The Netherlands is one of the largest of the smaller European countries. With 16.8 million inhabitants, it has three times more inhabitants than for example Norway, Denmark or Finland, and a little over a fourth of the inhabitants of the UK or Italy. With 486 inhabitants per square kilometre, the Netherlands is also a densely populated country. In a ranking of the population density, the Netherlands is in the top 30 of all countries worldwide. The 16.8 million Dutchmen and women live in any of the Dutch 390 municipalities. (CBS, 2016.)

Dutch culture is characterized by a great deal of social capital. Even though in recent years, changes have occurred quickly, overall in the Netherlands, social relations are rather stable. Wage differences are not excessive, strikes are rather uncommon, governments are formed by political coalitions and social trust is high. Part and parcel of the strong and stable social networks are the numerous clubs and informal associations, some of which date back to the seventeenth and eighteenth century. Non-profit private initiatives have always played a central role in shaping the Dutch culture. They have often stood at the origin of the social and cultural institutions such as of museums, schools, libraries and homes for the sick and the elderly. (Breedveld & Tiessen-Raaphorst, 2011; Hoekman & Breedveld, 2013.)

Also in the sport sector, non-profit private initiatives have played an important role in shaping today's sport landscape. Currently, 27% of the Dutch are members of a sport club, well above the EU-average of 12% making the Netherlands the country with the highest sport club membership density. With 18% of the population involved in volunteering in sport, the Netherlands rank second in the EU, after Sweden and together with Denmark. (European Commission, 2014.) It is estimated that some 4.4 million Dutchmen and women are members of any of the 24,727 NOC*NSF sport clubs[1] in the Netherlands (NOC*NSF, 2015.) Most of those sport clubs belong to any of the 75 sport federations that together constitute NOC*NSF. Even though many clubs nowadays employ paid workers as well, most are still governed by the estimated 1.5 million sport volunteers. Roughly a third of the club members take part in voluntary work. On average, within each sport club, sixty volunteers are active, turning sport in the Netherlands into the largest voluntary sector in the country. (Goossens, Kuipers, & Van den Dool, 2014.)

Typically, sport clubs in the Netherlands are funded by fees from their members and to some extent by their municipalities and by sponsors (in this order). Sport federations on the other hand are funded by the contributions of their members (clubs), their sponsors, media-rights and licenses, funds from NOC*NSF and sometimes grants from the government. NOC*NSF in turn is funded by sponsors, by revenues generated from the Lotto (lottery) and through grants from the government. (CBS, 2015; Goossens & Kuipers, 2014; Hoekman & Breedveld, 2013.)

Sport clubs still make up for the core of the Dutch sport system. However, over the past decades, this 'core' has started to give way to a new segment of the sport market: that of commercial sport providers and of people who organize sport activities on their own, or 'informally' with the help from friends and relatives. In fact, much of the growth of the sport participation in the Netherlands over the past decades has come from the growth in commercial and 'unorganized' sports (see Fig. 1). As in most EU countries, individual sports like fitness, running, swimming, walking and cycling are nowadays the most popular sports, with football ranking 'merely' sixth[2]. This is quite different from the picture in 1963, when the first statistics appeared on participation in specific types of sport, and in which the two most popular sports were swimming and football. (Breedveld, 2014.)

Today, fitness is the most practiced sport in the Netherlands. In 1963 however, there was no such thing as fitness-sport. Running was already a sport of course in

[1] The fact that there are so many sport clubs in the Netherlands partly has to do with the fact that the Netherlands is a society in which both the catholic and the protestant religion have a strong foothold. Historically, both religions had their own set of institutions. Hence, in any of the Dutch municipalities one would find a catholic football club, a protestant football club and a 'neutral' football club. Although with the declining importance of religion this pillar system lost much of its social significance, most institutions that grew out of that system still exist today – accounting for the fact that there are currently some 3149 formally registered football clubs – on average eight per municipality.

[2] Football is the sport with the most clubs (3149) and with the most members (1.2 million) (NOC*NSF 2015), well before tennis (1700 clubs, 0.6 million members). Other sports follow on considerable distance.

1963, as many people remember Fanny Blankers Koen winning four gold medals already at the 1948 London Olympic Games. Yet at that time only a few people practiced running, and running was not even a category in the statistics back then. Nowadays, it is estimated that some 2–3 million Dutch inhabitants run on a regular basis. (Hover, Van der Werff, & Breedveld, 2015.)

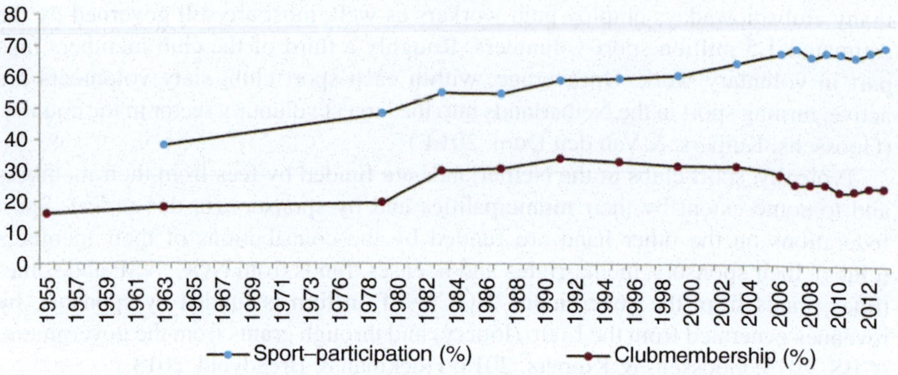

Fig. 1 Sport participation and sport club memberships in the Netherlands in 1955–2013, population of twelve years and older. Source: Breedveld (2014).

In addition to the sport clubs, sport federations and commercial providers, the other main actors in the Dutch sport sector are: at the national level the ministry of Health, Well Being and Sports (in short, in Dutch: VWS) who is responsible for sport policies, and the Ministry for Education and Culture (OCW) who is responsible for policies with regards to physical education.

Below the national level, sport policies are mainly the domain of the 390 municipalities. The 12 provinces in the Netherlands only play a minor role when it comes to sport. Over 90% of the government spending on sport, comes from the local governments. Out of this local spending, 90% is invested in building and maintaining sport infrastructure (e.g., stadia and pitches). (Goossens & Kuipers, 2014.) Typically, football fields and sport halls are built by local governments and rented out to sport clubs, sometimes also to schools for organizing competitions, trainings and physical education.

Swimming pools and ice rinks are built either by municipalities or by private companies. Some municipalities run their own facilities, others have privatized the management of the facilities to commercial organizations. In case the facilities are privately owned, the owners almost always receive considerable grants from the municipality to run the facility. In both cases, swimming clubs and skating clubs may rent the accommodation for their own club activities. The swimming pools and ice rinks themselves rent out their facilities directly to the general public. Tennis courts are usually owned by clubs, although some private companies operate tennis courts as well, especially indoor courts. Golf courses, fitness centres and bowling allies are owned exclusively by private companies. (CBS, 2015; Goossens & Kuipers, 2014; Hoekman & Breedveld, 2013.)

Swimming pool 'De Kromme Rijn' in Utrecht is a good example of the Dutch sport economy. The municipality of Utrecht owns the swimming pool and pays for its maintenance. The municipality also manages the swimming pool during the summer period. From October to May the swimming pool is managed by its main user, the local swimming club. Several commercial swimming schools hire space in the pool to give lessons. The building also hosts a commercial fitness center. Thus, the facility is indeed a collaboration between the municipality, a sport club and private companies. *Photo: Mulier Institute.*

In addition to building or funding facilities, municipalities support local sport clubs financially by providing grants to specific programs and projects. Municipalities also invest in programs for community sport for minority groups, for example retired people, single mothers, ethnic minorities and unemployed. Some of these programs are run by the municipality itself, others by sport clubs or by other public-private organizations. Schools receive their funding for physical education (PE) from the Ministry of Education and Culture. Municipalities, especially those in larger cities, supplement these budgets with extra hours of PE, swimming classes or hiring dedicated PE teachers. In addition to all this, a whole range of policies, knowledge and lobby organizations are woven into this network, each with its specific tasks and duties. (Hoekman & Breedveld, 2013.)

Finally, private foundations with their own funds, like the Cruyff Foundation or the Krajicek Foundation, as well as charity organizations operate in the sport sector. As for sport gambling, NOC*NSF runs a Lotto of which it reaps 70–75% of its benefits. Legally, other formal gambling providers are also obliged to contribute part of their revenues to charity – although not necessarily to sport. Commercial sport providers can be fitness centres or any other owners of commercially run facilities, like marinas, riding schools, bowling allies, tennis halls, squash courts, sport event organizers or sport instructors. In addition to the sport providers themselves, other branches of industry contributing to the sport economy are trade companies, accommodation-owners or managers, food services, travel and insurance companies, media companies and construction companies. The Dutch sport economy has also a fair share of companies producing specific sporting goods (e.g., boats, horses and artificial grass), but a substantial amount of the sporting goods and sportswear is imported. (CBS, 2015.)

Sport Economy: Main Overview[3]

One way to look at sport in economic terms is by means of a sport satellite account. This sport satellite account is extracted from the national accounts of the Dutch economy. Thus, characteristics of the sport economy can be compared to those of the total economy.

How do we define sport economy? Can it be described as a 'normal' branch of industry? Athletes and spectators spend money on participating and watching sport. Companies and organizations produce goods and services to facilitate this, thereby generating money, and 'value added' to the economy. All flows of goods, services and money related to sport are referred to as the 'sport economy'. More abstractly formulated, the sport economy consists of the sporting services, all products and services which are necessary as inputs for 'doing sport', and all products and services that have direct or indirect relations to any sport activity, either by active participation or by spectatorship. Examples of the indirect sport impact are the sport coverage in the media and healthcare related to sport injuries. The sport economy is outlined by an international definition of sport: the Vilnius definition (European Commission, 2013). In this paragraph the results of the sport satellite account are presented by giving an overview of the characteristics of the sport economy and its contribution to the total Dutch economy.

Share of Sport Economy in the Total Economy

The total gross value added of the Dutch sport economy, as defined above, is 6.6 billion euros – contributing to 1% of the total Dutch economy (expressed as the total gross domestic product; see Table 1). This has roughly been the case since

[3] If not cited explicitly, data in this paragraph come from the Dutch Sport Satellite Accounts 2006-2012. See for the full report (in Dutch) CBS (2015). A next Sport Satellite Account is expected to be published in 2018 (data from 2015).

Statistics Netherlands started putting together sport satellite accounts in 2006. With this 1%, the size of the Dutch sport economy is comparable to that of the metal production industry (1.1%) and double the size of the pharmaceutical industry and the publishing industry (both 0.5%).

The share of sport goods and services in imports and exports is relatively small. The consumption of the sport goods and services is 11.7 billion euros, which accounts for 2.5% of the total Dutch consumption. Large part of the sport economy is related to local services, for example sporting activities and providing sport facilities. This partly explains the small shares in international trade and the larger parts in final consumption. Other characteristics of the Dutch sport economy are that 88% of the total supply of sport goods and services come from domestic production and 85% of the demand side is consumption by households and government. (CBS, 2015.)

Table 1 Size of sport economy and shares in total economy in the Netherlands in 2012.

	MEUR	% of total economy
Gross domestic product (GDP)	6630	1,0
Production value	11,520	0,9
Imports	1630	0,3
Final expenditures of which	13,760	1,2
consumption	11,720	2,5
exports	1720	0,3

Source: Statistics Netherlands, Dutch sport satellite accounts 2006–2012. CBS (2015).

With 90,000 full time equivalents (FTE), the share of the sport economy in the total employment is 1.3% (figures not in the table above). In 2010, the share in the total employment was 1.4%. The share of the sport economy in the total employment is a little larger than the share in the gross value added (1.0% – see Table 1). The reason why the contribution of the sport economy to total employment is larger than its contribution to total value added (GDP) is that wages in the sport sector are generally below average. Another reason is that the capital intensity of the sport sector is lower than in other industries.

The work of the estimated 1.5 million volunteers have not been included in these numbers, as volunteers are not seen as employed persons. It is estimated that the joint input from sport volunteers account for some 56,000 FTE of unpaid work, as against 90,000 FTE in paid work.

Constitution of the Sport Economy: The Importance of Sport Services

From the perspective of the supply side it can be seen that sport and recreational services account for the largest share of the sport industry. Close to 25% of the total supply of sport goods and services consists of sport and recreational services

(Fig. 2). These services are almost entirely produced domestically. Education comes second. This concerns mainly physical education at primary and secondary schools. Third are the hotel and catering services. These services are partly provided by private overnight accommodations, hotels and restaurants in large sport events such as world championship beach volleyball or the take-off of the Tour the France. These services include also for example the consumption of drinks in the canteens of the sport clubs. Public goods and services consist mainly of the supply of the sport facilities by the local government, as stated earlier.

Trade and transport services amount to a substantial part of the sport goods and services. The trade and transport sector earn money by selling and re-exporting sport goods and clothing. Sport goods and sportswear are mainly imported. Thus, growth of the demand for these products benefits the trade and transport sector more than it does the domestic industry. (CBS, 2015.)

In the Netherlands, the goods and services that dominate the sport economy are not mainly provided by the private business sector. Many sports and recreational services are provided by sport clubs, which are partly non-market producers. This means that the fees that sport clubs charge from their members, do not necessarily have to cover all the costs involved. As stated earlier, most sport clubs are subsidized somehow by their local governments. Education is almost entirely financed by tax income. Another example of the government concern is the sport media. The public broadcasting company NPO is financed in part by the government, through taxes. Currently, there is debate going on in the Netherlands about which sport events need to be made freely available to the general public through the NPO, and which events can be left to the market to be broadcasted – and therefore might end up after a decoder. (CBS, 2015; Sonck & Van den Dool, 2014.)

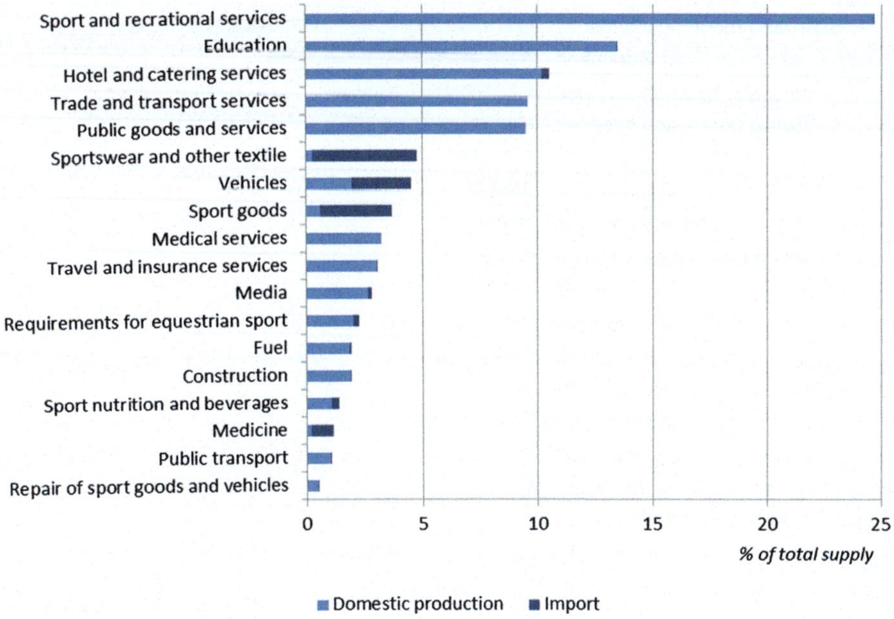

Fig. 2 Supply of goods and services in the Dutch sport economy in 2012. Source: Statistics Netherlands, Dutch sport satellite accounts 2006–2012. CBS (2015).

Households Spending

As mentioned earlier, 85% of the total expenditures of sport goods and services consists of the consumption by households (61%) and government (24%). Expressed as an average, households spend annually 1100 euros on sport goods and services. Out of these expenditures the most important part is spent on sport activities. Education and public goods and services are "consumed" mostly or entirely by the government 'on behalf' of the households because these services are financed by the tax income (Fig. 3). In reality it is of course the households who enjoy physical education at schools and sport activities in accommodations facilitated by local governments.

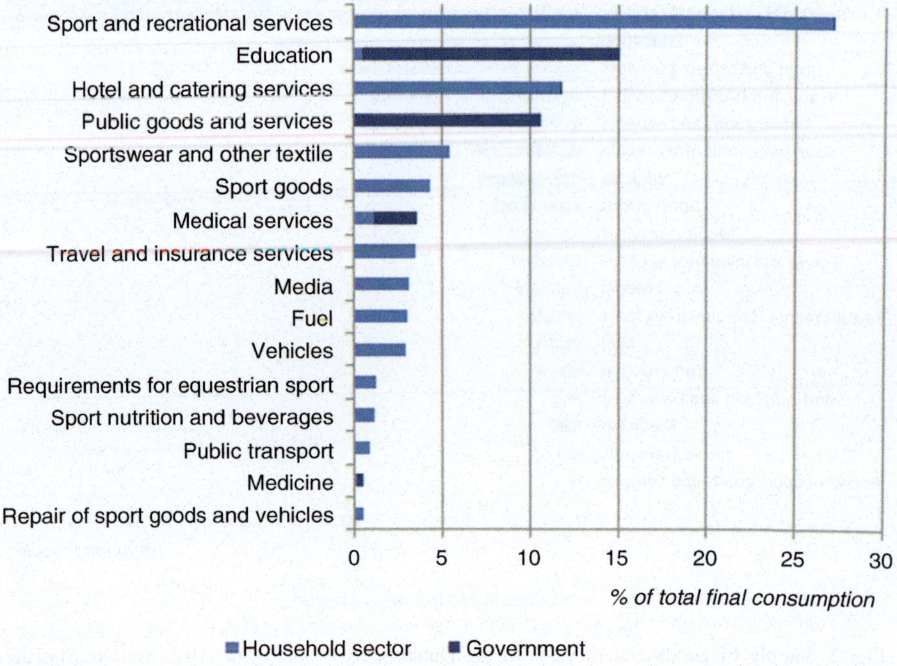

Fig. 3 Final consumption of sport goods and services by households and government in the Netherlands in 2012. Source: Statistics Netherlands, Dutch sports satellite account 2006–2012. CBS (2015).

Education is the Largest Sector in the Sport Economy

This chapter looks at the most important branches of industry for the sport economy in the Netherlands. Of the total sport economy, sport-related education takes up the largest part (25%), closely followed by the sport and recreational sector (22%), and, at some distance the government – either local or national (13%). Truly commercial sectors like trade (10%) and accommodation and food services (10%) only come fourth and fifth. Together, these five sectors account for 83% of the Dutch sport economy. The remaining 17% is made up of healthcare (5%), and seven sectors that each account for 3% or less. Thus, taking into consideration that the sport and recreational sector itself consists to a large extend of non-profit sport clubs, the most important sectors within the sport economy are mixtures of businesses and public institutes. To a certain extent then sport is treated as a public good and as such causes certain interferences with the government. (Hoekman & Breedveld, 2013.)

The Sport Economy in Detail

In this chapter, extra light is thrown to some specific sectors of the Dutch sport economy. This will be done by looking at the numbers and sizes of the companies involved, which are presented in the available data[4] (Table 2). These are the sectors whose main activity is to provide sport goods and services. This does not however, mean that all sport goods and services are provided by these sectors. Sometimes other companies are active in the sport market as well, even though their main focus lies elsewhere. This goes also the other way around: not all goods and services provided by the companies classified as part of the sport sector are sport goods and services. These companies may also produce goods and services for other markets for example to recreational goods and services and leisure.

The Production of Sport Goods

The Netherlands does not possess a large sporting goods manufacturing industry. Most of the sporting goods are imported (see Fig. 2). A little over 200 companies are involved in the manufacturing of the sporting goods in the Netherlands, employing a rather negligent of 670 FTE. Examples of these sporting goods are hockey sticks, footballs, tennis rackets and bats. As shown in Fig. 2 most of these sport goods are imported (domestic production around 80 million euros).

However, there are other sport goods in which the domestic production in the Netherlands is more substantial. These include for example the production of vehicles such as bicycles and sport boats (domestic production around 270 million euros) and the breeding of horses (domestic production around 140 million euros). These products are not, however part of the branch of industry classified as part of the sport industry. Breeding horses is part of the agriculture. Building sport boats and manufacture sport bicycles on the other hand are part of the industry, which build ships and manufacture vehicles respectively. (CBS, 2015.)

There are also other examples that show that sportrelated goods are frequently not being produced within the sport industry. For instance, the Ten Cate company in Almelo is one of the global market leaders in the production of the synthetic turfs (artificial grass). Yet, its main aim is to 'protect people'. As such the production of synthetic turfs is only a fraction of its 1.2 billion euro's revenues, in addition to the fabrics being produced for example for the military or to protect firemen. In 2015, Ten Cate generated 22% of its revenues from the 'sport and leisure' market (Ten Cate, 2016). Another example could be a leading construction company like Ballast Nedam, which is famous for its football stadiums. These examples illustrate

[4] It was not possible to present data for all categories. For some categories, Statistics Netherlands has decided not to disclose numbers (mostly because of insufficient cases and to safeguard the anonymity of the responding units/companies). These data are being reported to Eurostat and are as such integrated into EU-statistics, but without giving specifics on numbers for the Netherlands.

that a commodity approach – in which goods and services are classified as sport goods and services or related to sport – draws a more complete and richer picture of the sport economy than the one based on a limited number of industries classified as being part of the sport industry.

Wholesale and Retail of Sport Goods

One of the largest sectors in the Dutch sport economy is within the trading of sport goods. This is quite in line with the tradition that the Netherlands holds as a trading nation dating back to the seventeenth century when Dutch entrepreneurs sailed out to the East and West of the world to buy and trade spices. Some 1500 companies are nowadays involved in business-to-business trading of sport goods (wholesale). For example, the headquarters of Nike Europe and Asics Europe are located in the Netherlands, in Hilversum and in Amsterdam respectively.

Some 4400 companies are involved in the retail and repairs of the sport goods, with the total revenue of some 2.5 billion euros and an employment of a little less than 11,000 FTE. The average size of a company in this sector of the sport economy is 2.5 FTE. Around 95% of the enterprises in this branch have less than ten employed persons and thus only one or a limited number of establishments. Around ten enterprises have over 100 employed persons. This indicates that the retail sector is predominantly a small business economy, although some larger companies and chains of companies exist in the field.

Next to the well-known international chains like Intersport and Decathlon, Perry-Sport is probably the largest Dutch-based sport retailer. This chain dates back to 1866 and currently operates in some 50 locations with 800+ staff. Over time it has had multiple international owners. One of the leading figures of the chain was Leo van der Kar, a well-known Dutch athlete in the 1930's and sport trainer in the 1940's and 1950's. The company went bankrupt in February 2016, and in March 2016, a new owner took over the brand name, most of the stores and the inventory. A small, yet not insignificant legacy of the Perry Sport culture involved the game of Monopoly. In 1936, Perry Sport was the importer of game. When they created the Dutch version, in 1941, Perry Sport decided to use the names of the cities and streets where there were Perry stores. So, even though the future of the Dutch largest sport retailer remains anything but sure, through the Monopoly game, Perry Sport will always remain a part of Dutch culture. (See Perry Sport, 2017.)

Education and Instruction in Sport

The main part of the education and instruction comprises physical education that is being taught at primary and secondary schools in the Netherlands, roughly two hours per week, by teachers with a bachelor degree (Lucassen & Reijgersberg, 2014). Outside of the school system, some 7200 companies are involved in providing coaching and training to sportsmen and women. With 4320 employed persons (FTE) of which 2740 FTE employees, the sector consists of a substantial part of self-employed without employees. The total revenue of 454 million euros means an average revenue of 62,000 euros per organization. Thus it is clear that this part of sector of the sport economy relies mostly on (very) small businesses. It is estimated that some 5600 companies that are involved for example in sport instruction are found in the fitness sector. (Goossens et al., 2014). Paid and independent sport instructors are also typically employed in tennis (some 300+ tennis schools) (Lucassen, Reijgersberg, & Van Fraayenhoven, 2015); in water sports (165 sailing and surfing schools) (Goossens & Kuipers, 2014); in swimming (some 100 commercially operating swimming schools) (Van der Werff, 2013); and in golf (no numbers available). Most of the 1450 riding schools provide paid instruction. In other sport branches, for example in football, hockey and track and field, most of the instruction at the lower levels is still done by volunteers, while at the higher levels, instructors and trainers may be hired by clubs. There appears to be a general trend, in all sports, to hire paid staff to provide training and instruction. In running, not a lot of people join clubs. Most people run on their own or join running groups that are either informal (friends) or are being organized by the growing number of independent running instructors (Breedveld, Scheerder, & Borgers, 2015).

Sport Facilities

The close to 2000 private companies that run sport facilities (other than fitness centres) together 'possess' 2800 facilities. Among these, there are a little less than 500 swimming pools. This is 68% of the total number of swimming pools in the Netherlands. The rest (32%) of the swimming pools are owned by local governments. In general, 42% of all sport facilities are run by private companies and organizations, including non-profit foundations. In open air facilities, the share of the private sector is 29%, in sport halls it is 55%. Sport halls, football, hockey and rugby pitches and track and field -arenas are usually built and owned by municipalities. Tennis courts on the other hand are usually owned by tennis clubs, with an exception of the indoor tennis courts that are usually operated commercially (as is squash). Bowling allies, climbing walls and golf courses are all commercially operating. Ice rinks and swimming pools may be owned by municipalities or by private companies, but in both cases they heavily depend upon grants by the municipality to financially secure their existence.

With a total revenue of 1.2 billion euros (617,000 euros per company) and an average staff of 5.2 FTE, sport facility companies are bigger players than sport instructors. Major companies in this field are Sportfondsen, Optisport and Laco. The Sportfondsen company arose out of an initiative of 'crowd source' money for a swimming pool in 1923 in Amsterdam (Kemper, 2013). This swimming pool was originally built in 1927 and it still exists as Sportfondsenbad Amsterdam Oost. Nowadays, the Sportfondsen company runs 300 sport facilities, of which 100 are swimming pools. In addition, the company offers advice and support to the municipalities in their plans for managing of and investing in the facilities (ibid). Optisport was established in 1994, and has nowadays a revenue of some 70 million euros. This is generated by operating some 300 facilities which to a great number consists of swimming pools and sport halls and increasingly of health centres. Optisport employs 1600 people and is owned by private investors. The third main company involved, Laco, is a family-run business that has been in operation since 1987 and runs some 40 swimming pools, fitness centres and other sport facilities, mostly in the south of the Netherlands.

Sport Clubs

Although over the past decades the biggest increase has been in people participating in sport individually or in self-organized forms, sport clubs still play a major role in sport participation in the Netherlands, especially for the youth. As a member of a sport club one can practise sport at a competitive level. In the Netherlands there are around 28,000 sport clubs with 5.5 million memberships[5], which equals to an average of 193 memberships per sport club. There is a variety in sport clubs and their characteristics. Outdoor football is still the largest activity with 2770 clubs[6] and on average 425 members per club. Sport clubs include also fishing and golf clubs and smaller clubs such as chess, bridge, strength and combat sports.

The total revenues of all sport clubs in the Netherlands is 1.3 billion euros, which equals to an average of 46,000 per club and roughly speaking 240 euros per membership. Only 12% of the sport clubs have employees with the total number of FTE equalling 3910. More than 80% of the sport clubs use volunteers. The volume of these voluntary activities is estimated at 56,000 FTE. Compared to the number of employees, one can safely state that the Dutch sport clubs are run by the volunteers. This illustrates that sport clubs, although not actually belonging to the public sector, operate largely in the 'public domain', outside of the business sector, as non-profit private organizations.

Roughly half (52%) of total revenues of sport clubs consists of fees and subscriptions of the members. Almost a quarter of the revenues of the clubs consists of income from canteens (sales of food and beverages). Canteens are often part of the sport clubs' operations and are run by the volunteers. For a large number of sport clubs these canteen revenues are an important source of income. For example, for outdoor football, incomes out of canteen sales are more important than the revenues from the membership-fees (resp. 39% and 32% of football clubs' total incomes). On average 9% of the revenues of sport clubs are subsidies, mostly from the local governments. (Goossens & Kuipers, 2014.)

[5] The numbers deviate slightly from the numbers as reported by NOC*NSF. The main reason behind this, is that Statistics Netherland also records sport-clubs that are not members of NOC*NSF. Often, these are smaller clubs.

[6] This number is somewhat smaller than what the football association KNVB reports itself (see note 3), largely because the football association also takes into consideration clubs that are not football clubs per se, but that do have a football department (like a tennis club with a football section).

Table 2 Key variables of sport and related sectors in the Netherlands.

	Period	Number of enterprises	Employed persons	Employees		Revenue	Purchases of goods and services
Branches of industry by NACE Rev. 2[a]		n	n	n	FTE	MEUR	MEUR
MANUFACTURING							
3230 Manufacture of sport goods	2013	205	940	830	670	.	.
WHOLESALE AND RETAIL TRADE; REPAIR OF MOTOR VEHICLES AND MOTORCYCLES							
4694 Wholesale of other household goods of which	2013	8350	34,280	29,415	24,500	.	.
46942 Wholesale in watersport goods	2013	455	.	.	.	.	.
46946 Wholesale in sport goods	2013	1150	.	.	.	.	.
4764 Retail sale of sporting equipment in specialised stores of which	2013	4400	19,615	14,995	10,940	2551	1987
47642 Retail sale in watersport goods	2013	450	.	.	.	.	.
47643 Retail sale in sport goods	2013	1330	.	.	.	.	.
ADMINISTRATIVE AND SUPPORT SERVICE ACTIVITIES							
7721 Renting and leasing of recreational and sport goods	2013	1140	1910	1045	575	.	.
EDUCATION							
8551 Sport and recreation education[b]	2012	7225	4320[c]	6770	2740	454	332
ARTS, ENTERTAINMENT AND RECREATION							
9311 Operation of sport facilities	2012	1940	1430[c]	17,800	8830	1198	1142
9312 Activities of sport clubs	2012	28,800		12,460	3910	1321	1281
9313 Fitness facilities	2008	1255	6000[d, c]	.	.	986[d]	.
9319 Other sport activities	2012	2480	.	.	.	.	.

Source: Datasets Statistics Netherlands (StatLine) and Eurostat (Structural business statistics).
[a]Dutch equivalent of NACE Rev. 2 is called SBI 2008 - Standaard Bedrijfsindeling 2008.
[b]Data for school for martial arts based on 2009.
[c]Full time equivalent units.
[d]Source: Hover et al. (2012).

Undoubtedly, there are differences between different kinds of sport clubs. For example, one third of the golf clubs have employees. Another example is that golf clubs only rely for 3% of their incomes on subsidies, as against 9% for the clubs on average. In addition, 74% of the revenues of the golf clubs consist of subscriptions/membership fees, as against 52% for the average sport club. Canteen sales represent merely 7% of the golf clubs' total revenues. This is because the canteens in most cases are not owned and run by the golf clubs, but by the owners of the facilities.

In general, there is a difference between outdoor and indoor sport clubs. In most cases outdoor clubs run their own canteens. Indoor sport clubs on the other hand usually rent space in facilities that are run by the local governments and that operate their own canteens. Smaller sport clubs such as swimming and diving clubs receive proportionally more subsidies from the local governments than larger sport clubs (up to 17%). Thus, there is a certain interference of the (local) government also for the sport clubs. However, this interference is not the same for all sport clubs, both for historic and financial reasons. For example, football has traditionally always enjoyed subsidies, while a new sport like hockey has not. On the other hand, tennis clubs do well enough on their own, while swimming clubs cannot afford to build their own swimming pools.

Fitness

The fitness sector has surely been the fastest growing segment of the sport market for the last decades – at least until a couple of years ago before the recession started to kick in. Between 1996 and 2011, the number of fitness centres more than doubled in the Netherlands. In 2008/2010, statistics registered 1255 fitness companies altogether generating estimated revenues of slightly more than one billion euros and employing some 6000 people (Hover et al., 2012). A large section of these companies is run by larger chains, for example by Basic-Fit (140 locations in the Netherlands), Fit for Free (77 locations), Sport City (19 locations), Achmea Health Centres (38 locations), Laco (18 locations), Health City (11 locations) and David Lloyds (7 locations in the Netherlands and 78 locations in the U.K.). Ownerships of these chains change frequently. For example, stocks of the Basic-Fit company are being exchanged at the Amsterdam Stock Market, although the majority of the stocks are still owned by a British investment company (Molenaar, 2016).

Conclusions

In the Netherlands, sport is rooted in a long-lasting tradition of the non-profit private initiatives. As early as in the seventeenth century, citizens started to build facilities and establish voluntary organizations. These origins are still visible in the great number of sport clubs and volunteers that shape today's Dutch sport landscape. In addition, central government as well as local municipalities and schools have played substantial roles in financing and organizing sport and physical education.

These last decades have seen a growth of the commercial initiatives in the sport sector. New sports have arisen or taken the floor much more than before. In the commercial sector, fitness appears to be the most important representative. Today, the Netherlands counts for over 1000 fitness companies and over 5000 fitness instructors. In other sport-related branches, like outdoor pitches for football or sport halls, municipalities provide funding and maintaining facilities. In addition, there are a number of other branches of sport where companies and municipalities line up together to fund, build and manage sport facilities.

All in all, sport takes up 1.0% of the Dutch economy and 1.3% of its labour force. Sport exports and imports are rather low (both 0.3% of total economy). Most expenditures in sport are created by households (61%) and by the national and local governments (24%). Manufacturing sporting goods is not a large part of the sport economy in the Netherlands, although some companies outside of the sport sector play an important role in this field (e.g., in synthetic turf, construction, production of bicycles and boats and breeding of horses). As for the wholesale and retail, sport-related markets mostly consist of rather small domestic players. This is even more the case when private education and instruction in sport is observed, as they mostly consist of self-employment. As far as sport-related facilities, a few larger companies have a leading position in the market, although especially football pitches, indoor sport facilities and sport halls for schools are almost always run by local governments. Nevertheless, the 25,000–28,000 sport clubs still represent an important economic factor in the Netherlands. To further state this point: the 56,000 FTE volume of the voluntary activity in the sport clubs is 14 times more than the volume of paid work in the sport clubs.

All in all, the sport sector is a substantial sector of the Dutch economy. Its core of non-profit initiatives has by no means fully disappeared. Neither is it expected that sport in the Netherlands will ever become a full-blown commercial enterprise. In the end, municipalities, schools and sport clubs will continue to play important roles in shaping the Dutch sport-landscape, keeping costs for the final consumers low, and adding to the accessibility and sustainability of the sport system as well as to the social ties between the citizens.

References

Breedveld, K. (2014). *Sportparticipatie: uitdagingen voor wetenschap en beleid* [Sport-participation: Challenges for science and policies]. Nijmegen, The Netherlands: Radboud Universiteit Nijmegen.

Breedveld, K., & Tiessen-Raaphorst, A. (2011). Low countries, high performances. In C. Sobry (Ed.), *Sports governance in the world. A socio-historic approach* (pp. 347–374). Paris, France: Editons le Manuscrit.

Breedveld, K., Scheerder, J., & Borgers, J. (2015). Running across Europe: The way forward. In J. Scheerder & K. Breedveld (Eds.), *Running across Europe* (pp. 241–264). Basingstoke, UK: Palgrave Macmillan.

CBS. (2015). *De Nederlandse sporteconomie. De bijdrage van sport aan de Nederlandse economie in 2006–2012* [The Dutch sport economy. The contribution of sport to the Dutch economy 2006–2012]. Den Haag, The Netherlands: Centraal Bureau voor de Statistiek.

CBS. (2016). *Aantal gemeenten in 2016 daalt naar 390* [Number of municipalities drops in 2016 to 390]. Published January 4, 2016. Retrieved July 31, 2016 from https://www.cbs.nl/nl-nl/nieuws/2016/01/aantal-gemeenten-in-2016-daalt-naar-390

European Commission. (2013). Definition of Sport – Version 2.0 ("Vilnius Definition 2.0") according to CPA 2008. Brussels, Belgium: European Commission.

European Commission. (2014). *Sport and physical activity*. Special Eurobarometer 412/Wave 80.2. Brussels, Belgium: D-G Education and Culture.

Goossens, R., & Kuipers, A. (2014). Economie van de sport [The sport-economy]. In A. Tiessen-Raaphorst (Ed.), *Rapportage sport 2014* (pp. 143–165). Den Haag, The Netherlands: Sociaal en Cultureel Planbureau.

Goossens, R., Kuipers, A., & Van den Dool, R. (2014). Sportinfrastructuur: organisaties, accommodaties en vrijwilligers [Sport infrastructure: Organizations, facilities and volunteers]. In A. Tiessen-Raaphorst (Ed.), *Rapportage sport 2014* (pp. 122–142). Den Haag, The Netherlands: Sociaal en Cultureel Planbureau.

Hoekman, R., & Breedveld, K. (2013). The Netherlands. In K. Hallmann & K. Petry (Eds.), *Comparative sport development: Systems, participation and public policy* (pp. 119–135). New York, NY: Springer.

Hover, P., Hakkers, S., Breedveld, K., Elling-Machartzki, A., & Lucassen, J. M. H. (2012). *Trendrapport fitnessbranche 2012* [Trend report on fitness 2012]. Utrecht, The Netherlands: Arko Sports Media/Mulier Instituut.

Hover, P., Van der Werff, H., & Breedveld, K. (2015). The Netherlands: Participation rates, shifting segments. In J. Scheerder & K. Breedveld (Eds.), *Running across Europe* (pp. 187–207). Basingstoke, UK: Palgrave Macmillan.

Kemper, F. (2013). Van nood naar deugd [From necessity to blessing]. In H. van der Werff & K. Breedveld (Eds.), *Zwemmen in Nederland. De zwemsport in al zijn facetten nader belicht* (pp. 20–33). Utrecht, The Netherlands: Mulier Instituut/Arko Sports Media.

Lucassen, J., & Reijgersberg, N. (2014). Sport en onderwijs [Sport and education]. In A. Tiessen-Raaphorst (Ed.), *Rapportage sport 2014* (pp. 201–223). Den Haag, The Netherlands: Sociaal en Cultureel Planbureau.

Lucassen, J., Reijgersberg, N., & Van Fraayenhoven, F. (2015). Leren tennissen [On learning tennis]. In H. van der Poel & S. Bakker (Eds.), *Tennis in Nederland* (pp. 58–77). Utrecht, The Netherlands: Mulier Instituut/Arko Sports Media.

Molenaar, J. (2016). Balen bij beurs-debuut Basic Fit [Disappointment over introduction to stock exchange Basic Fit]. In *Financieel Dagblad*, June 10, 2016. Retrieved July 31, 2016 from https://fd.nl/economie-politiek/1155615/basic-fit-daalt-bij-beursdebuut

NOC*NSF. (2010). *Studie top 10* [Study top ten]. Arnhem, The Netherlands: NOC*NSF.

NOC*NSF. (2015). *Ledentallenrapportage 2014* [Report on club membership 2014]. Arnhem, The Netherlands: NOC*NSF.

Perry Sport. (2017). Over Perry [About Perry]. Retrieved January 27, 2017 from https://www.werkenbijperrysport.nl/over-perry.html

Sonck, N., & Van den Dool, R. (2014). Sportfans: volgen van sport via de media [Sport fans: Following sport through the media]. In A. Tiessen-Raaphorst (Ed.), *Rapportage Sport 2014* (pp. 85–100). Den Haag, The Netherlands: Sociaal en Cultureel Planbureau.

Ten Cate. (2016). *Annual report 2015*. Almelo, The Netherlands: Ten Cate NV.

Van der Werff, H. (2013). Zwemlesaanbieders [Swimming schools]. In H. Van der Werff & K. Breedveld (Eds.), *Zwemmen in Nederland. De zwemsport in al zijn facetten nader belicht* (pp. 200–213). Utrecht, The Netherlands: Mulier Instituut/Arko Sports Media.

PORTUGAL: A Growing Sport Market in a Dominant State Model

Rui Gomes, Nuno Gustavo, Ricardo Melo, and Vera Pedragosa

Selected country facts (in 2013)	
Capital	Lisbon
Geographical size (km^2)	92,226
Population (million)	10.49
GDP (euro per capita)	16,300
GDP (per capita in PPS)	77
Annual net earnings average (€)	12,807

The Configuration of the Portuguese Sport System

Sport has become a generic term designating almost the entire range of contemporary physical activities. However, most historians agree that modern sport was born in the United Kingdom in the mid-nineteenth century (McIntosh, 1963), as a pedagogical treatment of the traditional and popular games and their transformation into an instrument of education within English schools. The sportisation of the

R. Gomes (✉)
Centre for Social Studies, University of Coimbra, Coimbra, Portugal
e-mail: ramgomes@gmail.com

N. Gustavo
Estoril Higher Institute for Tourism and Hotel Studies, Estoril, Portugal

R. Melo
Coimbra Education School, Polytechnic Institute of Coimbra, Coimbra, Portugal

V. Pedragosa
Autónomous University of Lisbon, Lisbon, Portugal

A. Laine, H. Vehmas (eds.), *The Private Sport Sector in Europe*, Sports Economics, Management and Policy 14, https://doi.org/10.1007/978-3-319-61310-9_16

traditional physical activities involve formalisation of the structures organising competitions according to written, universal rules, and to a specific temporal, organisational and spatial format.

One of the characteristics of the modern sport was that it gave rise to a high number of international non-governmental organisations. This worldwide sport system created a network of sport activities and organisations of sporting disciplines that coordinate the activities of the federations and comply public authorities with standards drawn up internationally. Nonetheless, the federated voluntary sport movement depends on the public funding and can be subject to rules and pressures from the public authorities. Portugal represents a typical reference of the "bureaucratic configuration" of sport system (Camy, Clijsen, Madella, & Pilkington, 2004, 53) characterised by "the active role that the public authorities take in regulating the system".

The traditional integration of sport into research regarding the welfare state is based in two main ideas. First, sport practices have contributed to building the welfare state through integration, social networks and the promotion of equality of opportunities. Second, it is assumed that the opportunities to participate in sport activities are linked with the way welfare state subsidies and develops sport facilities and sport participation. For many years the political debate and the academic literature have been dominated by the logic of state versus market as the way to understand the social dynamic. However the organisation of welfare in modern societies is much more complex if we want to give a comprehensive analysis of sport.

In comparative social analyses the Portuguese welfare is called as a *family solidarity model* which has some characteristics of the Bismarckian model (Esping-Andersen, 1990), as the organisation on the basis of occupational categories and the level of social protection have been offered by the market performance and employment situation. The particularities of Portugal and other Southern countries enable to analyse the central characteristics of the institutionalised welfare model as similar but partly different from the German model. Two distinguished characteristics are the principle of subsidiarity based on the *welfare society*, mainly by the for free women's work in the family. A strong asymmetry between the family provisions and other social provisions characterize Portugal as a dual welfare state providing national solidarity schemes to health care and protection of core sectors of the workforce on one hand, and rudimentary levels of protection to family and social benefits to housing and pensions of a large part of society on the other hand.

Sport sector includes several segments that are organised around the production of services by different dominant social actors. These are sport entertainment that is increasingly organised by commercial enterprises integrated in international financial groups; competitive sport mainly organised by sport clubs; leisure sport, which takes place in commercial companies or self-organised groups in outdoor or in public facilities; and social sport that corresponds to the welfare ideal of *sport for all* by using sport as a means to integrate differentiated populations traditionally discriminated such as disabled, ethnic minorities, socially excluded and elderly. Taking into consideration the long-term historic and cultural specifics that give each country its own identity, Camy et al. (2004) proposed a typology characterising the Portuguese sport system as a bureaucratic configuration, whose main features are a legislative framework and rules dominated by the public agencies, a voluntary sport movement funded and acting by the delegation of the state, and a low contribution of the social partners. In the core areas of the welfare state, the public sector is totally dominant, while the sport associations and organisations possess a large degree of autonomy.

Tendency Towards the Individualisation of the Body Culture

Lifestyles and ways of life have changed during the last two decades. Promotion of health has been brought to contemporary households by TV campaigns, and showcased in supermarkets and shopping malls, where it catches our eyes for example in cosmetic advertising. It is displayed in fitness and health clubs, and flows freely within cybernetic space. The health versus illness issue is no longer confined to the hospital environment and medical centres, nor is it confined to the traditional doctor-patient relationship. This issue is nowadays spread to other social and commercial arenas in many parts of the world. Nowadays, we witness the demolishing of the last frontiers that have long resisted the differentiation between health production and health consumption. (Gomes, 2010.)

This cultural trend amplifies the risk-safety paradox and the ideology of the human health perfection that has drawn societies to increasing medicalization. In a medicalized society, physical activity is presented as the best way to control one's body and life. Bodies in control and bodies out of control become not only physical markers, but also targets of the ethical focus and ways to reach self-responsibility. The attribution of the social responsibility to the active pursuit of health has moved forward since the healthism of the 1980's when themes such as individual effort, discipline and will came together with the deregulation of public health programs in Portugal. (Gomes, 2010.)

The normalizing ethical power of the model is proposed by the rhetoric of free choice and personal autonomy. Such thinking is typical in countries that attempt to replace the former welfare models of regulating health. These new dimensions and interpretations of the health concept arise from the reflex of the new healthist model (Crawford, 1980), where wellbeing is the prime motto. As a consequence of the new discourses and novel interpretations of well-being endorsed by the new health players the individuals are encouraged to assume that they want to be healthy and can freely choose the ways of living for the purpose of promoting their own health. The increasing individualism and the demand for greater respect for the individual needs, challenge the standardized services of the welfare state. (Gomes, 2010.)

While the public educational politics of Portugal have depreciated physical education in schools, the marketplace alternatives go on in the last decade by increasing the number of health centres and fitness clubs as a direct result of the body consumer culture, and/or the home workout by means of personalized machines.

Evidence suggests that the implementation of such private projects is constitutively linked with the rise of expert languages and the media through which to spread them. The proliferation of the new magazines, self-help packages, and exercise videos are results of the new alliances between professionals, claiming to provide rational answers, and of the individuals, seeking to shape the lifestyles in the hope of personal recoveries. Therefore, the state bureaucracy is losing its traditional role in ruling healthy habits, but instead the private sector is growing through the tendency towards individualisation of the activities and the ways people engage in them. This tendency may be reinforced by the growing political interest in promoting public health by individual self-determination. (Gomes, 2010.)

As a consequence, the private sector has become more involved in the privatisation of sport public services, tasks and user-payments for certain public services at local level. However, the argument for the respect of the individual needs and desires, the main rhetoric against the state provision of sport activities, do not have evident impact in sport participation. Compared with the levels of sport participation between EU member states' profiles Portugal appears to be a sedentary country with low levels of participation, intermediate levels of frequency, and low engagement in voluntary work that support sporting activities (European Commission, 2010).

Eurobarometer (European Commission, 2014) also states that Portugal has one of the lowest sport participation rates, indicating that 64% of the population participates in some type of sport activity, and only 28% do so regularly or with some regularity (8% and 20% respectively). Portugal is also one of the countries with higher proportion of respondents not members at any sport club or health/fitness centre (88%; 74% in EU28) (European Commission, 2014).

General Data About Sport Business Fields

The results of the directly sport-related business fields, according to the Portuguese equivalent (CAE Rev. 3) of the *Statistical classification of economic activities in the European Community* (NACE Rev. 2, 2008) show a trend towards the growth of the private sport supply (see Table 1). These results coincide with the trends shown in the three most relevant sectors (fitness centres, golf and nature sports) and in other sectors (e.g., private football schools and sport events). However, the growth trend of the private sport it is also influenced by the self-determinate lifestyles, at least in the case of nature sports which shows a tendency towards autonomous practice. The Eurobarometer also indicates that, contrary to the European average, sport participation in Portugal has grown in parks and outdoors, and decreased in schools and universities. On the other hand, in line with the European trend, the participation in fitness centers and sport clubs has increased (European Commission, 2014).

Table 1 Directly sport-related business fields in Portugal in 2013.

Business field	NACE code	Companies (n)	Staff (n)	Revenue (1000 €)	Revenue/ Company (1000 €)	Average salary (1000 €)
Retail sale of sport equipment	47640	1829	5271	598,783.1	327.4	10.1
Activities of sport clubs	93120	46	1356	179,927.7	3911.5	110.1
Operation of sport facilities	93110	449	3192	177,023.1	394.3	13.4
Manufacture of sport goods	32300	69	267	147,322.8	2135.1	14.3
Activities of tourism animation	93293	868	1212	54,375.9	62.6	9.1
Sport and recreation education	85510	4273	376	29,959.2	7	6.2
Renting and leasing of sporting goods (77210)	77210	461	285	14,568.2	31.6	7.2
Activities of recreational ports	93293	11	91	10,901.5	991	15.9
Activities of fitness	93130	947	n/a	n/a	n/a	n/a

Source: Statistics Portugal INE (2016a).

Three Relevant Cases: Fitness, Golf and Nature Sports

Fitness

Fitness is a worldwide accepted concept. It refers to individual's capacity to do physical activities, from moderate to a high level, without fatigue, and the ability to keep this capacity during one's lifetime (ACSM, 2014). Fitness is also used to describe the physical activity exercised in the fitness facilities: gymnasiums, health clubs and organizations related to this field's services (Correia, Costa, Mamede, & Sacavém, 2000).

The regular practice of physical activity results in physical and physiological well-being (Calmeiro & Matos, 2004). The acceptance of the concept of well-being combined with the benefits have led to the development of the fitness industry. The fitness industry originates to the United States of America (USA) in the 1940's (Bates, 2008). In the 1980's Portugal started importing programs and physical exercises from the USA (Santos & Correia, 2011) and fitness industry began to obtain market space and importance (Pedragosa, Biscaia, & Correia, 2015).

Fitness can be divided in two periods in Portugal: the initial period (between 1980 and 1998) and the modern period (from 1998 until now) (Santos & Correia, 2011). The initial period was characterized by technical orientation, low human skills and obsolete ways of management without marketing fitness strategies. This period was the first step of the fitness in Portugal, where fitness facilities started to appear and memberships were mainly for men, who performed structured physical activities (bodybuilding) (Pedragosa, 2012). The modern period was characterized for example by an improvement of human skills, marketing strategies, sales, service experiences, fitness regulations, consumer's rights, academic degrees, training, finances, and creation of fitness associations. In the end of the 1990's the first foreign fitness facility Holmes Place was established in Portugal. The modern period began with this fitness facility, which led the fitness market to a new organizational and marketing culture. At the same time, women's participation increased and fitness facilities started to offer group classes and mix-fitness facilities for men and women. Fitness facilities became bigger, with an offer of differential services: for example exercise rooms, group classes, spas, personal training, parking restaurants and baby-sitting (Pedragosa, 2012). Therefore, during the 2000's the fitness industry had five important occurrences which explain the evolution of the industry: Fitness Association (AGAP – Associações de Academias e Ginásios de Portugal); VAT (value-added tax) impact; instructor academic degree impact; academic sport management programs and training schools; economic crisis. In the Table 2 the evolution of the fitness market is seen from 2004 until 2012. In 2013 the fitness market had 947 fitness facilities (companies) (Statistics Portugal INE, 2016a; 2016b).

Table 2 Fitness market in Portugal in 2004–2012.

Year	Companies (n)	Staff (n)	Revenue (1000 €)	Revenue/Company (1000 €)	Average salary (1000 €)
2012	894	2108	82,205.9	91.9	11.3
2011	886	2199	89,052.7	100.5	11.5
2010	858	2070	107,553.2	125.3	13
2009	697	1862	88,589	127.1	11.5
2008	577	1488	68,047.9	117.9	10.6
2007	413	1291	60,494.3	146.5	10.8
2006	356	1039	53,970.2	151.6	11.3
2005	310	900	52,198.8	168.4	12
2004	282	802	45,284.9	160.6	12.3

Sources: Statistics Portugal INE (2016a; 2016b).

First, AGAP started its activities in 1999, and the majority of the fitness facilities (60%) were affiliated in it (AGAP, 2015). The mission of the AGAP is to defend the rights and promotion of this industry. This includes memberships, instructors, companies and owners. The increase of the fitness facilities can be explained, partially, by the credibility of the AGAP in the market. The number of fitness facilities increased more than 200%, between 2004 and 2013 (Table 2).

Second, the increase of the numbers of fitness facilities can be explained by the VAT impact. In Portugal, between 2008 and 2011, the governmental officials introduced a 5% VAT. This measure enabled big investments in the number of fitness facilities. As Table 2 presents, the number of fitness facilities increased by 40% between 2007 and 2008, and it continued to grow until 2010. Government increased the VAT from five to 23% in 2011. After 2011 a minor increase in the number of fitness facilities has been detected.

Third, the level of the academic degrees and technical training of the instructors changed due to the Decree 271/2009, 1 October (Conselho de Ministros, 2009). All physical activity instructors must nowadays have a professional certificate with a sport academic degree. This measure had a negative impact in the professional market. Despite the growing number of the professionals, the market had to experience an adaptation period in order to assess all the professionals who did not have a professional academic degree in the sector. This explanation can be seen in the Table 2 between 2010 and 2012. Between 2010 and 2011 there was only an increase of 6% and between 2011 and 2012 a decrease of 4%. To complement these government official measures, university sport programs and training schools started to offer services in order to increase the skill level of the fitness professionals, both instructors and management. The number of fitness professionals increased by more than 150%, between 2004 and 2012.

Fourth, Portugal has suffered from the economic crisis between 2010 and 2013. Therefore, the government introduced austerity measures before and after *Troika* period that had an impact in the unemployment rate and consumer purchasing power. The increase of the unemployment rate was very high, more than 10%, between the analyzed periods. In 2004 the unemployment rate was 6.6% and 15.5% in 2012. This rate continued to increase until 2013, reaching 16.2%. In 2014 it decreased again to 13.9% and in 2015 to 12.4% (PORDATA, 2016). Consequently, the consumer purchasing power decreased in the same analyzed period.

Fifth, the salaries of companies in the fitness industry increased in the above mentioned period, which was expected because the number of fitness facilities and instructors also increased during this same period. Personal costs increased by more than 140%, between 2004 and 2012. The maximum value in personal costs was reached in 2010 with an average decrease of 6% between 2010 and 2012 (Table 2). Curiously, the average salary per person did not increase during the same period. From 2004 until 2012 the average salary in the fitness sector decreased 8%.

Finally, fitness facilities revenue increased more than eighty per cent, between 2004 and 2012. The average increase per year was 9% with a standard deviation of 14%. The maximum value was reached in 2010. There was a decrease of 17% from 2010 to 2011, followed by a decrease of eighth per cent from 2011 to 2012. Contrarily, the revenue per fitness facilities decreased more than 40%, between 2004 and 2012. Only the period of 2008 and 2009 showed positive revenue per fitness facility (Table 2).

A recent report from the International Health, Racquet & Sportsclub Association (IHRSA, 2013; 2015) provides information about the size and the scope of the fitness industry. Thus, the Statistics Portugal INE data can be complemented with the information about the memberships, average gross prices per month and the penetration rates (Table 3). Between 2005 and 2009 all the values increased, except the average gross price per month. After 2010 until 2013 all the values decreased, that meets the INE data.

Table 3 Fitness market in Portugal in 2005–2013.

	Membership (n)	Average gross price (Per month in euros)	Penetration rate (%)
2013	500,000	39	4.6
2010	600,000	46	5.7
2005	500,500	48	4.8

Sources: IHRSA (2013; 2015).

Additionally, the INE data can be also complemented with the leading actors in Portugal (IHRSA, 2013; 2015). Table 4 presents the number of fitness facilities per leading actor (clubs) and the market share percentages. From 2005 to 2010 the market share increased by more than 100%. Fitness facilities only for women increased considerably.

Table 4 Leading actors in the fitness sector in Portugal in 2005 and 2010.

2010		2005	
Brands	**Clubs (n)**	**Brands**	**Clubs (n)**
Holmes Place Iberia	19	Holmes Place	12
Solinca	9	Solinca Health & Fitness	5
Fitness Worx	6	Premier Group	6
Vivafit[a]	102		
WomanFit[a]	22		
Curves[a]	13		
GoFit[a]	13		
Market Share 7.9%		**Market Share 2.3%**	

Sources: IHRSA (2013; 2015).
[a]Only for women.

Golf

Golf in Portugal assumes a relevant position, mainly due to its strategic role and contribution to tourism. However, as a cultural and local form of leisure, golf has low participation rates among the Portuguese. There are only 14,198 (2013) affiliated players in Portugal (24.1% of whom are foreign but with a second home in Portugal).

The relevant economic and social impact of golf in Portugal result from the high international demand, and from the high level of supply. Currently (2014) Portugal has a significant supply of about 88 golf courses (EGA, 2014). The economic and social impact of golf in Portugal stems essentially from two vectors: tourism and real estate. Tourism and real estate as satellite activities of golf (Hudson & Hudson, 2010) create a significant set of indirect and induced jobs. For example tourism has an indirect influence on the property development. The increase in tourism also increases the number of golf courses, which in turn increases property development, which in turn increases the number of golf courses (Woodside, 2009) (Fig. 1).

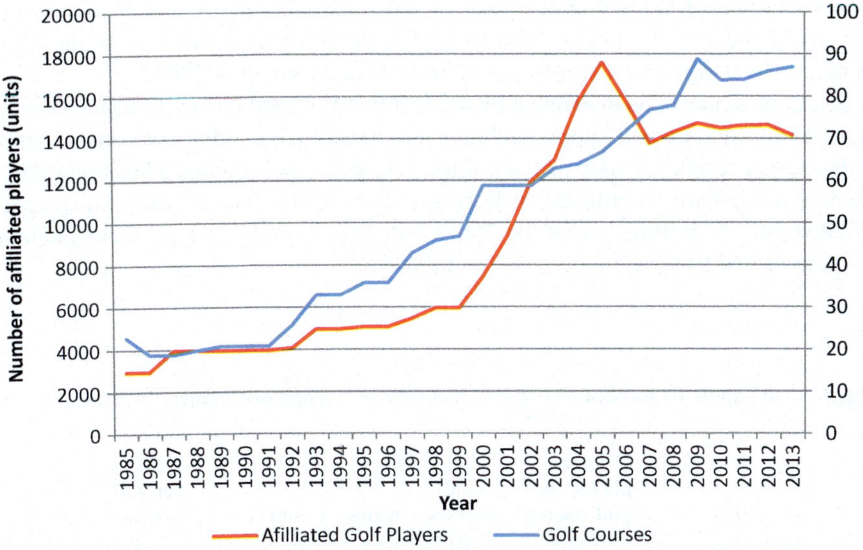

Fig. 1 Affiliated golf players vs. golf courses – evolution in Portugal in 1985–2013. Source: EGA (European Golf Association) (2014).

According to KPMG and Oxford Economics (2008), Portuguese destinations in golf real estate represents about 70% of the business, in golf tourism 15% and in other golf businesses (e.g., tournaments, golf facilities, capital investment and golf supplies) 15% of the volume of businesses associated with the sector.

Regarding the demand, it is noteworthy that golf is considered to be one of the top ten strategic products of the national strategic plan for the Portuguese tourism (Ministério da Economia e Inovação, 2007). Due to its geographic and weather conditions, Portugal is recognized internationally as a sunny sea tourism destination. However, Portugal is also currently recognized as a golf tourism destination (Hudson & Hudson, 2010). Due to these circumstances, golf is today strategically taken as a core activity for tourism development in Portugal. Golf has become associated with the image and brand of Portugal at the international level, highlighting the country's potentials, such as the excellent climate and hospitality conditions (Hudson & Hudson, 2010).

Also from the strategic tourism destination management perspective golf is very relevant in Portugal. Given the seasonal nature of tourism in Portugal, and the high structural weight of sun and sea tourism products, especially during the summer months of June-September, golf has been used as an anti-cycle product. This is particularly evident in Algarve, the main tourism region of Portugal, well known for its sunny beaches and where near 50% of the golf courses in Portugal are concentrated.

On the other hand, the justification of the golf courses in Portugal stems from the real estate market. Golf courses have been used as a differentiating factor in housing sales, not only for foreign golf customers and residential tourism, which are considered among the top ten strategic products in Portugese tourism, but also for the local population as first homes (Ministério da Economia e Inovação, 2007).

This condition can be evidenced by the fact that Portugal currently has a chronic discrepancy between golf supply and demand, which is typical also in other southern European countries, such as Italy, Turkey, Greece and Croatia. This situation is however particularly significant in Portugal since in the ratio of the golf course/affiliated golfers, Portugal is on the 25th position in a total of 31 countries, with a 167 ratio of resident golfers per course (Table 5).

Table 5 **Golf supply by local players per golf course in Europe per country in 2014.**

Rank	Country	Local players per golf course	Golf courses	Rank	Country	Local players per golf course	Golf courses
1	Netherlands	1749	201	17	Italy	368	273
2	Finland	1128	126	18	Latvia	300	3
3	Sweden	1082	454	19	Turkey	297	19
4	Spain	941	349	20	Estonia	261	8
5	Germany	862	708	21	Iceland	243	66
6	Switzerland	849	94	22	Greece	223	8
7	Denmark	835	181	23	Serbia	220	2
8	France	705	578	24	Croatia	183	3
9	Norway	704	173	25	Portugal	167	88
10	Austria	701	149	26	Hungary	156	13
11	Belgium	699	79	27	Romania	138	4
12	Luxembourg	671	6	28	Cyprus	123	10
13	Slovenia	653	13	29	Poland	95	29
14	Czech Rep.	560	89	30	Bulgaria	89	6
15	Slovakia	518	13	31	Lithuania	68	6
16	UK & Ireland	444	2989				

Source: EGA (European Golf Association) (2014).

This is a very low participation rate for Portugal. From the business point of view, to provide (some) stability for the operators, it is estimated that the number of resident golfers per course should reach a minimum of 1850 (Hatami, 2013).

From the supply perspective, this level and profile of the demand have direct consequences for the business (Table 6). Despite the better performances during the most recent years, the EBITDA (Earnings Before Interests, Taxes, Depreciation and Amortisation) shows that the profit to pay all the other financial expenses is very limited. A more dynamic internal market could contribute to improving the business performances of the Portuguese golf courses.

Table 6 Supply business performance (average per golf course) in Portugal in 2010–2014.

Average per golf course	2010	2013	2014
Golf rounds and % Portuguese	25,392 (16,2%)	25,313 (17%)	26,247 (22%)
Golf course members	207	217	243
EBITDA	−208,956.00 €	114,998.00 €	160,984.00 €
Revenue	1,263,392.00 €	1,323,643.00 €	1,564,166.00 €
Expenses	1,472,348.00 €	1,247,634.00 €	1,403,182.00 €
Staff	34	27	32
Golf course (total)	**88**	**87**	**89**

Source: National Golf Industry Council (2015).

Nature Sports

Nature sports is a concept that has emerged in the recent years to define the sport field related to leisure and tourism industries. Nature sports comprises a group of sport activities that have developed in natural or rural areas, presenting different scope of practices, ranging from formal to non-formal and informal practices, and which contribute to sustainable local development in the environmental, economic and socio-cultural dimensions. (Melo & Gomes, 2017.)

Nature sports are incorporated in the sport tourism sector. The relationship between sport and tourism is evident in the economic impacts generated in the touristic/tourism destinations, and visible in all scopes of nature sports practices (associative, business and free or autonomous). A significant part of these activities have been developed in places away from the residential areas and urban centers, especially in natural places and rural zones, requiring a travel and tourism consumption (e.g., accommodation, food, purchase of services and equipment) (Melo & Gomes, 2016).

Portugal has great potential to develop nature sports, considering its geomorphologic and climatic characteristics that allow the development of a wide range of nature sports activities, under optimal conditions throughout the year. Worldwide, it is not easy to find such a variety and density of specific places to develop nature sports activities in small areas. Portugal has extensive rural areas and natural spaces, with or without special protected areas, together with sea and beaches, rivers and other aquatic spaces, mountains and cliffs.

With this in mind, nature sports are becoming a potential factor for tourism development. It must be highlighted that nature tourism, that includes soft (e.g., trekking) and hard (e.g., rafting, kayaking and hiking) nature sport activities, induces a market of 22 million travels by year, with an average annual growth of 7% (1997–2004), representing 9% of the total amount of visits made by the European travelers (Turismo de Portugal, 2006a). On the other hand, nautical tourism that includes nature sports activities, such as surfing, windsurfing, sailing and other nautical sports, represents almost three million travels, which is approximately 1.2% of the total amount of visits made by the Europeans, with a market growth from eight to 10% per year (Turismo de Portugal, 2006b).

It is estimated that nature tourism market (including outdoor recreation and nature sports) is globally a tourism sector that presents the highest growth rate for the next decades (Bell, Tyrvainen, Sievanen, Prbstl, & Simpson, 2007). In 2014 tourism in Portugal represented 4% of the GDP, generating an income of 10,394 million euros, and a positive touristic balance of seven billion euros (Statistics Portugal INE, 2015). These figures lead to expect that nature sports that have been consolidating since the 1970's as one of the most solid group of sport activities, will have a strong growth with more potential also in the future (Dias, Melo, & Junior, 2007). This growth has been associated with the gradual appreciation of the outdoor leisure (Costa, 2007), greater need for nature contact, search for sensations and emotions in a routine and controlled society, and with a demand for new states of the consciousness in a secular and desecrated society (Miranda, Lacasa, & Muro, 1995).

Nature sports is one of the growing areas of private sport sector in Portugal. A properly equipped group canyoning in Portuguese nature. *Photo: Luís Campos/FCDEF-UC*.

With the growth of the touristic/tourism animation (including nature sports) segment, the government established for the first time in 2000 (updated in 2002) a legal framework for touristic/tourism animation activities (Ministério da Economia, 2002). Almost one decade later, noting that the law was outdated, a new legislation was created, which defines the access and exercise conditions for the touristic/tourism animation companies and maritime-touristic/tourism operators. This law was first updated in 2013, and more recently in 2015 (Ministério da Economia, 2015).

According to Melo (2013), it is difficult to exactly estimate the demand for nature sports in Portugal, because majority of the practitioners participate in the activities autonomously and unorganized. However, there are some indicators that reflect the increasing number of practitioners, and the sector's growth in Portugal (Melo, 2013). These are: (a) higher participation rates of the informal/unorganized practitioners, which indicate a growing independence of the practitioners, and therefore a greater autonomy in participation; (b) greater participation of young people who begin to practice these activities at an earlier age, probably influenced by the integration of these activities in the curricula of primary and secondary education; (c) women's increasing participation, particularly in younger age groups; (d) diversified supply that allows to offer different sport projects, ranging from more formal activities under the federative model (e.g., sport clubs of canoeing and oriented for competition), to the more informal/unorganized structures (e.g., mountain biking (MTB) clubs oriented for recreational practices), depending on the different motivation of the practitioners; (e) growth of the specialized supply, targeted for education and training of the practitioners, as in the case of the most surf clubs; (f) increase of the number of formal/organized sport events, such as orienteering federative competitions, but also the informal events, such as MTB events organized by practitioners' clubs and associations; (g) creation of new spaces for practices, such as networks of walking paths, nautical centers and centers of surfing high performance; (h) creation of a positive image in the territories associated with mediatic sport events such as the case of Peniche from the surf world championship or Nazaré from the largest wave surfed (by Garrett McNamara) and (i) growth tendency of the sector pointed by the leaders of the nature sports organizations (Melo, 2013).

Data from the Statistics Portugal INE (2016a) show the growing tendency of the private sector of nature sports in Portugal (Table 7). Generally, one can observe that in almost all indicators there is a tendency for growth every year, from 2004 until 2013, particularly in the number of companies and in the number of staff.

Table 7 Organization of touristic/tourism animation activities in Portugal in 2004–2013.

Year	Companies (n)	Staff (n)	Revenues (1000 €)	Revenue/Company (1000 €)	Spending with staff (1000 €)	Average salary (1000 €)
2004	116	226	12,637.1	108.9	1372.5	6.1
2005	129	253	17,102.8	132.6	2079.4	8.2
2006	148	379	22,460.9	151.8	3577.5	9.4
2007	172	406	22,362.4	130	3327.2	8.2
2008	293	593	27,936	95.3	4417.9	7.5
2009	383	730	31,157.8	81.4	5735.2	7.9
2010	496	888	48,500.9	97.8	8838.4	10
2011	592	1034	46,045.5	77.8	9446.1	9.1
2012	711	1156	46,223.9	65	9425.6	8.2
2013	868	1212	54,375.9	62.7	11,024	9.1

Source: Statistics Portugal INE (2016a).

In a recent study, Melo and Gomes (2016) found differences in the supply and demand of the nature sports organizations, when comparing the civic/voluntary actors with the private sector of nature sports. The following evidences can be presented about the companies in the field: (a) companies operating in the nature sports sector in Portugal are mostly constituted as limited companies, and sole proprietors; (b) companies are mainly recently founded family based microenterprises; (c) companies present a high seasonality on demand, high number of nature sports activities in their offerings, and consequently a little specialized supply, which can be explained by the attempts to combat seasonality (Melo & Gomes, 2016).

Although education/training was not initially a goal for the entrepreneurs, this seems to be changing, as evidenced by the increasing supply of courses/training for the practitioners, as in the case of surfing schools and surf camps. In this regard, companies in the field seem to be the organizations willing to adapt to the changing demands of the nature sports. (Melo & Gomes, 2016.)

Conclusions

Sport participation levels in Portugal are lower than in most other European countries. The growing acceptance of the commercial sector as a provider of the solutions to physical activities, especially in promoting public health, reveals a scenario of the commodification of the services, individualization of the demand and irregularity of the practices. One of the challenges in the future in Portugal will be the way public authorities are able to regulate the commodification of sport services and the equality of access to facilities and other sport practices.

During the period of 2004–2013 there were occurrences in the fitness and economic industry that explain the sector's evolution. In general terms, the fitness market in Portugal grew in between 2004 and 2012, except for the revenue per fitness facilities and the average salary per person. The creation of the AGAP, the decrease and the increase of VAT, the sector regulations, together with the economic crisis, were among the key factors that have had an impact in the development of the private sport sector in Portugal, mainly after 2009.

As the statistics show, some of these occurrences have reduced the main indicators of the fitness industry: companies, staff, revenue, revenue/company, salaries of the employees, and the average salary. Complementarily, the fitness industry have promoted low price strategies in order to continue selling their products and services. In a short term, the fitness facilities' costs did not follow the low price strategies, which led to a decrease in the sector. After 2010 new fitness business models and services appeared to counteract the downward market fitness trend and take advantage of the market opportunities. These are for example low-cost fitness facilities, nutrition and physiotherapy services, virtual classes and CrossFit studios.

From the demand point of view, golf business is structured in a binomial market. On one hand there is golf as a leisure sport, and as a sociocultural sport practice of the host community. On the other hand, golf is associated with tourism and thus dependent on international tourism markets, mostly from the northern to the southern countries of Europe where, in most of the cases, there is a limited connection to the local community (Bull, 2005; Higham, 2005; Moital, Dias, & Machado, 2013).

Increasing of the sport activities' commercialization, in particular among nature sports is closely associated with the growth of leisure and tourism industry, especially of the new tourism segments that have arisen along the growing demand for active holidays (Melo & Gomes, 2016). This is due to the fact that sport clubs have mainly focused on the values of effort, competition and technique learning, failing to meet the expectations from the leisure sport field. Thus, several sport commercial structures have emerged and are being established to meet the needs of the consumers by commercializing their products with emphasis on playful, accessible and unrestricted sport practices (Leblanc, 2001; Paget, Mounet, & Guilhon, 2007; Pigeassou & Garrabos, 1997). The business creation process follows a logic that began with the discovery of the sport activities, and was later reinforced by the emergence of an increasingly dynamic market (Bouhaouala, 2004). This process emerged from the late 1980's until the mid-1990's, due to the favorable socio-economic conditions for the development of nature tourism (Bouhaouala, 2004; Viñuelas, Betrán, & Plantalamor, 1995). The commitment of the local and regional government bodies regarding socio-economic development (e.g., job creation for the local population), and the increased demand for new forms of tourism contributed also to the consolidation of the sector.

References

ACSM. (2014). *ACSM's guidelines for exercise testing and prescription* (9th ed.). Philadelphia, PA: Wolters Kluwer-Lippincott Williams & Wilkins Health.

AGAP. (2015). *Associação de empresas de ginásios e academias de Portugal: barómetro 2015* [AGAP: Barometer 2015]. Lisbon, Portugal: Edições AGAP.

Bates, M. (2008). *Health fitness management: a comprehensive resource for managing and operating programs and facilities*. Champaign, IL: Human Kinetics.
Bell, S., Tyrvainen, L., Sievanen, T., Prbstl, U., & Simpson, M. (2007). Outdoor recreation and nature tourism: A European perspective. *Living Reviews in Landscape Research, 1*(2), 1–46.
Bouhaouala, M. (2004). Les Sports de nature comme outil de developpement socio-economique: creation et developpement d'entreprises [Nature Sports as a tool for the socio-economic development: Rise and improvement of entreprises.] In P. Bouchet & M. Kaach (Eds.), *Afrique francophone et développement du sport: du myth à la realité?* (pp. 173–184). Paris, France: L'Harmattan.
Bull, C. (2005). Sport tourism destination resource analysis. In J. Higham (Ed.), *Sport tourism destinations-issues, opportunities and analysis* (pp. 25–38). Oxford, UK: Elsevier Butterworth-Heinemann.
Calmeiro, L., & Matos, M. G. (2004). *Psicologia do exercício e saúde* [Exercise and health Psychology]. Lisbon, Portugal: Visão e Contextos, Lda.
Camy, J., Clijsen, L., Madella, A., & Pilkington, A. (2004). *Vocasport. Improving employment in the field of sport in Europe through vocational training. Vocational education and training in the field of sport in the European Union. Situation, trends and outlook*. Lyon, France: Université Claude Bernard Lyon 1.
Conselho de Ministros. (2009). Decreto-Lei 271/2009, de 1 de Outubro [Law 271/2009, October]. *Diário da República n.° 191 - 1.ª Série*.
Correia, A., Costa, C., Mamede, P., & Sacavém, A. (2000). *Serviços de qualidade no desporto de piscinas, polidesportivos e ginásios* [Quality in swimming pools, multisport facilities and gym services]. Lisbon, Portugal: Centro de Estudos e Formação Desportiva.
Costa, L. (2007). Princípios do esporte para todos [Principles for sport for all]. In A. Almeida & L. Costa (Eds.), *Meio ambiente, esporte, lazer e turismo. Estudos e pesquisa no Brasil: 1967–2007* (pp. 97–99). Rio de Janeiro, Brazil: Editora Gama Filho.
Crawford, R. (1980). Healthism and the medicalization of everiday life. *Journal of Health Services, 10*(3), 365–388.
Dias, C., Melo, V., & Júnior, E. (2007). Os estudos dos esportes na natureza: desafios teóricos e conceituais [The Nature Sports studies: Theoretical and conceptual challenges]. *Revista Portuguesa de Ciências do Desporto, 7*(3), 358–367.
EGA. (2014). *Golf participation rate statistics*. Epalinges, Switzerland: EGA.
Esping-Andersen, G. (1990). *The three worlds of welfare capitalism*. Cambridge, UK: Polity Press.
European Commission. (2010). *Sport and physical activity*. Special Eurobarometer 334/Wave 72.3. Brussels, Belgium: D-G Education and Culture.
European Commission. (2014). *Sport and physical activity*. Special Eurobarometer 412/Wave 80.2. Brussels, Belgium: D-G Education and Culture.
Gomes, R. M. (2010). The visible body: Health representations in a consumer society. In E. Ettorre (Ed.), *Culture, bodies and the sociology of health* (pp. 85–105). Farnham, UK: Ashgate.
Hatami, D. (2013). *Thoughts from the golf industry show (Part 3)*. Boulder, CO: HVS Golf Services.
Higham, J. (2005). Introduction to sport tourism destination marketing and management. In J. Higham (Ed.), *Sport tourism destinations-issues, opportunities and analysis* (pp. 53–162). Oxford, UK: Elsevier Butterworth-Heinemann.
Hudson, S., & Hudson, L. (2010). *Golf tourism*. Oxford, UK: Goodfellow Publishers Limited.
IHRSA. (2013). *European health club report: Size and scope of the fitness Industry*. Boston, MA: IHRSA Publications.
IHRSA. (2015). *Global report*. Boston, MA: IHRSA Publications.
KPMG & Oxford Economics. (2008). *The economic value of golf to Europe*. Retrieved March 17, 2016 from http://www.bgia.org.uk/upload/public/documents/news/KPMG%20Golf%20Economy%20report_final.pdf
Leblanc, M. (2001). *O clube do ano 2000* [The clubs in the 2000's]. Lisbon, Portugal: CEFD.
McIntosh, P. (1963). *Sport in society*. London, UK: Watts.

Melo, R. (2013). *Desportos de Natureza e Desenvolvimento Local Sustentável: Análise dos praticantes e das Organizações Promotoras dos Desportos de Natureza* [Nature sports and sustainable local development: Analysis of the practitioners and organisations] (Unpublished Doctoral Dissertation). Universidade de Coimbra.

Melo, R., & Gomes, R. (2016). Understanding Nature Sports Organizations in Portugal. *The Open Sports Sciences Journal, 9*(Suppl-1, M3), 13–25.

Melo, R., & Gomes, R. (2017). A sociocultural approach to understanding the development of nature sports. In R. Melo & C. Sobry (Eds.), *Sport tourism: New challenges in a globalized world* (pp. 60–90). Cambridge, UK: Cambridge Scholar Publishing.

Ministério da Economia. (2002). Decreto-Lei n.° 47/99, de 16 de Fevereiro, alterado pelo Decreto-Lei n.° 56/2002, de 11 de Março [Law 56/2002, March 11]. *Diário da República, 1ª Série A, n.° 59*, 2112–2129.

Ministério da Economia. (2015). Decreto-Lei n.° 186/2015, de 3 de Setembro [Law 186/2015, September 3]. *Diário da República, 1ª série, n.°* 172, 6947–6982.

Ministério da Economia e Inovação. (2007). *Plano Estratégico Nacional do Turismo para o desenvolvimento do turismo em Portugal* [Tourism national strategic plan for the Portuguese tourism development]. Lisbon, Portugal: Turismo de Portugal.

Miranda, J., Lacasa, E., & Muro, I. (1995). Actividades físicas en la naturaleza: un objeto a investigar [Nature physical activities: A research topic]. *Apunts: Educación Física y Deportes, 41*, 53–69.

Moital, M., Dias, N., & Machado, D. (2013). A cross national study of golf tourists' satisfaction. *Journal of Destination Marketing & Management, 2*(1), 39–45.

National Golf Industry Council. (2015). *Annual report – 2015*. Grândola, Portugal: CNIG.

Paget, E., Mounet, J., & Guilhon, A. (2007). Les petites entreprises prestataires de sport et leurs dirigeants: spécificités et stratégies [The small sport companies and their managers: Specifities and strategies]. *Revue Européenne de Management du Sport, 17*, 1–13.

Pedragosa V. (2012). *Satisfação e fidelização em ginásios e health clubs: estudo das expetativas, das emoções e da qualidade* [Satisfaction and loyalty in gyms and health clubs: Study of expectations, emotions and quality] (Unpublished Doctoral Dissertation). Universidade Técnica de Lisboa.

Pedragosa, V., Biscaia, R., & Correia, A. (2015). The role of emotions on consumers' satisfaction within the fitness context. *Motriz: Revista de Educação Física, 21*(2), 116–124.

Pigeassou, C., & Garrabos, C. (1997). *Management des organisations de services sportifs* [Sport organisations management]. Paris, France: PUF.

PORDATA. (2016). *Taxa de desemprego: total e por sexo* [Unemployment rate: Total and by sex]. Retrived February 18, 2016 from www.pordata.pt

Santos, E., & Correia, A. (2011). *Evolução do Fitness em Portugal: mudanças e desafios* [Fitness evolution in Portugal: Changes and challenges]. Lisbon, Portugal: Visão e Contextos, Lda.

Statistics Portugal INE. (2015). *Estatísticas do Turismo 2014* [Tourism statistics 2014]. Lisbon, Portugal: Instituto Nacional de Estatística.

Statistics Portugal INE. (2016a). *Informação Estatística* [Statistics information]. Lisbon, Portugal: Instituto Nacional de Estatística.

Statistics Portugal INE. (2016b). *Fitness companies by economic activity (CAE Ver. 3)*. INE Portal. Retrieved February 17, 2016 from www.ine.pt

Turismo de Portugal. (2006a). *Turismo de Natureza* [Nature tourism]. Lisbon, Portugal: Turismo de Portugal.

Turismo de Portugal. (2006b). *Turismo Náutico* [Nautic tourism]. Lisbon, Portugal: Turismo de Portugal.

Viñuelas, J., Betrán, J., & Plantalamor, A. (1995). Análisis del ámbito empresarial y de la difusión sociocultural de las actividades de aventura en la naturaleza [Analysis of the business scope and the socio-cultural diffusion of outdoor challenge activities]. *Apunts: Educación Física y Deportes, 41*, 130–136.

Woodside, A. (2009). Applying systems thinking to sustainable Golf tourism. *Journal of Travel Research, 48*(2), 205–215.

ROMANIA: Private Sport Sector at the Crossroads of Past Socialism and Present Capitalism

László Péter

Selected country facts (in 2013)	
Capital	Bucharest
Geographical size (km^2)	238,391
Population (million)	20.02
GDP (euro per capita)	7200
GDP (per capita in PPS)	55
Annual net earnings average (€)	4147

Focusing on Romanian Realities – Theoretical Dimensions

The core of this article is made up of the presentation and interpretation of those descriptive statistics that are marked by the most important economic indicators of the operators interested in sport. An emphasised sociological view has been also asserted, primarily to present the social particularities and the contextualisation, and to raise new questions and problems. I also included historical informations to avoid an ahistorical interpretation.

The perspective is a combination of conflictualism (Collins, 1994) and critical theory (Ritzer & Stepnisky, 2007). The former approach states that the interests of the external economic operators overwrite the direct interests of the actors that are involved in the internal practices of sport. For instance, the interests of the owners of ventures operating football pitches in small towns prevail over the sporting opportunities of the people partaking in mass sport, especially when alternatives

L. Péter (✉)
Department of Sociology, Babeș-Bolyai University, Cluj, Romania
e-mail: peterlaci@yahoo.com

A. Laine, H. Vehmas (eds.), *The Private Sport Sector in Europe*, Sports Economics, Management and Policy 14, https://doi.org/10.1007/978-3-319-61310-9_17

(community facilities) are absent. Thus, those individuals, organisations and institutions that have the power, benefit of the profit from sport, to the detriment of the potential participants and the disadvantaged. All these are important because most of the companies operating in the sector are geographically concentrated in cities and regions with higher economic potential, producing a new type of social inequality: the inequality of access to commodified sport or services.

According to the critical theory sport is not simply a mirror of society but also a good opportunity and an effective tool, or a possibility to change society and making it better (Woods, 2011, 21). The fact that the private sport sector began to develop dynamically and diversified in the past years also bears the possibility that it becomes more inclusive and democratic.

The methodology of this article is organised around secondary statistical data analysis. The framework used is the Romanian equivalent (CAEN Rev. 2) of the *Statistical classification of economic activities in the European Community* (NACE Rev. 2, 2008). This is completed by case studies, observations in the field and semi-structured interviews, and content analysis. Primarily in connection with the presentation of the conditions of the sport sector before 1989 and after 1990, respectively with regard to the identification of the background factors of the Halep phenomenon, I wanted to demonstrate the radical changes and the different factors within the sport sectors that made the successes of the tennis star Simona Halep and gymnast Nadia Comăneci possible.

The data has been recorded by the official institutions listen in reference list. On the validity and the reliability of the data it must be remarked that the data acquisition was not simple, yet the information can be considered relevant. I have not worked on a selective sample, but under the given objective circumstances that I consider the circle of analysed units to be exhaustive. As a result of the time consuming and laborious process that included thoughtful data selection and multiple cross-checking, a comprehensive, constructed database was created.

It must be recognised that the selection of data also meant an interpretation, of "data construction". This is especially true for Romania, where a usable data set could never have been gathered without the selection of the adequate information, but neither without their cross-checking or completion. The most important decisions of the process arose in connection with the following issues. First, missing data raised questions, as it was not clear in every case what their significance was: suspended activity, failure to turn in the balance sheet or other errors of registration. Frequently a given venture appears in the records of the Trade Registry as an active company, yet it does not provide an annual balance sheet to the Ministry of Finance. If I was unable to complement the missing data from any other source, I considered it 0, and if there was no available data for the company during the entire examined period, I took that for a firm that had been closed down. Contradictory information about the same commercial entity, but from different sources, represented further problems. For example, there was a figure in the balance sheet submitted to the Ministry of Finance, and an entirely different figure appeared in another available source. In such cases I always relied on the data obtained from the Ministry of Finance.

Second, the resulting data still includes deficiencies. I foremost refer to the fact that the records only contain the primary activities of the companies, whereas law allows the registration of further secondary activities. Thus, the ventures having sport activities mentioned as secondary or supplementary activities were left out of the analysis. Similarly, my data does not include illegal ventures that carry out sport activities within the realms of the black economy. I am aware of the fact that the number of analysed entities can change rapidly under the conditions of the market economy. This may be important as the examined period represents the period of the economic crisis with negative impact upon small sized companies.

The questions are relevant also from the epistemological point of view. As part of the source criticism I must remark that the collection of data raises questions, from the philosophy of science (Léderer, 2002) and sociology of knowledge perspective: "whose data are we talking about?" What is the role of the researcher in the "construction of data and facts" (Bijker, Hughes, & Pinch, 1987) under the circumstances when the state record systems function inaccurately? This is hardly a question for the positivists because they automatically consider that the registered data by qualified institutions are automatically objective facts, limiting itself to the search of the relations between them. The construction of the database – as a construction of facts and data controlled by this research perspective – has been an interactive process, during which an empirical universe was validated and crystallised in a triangle defined by the statistical data–data source–the perspective of the researcher, based on which I formulated my statements maintaining their validity under the defined circumstances.

The units of the analysis consisted of the active private companies, formally registered as legal entities, operating in the private sport sector in accordance with their primary NACE codes, with official financial accounting balance sheets for fiscal year 2013.

Features of the Sport Sector

The present state of the sport sector in Romania is defined by the consequences of the policy of the socialist period. That regime appropriated sport, and instrumentalised it for political purposes (Ciobotaru, 2015; Tismăneanu, 2006), degrading it into a tool of control and propaganda. By the 1950's the communist power succeeded to completely get away with community institutions, brutally liquidating their functioning. In order to increase the prestige and legitimacy of the political system reaching the peak at the Olympiad in 1984 it fully subjugated competitive sport from a financial perspective (Petracovschi & Terret, 2013), making the entire sport system completely dependent of state funding. At the same time, mass sport had been institutionalised with the creation of Daciada.

Daciada became an institutional framework of the nationalist-communist mass sport, initiated by the leadership in 1977, under the slogan of "*First in sport, first in work*" (Bogdan, 2014). It was the "Romanian winter and summer Olympic Games" named to evoke the two thousand-year statehood of Romania, organised on a biannual basis under the slogan of *"Sport for everyone!"*, compulsory for everybody, where amateur athletes had to compete with each other in almost all sport branches. The officially declared aim of the mass movement was to promote a healthy physical training, but in fact it meant institutional practices of the symbolic occupation of the physical body, besides obvious political indoctrination. The patriotic sport movement organised by the CNEFS, the National Council for Physhical Education and Sport, was meant to shape the "New Man", a means to enforce social control in a refined way, and to colonisate the free time of the people. Competitions went on among schools, companies and state institutions. But it is true that the sporting bases that were built provided good opportunities for leisure sport participation. It undertook some kind of a talent scout function, it constituted a recruitment basis for professional athletes. This institutional framework and ways of sport automatically ceased to exist after 1989 when the competition was abolished. Lately public sporting bases were privatised, or left to deteriorate (Péter, 2016, 54).

Daciada had mostly negative effects. Due to its compulsory character, involving six million people, no true grassroots mass sport movements evolved in Romania. Daciada was just a pseudo-movement of mass sport, sort of a political theatre. It is largely due to its effects that there is no mass sport culture in Romania today (Massiera & Ionescu, 2005). It is also the reason why there is almost a complete lack of community based sector formally organised or freely available facilities. Furthermore, without state funding the public sport drastically deteriorated, creating a peculiar situation that was also recognised by the government.

The Romanian Sport Strategy (MTS, 2016) stipulates that the main institution of the sport administration is the Ministry Sport, in co-operation with COSR (Romanian Olympic Sports Committee) and the professional associations. This stipulates that regulating is the role of the state (MTS, 2016, 15), to which Law No. 69/2000 on Sport (Romanian Government, 2000) and articles 3 and 42 of Law No. 1/2011 on Education (Romanian Government, 2011) provide. The strategy recognises underfinancing, the lack of mass sport and of sport facilities as reality, as well as the problems of the access to sport opportunities, and the deplorable state of public infrastructure (MTS, 2016, 30, 44). As a consequence, in of all these Romania is the last in the EU when it comes to physical activity of the population: 60% never exercise or play sport at all; only 1% are members of sport club; only 6%, respectively 15% exercise or play sport more or less regularly (European Commission, 2014).

With these antecedents and consequances, only the private sport sector plays a considerable role today. The previous political system caused a boomerang type of effect both in the case of mass sport and professional sport after the change of the regime (Bogdan, 2014): the public sector plays a minor role.

Commercialization of sport has produced new forms of inequality in Romania. A tennis court just next to the exclusivist estate in Cluj/Kolozsvár is an eloquent example. Accessing such gated communities is impossible for the majority of the population, especially for lower income families. Nevertheless, exercising is a universal human right beyond the almost invisible, yet very palpable fence is whole different reality. *Photo: Tamás Gönczy*.

The Private Sport Sector Reflected by the Statistics

During the 1990's, only a very few private companies with sport-related activities were created. In the following I concentrate only on the directly sport-related NACE classes. So all the figures/tables are about these companies. The number of registered ventures started to grow dynamically in the beginning of the first decade of the 2000 (Fig. 1). The private sport companies represent 0.35% of the total of 746,758 Romanian private companies (Romanian Ministry of Public Finance, 2016).

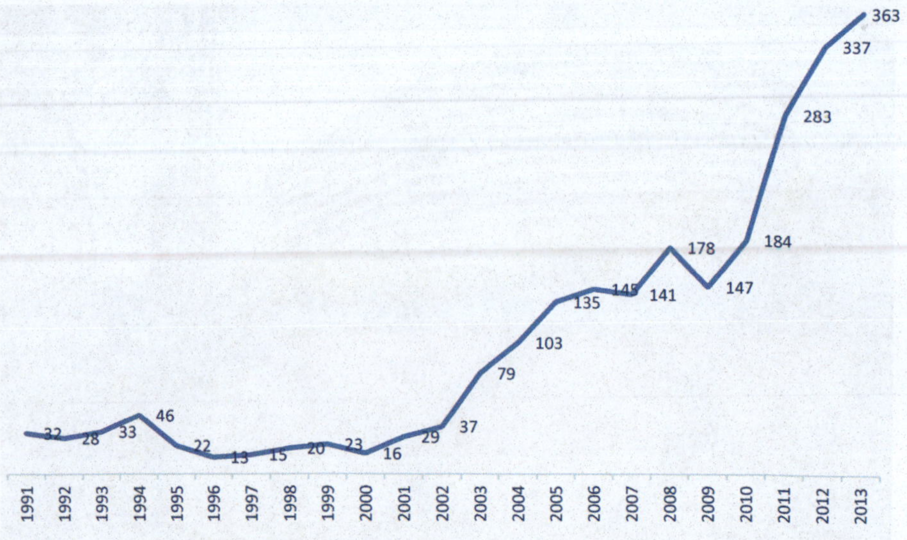

Fig. 1 Number of active companies in the sport sector in Romania according to their years of establishment. Source: List of Companies (2015).

These companies are obviously not distributed evenly in the territory of the whole country. The largest numbers are located in Bucharest, the capital city and its vicinity (748), and in the North-Western (445), Western (284) and Central (378) regions of Romania. All these represent 71% of all companies that operate in the sport sector. A similar break up can be found when the density of the distribution on county level is examined, compared to the population of the county.

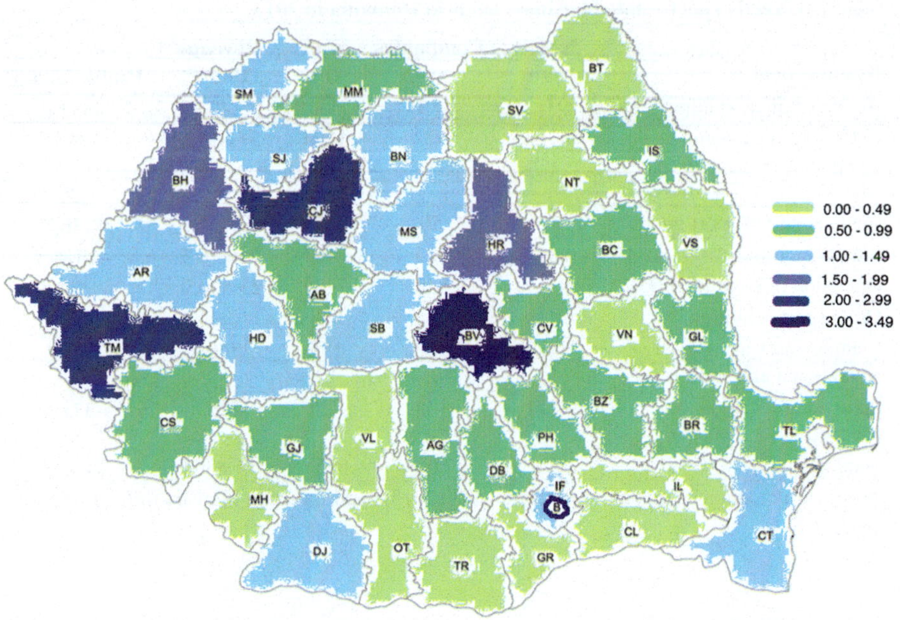

Fig. 2 The territorial distribution of companies active in the sport sector in Romania in relation to the population (per 10,000 inhabitants). Sources: Calculation based on List of Companies (2015) and INSSE (2016).

The distribution map (Fig. 2) shows that the density of sport companies is higher in the capital city and its vicinity, as well as in the counties of the North-Western, Western and Central regions. More specifically the companies are found in Braşov (3.05 companies/10,000 inhabitants), Bucharest (3.0 companies/10,000 inhabitants), Cluj (2.06 companies/10,000 inhabitants), Timiş (2.06 companies/10,000 inhabitants), Harghita (1.67 companies/10,000 inhabitants), and in the Bihor county (1.57 companies/10,000 inhabitants).

Table 1 Directly sport-related business fields in Romania in 2013.

Business field	NACE code	Companies (n)	Staff (n)	Revenue (1000 €)	Profit (1000 €)
Activities of sport clubs	9312	80	468	55,403.8	4331.0
Retail sale of sporting equipment in specialized stores	4764	522	1104	51,811.6	−454.7
Manufacture of sport goods	3230	50	1683	39,875.4	1330.7
Fitness facilities	9313	635	1402	25,276.5	−2515.5
Operation of sport facilities	9311	549	1337	23,500.9	−1558.8
Other sport activities	9319	474	593	11,994.3	−442.3
Renting and leasing of recreational and sport goods	7721	182	155	3540.7	568.7
Sport and recreation education	8551	103	226	3426.8	−371.9
Total		2595	6968	214,830.0	887.1

Sources: Calculation based on List of Companies (2015) and Romanian Ministry of Public Finance (2016).

As the Table 1 shows, almost a quarter of the companies (635) provide sport opportunities (fitness facilities), over one fifth (549) operate sport facilities, almost one fifth carry out retail sales of sporting equipment (522) and 182 companies rent and lease recreational and sport goods. All of these activities make up 73% of the active companies in the sport sector. With respect to the number of employees the distribution of sport companies is presented in Table 2.

Table 2 Staff per directly sport-related business field in Romania in 2013.

Business field	NACE code	Total staff (n)	Average staff (n)
Manufacture of sport goods	3220	1683	33.7
Fitness facilities	9313	1402	2.2
Operation of sport facilities	9311	1337	2.4
Retail sale of sporting equipment in specialized stores	4764	1104	2.1
Activities of sport clubs	9312	468	5.9
Sport and recreation education	8551	226	2.2
Renting and leasing of recreational and sport goods	7721	155	0.9
Other sport activities	9319	593	1.3
Total		6968	2.7

Sources: Calculation based on List of Companies (2015) and Romanian Ministry of Public Finance (2016).

Companies that manufacture sport goods require the highest number of employees, a total of 1683, which means an average number of 33.7 employees per company. This exceeds by far the average number of 2.7 employees, as well as those needed by all the other areas of activity. (Table 2). The evolution of the number of employees can be regarded as favourable in the past five years, with an increase of over 50% from 4559 to 6968. Broken down according to business fields, the largest increase is shown in the retail sale of sporting equipment (NACE code 4764, 101.8%), where the number of employees doubled. Similarly, the increase of the employee numbers exceeded the average in the cases of companies that operated sport facilities (NACE 9311, 79.2%) and those that rented and leased recreational and sport goods (NACE 7721, 68.5%). The smallest increase was registered in the area with the largest need of workforce, the manufacture of sport goods (NACE 3230, 24.8%). (Fig. 3.)

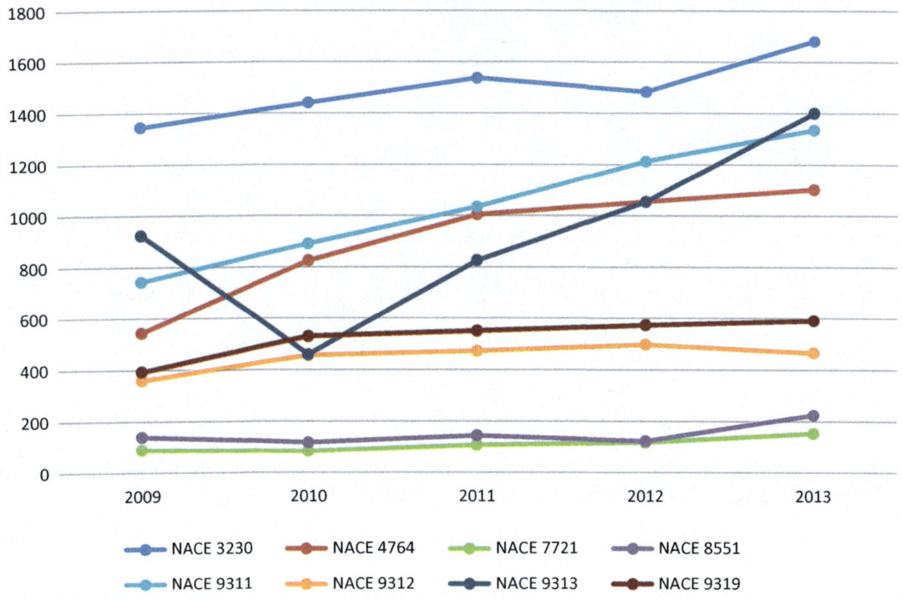

Fig. 3 Evolution of the number of employees per directly sport-related business field in Romania in 2009–2013. Sources: Calculation based on List of Companies (2015), Romanian Ministry of Public Finance (2016) and Romanian Trade Registry (2016).

The total value of the revenue of the examined companies in 2013 was 215 million euros. A significant part of that (63.5%) was made up of the companies that are registered in the capital city and its vicinity (Ilfov county), reaching a sum of 63.5 million euros. In territorial distribution the counties with the best performance were Mureş (12.2 million euros), Cluj (9.1 million euros), Prahova (6.2 million euros), Timiş (6.1 million euros), Braşov (5.7 million euros), Vaslui (3.9 million euros), Constanţa (3.9 million euros) and Harghita (3.6 million euros) (Figure 4). These together represented almost 90% of the revenue of all the sport companies.

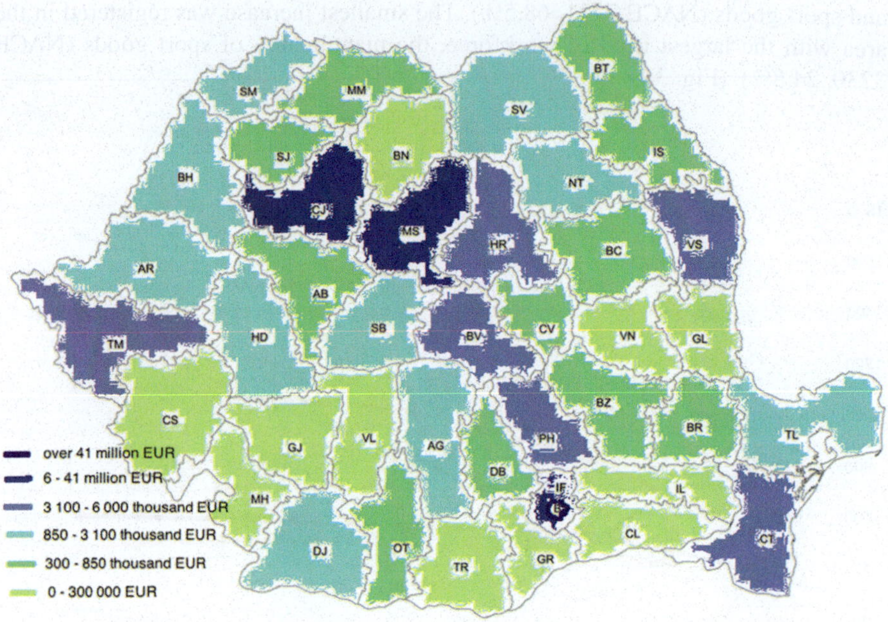

Fig. 4 Territorial distribution of the revenue of private sport companies in Romania. Sources: Calculation based on List of Companies (2015) and INSSE (2016).

When broken down per industry field the largest share of the total financial revenue is created by the activities of sport clubs (NACE 9312, 55 million euros), the retail sale of sporting equipment (NACE 4764, 52 million euros) and the manufacture of sport goods (NACE 3220, 40 million euros) (Table 1). Among other things the uneven territorial distribution can be explained by economic indicators. The financial revenue realised by sport companies is positively correlated on level 0.01 (the value of Pearson correlation is 0.896) with the general economic performance of the counties (GDP) (TEMPO Data Series, 2016). The higher the economic performance of the given county, the higher the economic performance of the sport companies, too.

The past 5 years brought about an average of 90% increase in the revenue of the examined companies. Within this figure the largest growth was registered by the companies providing opportunities to pursue sport activities (fitness facilities) (NACE 9313), which increased their financial revenue three times in that period (203.6%). The smallest growth was registered in the companies that are renting and leasing recreational and sport goods (NACE 7721, 54%), and which provide sport and recreational education (NACE 8551, 68.6%) (Fig. 5).

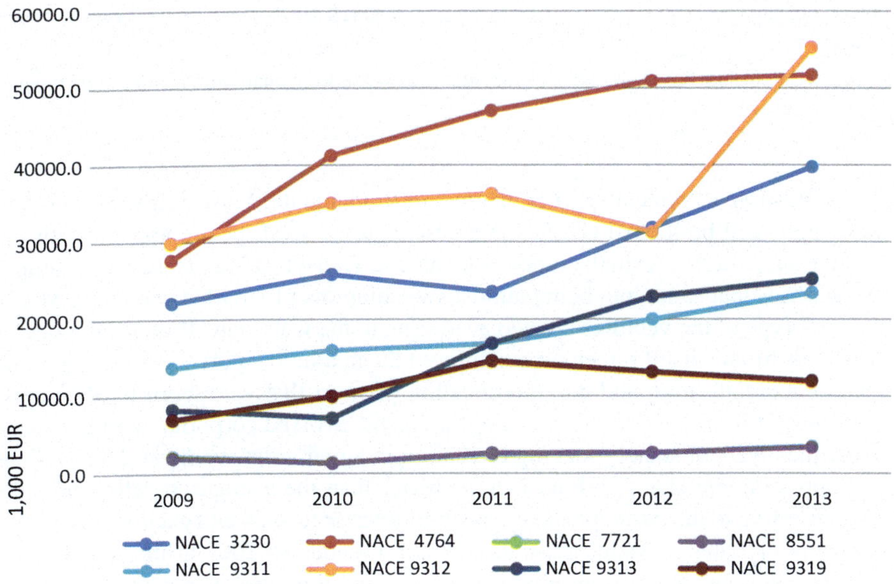

Fig. 5 Evolution of the value of total revenue per directly sport-related business field in Romania in 2009–2013. Sources: Calculation based on List of Companies (2015) and Romanian Ministry of Public Finance (2016).

Among the companies operating in the field of sport 63.5% showed a deficit in 2013. The value of the annual total profit was around 887 thousand euros, the average profit was 342 euros (Table 3), by far the most profitable industries are the activities of sport clubs followed by manufacture of sport goods. The largest profit obtained was 11.6 million euros realised by Football Club Steaua Bucuresti (Table 4).

Table 3 **Total and average profit by directly sport-related business field in Romania in 2013.**

Business field	Profit (1000 €)	Profit (1000 €/Company)
Activities of sport clubs	4331.0	54.1
Manufacture of sport goods	1330.7	26.6
Renting and leasing of recreational and sport goods	568.7	3.1
Sport and recreation education	−371.9	−3.6
Other sport activities	−442.3	−0.9
Retail sale of sporting equipment in specialized stores	−454.7	−0.9
Operation of sport facilities	−1558.8	−2.8
Fitness facilities	−2515.5	−4.0
Total	887.1	0.3

Sources: Calculation based on List of Companies (2015) and Romanian Ministry of Public Finance (2016).

To illustrate a "typical sport company" in Romania the Master Adventure (MA) case study will be looked at. This is a case of a classical local company with the "Protestant pattern". A small company located in Transylvania is a talkative example of the series that came into being amidst switching over to market economy. MA is the prototype of the ventures created according to the weberian "Protestant model", which positioned itself rather successfully to the market of sport services, as part of the commercialisation and commodification of sport that were born by their own resources. It is oriented to the actors of the freshly evolved corporate world, respectively the layers of society seeking recreation in larger cities, younger than average and upper middle class, with an income better than the average. It sells adrenalin and adventure to the participants of team buildings or to weekend excursionists. The company operates in Vadul Crişului and was founded in 2007 at the initiative of friends, who enjoyed adventurous watersport, and thus discovered the Criş River close to Oradea suitable for rafting. With three employees in 2010 they floated around a thousand people on the river. In 2014 they had six trained staff members, helped by two drivers to carry the tourists. Their clientele grew gradually; in 2011 they served approximately 1500 persons; in 2013 the number of those seeking adventure grew to 4000 according to the MA owners.

MA is a prototype of an average actor in the sport sector: the initiators started the company out of their personal motivation and for making financial profit. Thus they found a market niche in which the demand is continuously increasing as large companies are settling down in the region and as the middle class is getting stronger. Also the corporate organisational culture is spreading and increasing the role of team buildings in natural settings. More and more back-packer tourists arrive in the region, just like the so-called 'escapists', who wish to go to nature. These special categories constitute a good and sound demand. Unfortunately, MA's contribution to the development of mass or competitive sport is almost non-existent. Due to their high prices, they are available only for a narrow segment of the population. In spite of their successful operation, the market actors providing similar narrow targeted services like MA also appear as bearers of the inequalities with respect to access to sport.

Regarding the invested capital 6.8% of the sport companies that are active in Romania have also foreign capital. Although the number of these companies is relatively small, the influence of foreign investment is significant for these companies. In comparison with the companies disposing solely on the domestic capital, the companies that have also gotten foreign capital have a double revenue (Fig. 6). Similarly, the average number of employees of the companies with foreign capital (4.8%) exceeds by far the average number of employees in the case of companies with exclusively domestic capital (2.5%) (Fig. 7).

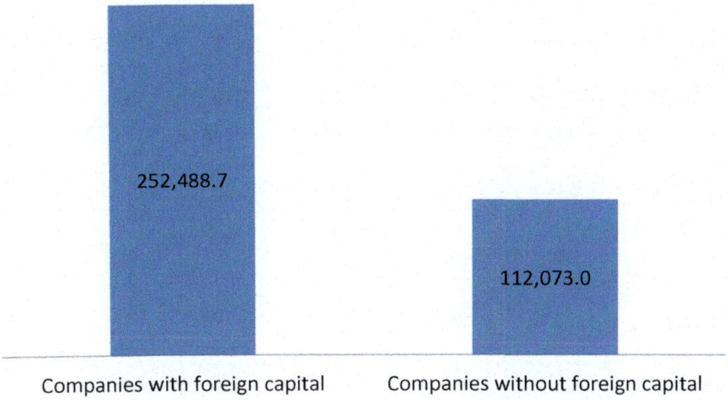

Fig. 6 Average financial revenue (EUR) of the private sport companies with and without foreign capital in Romania in 2013. Sources: Calculation based on List of Companies (2015) and Romanian Ministry of Public Finance (2016).

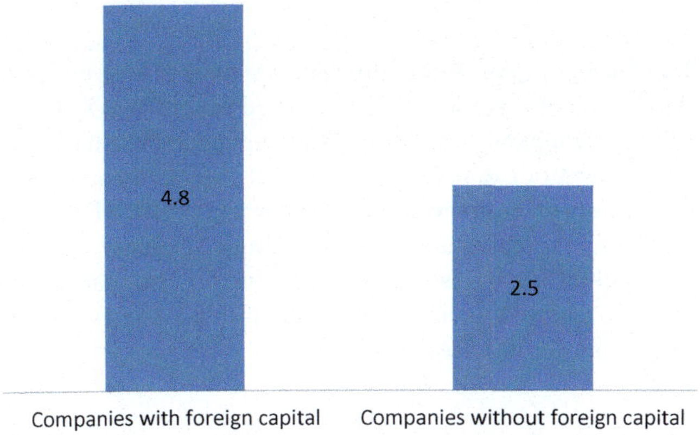

Fig. 7 Average number of staff in companies with and without foreign capital in Romania in 2013. Sources: Calculation based on List of Companies (2015) and Romanian Ministry of Public Finance (2016).

The profile of the biggest private sport companies by revenue (Table 4) supports the initial statement that the formation of the sector follows four major patterns. These are the privatization of the former state-owned entities, direct foreign investments, new local companies and other atypical patterns.

Table 4 Biggest private sport companies by revenue in Romania in 2013.

Company	NACE code	County	Year of foundation	Staff (n)	Revenue (1000 €)	Profit (1000 €)
Fotbal Club Steaua Bucuresti SA	9312	IF	2003	48	36,052.8	11,606.6
Hervis Sports and Fashion SRL	4764	B	2013	154	15,607.4	−12.0
Transilvania Sport Equipment SRL	3230	B	2006	597	12,742.2	352.2
Natural Studio SRL	3230	MS	2007	192	9988.1	−155.0
World Class Romania SA	9313	B	2004	128	8199.3	445.7
Dinamo 1948 SA	9312	B	2001	82	7888.4	−1629.5
Desaga Design SRL	3230	B	2005	170	6456.3	274.0
Fotbal Club Petrolul SA	9311	PH	1999	65	3874.2	1481.8
Ramisa Universal SRL	3230	B	2009	293	3775.2	543.5
Sporting Club SA	9312	VS	2005	36	3664.9	−1270.9

Sources: List of Companies (2015); Romanian Ministry of Public Finance (2016).

Leading Football Clubs

The football sector is complex. Officially there are three NACE codes regulating the football. Based on the observations it is also usual for clubs to hide the revenues in complex circles of companies and non profit organizations. It is common to use caritative foundations, for example Fundatia CFR 1909 Cluj, and other NGOs connected to club owners or political parties to hide the profit. Moreover, we can see that nine Premiership football clubs are not profitable, and only six of them declared some profit. Four clubs are in insolvency, and/or under criminal investigation. This is why there is no data on their revenue and profits. The main features of the Premiership clubs are summarized in Table 5.

Table 5 Romanian Premiership football clubs in 2013.

Club	Formal name	City	NACE code	Staff (n)	Revenue (1000 €)	Profit (1000 €)
Astra	As. FC Astra	Giurgiu	9313	53	566.2	−2933.2
Ceahlaul	FC Ceahlăul SA	Piatra Neamț	9319	40	1925.8	−157.9
CFR 1907	Fotbal Club CFR 1907 Cluj SA	Cluj-Napoca	9312	73	3662.0	−2877.9
Concordia	Clubul Sportiv Concordia Chiajna	Chiajna	9312	44	2967.6	534.3
CSMS Iasi	As. "Club Sportiv Municipal Politechnica Iași"	Iasi	9313	n/a	n/a	n/a
Dinamo	Dinamo 1948 SA	Bucharest	9312	82	7888.4	−1629.5
FC Brasov	FC Brasov SA	Brasov	9319	37	1698.0	76.2
FC Vaslui	Sporting Club SA	Vaslui	9312	36	3664.9	−1270.9
Gaz Metan	Club Sportiv "Gaz Metan" Medias	Medias	9319	n/a	n/a	n/a
Gloria	As. Club Fotbal Gloria 1922 Bistrita	Bistrita	9319	30	478.6	−480.9
Otelul	FC Oțelul SA	Galati	9312	70	2558.9	−339.1
Pandurii	Clubul Sportiv "Pandurii" Tg-Jiu	Târgu Jiu	9312	n/a	n/a	n/a
Petrolul Ploiesti	FC Petrolul SA	Ploiești	9311	65	3874.2	1481.8
Rapid	FC Rapid SA	Bucharest	9319	16	1801.2	n/a
Steaua	FC Steaua Bucutești	Mogosoaia	9312	48	36,052.8	11,606.6
Turnu Severin	FC Drobeta-Turnu Severin SA	Turnu Severin	9312	n/a	n/a	n/a
U Craiova	Club Sportiv U Craiova SA	Craiova	9312	16	263.3	−1042.2
U Cluj	FC Universitatea Cluj SA	Cluj-Napoca	9312	33	1505.1	−835.1
Viitorul	FC Viitorul SA	Constanta	9312	42	1427.1	647.8

Sources: List of Companies (2015); Romanian Ministry of Public Finance (2016).

The average number of staff is 49, which relatively low. In the Premiership clubs altogether there are 685 employees, which represent almost 10% of all workforce engaged in the private sport sector. Taking into the consideration the declared total revenues we find 70.3 million euros, responsible for almost one third of the total revenue registered in the private sport sector (Table 5). The close relation with the political field and corruption scandals (Péter, 2014) is another feature of football sector.

The Story of the Privatisation of FC Steaua: How the "Voluntary" Creditor Became a "Happy" Owner

FC Steaua is the biggest and the most popular football club in Romania, created as an important bastion of the communist power under the patronage of the Ministry of Defence, in 1947, following the Soviet model (Péter, 2014). The communist system assigned a strategic role to sport in the formation of the "New Man". The army had a crucial role in the process of Stalinisation of the society, and later on, it excelled in the spreading and strengthening of the national-communist ideology and personality cult after 1971 (Tismăneanu, 2006). Steaua won the European Champion Clubs' Cup in 1986, and was an integral part of the CSA sport club. CSA means Clubul Sportiv al Armatei, or the Army Sport Club. At that time, various individual figures connected to the communist power appeared around the team, many of whom became influential business people, politicians or sport leaders after the change of the regime. Among them was the young George Becali. Before 1989 he maintained good relationships with the players and provided them with fresh dairy products at the trainings, and thus became a rather popular person.

After 1989 the entire sport sector was reorganised. The Romanian Government Decree No.124/1991 regulated the reorganisation of the Romanian Olympic Committee, and promoted private sport clubs, especially football associations with an independent status (Romanian Government, 1991a). The Romanian Professional League (LPF) was formed in 1992, with only professional and private clubs among its members. Concurrently the reorganisation of the new football championship took place. The main point was that football sections needed to be separated from the CSA sport clubs and continue as independent entities.

Real changes happend in 1998, when the football section of the CSA was formally separated from the mother association in the ownership of the Ministry of Defence, and the Steaua București Not-for-Profit Sports Association was formed confirmed by Government Decree No. 66/1991 (Romanian Government, 1991b). The Association with 89 members at the moment was chaired by Viorel Păunescu, a businessman with close ties to political power. The association had to be financially self-reliant. Financial balance sheets however, showed continuous losses, and the transfer values of the players were marked down and displayed it as losses. This practice was considered as intentional financial manoeuvre and artificial by the sport press of the time. Under the given circumstances, Gigi Becali offered a credit to the team, which the association failed to pay off. According to some sources the credit amounted 200,000 euros while according to Fanatik Sportspaper (2015) the later owners talked about 30 million euros. The real figures were never made public.

In January 2003 the nonprofit association in community ownership was reorganised: it become a commercial association completely in private ownership, called SC FCSB SA owned by Gigi Becali as its majority shareholder. The financial basis for the transaction originated from the compensation of the unpaid credit of the

Association. The transaction was approved by the Government Decree No. 128/2003 (Romanian Government, 2003). Later on the share of the association ended up in the ownership of Gigi Becali.

This case is instructive and demonstrates well one, but by far not the only example of the mechanisms of the evolution in the sport sector. In this scheme, a public-private partnership was created in the first step with the support of the high-ranking army generals and politicians with close ties to the power, in a changing legal environment, that referred to mutual benefits. In fact, they establish an independent legal entity from the marketable part of the public proprietorship. In this case, it is a sport association in corporate ownership, which is separated from the mother entity. In the second step this is intentionally devaluated, made to show a deficit, driven close to a bankruptcy situation. In the third step, the presumptive owner credits the association with a credit, which the latter is obviously unable to pay back. In the fourth step, the parties reach a peaceful agreement, out of court, in which the creditor accepts the "aided entity" in exchange for the credit, thus becoming its fully qualified owner. This state of affairs must only be validated by the law-makers, which, due to the existing political connections, is a mere formality. This is one of the patterns along which some of the actors of the current private sport sector – especially in highly popular football – appear. With this case, an important mechanism is shown how some of the units functioning in the current private sport field came to exist.

The Big Picture is Completed with the Third Case Study – Tennis Player Simona Halep Phenomenon

Simona Halep is the best-known sportswoman of the Aromanian sub-ethnic group, reached to be the distinguished fourth on the Women Tennis Association ranking by 2016 (her best position was the second place in 2014). As a tennis star, she called forth the admiration of many with her determination and modesty since 2013. Yet she is not interesting for this case because her exemplary habitude, but rather because her rise and the factors of her career are evocative from the perspective of the present functioning of the sector. She is an example for the exceptional case when someone becomes highly successful as a result of the support from the family and the relatives – both professionally and financially. Halep is "fanatic" in following an individual journey and a "one-person company" pattern. By that she is also indicative for the number of reasons why the present Romanian sport sector could not become professionalised (Petracovschi & Terret, 2013) and why the failure of the Romanian sport dominated by the private sector was inevitable at the Olympic Games in Rio (Paul, 2016b). The Halep phenomenon is a positive exception that proves the rule of insufficient functioning.

The focus will be on the social factors, which have defined her career, and on the functions that the private sport sector could hardly fulfil by itself (i.e., without the support of the state). Halep was born in 1991 in the Constanța, to a family of entrepreneurs. Her father wanted to fulfil his sport-related dreams with great sacrifices. The talented girl took up tennis at the age of four, and until she turned 15, the family paid for all the expenses related to her sport equipment, trainings and the increasing expenses of her participation at competitions. The family even contracted a loan to cover the annual expenses of 30 50,000 euros (Paul, 2014), which was a heavy burden to the family venture. After that, Corneliu Idu, the owner of Tennis Club Idu Mamaia took Simona under his wings, with undertaking financial sacrifices. Later on, another Aromanian, a football star Gică Hagi also privately sponsored Halep reputedly with half a million euros. The success did not fail to come, private investments were refunded, because by 2008 the girl had won the junior category of the Roland Garros. Now she is managed by the 1978 Rolland Garros winner Virginia Ruzici. Quite successfully, since 2013 Simona has been in the forefront of WTA.

The story is instructive in the light of the function of the private sport sector. There are no tennis academies in Romania (Paul, 2016a). The personal undertaking is an exclusive "grassroots organisation" that is organised as a network along almost fanatic determination, together with family and friendly ties, and with the central nucleus being the Halep family itself. The ethnic component is not to be neglected either. Other Aromanians helped her to reach success based on solitarity and common trust, which is a valuable capital in such network companies (Csata, 2015). Her carrier was strengthened by local gym teachers with a sense of vocation, offering their help on a quasi-volunteer basis, and who recognised her talent.

The role of the state is nil in this equation and the community sport sector only played a role in it insofar the elementary and secondary schools did not obstruct her sporting career, respectively the gym teachers supported the outstanding talent voluntarily. The inadequate development of the private sport sector was well shown with the fact that until 2013 Halep's career evolved in parallel with that, mostly abroad and its crucial actors did not play a significant role either in the cultivation of the talent of the tennis player or in her promotion. The case shows well that the financially important actors of the sport sector do not form an integrated cluster that could be able to co-operate with the sport sphere owned by the state in discovering talents, their sponsorship, nurturing and promotion. The latter has largely withdrawn from supporting of sport, only sustaining football, which pays off politically.

The defining elements of the Halep pattern become even more apparent if the phenomenon is compared with the patterns of the centralist and elitist system of the sport sector operated by the previous political regime, also for propagandistic reasons, and which facilitated the success of gymnast Nadia Comăneci. The comparison is done with the dimensions of the essential significance. Nadia became a world star for the state reasons and at public expense, was trained in the school of gymnastic in Deva, in a rigorously strict system similar to military training, far from the family (Massiera & Ionescu, 2005, 382), whereas Simona was training in clubs that were exclusively funded by the uncertain family funds and operated by personal resources. The international success of Nadia is a common cause, a national interest, backed up by the entire state apparatus (Meyers, 2016), whereas in the case of Simona the role of the state has been insignificant, and only started to exploit the success at the time when Halep was a global superstar in order to acquire political capital. Interestingly, also the general judgment of the two excellent sportswomen is different. Following her 10 points in the 1976 Olympic Games in Montreal the whole society uniformly and sincerely looked up to Nadia, respected her deeply and could identify with her. Strangely this is not happening in the case of Simona: although she is also surrounded by recognition, the audience often bursts out into indignation over her lost matches. Moreover, the earlier ATP winner (1973) Ilie Năstase, one of the most vehement critics of Halep, passed on sexist remarks about her.

What is the lesson to be learned from all this? Although both cases are about successful sport careers, they are both unsustainable and extreme models of operation, which can only occasionally lead to outstanding success. In the case of Nadia, the centralised operation of the sport sector organised strictly under the principles of the state monopoly brought success. In Halep's case, a non-reproducible family venture created conditions of the decentralised and fragmented operation of a private sector that was left alone following the total withdrawal of the state from sport, an eventually brought success for a champion grown out from a talented little girl.

The true problem is that in the present day private sport sector lacks the structural conditions that could lead to the success of an athlete arriving from a functioning mass sport. The spectacular failure of Romanian sportsmen and -women at the Olympics in Rio talks for itself.

Conclusions

Based on the statistical and qualitative data it can be concluded that the private sector is underdeveloped when its share among the active commercial entities is looked at. However, since 2000 it has represented a dynamically expanding domain. Most sport-related companies are found in the areas of industries like fitness services, the operation of sport facilities (e.g., pitches and gyms), as well as the retail sale of sport equipment. The number of sport clubs, that are considered to be among the most important actors of sport activities is low.

When analysing the budgets of the sport companies, it becomes clear that the first cluster is formed by the sport clubs, companies dealing with the retail sale of sporting equipment and those interested in the manufacture of sport goods. The clubs on the top of the list include those that operate in professional football. This denotes that the population is rather passive than active in sport pursuers. The other two well accomplishing branches support the initial assumption of this article that sport sector got commercialised and commodified and denote layer specific leisure sport. A sign of that is the economic importance of the companies that sell and produce sport goods. The second cluster is formed around the fitness services and facilities used by the middle class. These two branches give the largest number of companies. While in terms of their revenue these are smaller, yet by their large number they have a strong impact in the sector.

The private sector has taken over the role of the monopolist state in organising sport. The emphasis of the state sector has drastically declined and the state practically withdrew from the organisation practices of sport. In the meantime, the community sport sector remains weak, and primarily functions informally. Metaphorically it could be stated that the sport sector is still struggling in the trap of socialism (or its inheritance) and (wild) capitalism.

Moreover, due to the commercialisation and commodification, sport has become a needy stock: the elderly, the rural inhabitants, the poor, people low income have been forced to gradually give up in sport: the current sport sector serves a narrow, urban layer, with higher income. A new type of inequality has come into being with respect to the access to sport services, a phenomenon that can have a negative impact in the health of society in general.

Lacking mass sport culture, the slowly shaping civil society was unable to rebuild the community sport sector that had been wound up between 1945 and 1947. Therefore, the defining part of the internal structure of the entire sport sector is made up of the units that are shaped by the capitalist logic. As a result of deindustrialisation after 2000 (Pásztor, 2015) the sport establishments were either privatised or incorporated into real estate developments, demolished, and office buildings, or residential parks were built on their locations. This reshapeed the urban landscape (Pásztor, 2006), but also led to the disappearance of the sport facilities that could be used by the masses.

To sum it up: the sport sector in Romania is relatively underdeveloped and fragmented with a low number of actors, who have become strongly commercialised and commodified. This has generated new type of inequality, while also showing a tendency concentrated geographically and in space. At the same time, it is a dynamically a developing sector, which is estimated to become diversified and bearing the possibility to generate mass sport.

References

Bijker, W. E., Hughes, T. P., & Pinch, T. (1987). The social construction of facts and artifacts: Or how the sociology of science and the sociology of technology might benefit each other. In W. E. Bijker, T. P. Hughes, & T. Pinch (Eds.), *The social construction of technical systems: New directions in the sociology and history of technology* (pp. 17–50). Cambridge, MA: MIT Press.

Bogdan, G. (2014). Daciada. *Revista Historia*. Retrieved June 11, 2016 from http://www.historia.ro/exclusiv_web/general/articol/daciada-olimpiada-romaneasca

Ciobotaru, D. (2015). Sportul–mijloc de implementare a comunismului [Sport as Instrument to Implement Communism]. *Revista Historia*. Retrieved June 10, 2016 from http://www.historia.ro/exclusiv_web/actualitate/articol/sportul-mijloc-implementare-comunismului-n-rom-nia

Collins, R. (1994). *Four tradition of sociological theory*. New York, NY/Oxford, UK: Oxford University Press.

Csata, Z. (2015). Ethnicity and economy. A reserach agenda for Transylvania. *Erdélyi Társadalom, 13*(3), 9–24.

European Commission. (2014). *Sport and physical activity*. Special Eurobarometer 412/Wave 80.2. Brussels, Belgium: D-G Education and Culture.

Fanatik Sportspaper. (2015). *STEAUA. Hagi între Becali și Armată: "A luat clubul pe NIMIC!"* [STEAUA. Hagi between Bacali and the Army: He took the Club for FREE]. Retrieved June 12, 2016 from http://www.fanatik.ro/steaua-hagi-intre-becali-si-armata-luat-clubul-pe-nimic-424098

INSSE. (2016). Institutul National de Statistica [National Institute of Statistics]. Retrived March 17, 2016 from http://www.insse.ro/cms/

Léderer, P. (2002). *A szociológus, a módszerei, meg a szövege. Rögeszme-félék a mesterségről* [The Sociologist, his methods and its texts. Obsessions on profession]. Budapest, Hungary: Új Mandátum.

List of Companies. (2015). *CD data*. Bucharest, Romania: Borg Design.

Massiera, B., & Ionescu, S. (2005). Practica sportivă în România sub Influența politică a istoriei [Sport practice in Romania under political influence of history]. *Analele UVT-Seria EFS, 62*(7), 376–384.

Meyers, D. (2016). *The end of perfect ten. The making and breaking of gymnastics' tops scores: From Nadia to now*. New York, NY: Touchstone.

MTS. Guvernul României. (2016). *Strategia de dezvoltare a sportului în Romania 2016–2032* [Development strategy on sport in Romania 2016–2032]. Bucharest, Romania: MTS.

Pásztor, G. (2006). *Városszociológia. Elméletek és problémák* [Urban sociology. Theories and problems]. Cluj, Romania: Cluj University Press.

Pásztor, G. (2015). Changing reality. Deindustrialization and its narratives. In A. Lošonc & A. Ivanišević (Eds.), *Institutional assumptions about socio-economic dynamics in East and Central Europe* (pp. 23–38). Novi Sad, Serbia: Faculty of Technical Sciences.

Paul, L. (2014). Talent în mișcare [Talent on the move]. *Sinteza, 1*(4), 178–180.

Paul, L. (2016a). Prăbușirea de pe bârnă [Crashing down from buck]. *Sinteza, 3*(28), 202–208.

Paul, L. (2016b). Rio 2016, Strigătul Medaliilor [Rio 2016, Medals shout]. *Sinteza, 3*(32), 223–228.

Péter, L. (2014). *Football and society in Romania. Issues and problems in soccer discourses* (PhD dissertation). University of Jyväskylä, Jyväskylä.

Péter, L. (2016). *A labdarugás szociológiája* [The sociology of football]. Cluj, Romania: Cluj University Press.

Petracovschi, S., & Terret, T. (2013). From best to worst? Romania and its nostalgia for Olympic successes. *The International Journal of the History of Sport, 30*(7), 774–788.

Ritzer, G., & Stepnisky, J. (2007). *Sociological theory*. New York, NY: McGraw-Hill Companies.

Romanian Government. (1991a). *Hotărârea nr. 124/1991 privind organizarea şi funcționarea Comitetului Olimpic Român* [GD 124/1991 on Organization of Romanian Olympic Committee]. Bucharest, Romania.

Romanian Government. (1991b). *Hotărârea nr. 66/1991 privind infiintarea Asociatiei de sportive de fotbal Steaua Bucuresti cu scop nepatimonial* [Government Decree No. 66/1991 on the foundation of Steaua Bucuresti Not-for-Profit Sports Association]. Bucharest, Romania.

Romanian Government. (2000). *Legea sportului 69/2000* [Law of Sport 69/2000]. Bucharest, Romania.

Romanian Government. (2003). *Hotărârea nr. 128/2003 cu privire la abrogarea Hotararii Guvernului nr. 66/1999 privind transmiterea in folosinta gratuita a unui imobil situat in municipiul Bucuresti* [Romanian Government Decree No. 128/2003 on the Revocation of Government Decree 66/1999 on the free usage of a real estate building situated in Bucharest]. Bucharest, Romania.

Romanian Government. (2011). *Legea Educației 1/2011* [Law of Education 1/2011]. Bucharest, Romania.

Romanian Ministry of Public Finance. (2016). *Agenti economici si institutii publice – Date de identificare, informatii fiscal, bilanturi* [Economical entities and public institutions – Identification data, fiscal informations, balance sheets]. Retrieved March 22, 2016 from http://www.mfinante.gov.ro/pjuridice.html?pagina=domenii&cs=5705570d

Romanian Trade Registry. (2016). *Inmatriculari de persoane fizice si juridice* [Registrations for individuals and companies]. Retrieved March 28, 2016 from http://www.onrc.ro/index.php/ro/statistici

TEMPO Data Series. (2016). *Anuarul statistic al Romaniei – Serii de timp* [Statistical yearbook of Romania – Time series]. Retrieved August 21, 2016 from http://statistici.insse.ro/shop/?page=publD&lang=ro&publ_id=22

Tismăneanu, V. (2006). *Raport final. Comisia prezidențială pentru analiza comunismului* [Final report: Presidential Commission on the Analysis of Communism]. Bucharest, Romania: Presedinția României.

Woods, R. (2011). *Social issues in sport*. Champaign, IL: Human Kinetics.

SPAIN: Evolution and Characteristics of the Private Sport Sector – Focus on Fitness Centres and Gyms

Ramón Llopis-Goig, Anna Vilanova, and Jorge Martín Sánchez

Selected country facts (in 2013)	
Capital	Madrid
Geographical size (km^2)	505,944
Population (million)	46.73
GDP (euro per capita)	22,000
GDP (per capita in PPS)	90
Annual net earnings average (€)	20,062

The Organisational Framework of Sport in Spain

The Spanish sport system is an outcome of the collaboration between the public, voluntary and private sectors. Public institutions make up a coherent network of organizations, and play a predominant role in the sport system. This phenomenon can be explained by the social-historical nature of Spain, which was late in becoming developed as a democratic society and over-relying on the public sector (Burriel & Puig, 1999; Puig, Sarasa, Junyent, & Oró, 2003). The voluntary sector is associative by nature, and it includes the Spanish Olympic Committee, sport federations, sport clubs, the groupings of clubs and sport federations, sport promotional entities, and professional leagues. The private sector encompasses sport service companies,

R. Llopis-Goig (✉)
Faculty of Social Sciences, University of Valencia, Valencia, Spain
e-mail: ramon.llopis@uv.es

A. Vilanova • J. Martín Sánchez
National Institute of Physical Education of Catalonia, Catalonia, Spain
e-mail: anna.vilanova@inefcgiseafe.com; jsanchezmartin@hotmail.com

A. Laine, H. Vehmas (eds.), *The Private Sport Sector in Europe*, Sports Economics, Management and Policy 14, https://doi.org/10.1007/978-3-319-61310-9_18

professional sport clubs, fitness and wellness centres, and gyms. The composition of these three sectors is presented in detail in Fig. 1.

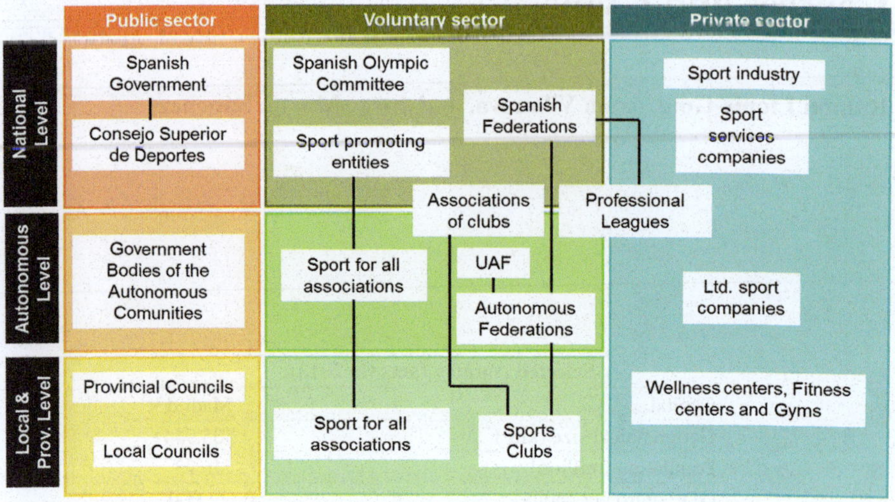

Fig. 1 The Spanish sport system. Source: Adapted from Puig et al. (2003).

The Public Sector

The public sector has a decentralized political structure and it operates at three levels: national, regional and local. There is no ministry of sport in Spain. Instead, the highest responsible organism for the sport sector is the National Sports Agency CSD (Consejo Superior de Deportes). The CSD disperses the government's sport-related mandates to the various sport federations and sport organizations throughout the Spanish territory. It is also responsible for authorising and revoking the Spanish sport federations' licensing. In addition, the CSD, in conjunction with the federations, develops the federations' goals, programmes, budgets and structures. It also grants economic subsidies to the federations, as well as to other sport organizations and associations.

The CSD interacts in collaboration with other autonomous communities, which are self-governed Spanish regions. It also represents Spain in sport-related issues at the European Union level. Due to the fact that sport is included in the Treaty of Lisbon, the Spanish Secretary of State for Sport attends the EU Council of Sport Ministers when it meets formally (Puig, Martínez, & García, 2010).

Despite the differences that exist between the autonomous communities, they have the following common responsibilities at a regional level: the promotion, construction and management of sport facilities; the overseeing and coordinating of the sport federations on a regional scope; the coordinating, promoting and overseeing of the sport associations; the legislative authority overseeing sport policies at a regional level; the granting of sport subsidies; physical education, and other school-related sport activities. Similar responsibilities are also undertaken in relation to the so-called 'diputaciones provinciales' (provincial or district councils), but they mainly focus on supporting local councils. (Puig et al., 2010.)

Municipal governments play an essential role within the sport sector at the local level. Municipalities not only have an implementing role, but they actively intervene with the sport policy as well. The local entities have the authority to construct and manage local sport facilities, as well as develop sport programs at all age levels, and assist the sport clubs that are located in their area. The municipal governments' sport councils offer sport facilities to clubs and individuals, and they organise local competitions and manage municipal sport training centres. (Lera-López & Lizalde-Gil, 2013.)

The Voluntary Sector

The voluntary sector is also present at the national, regional and local levels. Sport clubs at the local level constitute the framework of the voluntary sector. Each club may be assigned to one or several governing bodies for sport at the regional level (regional federations), which in turn are linked with the governing bodies at the national level. Since 2015, the Spanish Federal Sport Association (Asociación del Deporte Federado Español) has been acting as an umbrella organisation at the national level, coordinating some of the governing bodies (CSD, 2015).

The Spanish Olympic Committee is a non-profit legal entity, and serves the public interest at large. Some of its objectives include developing the Olympic movement, and the diffusion of the Olympic ideals. It integrates 30 federations corresponding to the various Olympic categories, and represents Spain in the International Olympic Committee. The Spanish Paralympic Committee was founded in 1995 (Ramos & Martínez de Haro, 2009).

Sport Federations are private legal entities that function at the national level. Sport federations include sport clubs, regional federations, professional leagues, and other entities that are interested in the promotion and development of a specific sport on a national scope. Contrary to what happens in other European countries, there is not one unique coordinating entity that collects the petitions from the different regional federations, therefore, each regional federation must handle the negotiations with the proper public authorities. The exception is in Catalonia, where the Sports Federation Union of Catalonia (UFEC – Unió de Federacions Esportives Catalanes) handles this task (Iglesias & Tarragó, 2012).

Professional leagues are entities included in the sport federations, as mentioned in the previous paragraph. Professional leagues are private legal entities that are autonomous organizations, operating out of their corresponding federation. They are made up of those clubs that participate in the official professional competitions at the national level. The main professional leagues are The National Professional Football League (LPF), The Association of Basketball Clubs (ACB), and The Association of Handball Clubs (ASOBAL).

In accordance with the 1990 "Law of Sport" (Ley del Deporte, 1990), *sport clubs* are private legal associations consisting of self-employed owners and companies, whose objective is to promote one or more types of sport; to promote sport among their members; and to participate in sport activities and competitions. Sport clubs are classified into "elementary" clubs, "basic" clubs, and Sports Corporations (SAD – Sociedades Anónimas Deportivas). Elementary clubs have a simple legal structure, and they are dedicated to practising sport and participating in competitions at the local or regional levels. Basic clubs have more complex legal structures, as they are incorporated entities. Both may participate in sport competitions if they sign up with their corresponding federation. On the other hand, those clubs that participate in the official sport activities professionally, or at a national level, must form a Sports Corporation, as described in Article 15 of the Spanish Sports Act. (Ley del Deporte, 1990.)

It behoves to mention the existence of *sport clubs' associations* and *sport promotion entities* – both described in the Spanish Sports Act – which are both under national regulations and operate outside the regions. The sport clubs' associations have the exclusive objective to develop sport proceedings in those events and activities which are not contemplated by the sport federations; the sport promotion entities function as promoters and organisers of sport and physical activities that are leisure, educational or social in nature. (Ley del Deporte, 1990.)

The Private Sector

The Spanish private sport sector is made up of the sport industry, sport services companies, professional sport clubs, and fitness and wellness centres and gyms. While the sport industry operates at a national level, the gyms and wellness centres are based locally, although they frequently form chains that operate at the national level. In 2015, there were 31,139 organisations in the Spanish private sector whose main economic activity was sport-related (DIRCE, 2015). This figure represents 0.98% of the total companies registered in the country (DIRCE, 2015).

After describing the structure and organizational framework of the Spanish sport sector, the next section offers an analysis of the evolution and principal characteristics of the private sport sector in Spain during the last years and it includes information pertaining to the number of existing organisations, legal structures, number of employees, and territorial layouts. As a complement to this analysis, the third section focuses on studying the emerging and developmental processes of a specific type of private sport organisation in Spain: the fitness centres and gyms. An in-depth analysis of this kind of organisations has been undertaken as they have become especially successful in Spain in the last decades. A second reason to choose this kind of organisations has been the availability of data. The chapter concludes with a section that discusses the results, integrating the various empirical findings.

Muscle and Fitness Room in the Centre Esportiu Municipal Horta (Municipal Sports Centre, CEM Horta) in Barcelona. This centre is an example of the collaboration between private and public sport sectors in Spain. It is managed under the government concession by the company Horta Esportiva. In addition to the Muscle and Fitness Room, the facilities of CEM Horta include a football turf pitch, used by more than 250 players who form all the teams of Unió Atlètica d'Horta, and 33 × 25 m swimming pool, used by the swimming and water polo teams of Unió Esportiva d'Horta. The swimming pool is also used by all neighbourhood schools as the students attend swimming courses. *Photo: Horta Esportiva.*

The Private Sport Sector Development

Most (77.1%) of the 31,139 sport organizations in Spain in 2015 carried out activities as classified in the Section 931 of the "National Classification of Economic Activities Code" (CNAE-2009)[1]. The number of organizations associated with sport activities in Section 931[2] has continually risen during the last years, increasing from 16,291 entities in 2010, to 24,003 in 2015, which is equivalent to a growth of 47.3%. Of the remaining organizations, 6932 (22.3%) were specialty sport retailers (Section 4764) and 204 (0.7%) sport articles manufacturers (Section 323), as illustrated in Table 1[3].

[1] CNAE-2009 is the Spanish equivalent of the *Statistical classification of economic activities in the European Community* (NACE Rev. 2, 2008). Section 931 of CNAE 2009 does not include the development of marinas, nor ski resorts (included in Section 9329).

[2] Section 931 of the CNAE 2009 includes the activities referred to the management of sports facilities (931.1), sport clubs' activities (931.2), private sport centres or gyms (931.3), and other sport activities (931.9).

[3] It has not been possible to include other sport activities, as the statistical sources available do not provide further breakdowns.

Table 1 Evolution of the number of organisations linked to sport in Spain in 2010–2015.

Type (CNAE-2009 section)	2010	2011	2012	2013	2014	2015
Sport Activities (931)	16,291	16,827	18,167	19,270	21,506	24,003
Sport articles manufacturing (323)	188	175	175	174	177	204
Retail commerce of sport articles (4764)	7743	7653	7669	7253	7052	6932
Total	**24,222**	**24,655**	**26,011**	**26,697**	**28,735**	**31,139**

Source: Research findings based on data obtained from DIRCE (2015).

As to their legal stature, 26% of the sport organisations correspond to self-employed owners (see Table 2), while the remaining 74% correspond to companies. Within the latter, the number of corporations has slightly declined in the last few years, from 500 existing in 2010, to 498 in 2015, representing 2.1% of the total. Limited Liability Corporations are the most common type of sport companies, which in 2015 accounted for 36% of the total, after having experienced a steady growth since 2010. Other legal structures, such as associations and institutions connected to sport, as well as different types of legal Spanish companies – civil associations, cooperatives, partnerships or joint ownerships – have steadily increased during the last few years, comprising 35.9% of the overall total.

Table 2 Evolution of the number of organizations of sport activities in Spain according to the number of workers employed in 2010–2015 (Section 931).

Type of organization	2010	2011	2012	2013	2014	2015	% 2015
Individuals	4117	4250	4636	4639	5399	6243	26.0
Companies	12,174	12,577	13,531	14,631	16,107	17,760	74.0
Corporations	*500*	*504*	*503*	*500*	*488*	*498*	*2.1*
Limited Liability Co. (LLC)	*5858*	*6041*	*6679*	*7320*	*7966*	*8642*	*36.0*
Other legal entities	*5816*	*6032*	*6349*	*6811*	*7653*	*8620*	*35.9*
Total	**16,291**	**16,827**	**18,167**	**19,270**	**21,506**	**24,003**	**100**

Source: Research findings based on data obtained from DIRCE (2015).

Taking all this data into consideration, it is not surprising that a study about sport economics unveiled that it is very difficult to obtain reliable information from smaller sport companies and self-employed sport businesses (Arruza et al., 2011). Self-employed individuals make up a fourth of the total of these businesses. Most could be included within the special regime of self-employed workers that carry out their activities in one of the three groups in the Tax on Commercial and Professional Activities that are connected to sport. One may assume that sport trainers, coaches and sport professionals, as well as referees, retail workers, administrative personnel or sport betting business managers, are all included in the Tax on Commercial and Professional Activities (Martínez-Lemos & Romo-Pérez, 2015). Individual business people who are in charge of the gyms and adventure sport companies would have to be included in this special regime as well. The first economic studies on outdoor sport activities that were conducted in Catalonia (Olivera & Olivera, 1999) dealt with adventure sport companies. The researchers pinpointed the existence of a high percentage of sole proprietorships.

Regarding the number of workers within these sport organisations in Spain, 41.6% of the 24,003 of said organisations lack employees (see Table 3). This is a high percentage, but less than the average of the overall Spanish corporate industry; organisations without workers in 2015 made up 55% of the total amount.

Table 3 also shows that 41.8% of the organisations are small businesses with less than six workers, out of which 15.4% have between six and 49 workers, and the remaining 1.2% of the organisations employ 50 to 399 workers. On the other hand, between 2010 and 2015, sport organisations without any employees grew by 47.3% – the same growth as all the organisations combined – and the sport organisations with one or two workers had a slightly higher growth (47.9%) than those without employees. The growth in this same period was even greater among those companies that had three to five workers or six to nine workers, with increases of 59.2% and 83.3% respectively. Taking this data into consideration, one cannot conclude that only those sport organizations without workers have experienced growth in Spain during the recent economic downturn (Rocha & Aragón, 2012).

Table 3 Evolution of the number of sport activity organisations in Spain by number of employees in 2010–2015 (Section 931).

Number of employees	2010	2011	2012	2013	2014	2015	% 2015	% Δ 2015/2010
0	6786	7320	7857	7775	8828	9994	41.6	47.3
1–2	4737	4571	5041	5888	6484	7008	29.2	47.9
3–5	1901	1926	2060	2255	2592	3027	12.6	59.2
6–9	885	947	1044	1168	1452	1622	6.8	83.3
10–19	1132	1145	1210	1252	1356	1514	6.3	33.7
20–49	569	612	655	630	515	547	2.3	–3.9
50–99	146	170	179	164	141	153	0.6	4.8
100–199	108	104	90	87	86	89	0.4	–17.6
200–499	23	27	26	46	46	40	0.2	73.9
500–999	2	3	4	4	5	8	0.0	300.0
1000–4999	2	2	1	1	1	1	0.0	–50.0
5000 or more	–	–	–	–	–	–	–	–
Total	**16,291**	**16,827**	**18,167**	**19,270**	**21,506**	**24,003**	**100**	**47.3**

Source: Research findings based on data obtained from DIRCE (2015).

Among the larger sport organisations, those with 200–499 workers grew by 73.9%, from 23 to 40 entities, and those with 500–999 workers increased from two to eight entities. On the other hand, by 2015, the number of sport organisations with 1000–4999 employees shrank from two entities in 2010, to just one (see Table 3).

Regarding the sport organisations' territorial distribution, more than half (58.2%) is concentrated in four regions: 17% in Catalonia; 16.3% in Madrid; 14.7% in Andalusia, and 10.2% in Valencia. On the other hand, a study generated from the DIRCE using data from the year 2012 (Martínez-Lemos & Romo-Pérez, 2015), suggests the existence of a highly relative statistical correlation between the number of micro and small organisations within Section 931 (sport activities), the level of the Gross Domestic Product, and the autonomous communities' populations.

Structure and Characteristics of Fitness Centres and Gyms

During the last three decades in Spain, a new type of private initiative has evolved, consisting of fitness centres and gyms. This has instigated changes of how sport is perceived by a significant part of the population, leading to a large social demand for sport activities. This chapter is focused on the analysis of the evolution and current features of these centres, which constitute an essential part of the private sport sector in Spain.

At the end of the 1990's, fitness centres and gyms were attractive business activities from the economic standpoint. The fitness centre business was a developing market, generating a large return of investment, along with a clear growth trajectory. This was evidenced by the arrival of large multinational fitness centre companies at the Spanish market in the beginning of the first decade of the twenty-first century. Companies like Holmes Place, Esporta, Fitness First, and LA Fitness all had ambitious expansion plans, which covered the entire national territory, surpassing family gyms and small gym chains of the previous years, which were mainly dedicated to bodybuilding workouts.

Subsequently, a change in trends took place, leading to larger centres which were equipped with more advanced technology. Therefore, the activity and usage of the traditional free weight rooms – the previously focal activity – was pushed into the background. As a result of this new and upcoming trend, new centres emerged, offering a wider range of group classes and other services, such as cafeterias, hair salons, physical therapy, nutritional consultation, and day care facilities (Cámara, 2015). In addition, social gatherings, thematic activities and parties were offered, striving to obtain the users' further involvement in the centres (Dorado, 2006).

This business trend changed at the end of 2007 when the recession started, and it continues to have a lasting effect as of this writing. Subsequently, all sport business development plans were consequently altered. As a result, a new type of centre referred to as "low-cost gyms" started to emerge in Spain in 2009, shortly after the start of the recession, which had a major influence in the industry. During the same period, a new sport centre known as 'studios' or 'fitness boutiques' emerged into the private sport sector, having a huge influence on the sector's evolution. These *fitness boutiques* are specialised centres dedicated to a single physical sport activity, functional training, or as of 2013, a more personalised training through the utilisation of *whole body electromyostimulation*. (Cámara, 2015.)

Market research conducted by DBK[4] illustrates that, between 2000 and 2007, the fitness and gymnastic companies were growing at a constant rate of around 3%, comprising 4630 centres in 2007 (see Table 4). This growth was due to the expansion of the major chain operators, opening large fitness centres with a vast range of activities, and providing complementary and supplementary products and services. Additionally, as previously mentioned, there was a shrinkage in the number of smaller gyms – those that followed the traditional business model dedicated solely to martial arts or bodybuilding, or that failed to offer complementary services (Sánchez Martín, 2014).

In 2008 there were 4700 centres – 1.5% more than in the previous year – indicating the start of a slowdown in the growth rate, but still showing sustained growth in the expansion of large chains (see Table 4). The year 2009 was a turning point in the fitness centres' growth in Spain, since both the multinational fitness centres and the low-cost centre operators (which were introduced in Spain in 2009), started to halt their expansion plans as a consequence of the uncertainty created by the economic recession. Consequently, although fitness centres maintained a moderate growth rate, they were unable to counteract the large decline that caused the closing of the numerous centres affected by the recession. The effects of the economic downturn continued to ripple throughout the sector; in 2015 there were only 3900 fitness centres and gyms, 17% fewer than in 2008.

[4]This refers to the various editions of the *economic sector* studies conducted by the consulting company DBK about the private sport centres, classified as *gyms* (information available at: www.dbk.es). This classification excludes all public sport facilities, including those that have been licensed out by the government. The information used in this paper comes from this source, unless otherwise specified. The economic data related to this sector varies considerably from one source to another. This is due, in part, to the fact that there is not a clear understanding of what the scope of this sector is or what it entails. As an example, the numbers provided by KPMG for the year 2007 state that this sector had 6,000 sport centres and total annual revenue around 1.7 billion euros (information available at www.kpmg.es). Meanwhile, the National Federation of Sport Facilities Owners calculated that the number of these companies surpassed 8,000 entities in 2006. However, their definition included "those (companies) that are in the business of leisure sport, physical exercise, physical sport activity, and lifeguards" (information available at www.fneid.es). The National Institute of Statistics estimated that this sector of Section 926 (sports activities) of the 1993 National Classification of Economic Activities Codes was composed of 13,778 companies with revenues amounting to 5.729 billion euros in 2007 (information available at www.ine.es).

Table 4 Evolution of the fitness centres and gyms sector in Spain in 2005–2015.

	2005	**2006**	**2007**	**2008**	**2009**	**2010**	**2011**	**2012**	**2013**	**2014**	**2015**
Number of centres (n)	4370	4500	4630	4700	4600	4450	4300	4100	3950	3900	3900
Variation in no. of centres (%)	3.0	3.0	2.9	1.5	−2.1	−3.3	−3.4	−4.7	−3.7	−1.3	0.0
Market (MEUR)	920	1000	1050	1065	980	920	865	800	785	800	825
Market variation (%)	8.8	8.7	5.0	1.4	−8.0	−6.1	−6.0	−.5	−1.9	1.9	3.1

Source: Research findings based on data obtained from DBK (2015).

Regarding the economic data, the DBK research points out that the total revenues for the fitness centres and gyms grew at an annual rate of around 8% between the years 2000 and 2007 (Table 4). As an example, total revenues for this industry increased by 8.8% in 2005, and by 8.7% in 2006, reaching one billion euros that year. In 2007 industry revenues increased by 5% over the previous year – nearly 4% points less than the growth rate in 2006 – and in 2008 there was a mere 1.4% increase. Furthermore, in 2009 the effects of the recession led to a reduction in home expenditures, with widespread negative consequences: private sport centres' revenues suffered a severe contraction. Revenues fell by 8% in 2009, declining to 980 million euros. This drastic decrease in revenues continued incessantly until the year 2013, although somewhat more moderate during 2010, when the industry's revenues fell by 6.1% – to 920 million euros – which was the same amount of revenues as in 2005 (see Table 4).

The economic situation continued to worsen in 2011 and 2012. Revenues dropped by 6% in 2011, falling to 865 million euros. Meanwhile in 2012, the contraction was even greater, declining by 7.5% to 800 million euros. The largest contraction in 2012's revenues can be partly explained by the negative effects that the increase in the Value Added Tax had on demand as a whole. The increase in the VAT went into effect on 1 September 2012 after the mandate of the governmental decree. This increase raised the VAT by 13 points, from 8 to 21%. Numerous centres were forced to make the decision to bear this burden either partially or in its entirety, at the cost of a reduction in their operating margins, in order to prevent a possible loss of users. Revenues hit bottom in 2013. However, the percentage decrease was moderate, at 1.9%. In 2014 this tendency reversed, starting a recovery in the sector, experiencing a 1.9% increase in revenues during 2014.

Regarding the revenue composition, revenues from sport activities (members' dues) in 2008 represented 88% of the total revenues from fitness centres and gyms. The remaining percentage corresponded to the revenues related to other activities and optional services offered by the centres. This included personal trainers, beauty services, sales of clothing or sport items, and items from the cafeteria and vending, for example. In 2012, 90% of the total revenues came from sport activities, while only 10% corresponded to optional services. Therefore, proceeds from optional and complementary services declined, resulting in an increase in the percentage of revenues generated from sport activities. This is a clear illustration of how the fitness centre and gym patrons chose to cut back in complementary services during the two worse years of the Spanish recession.

After analysing the decrease of the revenues and their composition in depth, one might deduce that the impact of the recession caused customers to move away from fitness centres and gyms into less expensive forms of physical and sport activities, such as working out in one's own home or in public outdoor spaces. This trend coincided with behavioural and dynamic social patterns, as a result from changes in the corporal culture, individualism and post-materialism (Llopis-Goig, 2014).

Nevertheless, the number of private gym members and users has not stopped increasing in the last decades, as illustrated in Table 5. This is contrary to what some economic experts had forecasted, who foresaw a shift from the private sector to the public-owned centres. This data also illustrates the appeal of the *low-cost* centres, which in many cases offer an even more economical alternative than the municipal sport centres (Sánchez Martín, 2014).

Table 5 Evolution of the membership and use of gymnastics facilities in Spain in 1990–2015 (%).

Spanish population older than 15 years old who ...	1990	2000	2005	2010	2015
Is a private gym member	0	3	8	10	18
Realises his/her physical or sport activities in a private gym	7	8	8	13	23

Base: population older than 15 years old. Sources: Research findings from García-Ferrando and Llopis-Goig (2011; 2017).

As a result, the low-cost centres (which include the fitness centres that have introduced low-cost pricing in their membership rates) have been responsible for taking in the 'wanderers' who were price sensitive, but preferred to utilise sport facilities for their routine workouts. Low-cost centres, such as the multinational operators Basic-Fit, VivaGym, and McFit, or national chains such as Dream Fit, Altafit, and Fitness 19, have positioned their dues around 20 euros per month[5].

Upon review of the economic data and analysing the variation of the average revenues per private sport centre (see Table 6), a 14.9% decline occurred between 2008 and 2012. Average revenues per private sport centre went from a high of 227,000 euros per centre in the years 2007 and 2008, down to 195,000 euros per

[5] According to the 'Annual Study of the Spanish Fitness Market' (Life Fitness, 2015), in 32 per cent of these centres, monthly dues were between 30 and 40 euros, while in 27 per cent of the centres, they were between 20 and 30 euros. As a group, six of every ten centres had monthly dues between 20 and 40 euros. As an example, the price of the monthly dues at Basic-Fit and VivaGym in May, 2016 was between 15.95 and 24.90 euros in both cases, with the VAT included, both having the same access and usage conditions (unlimited entry).

centre in the year 2012. This notable decline in business revenues cannot be singularly caused by a minor reduction in revenues from optional and complementary services, but must necessarily encompass a reduction in revenues generated from sport activities (membership dues). In other words, private sport centre users reduced their expenditures in said facilities, looking for more economical options, such as low-cost centres.

Table 6 **Evolution of the average revenues in fitness centres and gyms in Spain in 2005–2015.**

Revenues	2005	2006	2007	2008	2009	2010	2011	2012	2013	2014	2015
MEUR	0.211	0.222	0.227	0.227	0.213	0.207	0.201	0.195	0.199	0.205	0.212
Variation (%)	–	5.2	2.3	0.0	−6.2	−2.8	−2.9	−3.0	2.1	3.0	3.4

Source: Research findings based on data obtained from DBK (2015).

The revenues per centre during 2013 (Table 6) rebounded 2.1%; they continued rising in 2014, with a 3% increase; the increase in 2015 was 3.4%. These increases result from the change in the fitness centres' and gyms' revenue sources; revenues rebounded from the optional activities and services provided.

We may therefore conclude that the decline in the total revenue volume in the fitness centres and gyms was not so much due to the reduction in their total number of users, but to the decrease in the membership dues average, caused by a downward price pressure created by the *low-cost* centres.

That data presented within may be expanded by an *ad hoc* study published recently, containing a sampling of 1662 people who work in fitness centres in Spain (Boned, Felipe, Barranco, Grimaldi-Puyana, & Crovetto, 2015). According to the authors, the workers in Spain's fitness centre and gym industry are comprised almost equally of men and women (50.7% and 49.3% respectively), with an average age of approximately 32 years old. Regarding their education, 50.2% have a university education, and 27.9% have professional training. Finally, the authors conclude that these workers possessed a vast amount of professional experience and an adequate level of training for tasks they undertake in their respective work centres.

The fitness centres and gyms in the study have a total combined surface area of over three million square metres. Half of the establishments are small in size, occupying less than 500 square metres. However, the large size of centres built recently in the suburbs of large cities increased the average size to over 750 square metres per establishment.

This sector is characterised by a surprisingly large number of small companies. There are numerous companies dedicated to the management of just one centre, and along with them, a few holding companies that manage various centres. Nevertheless, this industry is consolidating, with the top ten companies going from a 27.7%

Table 7 **Consolidation in the fitness centres and gyms industry in Spain in 2009–2014.**

Business consolidation	2009	2012	2014
Top 5 companies in the sector (%)	19.3	21.7	24.9
Top 10 companies in the sector (%)	27.7	33.5	39.3

Source: Research findings based on data obtained from DBK (2015).

market share in 2009, to a third of the market in 2012, reaching a 39.3% market share in 2014 (see Table 7)[6].

Finally, Table 8 shows the main characteristics of the top ten companies of the fitness sector, ranked by their total number of members. *Serviocio* tops the ranking, with 111,800 members, although its average number of members per centre is not the highest. This company has the largest total surface area in square metres and is second in the number of centres. *Alta Fit* has the second largest number of members, although the average surface area of its centres is the lowest of the ten companies included in the table. Nevertheless, they have the most centres and the lowest average number of employees per centre.

Table 8 **Characteristics of the ten main companies in the fitness and gym industry according to their number of members in Spain in 2014.**

	Members (n)		Surface Area (m²)		Employees (n)		
Company	Total	Average	Total	Average	Total	By centre	Number of centres
Serviocio	111,800	3990	132,000	4700	900	30	27
Alta Fit (low cost)	83,300	2450	51,000	1500	272	8	34
Dir	80,000	4500	81,675	4537	1300	72	18
Metropolitan	70,000	3000	100,000	4500	1200	50	22
Go Fit	55,847	5077	55,000	5500	–	–	12
Basic Fit (low cost)	55,479	2920	36,241	1907	250	13	19
Duet Sports	47,245	4295	82,380	6865	–	–	12
O2 Centro Wellness	43,000	3071	80,000	5714	700	50	14
Fitness Place Centre	42,000	2100	80,000	4000	–	–	20
Fundació Claror	40,500	5785	57,600	8229	572	82	7

Source: Research findings based on data obtained from DBK (2015).

[6] *Tercer Informe Gimnasios Low Cost en España* (Valcárcel, López, & García, 2015) analyses the evolution of these centres in the country as a whole; low-cost centres are defined as those centres with maximum monthly dues of 19.99 euros + VAT, although the dues could be 2 to 4 euros higher. This publication reports that in 2014 there were 39 private companies in Spain operating 200 centres. Of these companies, 20 per cent controlled 72 per cent of all fitness centres in Spain.

At the bottom of the Table 8, one can observe that *Fundació Claror* has the fewest number of total members, but the highest average of members and employees per centre. This is somewhat related to the larger amount of square metres in their centres.

Conclusions

This chapter has presented an analysis of the Spanish private sport sector. Compared to the other two sectors that make up the sport industry – the public sector and the voluntary sector – the private sector has not been researched as much, due to the dominance of the public sector in the sport world.

The private sector of the Spanish sport is made up of sport services companies, professional sport clubs, fitness and wellness centres, and gyms. These organisations – integrated within Section 931 of the National Classification of Economic Activities Code – have experienced a 47.3% growth in the last five years, increasing from 16,291 organisations in 2010, to 24,003 in 2015. Together they represent 0.75% of the country's total existing companies. Of these sport organisations, 26% are sole traders, and 74% are companies. Within the latter, the majority are comprised of limited liability companies (36%), while corporations account for a mere 2.1% of the organisations. Out of all the sport organisations, 41.6% have employees, and of those, 41.8% have less than six employees and 15.3% have six to 49 employees. Nearly six out of every ten sport organisations are concentrated in four regions: Catalonia, Madrid, Andalusia, and Valencia.

Instead of analysing the entire Spanish private sport sector, this chapter discussed specific types of organisations such as fitness centres and gyms. These types of private organisations have emerged in the last three decades and subsequently have become successful, leading to noticeable changes in the perception and the meaning of sport for a large amount of the population. A description of the evolution and characteristics of these types of centres in Spain was compiled from the data taken from the DBK report on the Spanish gym sector.

The number of fitness centres and gyms grew at a constant rate between the years 2000 and 2007. Beginning in 2009, a contraction period in the number of centres took place, as a result of the recession. Said contractual phase continues, albeit reduced; as of 2015 there were 3900 fitness centres and gyms. Total revenues increased by almost 8% annually in these centres between 2000 and 2007. Nonetheless, revenue growth slowed starting in 2009, also due to the effects of the recession. Revenues continued plummeting until 2013. Currently, the industry's revenues have reached 825 million euros, which is below the amount obtained in 2005. However, this decline has not been an obstacle in the growth of the number of members and users of those types of centres. In fact, the decline in the total revenues of the fitness centres and gyms was due mainly to the decrease in the membership dues average. Said decline in revenues was a result of downward price pressure created by the *low-cost* centres, rather than due to the reduction in the total number of users of these facilities. This subsector is composed of a large number of small businesses, where many of them are dedicated to the management of just one centre. Along with the small businesses, there are a few holding companies that manage several dozen centres. In any event, this industry is consolidating; the top ten companies hold a 39.3% market share.

Acknowledgments This article has been translated into English by Gregory Alan Howard.

References

Arruza, J., Arteche, I., Olaizola, B., Parrón, C., Pérez, C., Ortiz de Urbina, R., & Balerdi, A. (2011). *Estudio de la Actividad Económica del Deporte en Guipúzcoa* [Study of the economic activity of sport in Guipúzcoa]. San Sebastián, Spain: Observatorio del Deporte de Guipúzcoa.

Boned, C. J., Felipe, J. L., Barranco, D., Grimaldi-Puyana, M., & Crovetto, M. (2015). Perfil profesional de los trabajadores de los centros de fitness en España [Professional profile of workers in Spanish fitness clubs]. *Revista Internacional de Medicina y Ciencias de la Actividad Física y el Deporte, 15*(58), 195–210.

Burriel, J. C., & Puig, N. (1999). Responsabilidades y relaciones entre el sector público y el privado en el sistema deportivo [Responsibilities and relationships between the public and private sector in the sport system]. In J. Subirats (Ed.), *¿Existe sociedad civil en España? Responsabilidades colectivas y valores públicos* (pp. 178–202). Madrid, Spain: Fundación Encuentro.

Cámara, M. A. de. (2015). El sector del fitness en España: análisis del gimnasio low-cost y los centros de electro estimulación integral [Fitness industry in Spain; analysis of low-cost and whole body electromyostimulation centers]. *Revista Euroamericana de Ciencias del Deporte, 4*(2), 47–54.

CSD. (2015). *Nace la Asociación del Deporte Federado Español* [The Spanish Sport Federation Association has been created]. Madrid, Spain: Consejo Superior de Deportes. Retrieved May 15, 2016 from http://www.csd.gob.es/csd/documentacion/01GabPr/Novedades/nace-la-asociacion-del-deporte-federado-espanol/view

DBK. (2015). *Estudio Sectores – Gimnasios* [Study of sectors – Gyms]. Madrid, Spain: DBK Informa. Retrieved March 27, 2016 from https://www.dbk.es/es/estudios/16265

DIRCE. (2015). *Directorio Central de Empresas* [Central business register]. Madrid, Spain: Instituto Nacional de Estadística. Retrieved June 22, 2016 from http://www.ine.es/dynt3/inebase/es/index.htm?padre=51&dh=1

Dorado, A. (2006). La gestión privada de las organizaciones deportivas [The private management of sport organizations]. In L. Gallardo & J. Lozano (Eds.), *Futuras claves en la gestión de organizaciones deportivas* (pp. 103–116). Cuenca, Ecuador: Publicaciones de la Universidad de Castilla la Mancha.

García-Ferrando, M., & Llopis-Goig, R. (2011). *Ideal democrático y bienestar personal. Encuesta sobre los hábitos deportivos en España 2010* [Democratic ideal and personal wellbeing. Survey on sports habits in Spain 2010]. Madrid, Spain: CSD/CIS.

García-Ferrando, M., & Llopis-Goig, R. (2017). *La popularización del deporte en España. Encuestas de hábitos deportivos 1980–2015* [Popularization of sport in Spain. Surveys of sports habits 1980–2015]. Madrid, Spain: CSD/CIS.

Iglesias, X., & Tarragó, R. (2012). *Modelos del deporte en España* [Sport models in Spain]. Barcelona, Spain: INFEC. Retrieved April 21, 2016 from http://www.gr.unicamp.br/ceav/revista/content/pdf/modelos_deporte_esp_iglesias_tarrago.pdf

Lera-López, F., & Lizalde-Gil, E. (2013). Spain. In K. Hallmann & K. Petry (Eds.), *Comparative sport development: Systems, participation and public policy* (pp. 149–166). New York, NY: Springer.

Ley del Deporte. (1990). *Ley 10/1990 de 15 de octubre del Deporte* [Sports Act 10/1990 of 15 October]. Retrieved May 3, 2016 from http://www.csd.gob.es/csd/informacion-en/legislacion basica/ley del deporte/

Life Fitness. (2015). *Estudio Anual del Mercado del Fitness en España* [Annual study on the fitness market in Spain]. Retrieved June 1, 2016 from http://lifefitness-pro.es/zoommercado2015/

Llopis-Goig, R. (2014). Sport participation and cultural trends. Running as a reflection of individualisation and post-materialism processes in Spanish society. *European Journal for Sport and Society, 11*(2), 151–169.

Martínez-Lemos, R. I., & Romo-Pérez, V. (2015). El sector privado del deporte en España. Relación con la población, la producción y la renta [The private sector of sport in Spain. Relationship with population, production and income]. *Retos, 28*(2nd quarter), 71–77.

Olivera, A., & Olivera, J. (1999). Las actividades físicas de aventura en la naturaleza. Estudio de la oferta y la demanda en el sector empresarial [Physical and adventure activities in the nature. A Study of supply and demand in the business sector]. *Apunts de Educación Física y Deportes, 57*(3rd quarter), 86–94.

Puig, N., Martínez, J., & García, B. (2010). Sport policy in Spain. *International Journal of Sport Policy, 2*(3), 381–390.

Puig, N., Sarasa, S., Junyent, R., & Oró, C. (2003). Sport and welfare state in the process of Spanish democratisation. In K. Heinemann (Ed.), *Sport and the welfare state* (pp. 295–350). Schorndorf, Germany: Hofmann & Schattauer.

Ramos, J. J., & Martínez de Haro, V. (2009). El deporte paralímpico [Paralympic sport]. In R. Ansón (Ed.), *El Olimpismo* (2nd ed., pp. 356–365). Madrid, Spain: Universidad Camilo José Cela, Cátedra Olímpica Marqués de Samaranch.

Rocha, F., & Aragón, J. (2012). *La crisis económica y sus efectos sobre el empleo en España* [Economic crisis and their effects on employment in Spain]. Colección Informes número 55. Madrid: Fundación 1° de Mayo.

Sánchez Martín, J. (2014). *Cómo aumentar los ingresos en los centros deportivos sin exprimir a los clientes* [How to increase revenues in sports centers without squeezing customers]. Barcelona, Spain: Editorial UOC.

Valcárcel, M., López, F., & García, J. (2015). *Tercer Informe Gimnasios Low Cost en España* [Third report on low cost gyms in Spain]. Retrieved May 7, 2016 from http://valgo.es/recursos/informes-estudios/132-tercer-informe-gimnasios-low-cost-espa%C3%B1a-2015

UNITED KINGDOM: Dominance of the Commercial Sector in the Sport Market

Chris Gratton and Themis Kokolakakis

Selected country facts (in 2013)	
Capital	London
Geographical size (km^2)	248,528
Population (million)	63.91
GDP (euro per capita)	32,000
GDP (per capita in PPS)	107
Annual net earnings average (€)	31,782

Introduction

The supply side of the sport market comprises three sectors: the government sector, both national and local, the voluntary sector, and the commercial sector. In the early stages of the sport market in the nineteenth century the government sector and the voluntary sector dominated the British sport market. There was little commercial activity in sport. Throughout the twentieth century increases in both income and leisure time led to increasing commercialisation of the sport market. In the twenty-first century the commercial sector dominates the sport market. In order to understand these changes it is useful to begin with a brief history of the development of the sport market in Britain charting the role of each of these three sectors and in particular the gradual growth of the commercial sector. We then move on to look at the sport system and the structure of organised sport in the United Kingdom (UK). What drives the sport market is the demand for sport and we look at recent changes

C. Gratton (✉) • T. Kokolakakis
Sport Industry Research Centre, Sheffield Hallam University, Sheffield, UK
e-mail: c.gratton@shu.ac.uk; t.kokolakakis@shu.ac.uk

A. Laine, H. Vehmas (eds.), *The Private Sport Sector in Europe*, Sports Economics, Management and Policy 14, https://doi.org/10.1007/978-3-319-61310-9_19

in sport participation. Finally, we measure the economic value of the commercial sector in sport with three specific case studies of sport betting, commercial health and fitness centres and sport broadcasting.

History of the Development of the Sport Market

If we go back to the early 1600's in England some sports (for example football, cricket, horse racing, boxing, cock fighting, bull-baiting and dog fighting), both participant and spectator, were highly popular but these activities were unrecognisable from the same activities today. Football as practiced then had no designated pitch or goals and the teams could contain hundreds of people. No sport market in financial terms existed. Nobody paid any money to take part in sport or to spectate. There was expenditure on gambling related to sport and on alcohol consumed either watching or playing it. (Malcolmson, 1973.)

The industrialisation process of the early nineteenth century saw the movement from agriculture to manufacturing industry, involving the movement of the population from rural to urban environments, which completely altered sport in Britain. The most significant change was in the availability of leisure. Factory work typically involved a six-day week, with working days of at least twelve hours for men, women and children alike. There was no seasonal rhythm to this work – every week was the same. Holidays also decreased. In 1750 the Bank of England closed on forty-seven holidays. By 1830 this had decreased to eighteen, and by 1834 it closed on only four days – Good Friday, Christmas Day, and the first days of May and November. During the same period many of the popular recreations of pre-industrial Britain virtually disappeared. Space was also a major constraint for sport activities. Many sports, football in particular, could not flourish in the new industrial towns because of the lack of space. These activities still survived in rural areas, but by 1851 the majority of the English population lived in towns and cities. (Walvin, 1978.)

Public schools played a crucial role in the development of sport in England. Holt (1989, 81) describes how the top public schools initially saw the potential of sport as a source of discipline and morality, but eventually "sport ceased to be a means to a disciplinary end and became an end in itself. The culture of athleticism steadily came to dominate the whole system of elite education." The top public schools had sport every day. Individual schools codified the rules and these eventually became standardised across the schools as they started to play each other in these sports.

As the nineteenth century progressed the twin constraints of time and money were gradually eased for the mass of the English population and leisure activities began to expand. By the 1850's, Saturday afternoon was no longer a regular work time and, because of the strong influence of the Sabbatarian lobby keeping Sunday a rest day, it became the regular sport and recreation afternoon (Walvin, 1978).

Voluntary sport clubs were formed and these clubs played each other on a Saturday afternoon in emerging sport leagues. Sport was encouraged by local government in providing parks, open spaces and swimming pools. One of the problems with the move from country to town was that there was no longer any space in the new urban areas for the conventional pre-industrial popular recreations. As the nineteenth century progressed local governments accepted the responsibility for the provision of both space and facilities for sport in the towns and cities.

Sport became more commercial during the second half of the nineteenth century. Football had been tamed by the public schools to become an organised, respectable sport with a rigid set of rules. In 1863 the Football Association was established and in 1872 came the first F.A. Cup competition. The game started to attract large numbers of spectators, and football stadiums were constructed to house them. By the 1880's professionalism in football was well-established. In 1895, professionalism also entered rugby when some northern clubs split away from the Rugby Union to form the new Rugby League because they wished to allow payments to players. (Mason, 1980.)

The nineteenth century saw the emergence of the two major players in the sport market, namely the government and the voluntary sport sectors. The twentieth century saw the increasing presence of the third player, the commercial sport sector. We have used the term commercial sector rather than the private sector in this chapter since the private sector consists of two sectors: the private for-profit sector (the commercial sector) and the private not-for-profit sector (the voluntary and charity sectors). We have only measured the commercial sport sector here.

Structure and System of Organised Sport

The principal UK government department responsible for sport is the Department of Culture, Media and Sport (DCMS). The DCMS funds both UK Sport and Sport England. These bodies administer sport policy. Elite sport including major sport events and the financial support of elite athletes, is the responsibility of UK Sport. Support for sport participation and grassroots sport, however, and the monitoring of this through collection of data on sport participation is the responsibility of agencies of the home countries of the UK: England, Northern Ireland, Scotland, and Wales. Each of these countries has its own sport council with responsibility for sport policy (e.g., Sport England) and each collects its own data on sport participation.

Gratton, Taylor and Rowe (2013) indicate the complexity of the structures for administering and delivering sport in England. The organisational network can be structured according to three levels: (1) national (government); (2) national (non-government) and (3) local. Individual sports are run by independent governing bodies, the majority of which are 'recognised' National Governing Bodies (NGBs). In the UK there are over 250 NGBs for just over 100 sports – many sports have more than one NGB. Some NGBs have a UK structure, some a Great Britain structure and most are constituted separately in England, Wales, Scotland and Northern Ireland. Many of the major NGBs receive substantial funds from the government, via the national sports councils. (Gratton et al., 2013.)

Local organisations include local authorities; schools; further and higher education institutions; local trusts and non-profit organisations; commercial sector owners and operators (e.g., health and fitness clubs) and local sport councils, sport clubs and associations. Local organisations are at the heart of the sport provision in England

and sport clubs and local authorities are the most significant actors. According to the Audit Commission (2006) there are 3489 sport and recreation facilities with public access in England, three-quarters of these being local authority owned.

Financing of Sport

Funding for sport comes from a variety of sources. These include central government; local government; National Lottery; sponsorships; SportsAid (formerly Sports Aid Foundation, a private charity set up to provide funding to promising sportspeople); commercial sector companies; voluntary sector, benefactors, donors and the public. According to the DCMS/Cabinet Office (2002), in 2000 nearly 90% of the central government funding for sport was distributed by local authorities, and this central government funding represented just over a half of local authorities' expenditure on sport (see Fig. 1). The rest was financed by fees and charges to the users (23%) and by local taxes (25%).

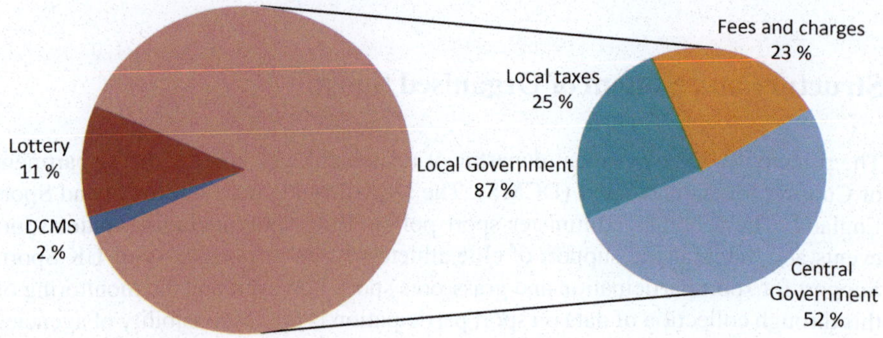

Fig. 1 Estimated government and lottery expenditure on sport in the UK in 2000. Source: DCMS/Cabinet Office (2002).

The National Lottery awards began in 1995 and sport has been one of the good causes throughout its existence. The DCMS website reveals a total of 89,079 grants awarded by the sport councils in the UK, totalling £5.844 billion in value between 1995, when the awards began, and the beginning of 2017 (DCMS, 2017), with Sport England grants dominating those of UK Sport. Given the relative population size of England to the UK, the majority of UK Sport grants will be in England. Many UK Sport grants are primarily for elite sport including elite training facilities, but in reality these facilities are also used for community purposes. One of the contentious issues with Lottery awards is that increasing amounts have been going to major projects, such as the 2012 Olympics facilities, leaving less money for community level sport. Another concern is that Lottery funding has not all represented a net addition to investment in sport because it has been used as an excuse to reduce normal capital funding of sport by central government and local authorities.

The Government, Voluntary and Commercial Sectors in Sport

The supply side of the sport market comprises three sectors, namely the government, voluntary and commercial sectors. The government sector is involved in sport because the sport market has aspects of market failure: that is, sport can generate social benefits over and above the private benefit to the individual participants. The most prominent of these is the health benefits generated by sport so government spending on sport may reduce government spending on health care. This and other market failures lead government to spend money to encourage more sport participation.

The government spends money also to enhance performance at the elite level since international sporting success for a country can be classified as a public good. These two areas, raising participation and enhancing elite performance, are the two areas the UK government intervenes in the sport market.

The largest element of the government expenditure on sport, however, is the local government subsidies to local sport facilities, which are predominantly provided by the local government. These facilities include swimming pools, indoor sport centres, outdoor pitches and golf courses. Since the global economic crisis in 2008 there has been severe squeeze on local authority budgets and these subsidies have been reduced considerably. Some sport facilities that were not economically viable have closed down. The ones that remain increasingly need to at least break even to survive in the new climate.

The voluntary sector also exists in sport because of the market failure but a type of market failure that is relevant only for a minority of the population. This means the market will provide less than is a socially optimum output. However, since it is only affecting a minority, governments also may not step in to provide a higher output. The voluntary sector provides a solution when a group of people who value the collective benefits provided by sport join together to increase the provision of opportunities.

We see this across sport but most notable in sport clubs. The motivation of club members is not to generate collective benefits for society in general but rather to maximise benefits for club members. Volunteer labour is a substantial resource to the voluntary sector and distinguishes this sector from the government sector. However, the volunteer labour is currently under threat by people feeling much more pressure on their time either through work demands or caring for children or older people. Some clubs are finding it more and more difficult to attract sufficient volunteers and some must resort to employing people to do jobs formerly done by volunteers. Thus both the voluntary sector and the government sector are currently under threat.

The rest of the sport market is supplied by the commercial sector where firms provide goods to the market for profit. Thus, sport equipment, sport clothing, sport shoes, sport gambling, professional team sports, most of sport broadcasting, and health and fitness clubs make up the main part of the commercial sector in sport. Later in this chapter we look at what has been happening in three of the largest of these sectors in recent years: sport gambling, commercial health and fitness centres, and commercial sport broadcasting.

Often we find all three sectors competing against each other in one segment of the sport market as we will see in the health and fitness centre market. Where this happens we are likely to see the voluntary and government sectors to provide a more basic product than the commercial sector but at a lower price, in the government sector because of public subsidy and in the voluntary sector because of volunteer labour. From the consumer's point of view the goods provided by the voluntary and government sectors are likely to be seen as inferior to that provided by the commercial sector since the latter is able to provide a higher degree of individual control for the consumer over the form of the good provided, type of availability and times of availability. Private market substitutes for collective goods will cater more to specific consumer demands. Since the degree of individual control desired by the consumer is likely to be positively related to income, the commercial supplier is likely to 'skim' the market and cater to the demands of the higher income consumer and charge a premium price for this service. This is exactly what happened in the health and fitness market in the early 1990's (see case study below).

Measuring Participation in Sport – The England Experience

The sport market, and in particular the commercial sector in sport, is driven by the demand for sport. The higher the demand for sport the larger the commercial sector in sport. This is particularly the case given the constraints on both the voluntary sector and government sectors since the global economic crisis in 2008. To understand the behaviour of the commercial sector in sport we need to also understand what is happening to demand.

Since 2005 Sport England has invested millions of pounds to carry out an annual survey of adult (aged 16 or older) participation in sport. The Active People Survey (APS) – the largest survey of its kind in Europe – involves around 170,000 telephone interviews each year (in 2005–2006 only the sample size was 363,000 and there was no survey in 2006–2007) to establish patterns of sport participation. The survey – which is run continuously throughout the year – includes at its core, measures of the types of sport people take part in, the frequency with which they take part (in a four week reference period), the intensity (in terms of energy expended – light, moderate or vigorous) and the duration (in minutes taking part per session). The survey also includes measures of the context in which participation takes place (club, competition and coaching/tuition); the levels of volunteering; the reasons why people do or do not take part in sport; and their future intentions. An extensive range of socio-demographic questions is also included, supporting complex social profiling and modelling. (APS, 2015.)

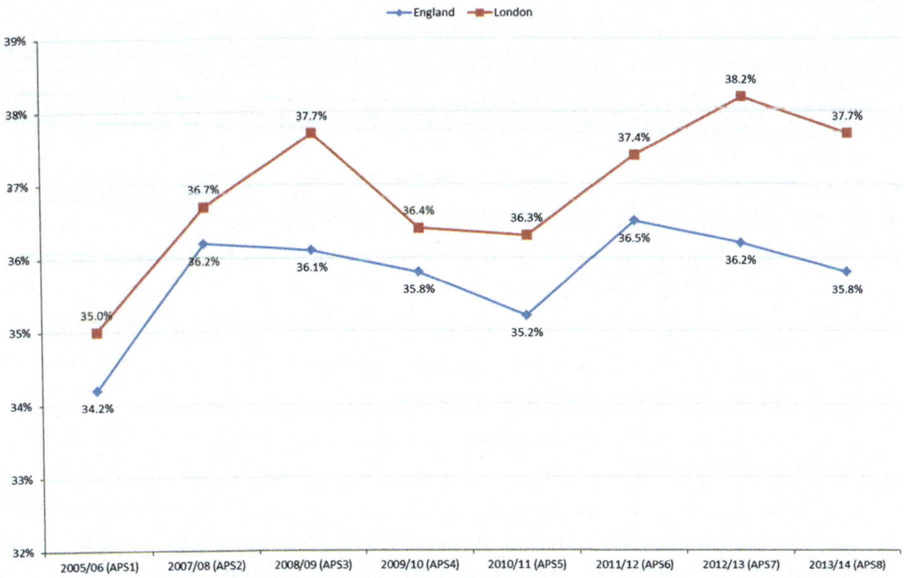

Fig. 2 Sport participation for England and London in 2005–2014. Source: Active People Survey (APS) (2015).

Figure 2 shows the trend in participation in England and London for those taking part in sport at least once a week for a minimum of 30 minutes (1 × 30 measure). The data do not relate to a calendar year but October to October. Thus the 2005–2006 data is from October 2005 to October 2006 and the same for the other years. The participation rate peaked at 36.5% in 2011–2012. There was a strong growth in participation between 2005–2006 and 2007–2008, but it dropped back in 2008–2009 and 2009–2010. This reduction could be due to the economic crisis because there was a sharp drop in the most expensive sports (golf, skiing and sailing) following the global financial crisis in 2008. From 2010–2011 participation recovered and then peaked in 2011–2012 in England. The 2011–2012 peak occurred in the period October 2011 to October 2012 that is in the period the Olympics were staged in London. Since then there has been a small reduction in participation, but it still remains above the 2010/2011 level (APS, 2015).

The Economic Value of the Sport Market

DCMS (2015) summarises the main results from the 2012 UK Sport Satellite Account, which shows official government statistics on the economic value of the sport market indicating the size of Gross Value Added (GVA), employment, and consumer expenditure in sport. All data in this section is from the sport satellite account for 2012.

GVA

- GVA for the sport sector economy grew in current prices (not adjusted for inflation) by 10.4% in 2011 and 4.4% in 2012 (7.2% and 2.7% in constant prices, adjusted to 2011 prices).
- The value of the sport economy was £38,891m in 2012 (current prices).
- In 2012, the largest sub-sectors by value (2011 prices) were sporting activities (£20,230m), telecommunications (£3677m), education (£1691m) and advertising business activities (£1578m).
- Sport-related GVA accounted for 2.6% of UK GVA in 2011 and 2012, compared with 2.4% in 2010.

Consumer spending

- Consumer sport-related spending increased from £26.4bn in 2010 to £29.2bn in 2012: a 10.6% increase in current prices (or 4.5% in constant prices).
- The highest spending sub-sectors within sport are wearing apparel (£3398m in 2012) and telecommunications (£3402m in 2012).
- Consumer spending on sport was 2.9% of all UK consumer spending in 2012, up from 2.8% in 2010 and 2011.

Employment

- Employment in sport increased by 55% in 2011 and a further 1% in 2012. There was a 66% increase between 2004 and 2012.
- Total sport employment in 2012 was one million, or 3.6% of UK employment (up from 2.2% in 2004).

Table 1 shows the growth in these three aggregates from 2009 to 2012.

Table 1 Value of sport in the UK in 2009–2012[a].

	2009	2010	2011	2012
Sport-related GVA, £m	29,455	33,736	37,252	38,891
as % of total GVA	2.2	2.4	2.6	2.6
Sport-related consumer spending, £m	24,845	26,405	27,754	29,207
as % of total spending	2.7	2.8	2.8	2.9
Sport-related employment, 000s	629.1	640.1	991.0	1000.5
as % of total employment	2.3	2.3	3.6	3.6

[a]GVA and consumer spending in current prices. Total number of people employed in the UK is taken from the *Labour Force Survey* and is calculated using full time equivalents (FTE). The GVA total is taken from the National Accounts and the consumer spending total from *Consumer Trends*.

The growth in the consumer spending and employment is associated with the hosting of the summer Olympics in 2012. This caused rising employment in the sport sector in the years before 2012, because of the construction of sport-related infrastructure. Also, as we have seen, sport participation increased strongly from 2010–2011, which led to a strong growth on expenditure on sport clothing, shoes and equipment.

In 2011 and 2012 sport-related GVA grew by 10.4% and 4.4% respectively in the current prices. The size of GVA increased from £33.7bn in 2010, to £37.3.5bn in 2011, and £38.9bn in 2012. Since 2009 the rates of growth in sport GVA were considerably higher than the growth rate for the economy overall. The majority of GVA was generated by the sport activities category. In 2011 and 2012 important contributions were also made by telecommunications, education, advertising and retail and other parts of the commercial sector. As in consumer spending, it is likely that the London 2012 Olympic Games influenced much sport-related activities.

The share of sport GVA as a proportion of the total UK GVA increased from 2.2% in 2009 to 2.6% of total GVA in both 2011 and 2012. In the period of 2006–2008 sport GVA growth was slower than growth in the economy as a whole. In 2009, when UK GVA reduced by 1.7%, it would have been expected that sport would also have declined, as in a recessionary period necessities become the priority for consumers. Instead, sport-related GVA rose slightly by 0.4%. This was followed by growth rates of 14.5% and 10.4% for the years 2010 and 2011 respectively. In 2012 there was a continued increase of 4.4%, compared to 2.4% for the UK economy as a whole.

In 2011 and 2012 sport consumption grew by 6.2% and 6.3% respectively, reaching £29.2bn in value in 2012. This has followed a gradual increase in spending each year from £23.4bn in 2004, with the exception of 2009 when there was a decrease of 11.5%, associated with the economic consequences of the recession. According to the National Accounts, in 2009 real GVA declined by 4.3%, representing the largest one-year fall in the last 60 years. In the same year, overall consumer spending, in current prices, declined by 2.0% compared to 2008.

Employment increased considerably during the years 2011 and 2012 as a result of projects and organisation of the Olympic and Paralympic Games. The greatest employment effect was in 2011 when sport-related employment increased by over 50%. During 2012 this was consolidated by a small rise of 1%. Total full time equivalent (FTE) sport employment reached 0.99 million and one million during the years 2011 and 2012 respectively.

The London Olympics and Paralympics had a considerable effect on consumption, a greater effect on GVA and the greatest effect on employment. This means that the generated GVA was weighted more heavily towards wages and employment than towards profits.

The share of sport employment (out of total UK employment) rose from 2.3% in 2010 to 3.6% in 2011 and 2012. This is a much greater than the share for GVA (2.6% in 2011 and 2012), implying that the sport economy is a labour intensive growth industry.

The Commercial Sport Sector in 2012

This section shows what proportion of the whole sport-related GVA, consumption, and employment is due to the commercial sector. In the UK there are official data on several aspects of the commercial sector (such as manufacturing through PRODCOM). However, as it happens throughout Europe, the details of these datasets are not sufficient to isolate the sport element. Other than using the National Accounting methodology, data can be generated through the Annual Business Survey (ABS), which gives information about the commercial sector at the four-digit *Standard Industrial Classification* (SIC) level, with the exception of financial services. SIC is the UK equivalent of the *Statistical classification of economic activities in the European Community* (NACE Rev. 2, 2008). The Annual Reports of the companies deposited at the Companies House are also used, together with questionnaires, for establishing a sport share per four-digit economic activity. The dataset of the Companies House includes around 3.5 million active UK companies; however, only a small subset of them submit Profit and Loss Accounts that can be used to derive GVA estimates. In some cases such as sport betting, the GVA share is derived from constructing in detail the sport element of betting and deriving afterwards profits and wages as parts of GVA. In other sectors such as in the boating industry data exists from independent commercial sectors that can be compared to the four digit SIC categories available through ABS. Overall since the 1980's the commercial sport sector in the UK has accounted for around 70% of the sport economy. However if we exclude the impact of the Olympics from the 2012 data, since it overstates the normal size of the public sector, the share of the commercial sector in the sport economy is nearer to 80%.

Table 2 Sport-related commercial sector: GVA, staff and wages in the UK in 2012.

Product areas (in brackets the UK sport satellite account codes)	GVA	Staff (FTE)	Wages
	£m	'000s	£m
Activities of sport clubs (93)	4231	112	3342
Producing and broadcastings TV/radio/ news sport programmes (60)	3207	43	1251
Operation of sport facilities/ other (93)	1955	90	1695
Retail sale of sport equipment and bicycles (47)	1867	64	714
Sport betting and betting tips services (92)	1730	33	660
Sport marketing and advertising services/R&D (72–74)	1653	28	1110
Administration (70, 82, 84, 92)	1400	35	1050
Boats/aircrafts/cycles/carts (30)	1185	29	904
Financial intermediation/ insurance (64–68)	1163	13	588
Fitness facilities/services (93, 96)	1059	35	547
Hotels and restaurants (55, 56)	888	39	558
Wholesale (46)	888	20	554.6
Travel agencies (79)	741	19	478
Sport centres, spa and mountain hotels (55, 96)	715	32	448
Publishing Services and printing (58)	508	9	330
Construction (41–43)	483	9	266
Agriculture (1, 10)	399	11	190
Manufacture of sport goods and repair (32)	371	9	200
Physical institutions and physiotherapists (96)	277	7	144
Manufacture and sale of motor vehicles for sport use (29, 45)	238	5	120
Transport (49)	212	5	140
Pharmaceuticals (21)	197	2	79
Machinery/weapons/optical instruments/ metal products (32, 33)	185	6	120
Manufacture of coke, petroleum for sport use (19)	160	6	150
Wearing apparel manufacturing (14)	144	5	95
Sport and recreation education (85)	144	8	174
Renting and leasing of recreational and sport goods (77)	135	3	50
Health and vet services (75)	120	4	87
Leather/footwear manufacturing and repair (14, 15, 95)	100	3	45
Maintenance of motor vehicles (45)	98	3	93
Other sport activities	519	21	529
Other personal service activities	345	12	219
Total	**27,317**	**720**	**16,931**
% of sport economy	**80%**	**73%**	**80%**

Source: Adapted from ONS (2015).

Table 2 shows how the commercial sport sector breaks down into its constituent product areas producing results consistent with the UK Sport Satellite account in 2012. Three of the largest areas of consumer spending on sport are sport betting, sport broadcasting and commercial health and fitness centres. The size of two of these, commercial health and fitness centres and sport broadcasting, in 1990 was very small although sport betting has always had an important share of the UK sport market. We now look at these three sectors in detail given their importance in overall consumer spending in the sport market.

Sport Betting

The UK is unusual in Europe having a large share of the gambling market centred on sport betting. Traditionally this has been dominated by football pools and horse racing betting. Although the latter is still important the former was almost destroyed by the introduction of the National Lottery in 1994. This expanded the total market of gambling but the consumers switched. People who used to spend Saturday evenings watching football results on television to see if they had won millions on the football pools switched to spending Saturday evenings watching the television to see if they had won millions by choosing the right combination of numbers in the National Lottery. However, betting on football has re-emerged as an important area of the market with the rise of online betting on mainly English Premier League football matches in the twenty-first century.

In the 1980's and early 1990's, sport betting accounted for over one quarter of consumer expenditure on sport. However, by 2000 its share had dropped to around one fifth of the total. Again much of this can be explained by the introduction of the National Lottery in 1994. Consumer spending on football pools was £633 million in 1994. By 2000, this was reduced to £124 million. Over 80% of the total consumer expenditure on gambling was sport-related in 1994. By 2000, this share had dropped to 43%. It is perhaps ironic that the lottery provides long-term investment funds for sport of around £200-£250 million a year, which will lead in the longer term to higher participation in sport and an expansion of the sport market. In the short term it actually reduced growth in the sport market by reducing the size of consumer spending on sport gambling. (SIRC, 2001.)

Since 2000, however, the market in sport betting has continued to grow. This has largely been fuelled by the strong increase in the online betting. Online betting is now the major part of the total sport betting market, which currently was worth just over £2.5 billion in 2015. Around 54% of this is online betting. The rest is accounted by retail betting in betting shops. Although the number of these shops has declined over the last 20 years it still dominates the horse racing betting sector, whereas online betting is dominated by football betting. (Mintel, 2016a.)

William Hill is the market leader with around 25% of the sport betting market, followed by Ladbrokes (18%), and Coral (13%). At the time of this writing, there is a talk of a merger between Ladbrokes and Coral where a new merged company would then become the market leader. However, this has not yet been confirmed. Bet 365 is the leading online betting company with 10% of the sport betting market. (Mintel, 2016b.)

Commercial Health and Fitness Centres

This sector of the sport market hardly existed until the 1990's, but there has been considerable growth since then so that it now accounts for a large share of the market for sport. The first major brand was David Lloyd Leisure, which opened its first club in 1982. This was a premium brand concentrated in London and the South East where incomes are higher. The club was based on tennis since David Lloyd was a well-known British tennis player. In addition to outdoor courts the clubs have indoor courts, the supply of which was very limited in the 1980's meaning that many tennis players only played in summer. In addition to tennis, the clubs also provided premium fitness facilities and a premium indoor swimming pool. David Lloyd set a new standard in health and fitness centres. Such facilities already existed to some extent in the new investment in public sector indoor leisure centres which expanded significantly in the 1970's and early 1980's together with some voluntary sector clubs, but the David Lloyd clubs were much more upmarket in the facilities that they provided and in the prices they charged for the memberships.

This trend of the commercial health and fitness centres to target the top end of the market continued in the strong growth period in the sector in the 1990's. In 1983 there were 20 new commercial facilities opened, and by 1990, this had increased to 60 new openings. By 1997, this number had doubled to 120 and in 2001, new openings peaked at over 170. In the years that followed, however new openings fell and by 2003 there were more commercial health and fitness facilities closing than opening. The market had reached its peak and started to decline. Between 2005 and 2010 consumer spending on commercial health and fitness clubs declined 19% in real terms. The market was hit particularly hard following the global economic crisis in 2008. (SIRC, 2011.)

However, from 2010 onwards the market started to grow again driven by the introduction of a new concept. The leader of this change was a brand called Pure Gym, a low cost operator that offers use of facilities without an annual contract and is open 24 hours a day. Whereas the premium brands often charged a hefty joining fee of around £400-£500 minimum and insisted on a minimum one year contract with fees starting at around £50 per month, Pure Gym typically has a monthly fee at around £18-£20 with no joining fees and no contracts. If the consumer wants to leave the club he or she can do so immediately and there is no liability. Another low cost brand is The Gym. Both of these brands expanded rapidly from 2010 with some of this expansion achieved by acquiring facilities from other operators including its takeover of 43 of LA Fitness facilities in 2015. In 2011, Pure Gym had 13 facilities and The Gym had 16. By 2015 Pure Gym became the market leader with 99 facilities, compared to the 63 owned by The Gym. (Mintel, 2015a.)

This expansion of the budget operators has not had a dramatic effect on consumer spending in the sector since 2010. The growth in the number of members has predominantly been in the budget sector with premium price operators either consolidating or reducing the number of facilities through sales to other operators. The result is that the larger number of consumers are not spending overall a lot more money. Consumer expenditure on commercial health and fitness centres grew by just over 3% between 2010 and 2015 to reach just under £2.7 billion, to make it one of the largest sectors in the sport market. (Mintel, 2015b.)

Sport Broadcasting

Up until 1992 there was little commercial activity in sport broadcasting in the UK. Consumer expenditure on sport broadcasting up to then was estimated by taking 7% of the BBC licence fee since the BBC had 7% of its expenditure in sport programmes. This was less than 1% of the sport market at that time. (Henley Centre for Forecasting, 1992.)

In 1992, the Premier League in the English football was introduced and a new satellite pay-per-view operator BskyB offered £191.5 million to televise 60 matches a season from 1992 to 1997. It then charged subscribers a monthly premium to watch these matches, the first time anybody had been charged directly to watch televised sport in Britain. From virtually nothing the size of the commercial sport broadcasting market has been growing strongly since then. In 1992, BskyB had 1.5 million subscribers and was making heavy losses. By 1997 it had seven million subscribers and was the most profitable broadcaster in Europe. Much of this success was due to its acquisition of sport broadcasting rights and most importantly its ownership of the broadcasting rights for Premier League football. There was a 250% increase in the level of fees for televised football in 1992 when BSkyB won the rights for 60 live matches of the Premier League at an average cost of £38 million per year. When the deal was renegotiated in 1997 there was a further 337% rise in the annual rights. Table 3, adapted from Gratton, Liu, Ramchandani and Wilson (2012, 86), shows how each contract renewal, with the exception of 2004, the amount paid by BSkyB rose considerably. Many argued that the 2004 deal proved the broadcasting rights escalation was over.

Table 3 English Premier League domestic TV rights in 1992–2016.

	1992	1997	2001	2004	2007	2010	2013	2016
Length of contract (years)	5	4	3	3	3	3	3	3
Broadcaster	BSkyB	BSkyB	BSkyB	BSkyB	BSkyB/ Setanta/ ESPN	BSkyB/ ESPN	BSkyB/ BT	BSkyB/ BT
Contract value (£m)	191.5	670	1100	1024	1702	1782	3400	5140
Annual rights fee (£m)	38.3	167.5	366.7	341.3	567.3	594.0	1133	1713
Live matches per season	60	60	106	138	138	138	138	138
Fee per live match (£m)	0.6	2.8	3.5	2.5	4.1	4.3	8.21	12.41

Source: Adapted from Gratton et al. (2012, 86).

During the life of the 2004–2007 contract the European Commission intervened on the grounds that BSkyB was in a monopoly position in relation to the control of broadcasting rights for live Premier League games. It insisted that when the rights for the 2007–2010 period were auctioned, at least one of the packages offered went to a different broadcaster. As a consequence, of the six packages offered by the Premier League for the 2007–2010 period, BSkyB only secured four of them consisting of a total of 92 live matches. BSkyB paid £1.3 billion for these games at a cost of £4.76 million per game compared with an average cost over the 2004–2007 period of £2.47 million per game. That is a 93% increase in the cost to BSkyB. The other two packages went to an Irish television station, Setanta. Their packages consisted of 46 live games per year at a total cost of £392 million, or £2.8 million per game, considerably less than the cost to BSkyB but more than BSkyB paid for each game over the 2004–2007 period. The total income to the Premier League from the new deal was £1.7 billion over three years, a massive 67% increase compared to 2004–2007. (Gratton et al., 2012.)

In 2013, a new aggressive competitor entered the bidding process for Premier League broadcasting rights, the newly set up BT Sport. The result was an almost doubling in the price of the domestic broadcasting rights to £3.4 billion. In 2016, this rose further to £5.14 billion (see Table 3).

Football retains a huge share of the sport market through clubs, apparel, participation, attendance, TV broadcasting and betting. The fee for a live Premier League match broadcasted has increased from £0.6m in 1992 to £12.4m in 2016. Liverpool fans in UEFA Champions League final Liverpool-AC Milan in Istanbul May 25, 2005. *Photo: Jussi Eskola.*

With each hike in the price of domestic broadcasting rights the subscription price to consumers went up by a similar percentage leading to massive increases in the consumer expenditure on sport broadcasting, a market that did not exist prior to 1992. Consumer expenditure on sport broadcasting in the UK was £3.1 billion in 2010, considerably more than either the sport betting market or the commercial health and fitness market both of which are around £2.5 billion. By 2012 the consumer expenditure had risen to £3.4 billion. (DCMS, 2015.)

This massive increase in the domestic broadcasting rights was also mirrored by the sale of international broadcasting rights. The Premier League has become a major sport market export. In 2007, the total international broadcasting rights sales amounted to £625 million. This rose to £1.4 billion in 2010, £2.3 billion in 2013, and £3 billion in 2016.

Conclusions

When the market for sport emerged in the nineteenth century, the major players in that were the voluntary sector and the government sector. However, today the commercial sector dominates the sport market as the government sector has been cut back in public expenditure that followed the global economic crisis of 2008. There has also been a decreasing role of the voluntary sector largely due to the constraints on time availability reducing the willingness of people to volunteer in sport. The commercial sector has filled the gap with consumers willing to pay a higher price for the commercial sector substitute for products and services previously supplied by the government and voluntary sectors. The largest share of the consumer expenditure on sport goes on three sectors: sport clothing, sport shoes, and sport equipment, the products necessary for a consumer to take part in sport. Although these three sectors dominate consumer spending on sport, their contribution to GVA and employment is relatively small since all these goods are predominantly manufactured outside of the UK and imported. The economic activity involved in wholesaling and retailing these goods is the main contribution to the GVA and employment. Sport services however, are predominantly supplied by the UK suppliers and the three sectors analysed in this chapter, namely sport betting, commercial sector health and fitness centres, and sport broadcasting, each take a major share of consumer spending, GVA and employment in the sport market. The future is likely to show a continuation of the trend identified in this chapter for the commercial sector to account for a larger and larger share of the sport market because of the continuing constraints on government expenditure and time availability for volunteers.

References

APS. (2015). *Active people survey*. London, UK: Sport England. Retrieved October 18, 2015 from https://www.sportengland.org/research/about-our-research/active-people-survey/

Audit Commission. (2006). *Public sport and recreation services*. London, UK: Audit Commission.

DCMS/Cabinet Office. (2002). *Game plan: A strategy for delivering government's sport and physical activity objectives report*. London, UK: DCMS.

DCMS. (2015). *UK sport satellite account, 2011 and 2012*. London, UK: DCMS.

DCMS. (2017). National lottery grants search – Grants awarded by distributing body. Retrieved March 17, 2017 from http://www.lottery.culture.gov.uk/GrantsByDistributingBody.aspx

Gratton, C., Liu, D., Ramchandani, G., & Wilson, D. (2012). *The global economics of sport*. Oxon, UK: Routledge.

Gratton, C., Taylor, P., & Rowe, N. (2013). UK: England. In K. Hallmann & K. Petry (Eds.), *Comparative sport development: Systems, participation and public policy* (pp. 167–180). New York, NY: Springer.

Henley Centre for Forecasting. (1992). *The economic impact and importance of sport in the UK economy in 1990*. London, UK: The Sports Council.

Holt, R. (1989). *Sport and the British: A modern history*. Oxford, UK: Clarendon Press.

Malcolmson, R. W. (1973). *Popular recreations in English society, 1700–1850*. Cambridge, UK: Cambridge University Press.

Mason, T. (1980). *Association football and English society, 1863–1915*. Brighton, UK: Harvester Press.
Mintel. (2015a). *Health and fitness clubs UK: Market share*. London, UK: Mintel.
Mintel. (2015b). *Health and fitness clubs UK: Market size and forecast*. London, UK: Mintel.
Mintel. (2016a). *Sports betting UK: Market segmentation*. London, UK: Mintel.
Mintel. (2016b). *Sports betting UK: Market share*. London, UK: Mintel.
ONS. (2015). *Annual business survey*. London, UK: ONS.
SIRC. (2001). *Sport market forecast 2001–2005*. Sheffield, UK: SIRC.
SIRC. (2011). *Sport market forecast 2011–2015*. Sheffield, UK: SIRC.
Walvin, J. (1978). *Leisure and society 1830–1950*. London, UK: Longman.

Development, Current Situation and Future Prospects of the Private Sport Sector in Europe

Antti Laine and Hanna Vehmas

This book aimed to outline the private sport sector in Europe. Altogether 18 European countries took part in this project to present *generally* how sport is organised in these countries, and *more precisely* what is the position, structure and characteristics of the private sport sector. What was meant by the private sport sector in this book, is the profit making, commercial companies and other organisations and events that produce and sell sport goods and services with the aim of making monetary profit. This encompasses all sport-related business fields, which are evident in operating commercial sport. Moreover, sport clubs and other sport activities, which aim to gain financial profit and operate as business entities, rather than non-profit associations, whose financial resources are mainly based on membership fees and government support, were defined as private sport sector.

In Europe sport and physical activity have traditionally been formed around the voluntary sport club activities and amateur ideology that have been supported by the government subsidies. This seems to be still the situation in many European countries, and it has consequently had direct implications for example to the job opportunities of the sport graduates. However, due to the socio-demographic and economic changes particularly in the post-industrial societies, there is more and more evidence nowadays about the public and non-profit sport sectors not offering employment as much as before (see e.g., Laine & Ilmola, 2016; Vehmas & Salmikangas, 2016).

As a basic framework of this book, all country contributors were asked to utilize the standardized *Statistical Classification of Economic Activities in the European Community* (NACE Rev. 2, 2008). NACE Rev. 2 is in use in all European countries, although the name of the classification varies. With the help of the NACE framework contributors were requested to provide country-specific information about the

A. Laine (✉) • H. Vehmas
Faculty of Sport and Health Sciences, University of Jyväskylä, Jyväskylä, Finland
e-mail: antti.laine@jyu.fi; hanna.m.vehmas@jyu.fi

A. Laine, H. Vehmas (eds.), *The Private Sport Sector in Europe*, Sports Economics, Management and Policy 14, https://doi.org/10.1007/978-3-319-61310-9_20

most significant directly sport-related business fields and the largest companies of those fields by using data from 2013 or another proximate year. The authors were also asked to outline the main changes in the private sport sector during the 2000s and to discuss what are the special cases that illustrate the development and future scenarios of the private sport sector.

There were surprisingly many similarities in the participating countries' private sport sectors. To a non-European observer this might not come as a surprise as geographically, culturally and economically Europe might seem like a coherent part of the Western world. Also when taking a closer glance at the differences and historical events that have shaped the European sport and physical culture, certain common features of globalisation (see e.g., Houlihan, 2016) can be indeed detected in the European sport business fields.

What seems to characterize if not all, at least most of the European countries, is the relatively clear division between the public, voluntary and private sport sectors. This was illustrated by different cases. First, the state and municipality authorities for example arrange and finance physical education at schools, subsidize sport participation possibilities of the citizens and construct public sport facilities. Second, it was evidenced that there was an increase in the retail sale of sport goods and equipment as well as in the number of fitness clubs and facilities in the commercially run profit-making sector. Third, non-profit sport clubs still provide physical activities to all age groups at various competition and recreational levels. Depending on how strongly and through what kind of historical processes these sectors have developed, the European countries can be classified as follows.

First, many of the European countries have historically and traditionally strong non-profit voluntary sport sectors, which have had implications to the ways how private sport sector has developed. This characterizes at least Belgium, Finland, Germany and the Netherlands. Especially in the Nordic countries, Finland being the only example in this book, promotion of sport and physical activity has been part of the Nordic model of welfare. Sport participation possibilities of the different population groupings have been an important aim of the sport policy in which for example both men and women should have equal possibilities in sport, from recreational to professional levels.

Voluntary sport organisations have been dominating also the German and Dutch sport systems for years. Even though these countries are profiled as major European sport markets, their physical cultures by origins are based on voluntarism. These countries can be defined as social market economies, which mean that they have economic systems that assign the state to undertake social-political corrections and work towards social balance within a 'capitalist competition' (Schubert & Klein, 2011). The provision of goods and services is coordinated by profit-making organisations, but voluntary sport organisations are dominating countries' sport systems. Even though sport clubs make up for the 'core' of sport, over the past decades this core has started to give way to a new segment of the sport market. The importance of the commercial sport providers and people who organize sport activities on their own, or ‘informally’ with the help from friends and relatives, has risen. (Breedveld, 2014; Breuer, Feiler, & Wicker, 2015.)

Second, former Eastern Bloc countries in this book, namely Czech Republic, Hungary, Romania and the Baltic states all share the history with the communist transformation after the World War II that influenced their political and economic systems fundamentally. The state sector became highly dominant without giving space to the civil and private sectors in all areas of society. During this period, a centrally articulated sport policy defined also the directions of the sport development, and the activities in sport were accompanied by centrally provided funding as well (Földesi, 1996).

As it was described in the country chapters for example in the Czech Republic many of the former or newly founded businesses succeeded in developing a competitive production of good quality sport equipment that did well on foreign markets. Even though the trade was oriented mainly to the Eastern Bloc countries, these experiences gave way to the adaptation of the market economy from 1990’s onwards. A specificity of that time was also that sport clubs were given a permission to conduct business operations, and thus, private sport services began to appear already in the 1980’s, with the permission of the communist regime. However, the private entities did not have the full characteristics of the independent enterprises at that time. (Kábele, 2011; Slepičková, 2007.)

A turning point for the future of the Eastern Bloc private sport sectors took place in 1989. This process was evidenced in the Central and Eastern European countries and initiated radical changes with respect to their political, economic and social systems. What seems to be characteristics in the varying degree in these countries is the experience of the relatively fast transformation of the sport and physical culture from the state monopolist organisation of sport to the privately run sport system. The importance of the state sector has declined and the state has also in many levels withdrawn itself from the organisation practices of sport. Consequently, the voluntary sport sector has remained weak and thus functions informally. Despite the positive cases of the growing areas, for example in team sports, the sport sector is still struggling in the legacy of socialism or its inheritance, and sometimes ‘wild’ capitalism, as illustrated in the Romanian chapter. Many population groupings, such as the elderly, the rural inhabitants and people with low income have been forced to give up sport participation as the current sport sector serves mainly a narrow urban layer with higher income. Thus, a new type of inequality has come into being with respect to the access to sport services, a phenomenon that can have a negative impact in the health of society in general. This situation is seen in Estonia where the average salary (monthly ca 1000 euros in 2014) is not enough to enable Estonians in general to consume many of the contemporary sport services, such as the commercial fitness club memberships.

Third, this book has shown that in many European countries sport is strongly wrapped around the commercial activities. This is seen foremost in the size and significance of the business field *retail sale of sporting equipment in specialised stores*, although this field appears to be rather vulnerable to economic fluctuations.

Also football and other team sports, which nurture fandom and consequently all forms of interconnected business activities and consumption, characterize the ways how sport is perceived in many parts of Europe. These forms of commercial activities might not necessarily promote actual sport participation of the citizens as they are often more related to the spectating sports. On the contrary, fitness boom is a strongly commercial field of the private sport sector whose growth is expected to result to people's increasing health promotion. At the same time however, there is a risk that sport participation becomes an exclusive opportunity for the better off cohorts of the society.

The Overall Importance of the Private Sport Sector in Europe

According the *broad definition of sport*, sport economy in Europe accounts for 1.76% of the total economic value added and 2.12% of the working population, but there are notable differences between the countries. For example, in Austria sport economy accounts for 4.03% of the total economic value added, which leaves traditionally strong sport countries such as the United Kingdom (UK) (2.33%), Germany (2.31%), France (1.40%), Spain (1.28%) and Italy (1.21%) behind. As far as sport-related employment is concerned the highest percentages are reported from Austria (5.38%), Germany (3.15%) and Finland (3.09%), whereas in Lithuania (1.10%), Portugal (1.41%) and Hungary (1.43%) shares are much smaller. (SportsEconAustria, 2012.) However, as it is presented in many articles of this book, the private sport sector contributes indirectly to many other industries (see e.g., Fig. 1 of chapter Getting A Grip on the Private Sport Sector in Europe) and thus the total economic impact of sport is difficult to estimate.

Although one of the original aims of this project was to gather comparable data about the private sport sector in Europe, not all countries were able to provide such data. Austria, the UK, and for the most part also the Netherlands, utilized other data sources (Sport Satellite Account system), Spain concentrated on fitness related data and Latvia was only able to provide data about the number of merchants working in the sport sector. With these limitations in mind however, all of the countries that took part in this project were able to present valuable data about the private sport sector in general and about selected sport business fields in particular. Based on this book, it is safe to say that in Europe sport is nowadays a huge retail and wholesale business, which influences millions of people's consumer behaviour. Sport clothing, footwear and equipment – for example bicycles, skies and golf gear – are items that are sold for millions of euros in different countries. Health and fitness boom especially in the 2000s has further increased sport-related consumption and can be seen as one of the drivers behind outstanding development within this sphere of sport business.

Large countries with higher purchasing power, such as France, Germany, Italy, the Netherlands and the UK, present naturally much higher figures in number of companies and their revenues than smaller European countries. It is worth mentioning that we as editors refrained from calculating any European averages on company numbers and revenues, because the participating countries are so different with regards to their population sizes and gross domestic products, as well as their histories and cultures. In order to avoid any misleading interpretations in this regard, we also felt that it is not useful to present comparative calculations about the average salaries of people working within the sport industry as countries' general income levels and purchasing powers vary substantially. However, with the help of selected facts presented in the beginning of each country article comparisons between countries can be made.

Sport Goods Sales Make the Core of the Private Sport Sector in Europe

According to the statistics provided by different countries in this book, the basis of the private sport sector business activities in Europe lies in the consumption of sporting goods and products. Measured by the revenues of the directly sport-related NACE business fields, largest field was *retail sale of sporting equipment in specialised stores* (the name of the class varied between countries). This was the case with eight countries out of 18, namely Cyprus, Czech Republic, Estonia, Finland, France, Italy, Lithuania and Portugal. Out of the individual countries, for example in Italy in 2013 the retail sale of sport goods field had, by far, the largest number of companies, almost one third of all companies in the directly sport-related business fields. Also the provision of employment was highest in this sport business field in Italy.

Retail sale of sport goods was the second largest sport business field in Austria, Belgium, Hungary, Romania, Germany and the Netherlands. In last three mentioned countries it was right behind NACE class *wholesale of sport goods*, a class which is not complied in all countries. It is also important to keep in mind that Greek, Latvian and Spanish contributors of this book were not able to provide retail sale of sport goods data. It is reasonable to expect that retail sale is among the largest sport business fields also in these countries. In the UK the retail sale was fourth largest sport business field.

Although in average retail sales represented the largest revenues among the directly sport-related NACE classes, there were differences in the significance and share of this business field. There was also variety regarding the number of companies and staff in this field. However, it seems that in general retail sale of sport goods field consists of a number of large international chains. There is proportionally smaller number of companies but relatively greater number of staff when compared to other directly sport-related business fields. A prime example would be an international sport retail sale company, for example Intersport International Corporation or XXL Sports & Outdoor. Those chains have shops in various locations and they also offer different kind of job opportunities, from full-time to part-time, permanent to fixed term, and from all around the year to seasonal contracts.

Sport goods retail market in Europe is concentrated on large international chains. Largest and fastest growing sport retailer by revenue in the Nordic region is XXL Sports & Outdoor. Photo from company's store in Vantaa, Finland. *Photo: XXL Sports & Outdoor/Teemu Ekholm.*

Top-Level Sport Clubs Functioning as Limited Companies

Sport club activities represent a significant part of the European private sport sector. In fact, in some countries, like Belgium, Cyprus, Romania and the UK, based on total revenues, NACE class *activities of sport clubs* was the largest directly sport-related business field. As presented for example in the Belgian chapter, in the Flemish Region and Brussels-Capital Region, between 2008 and 2015, *activities of sport clubs and federations* witnessed the clearest growth in the number of companies in the field, together with the *sport and recreation education*.

Out of the individual sport club activities football is particularly popular and significant for many European countries. In Cyprus it comprises the main pillar of the sport industry. In Italy on the other hand, sport clubs activities provide best salaries for their workers, with an average salary of around 176,000 euros per year, which is multiple more than both country average and averages in other sport business fields. This remarkable difference is mainly due to the huge revenues generated by men's top-level football clubs, not only in Italy, but also in the UK, Spain and France. The relative importance of football is unquestionable also in Hungary and Romania where the largest sport-related companies include four football clubs. Sport clubs activities was considerably large sport business field as well in Lithuania and Portugal ranking number two after retail sales, based on total revenues.

When drawing conclusions about the NACE class *activities of sport clubs*, it should be kept in mind, that it is not a very clear or coherent business field, when observed from the profit-making premises. This is because majority of the sport clubs in Europe still operate as registered associations, whose activities fit better to the non-profit domain than to the purely commercial sector. However, biggest top-level sport clubs are nowadays business entities, particularly in men's professional football. Professionalism has gained ground also in other men's team sports, for example in basketball in Lithuania, in handball in Hungary, and in ice hockey in Finland and Czech Republic.

One of the major concerns in running sport clubs as business entities is nowadays their poor profitability in several countries. Many major European football clubs in fact create constant losses to their owners. On a smaller scale this is seen also in periphery football countries, as well as in other sports, for example in ice hockey in Finland.

Sport Facilities as Business Entities

Activities of sport clubs is often connected with another directly sport-related NACE business field, namely *operation of sport facilities*. Many of the biggest football clubs own the stadiums, which are also used for purposes outside of sports. There are also companies that are concentrated in running sport facility businesses.

Operation of sport facilities comprise an important sport business field for many in this book examined countries. For example, in the UK, this field was the third largest sport business field, although it was measured by the Sport Satellite Account system, and is therefore not fully comparable with the NACE classification. However, it supports the idea of sport facilities being major business entities in the private sport sector. Also in the Netherlands there are close to 2000 private companies that run sport facilities (other than fitness centres) who 'possess' 2800 facilities.

In the Czech Republic *operation of sport facilities* companies comprised more than half of all the companies in the directly sport-related NACE business fields. In Romania *operation of sport facilities* was the third largest sport business field based on the number staff and it has shown a steady growth during the last few years. In Latvia, based on the number of merchants in the field, *operation of sport facilities* was the second largest sport business field after *other sport activities*.

Sport and Recreation Education Promote Personal Training and Top-Level Sports

NACE class *sport and recreation education* plays an important part of the profit-making sport sector in Europe, when looking at the number of companies and staff in this field. What makes the numbers somewhat surprising is the assumption that education in the European countries has been and still is either completely or for most parts free of charge and responsibility of the public sector domain. Thus, approaching education as a form of business is something new in many of the European countries.

As presented in the country chapters, for example in the Netherlands, *sport and recreation education* was the third largest sport business field when measured by the number of enterprises. Also in Lithuania, the number of companies in this field is remarkably high even though the revenues and average salaries remain low. In Estonia on the other hand, there are some 20 sport schools organised and supported by the local authorities.

Along with the expansion of the health boom and fitness culture, a new form of education and training system, namely personal training, has been developing and finding its establishment in the field. Thus, the relatively large share of companies in this field can be explained by the fact that there are nowadays an increasing number of personal training companies that are either forms of self-employment or hiring only a small amount of people. Also academies for top-level sport belong to this field. Especially in countries that highlight and appreciate careers in professional sport special training opportunities are offered by the profit-making providers.

Fitness Boom of the 2000s

The activities around NACE class *fitness facilities* have been a strongly developing market during this millennium, generating a large return of investment, along with a clear growth trajectory. *Fitness facilities* was also the most often and clearly mentioned sport business field in this book. This seemed to be the case even though by looking at the numbers of the companies and staff, as well as the average revenues, this field did not present exceptionally high figures. However, in line with the perception of most of the contributors, *fitness facilities* as a single niche market of sport is perceived as a significant sport business field that has showed a strong growth during the 2000s.

The number of *fitness facilities* represents average figures when compared to some other sport business fields. The ratio between the number of staff and companies' revenues indicates that this field comprises small companies that employ a relatively large amount of people. This however, might be explained by the high number of part time workers, because what is also seen increasingly in this field is the introduction of the budget-friendly facilities which often employ a very low number of people in their premises.

According fitness market study by Deloitte Sport Business Group, the German fitness market is clearly the biggest in Europe, accounting for nearly 20% out of the overall 50.1 million fitness centre members in 2014. However, as it was presented in the German chapter, the penetration rate (11.2%) was only average compared to some other European countries. The Netherlands on the other hand, has more members relatively to its population in the fitness facilities (16.0%). Regarding the revenues, Germany is ranked second with its 4.7 billion euros following Great Britain's 5.1 billion euros. (See Deloitte, 2015).

In Portugal the number of fitness companies and their staff had more than tripled between 2004 and 2012, and also the total revenues had more than doubled in that period. The revenues per company on the other hand had decreased which means that there are more than before smaller operators in the field. This indicates that fitness sector has come to offer business and employment opportunities that have relatively low start-up access and can easily open up self-employment possibilities.

It also seems that activities around *fitness facilities* have not been affected by the economic fluctuations as badly as around some other sport business fields, sales of sport goods for instance. Or at least the fitness businesses have found their ways to adapt to the new economic situations. What has been characteristics to the fitness boom in many parts of Europe is that the companies in the field have been able to reshape and diversify their activities. Many of the facilities have transformed from the 'old-school' bodybuilding gyms to trendy health and wellbeing centers that offer a wide variety of physical activities ranging from traditional group classes to individual personal training packages and other services. Today's fitness boom seems to be tied up with a holistic self-care ideology where people's bodies and minds have become at the same time channels and targets of consumption. Along with the ideas of 'disneyzation' fitness clubs illustrate the contemporary dependences between different forms of consumption, such as club memberships with interconnected services like physical therapy, nutritional consultation, and day care facilities (Bryman, 2004; de Cámara, 2015). In addition, social gatherings, thematic activities and parties are offered, striving to obtain the users' further involvement in the centres (Dorado, 2006).

What is also typical in the fitness business more broadly is that partly due to the economic recession in Europe in 2007–2009 the pricing and business opportunities in this field were altered. As a result new types of budget-friendly fitness centres, also known as 'low-cost gyms', often 24/7 accessible, started to emerge in many parts of Europe. These are offered both to consumers with lower economic backgrounds, and to those well-earning customers who prefer to have the flexibility in choosing the training hours and services.

Sport-Related Tourism Growing, but so far not a NACE Classified Business Field

In addition to the directly sport-related NACE classes, authors presented some other sport business fields, which are not statistically classified in NACE, but are seen to have potential in the commercial profit-making sport sector. One of them was sport-related tourism. Since the 1990's onwards, sport and activity-related tourism have become popular forms of tourism and niche markets in many destinations (see e.g., Higham & Hinch, 2009; Hinch & Higham, 2011; Hudson & Hudson, 2010). Visible examples of these are ski resorts and golf activities. However, NACE does not include sport-related tourism as a statistically classified business field and thus it is difficult to grasp an overview of this field purely based on the statistics. Out of the countries in this book, only Finland provided NACE classified statistics on *skiing centre activities* and Portugal on *activities of tourism animation / activities of recreational ports*.

Many of the countries have companies that carry on businesses around sport-related tourism, but those are classified to other sport business fields. For example, as presented in the Italian chapter, the leading company within the *operation of sport facilities* in Italy is Società Incremento Turistico Canazei (SITC) S.p.A., founded in 1947, mainly operating the ski lifts in Italy and promoting winter and summer tourism in areas of the Dolomiti Alps. Sport-related tourism, in particular winter tourism, is especially important to Austria. As shown in the Austrian chapter, together with sport goods retail, services around sport tourism dominate the private sport sector. However, these statistics were based on Sport Satellite Account system, not on NACE.

Traditional beach resorts are also nowadays offering a great variety of sport services to the holiday-takers. For example in Cyprus sport-related tourism is a growing field. Largest share of sport visitors in Cyprus come to the country for the sake of football, diving, cycling and swimming (Cyprus Tourism Organization, 2014). Sport-related tourism is also expected to contribute to the private sport sector growth in Greece as the country chapter outlines. Hotels and resorts invest in activities both in the summer and winter tourism in order to enhance their products and improve guests' experiences. Some resorts have also started to organize their own sport events. In Portugal nature-related tourism activities seem to follow a similar growth pattern with the fitness sector, especially when it comes to the number of companies and staff members in the field. Also golf is considered to be one of the top ten strategic products of the national strategic plan for the Portuguese tourism (Ministério da Economia e Inovação, 2007.)

Finally it can be concluded that the private sport sector has grown and gained a prominent position in the 2000s in all of the 18 countries that participated in this project. Even though the profit-making sport sector represents only a small share of the total economies in Europe, it is perceived as an auspicious business sector now and in the future. Even in countries with traditionally strong state and voluntary sport sectors, it is expected that the private sport sector will increase its significance as a sport service provider.

Out of the different sport business fields, this book gave an impression that there are high expectations especially towards the sport goods trade, fitness industry and sport-related tourism. However, in order to be able to give more accurate estimates of the future development, certain statistical shortcomings need to be solved. These mainly relate to the fact that in most European Union member states, the contribution of sport to the economy is still both underestimated and limitedly measured. Sport is still not fully understood and recognized as an important economic activity accumulating income and creating new jobs. Basic statistical publications of many European countries contain only little information on the sport sector, even though the contribution of sport to countries' economies is already considerable and it is growing. Since national statistics focus on a small fraction of what is generally understood as sport, the contribution of other than the limited amount of directly sport-related business fields covered in statistics are entirely left unaccounted for. There is also lack of accuracy and consistency in the statistics covered sport data, including the NACE classification that was used as a basic statistical framework of this book, as many of the contributors highlight. In the varying degree statistics about sport business fields and companies were limited, inconsistent and imprecise. As scholars in the field of social and economic sciences of sport we are hopefully able to shred light to these shortcomings so that in the near future the evidence-based knowledge also in the neglected fields of private sport sector will be increased. Concrete example is to expand and develop the Sport Satellite Account system in Europe.

References

Breedveld, K. (2014). *Sportparticipatie: uitdagingen voor wetenschap en beleid* [Sport-participation: Challenges for science and policies]. Nijmegen, The Netherlands: Radboud Universiteit Nijmegen.

Breuer, C., Feiler, S., & Wicker, P. (2015). Sport clubs in Germany. In C. Breuer, R. Hoekman, S. Nagel, & H. van der Werff (Eds.), *Sport clubs in Europe: A cross-national comparative perspective* (pp. 187–208). Cham, Switzerland: Springer International Publishing Switzerland.

Bryman, A. (2004). *Disneyzation of society*. London, UK: Sage.

Cámara, M. A. de. (2015). El sector del fitness en España: análisis del gimnasio low-cost y los centros de electro estimulación integral [Fitness industry in Spain; Analysis of low-cost and whole body electromyostimulation centers]. *Revista Euroamericana de Ciencias del Deporte, 4*(2), 47–54.

Cyprus Tourism Organization. (2014). *Sports tourism report for the year 2013*. Retrieved February 17, 2017 from http://media.visitcyprus.com/media/b2b_en/Research_Projects/Statistica_Athlitikos_Tourismos_2013_en.pdf

Deloitte. (2015). *Der deutsche Fitnessmarkt – Studie 2015* [The German fitness market – Study 2015]. Düsseldorf, Germany: Deloitte & Touche GmbH Wirtschaftsprüfungsgesellschaft.

Dorado, A. (2006). La gestión privada de las organizaciones deportivas [The private management of sport organizations]. In L. Gallardo & J. Lozano (Eds.), *Futuras claves en la gestión de organizaciones deportivas* (pp. 103–116). Cuenca, Ecuador: Publicaciones de la Universidad de Castilla la Mancha.

Földesi, S. G. (1996). Sport policy in Hungary. In L. Chalip, A. Johnson, & L. Stachura (Eds.), *National sports policies: An international handbook* (pp. 187–211). Westport, CT: Greenwood Press.

Higham, J., & Hinch, T. (2009). *Sport and tourism: Globalization, mobility and identity*. Oxford, UK: Elsevier.

Hinch, T., & Higham, J. (2011). *Sport tourism development*. Bristol, UK: Channel View Publications.

Houlihan, B. (2016). Sport and globalisation. In B. Huolihan & D. Malcom (Eds.), *Sport and society. A student introduction* (pp. 553–573). London, UK: Sage.

Hudson, S., & Hudson, L. (2010). *Golf tourism*. Oxford, UK: Goodfellow Publishers Limited.

Kábele, J. (2011). Sportpropag – nepravděpodobné místo pro studium společnosti: Osobní pohled [Sportpropag – Improbable place for studying society: Personal view]. *Sociální studia, 8*(1), 17–32.

Laine, A., & Ilmola, R. (2016). Liikunnan yhteiskuntatieteilijät työmarkkinoilla – vuosina 2000–2014 valmistuneiden maistereiden sijoittuminen työelämään [Social scientists of sport on the employment market – How the MSSc graduates from 2000–2014 are positioning themselves in working life]. *Liikunta & Tiede, 53*(1), 60–67.

Ministério da Economia e Inovação. (2007). Plano *Estratégico Nacional do Turismo para o desenvolvimento do turismo em Portugal* [Tourism national strategic plan for the Portuguese tourism development]. Lisbon, Portugal: Turismo de Portugal.

Schubert, K., & Klein, M. (2011). *Das Politiklexikon* [Encyclopaedia of politics]. Bonn, Germany: Dietz.

Slepičková, I. (2007). *Sportovní organizace. Teoretická východiska a situace v ČR po roce 1990* [Sport organizations. Theoretical background and situation in the Czech Republic after the year 1990]. Prague, Czech Republic: Karolinum.

SportsEconAustria. (2012). *Study on the contribution of sport to economic growth and employment in the EU*. Bruxelles, Belgium: European Commission, D-G Education and Culture.

Vehmas, H., & Salmikangas, A.-K. (2016). Higher education and employment in Sport management. Oral presentation in the 13th European Association for Sociology of Sport conference in Copenhagen, May 7, 2016.

Appendix: NACE Rev. 2 Directly Sport-Related Classes

SECTION	**C – MANUFACTURING**
Division	32 – Other manufacturing
Group	32.3 – Manufacture of sport goods
Class	**32.30 – Manufacture of sport goods**
	This class includes the manufacture of sporting and athletic goods (except apparel and footwear). This class includes:
	Manufacture of articles and equipment for sport, outdoor and indoor games, of any material:
	Hard, soft and inflatable balls
	Rackets, bats and clubs
	Skis, bindings and poles
	Ski-boots
	Sailboards and surfboards
	Requisites for sport fishing, including landing nets
	Requisites for hunting, mountain climbing etc.
	Leather sport gloves and sport headgear
	Basins for swimming and padding pools etc.
	Ice skates, roller skates etc.
	Bows and crossbows
	Gymnasium, fitness centre or athletic equipment
SECTION	**G – WHOLESALE AND RETAIL TRADE; REPAIR OF MOTOR VEHICLES AND MOTORCYCLES**
Division	47 – Retail trade, except of motor vehicles and motorcycles
Group	47.6 – Retail sale of cultural and recreation goods in specialised stores
Class	**47.64 – Retail sale of sporting equipment in specialised stores**
	This class includes:
	Retail sale of sport goods, fishing gear, camping goods, boats and bicycles

A. Laine, H. Vehmas (eds.), *The Private Sport Sector in Europe*, Sports Economics, Management and Policy 14, https://doi.org/10.1007/978-3-319-61310-9_21

SECTION	**N – ADMINISTRATIVE AND SUPPORT SERVICE ACTIVITIES**
Division	77 – Rental and leasing activities
Group	77.2 – Renting and leasing of personal and household goods
Class	**77.21 – Renting and leasing of recreational and sport goods**
	This class includes renting of recreational and sport equipment:
	Pleasure boats, canoes, sailboats
	Bicycles
	Beach chairs and umbrellas
	Other sport equipment
	Skis
SECTION	**P – EDUCATION**
Division	85 – Education
Group	85.5 – Other education
Class	**85.51 – Sport and recreation education**
	This class includes the provision of instruction in athletic activities to groups of individuals, such as by camps and schools. Overnight and day sport instruction camps are also included. It does not include academic schools, colleges and universities. Instruction may be provided in diverse settings, such as the unit's or client's training facilities, educational institutions or by other means. Instruction provided in this class is formally organised. This class includes:
	Sport instruction (baseball, basketball, cricket, football, etc.)
	Camps, sport instruction
	Gymnastics instruction
	Riding instruction, academies or schools
	Swimming instruction
	Professional sport instructors, teachers, coaches
	Martial arts instruction
	Card game instruction (such as bridge)
	Yoga instruction
SECTION	**R – ARTS, ENTERTAINMENT AND RECREATION**
Division	93 – Sport activities and amusement and recreation activities
Group	93.1 – Sport activities: This group includes the operation of sport facilities; activities of sport teams or clubs primarily participating in live sport events before a paying audience; independent athletes engaged in participating in live sporting or racing events before a paying audience; owners of racing participants such as cars, dogs, horses, etc. primarily engaged in entering them in racing events or other spectator sport events; sport trainers providing specialised services to support participants in sport events or competitions; operators of arenas and stadiums; other activities of organising, promoting or managing sport events (not elsewhere classified).
Class	**93.11 – Operation of sport facilities**
	This class includes:
	Operation of facilities for indoor or outdoor sport events (open, closed or covered, with or without spectator seating):
	Football, hockey, cricket, rugby stadiums
	Racetracks for car, dog, horse races

	Swimming pools and stadiums
	Track and field stadiums
	Winter sport arenas and stadiums
	Ice hockey arenas
	Boxing arenas
	Golf courses
	Bowling lanes
	Organisation and operation of outdoor or indoor sport events for professionals or amateurs by organisations with own facilities
	This class includes managing and providing the staff to operate these facilities.
Class	**93.12 – Activities of sport clubs**
	This class includes the activities of sport clubs, which, whether professional, semi-professional or amateur clubs, give their members the opportunity to engage in sporting activities. This class includes:
	Operation of sport clubs:
	Football clubs
	Bowling clubs
	Swimming clubs
	Golf clubs
	Boxing clubs
	Winter sport clubs
	Chess clubs
	Track and field clubs
	Shooting clubs, etc.
Class	**93.13 – Fitness facilities**
	This class includes:
	Fitness and body-building clubs and facilities
Class	**93.19 – Other sport activities**
	This class includes:
	Activities of producers or promoters of sport events, with or without facilities
	Activities of individual own-account sportsmen and athletes, referees, judges, timekeepers etc.
	Activities of sport leagues and regulating bodies
	Activities related to promotion of sporting events
	Activities of racing stables, kennels and garages
	Operation of sport fishing and hunting preserves
	Activities of mountain guides
	Support activities for sport or recreational hunting and fishing

Source: NACE Rev. 2. Statistical classification of economic activities in the European Community. Eurostat. Methodologies and Working papers. Retrieved January 15, 2017 from http://ec.europa.eu/eurostat/documents/3859598/5902521/KS-RA-07-015-EN.PDF

The manufacturer's authorised representative in the EU is Springer Nature Customer Service Centre GmbH, Europaplatz 3, 69115 Heidelberg, Germany. If you have any concerns regarding our products, please contact ProductSafety@springernature.com

Printed and bound by CPI Group (UK) Ltd, Croydon, CR0 4YY
01/10/2026
02225871-0007